Village Information System

Vol. Three
Development Planning

VILLAGE INFORMATION SYSTEM

VOLUME ONE: Innovation of Natural Infrastructure
VOLUME TWO: Innovation of Human Infrastructure
VOLUME THREE: Development Planning

About the Author

Hridai R. Yadav obtained degrees of M.Phil., Ph.D. from Jawaharlal Nehru University, New Delhi, worked with CSIR, Government of India as Pool Scientist for eight years, having authored 11 Books and 73 Research Papers. He has been the Member of the National Wastelands Development Board, Government of India and nominated as U.G.C. Observer for the selection of Professors in the various Universities and U.G.C. Nominee in the Board of Management of Autonomous Institute of Engineering and Technology (GBTU), Lucknow. He is also the Member, Governing Body, Madhya Pradesh Bhoj (Open) University, Bhopal. H.R. Yadav has been the members of various Government and Autonomous Institutions/Universities besides being Founder Member-Secretary-Director of the Institute of Wastelands Reclamation and Rural Development (1990) and Institute of Science and Technology for Rural Development (1994), Editor, Amethi Sangharsh (Hindi/Weekly) Newspaper and U.G.C. accredited RIWARD Post Graduate College, Hanumanganj, Sultanpur, U.P. (2004). Presently, he is engaged in the implementation of Agro-Afforestation on the Patta Banjar Lands, allotted to Scheduled Caste communities to promote MNREGA and Bhoomi Sena Programmes, Women Empowerment and Rural Health Mission Programmes in Amethi.

Village Information System

Vol. Three
Development Planning

[With 25 Coloured Maps]

Prof. (Dr.) Hridai R. Yadav

CONCEPT PUBLISHING COMPANY PVT. LTD.
NEW DELHI-110059

This Study has been supported by NRDMS, Department of Science and Technology, Government of India, New Delhi.

ISBN-13: 978-81-8069-940-5 (Set)
ISBN-13: 978-81-8069-941-2 (Vol. I)
ISBN-13: 978-81-8069-981-8 (Vol. II)
ISBN-13: 978-81-8069-982-5 (Vol. III)

First Published 2014

Published and Printed by

Concept
Since 1974

Concept Publishing Company Pvt. Ltd.
A/15-16, Commercial Block, Mohan Garden
New Delhi-110059 (India)
T: 25351460, 25351794, *F*: 091-11-25357109
E: publishing@conceptpub.com, W: www.conceptpub.com
Editorial Office: H-13, Bali Nagar, New Delhi-110 015, India.

Cataloging in Publication Data--Courtesy: D.K. Agencies (P) Ltd. <docinfo@dkagencies.com>

Yadav, Hridai Ram, 1957-
Village information system / Hridai R. Yadav.
3 v. cm.
Includes bibliographical references and indexes.
Contents: v. 1. Innovation of natural infrastructure — v. 2. Innovation of human infrastructure — v. 3. Development planning.
ISBN 9788180699405 (set)
ISBN 9788180699412 (v. 1)
ISBN 9788180699818 (v. 2)
ISBN 9788180699825 (v. 3)

1. Rural development projects—Geographic information systems—India—Amethi. 2. Infrastructure (Economics)—Geographic information systems—India—Amethi. 3. Natural resources—Geographic information systems—India—Amethi. I. Title.

DDC 307.141209542 23

Preface

The soul of India lives in the villages, where more than 76 per cent population survives on the Natural and Human (Socio-Economic), infrastructural resources in the remote rural areas. Development programmes for the remote rural areas has been pursued with genuine concern for human values. The development should ensure the betterment and welfare of all the deprived resourceless multitudes living in the remote rural areas.

The existing process of development has neither been true, nor good, nor beautiful, but it does not mean that everything is wrong. Really the development lies in the techno-scientific application for quantity and quality Agri-Horti-Forestry production for realizing the better quality of life by the village common people.

The process of development should be implemented *equally, effectively and efficiently* through people's participation, by the people with the people, and for the people for whom such development programmes have been formulated and planned for implementation the grassroots level.

The formulation of the plan based on the Human Resources has been adopted but at the grassroots level or village level or field level, the formulated and implemented plans did not yield the desired results due to inequities amongst the people mismanagement and disparities between rich to poor. Tremendous pressure on land, water and forest natural infrastructure and its over exploitation has led to deforestation, land degradation and environmental and socio-economic crises.

The nature has given bounty to us, land, water, forest resources, agro-climatic conditions and eco-system of the remote villages must be utilized optimally but not exploited in an unplanned system. The village development planning process for the appropriate management and optimum utilization of available water, land, forest, Natural, and Human (Socio-Economic-Institutional) Infrastructural resources has always been challenges to the policy makers and planners.

Thus, there is, an urgent need to evolve a planning strategy through evolving Village Information System and Innovation of Human (Socio-Economic-Institutional) Resources and the assessment of the ongoing development programmes and need based people participatory integrated village development planning.

In view of the above Natural (Human) Resources Data Management System (HRDMS), Department of Science & Technology, Government of India sanctioned a project on "Developing Village Information System in Amethi" which has been successfully implemented at village panchayat level in the Amethi Block.

The out come of the implemented project has been properly documented and an effort has been made to document the achievements of this study in the Book Form in three Volumes:

Vol. I :	Village Information System (Innovation of Natural Infrastructure)
Vol. II :	Village Information System (Innovation of Human Infrastructure)
Vol. III :	Village Information System (Development Planning)

The first Volume of this study has been related to Village Information System an innovation of the Natural Infrastructure, viz. land, water, forest and agro-climatic conditions of 44 Village Panchayats of Amethi Block covering 82 revenue villages and 377 purwas/tolas/hamlet villages based on the revenue records, Economic Register and other sources of Data and direct field level survey work has been carried out. In this volume an attempt has been made to analyse the socio-economic-institutional infrastructural available resources has been studied at village panchayat level in the Amethi Block.

In view of the above, an effort has been made in the second Volume of the Study to innovate and explain the available Human Infrastructural Resources, i.e. Socio-Economic-Institutional, Infrastructural Resources available at the village panchayat level in Amethi Block.

An attempt has been made in this Third Volume of the study to explain the regular policy planning initiated by the Government of India, State Government of Uttar Pradesh, District Planning, including Zila Panchyat, Block Panchayat, Village Panchayat. An effort has also been made in this study the assess the implementation of the various rural development programme being implemented at various levels including village panchayat level in Amethi. It has been attempted to analyse the village development planning and implementation of various planned village development programmes at District Level, Block Level, Village Level in Amethi.

In view of the above, I am sure the study on "Village Information System" in three volumes will serve as useful guide for policy-makers, planners while implementing institutions for the implementation of Village Development Programmes at grassroots level. This study will also be useful for academicians, research scholars and grassroots level village development programme implementing institutions and social workers, equally to understand field level or village level people's participatory development planning process and also the implementation of various integrated village development programmes, because it has been clearly indicated in our constituency that the fruits of the development must reach to the downtrodden deprived resourceless multitudes *equally*, *effectively* and *efficiently* at grassroots level.

Prof. (Dr.) Hridai R. Yadav

Acknowledgements

Natural Resources Data Management System (NRDMS), Department of Science and Technology, Government of India, sanctioned a project entitled "Developing Village Information System in Amethi" to the Institute of Wastelands Reclamation and Rural Development (RIWARD) Payagipur, Sultanpur, U.P. An attempt has been made to document the outcome of the sanctioned project in the form of Book "Village Information System (Development Planning) Volume-III for which Techno-Scientific assistance of Dr. Bhoop Singh, Director, NRDMS, Department of Science and Technology, Government of India has been highly appreciable because without his constant support this study would not have been successfully implemented.

Sincere gratitudes are recorded to the District-Block-Development authorities of the Amethi and Block Development Officer, Amethi and all Village Pradhans of the Amethi Block for providing need based support for the collecting the WORK PLAN of the Zila Yojana, Block Yojana and Village Panchayat Plans and Programmes of the Amethi Block.

Neeraj Kumar deserves heartiest thanks for supporting the collection of the needful information at village panchayat level in Amethi.

The tedious typing of the data and finalization of the manuscript and Maps etc. has been very carefully arranged by Sri Kamlesh Chandra Verma, who deserves special thanks.

I thank to all those, who directly or indirectly supported in the completion of this study. I acknowledge my sincerely gratitude to Sri Ashok Kumar Mittal, CMD, Concept Publishing Co. (Pvt.) Ltd., New Delhi for the publication of this study within the stipulated time.

Last, but not the least, I am highly obliged, grateful, indebted to Late Baba Sultan Shah Ji & Nafees Baba and my wife Reeta and lovely son Sahit Hridai, without whose support writing and completion of this study would not have been possible for me.

Prof. (Dr.) Hridai R. Yadav

Contents

List of Maps

List of Tables and Figures

TABLES

FIGURES

1
Introduction

1. INTRODUCTION

An economic development has been realized at National and State level in our country, commendable advances have been made in the diverse field of rural development programmes has been observed incomplete in reality, because such implemented rural development programmes failed to translate into better and dignified meaning for the life of the majority of the people surviving in the remote rural areas. The actions and aspirations for the better quality of life has been found comparatively better in the urban areas than the rural areas and rurban areas as well.

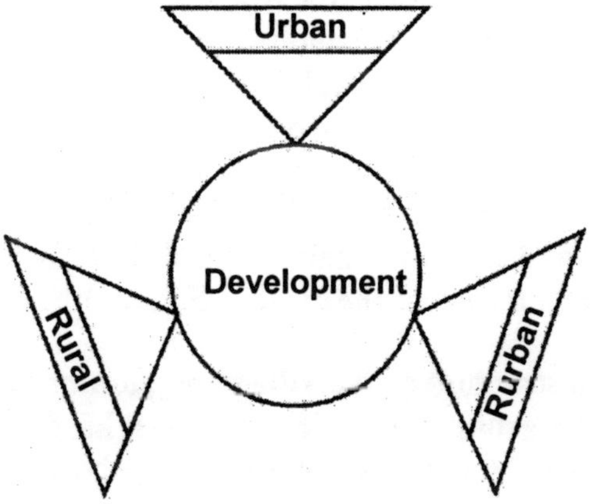

More than 76 per cent people live in the rural areas. The basic amenities and necessities of the rural people are much lower than that of the people living in the urban areas, rurban areas or city or town. It has been realized that generally, the rural poor people are isolated from the main streams and the villages are identified as an independent economic unit. The rural poor people's production and consumption activities takes place within a small units, usually households.

There are some difficulties in defining a village. The village in India, mean different things in terms of physical, economic and social structure. The village have some uniqueness in their structure socially, economically, institutionally, culturally, religiously, etc. It has also been noticed that at the same time villages have something in common too.

It has been observed that there are some general characteristics of a village:

- Village remoteness.
- Villages are settled together in a particular area.
- Purwas/Tolas/Hamlet Villages are settled by the people of some origin or indigenous people.
- Main occupation of the village people is agriculture or primary source of economic activities.
- Poor literacy ratio.
- Prevalence of traditional culture, belief, orthodoxy and conservation.
- Socio-Economic Backwardness.
- Poor infrastructure of the village.
- Purwas/Tolas/Hamlet Villages are main consisting of only one caste/community.
- Common economic behaviour, viz. cultivation, agricultural laboures, etc.

It has been noticed that there are few fundamental features common to all villages, though they have settled in the different revenue villages, purwas, tolas, hamlet villages. Villagers have some common features primarily in economic structure, basic physical infrastructure and more importantly village norms, systems and rituals.

In view of the above, this volume of study on Village Information System through development planning is a modest attempt to explore the problems and prospects of development planning and also developing the economic status of the village.

The Father of the Nation Mahatma Gandhi has stated that :

> "I would say that if the village perishes, India will perish too, India will be no more India. Her own mission in the world will get last. The revival of the village is possible only when it is no more exploited. Industrialization on a mass scale will necessarily lead to passive or active exploitation of the villages as the problems of competition and marketing come in. Therefore, we have to concentrate on the village being self-contained, manufacturing mainly for use. Provided this character of the village industry is maintained, there would be no objection to villagers using even the modern machines and tools that they can make and can afford to use. Only they should not be used, as a means of the exploitation of others."

The social structure of the **village** or **gaon** or **gram** is not just a physical space or **settlement** of a **group** of **people.** The social life in the village is organized along with definite rituals and secular principles, such as those of castes, kinship, politics, economy and religion and various other social activities.

The physical characteristics of all the villages is influenced by its dynamic interaction with these principles and patterns of settlement in the from of Purwas/Tolas/Hamlet Villages. A village could be clustered or dispersed in it different patterns of settlement.

The each and every village has a definite pattern of social relations based on traditional principles of kinship and marriage ceremony such as those of village exogamy. The social relations extend the interactive network and social space of village well beyond its boundaries into neighbouring villages. The real or fictive bond of kinship and marriage govern not only intra-familial interaction but also that between larger kins groups, often across village boundaries. It has been noticed that the trust is the social capital, which can reduce social transaction cost, community institutions and organizations are inflexible and fail to adjust to changing economic needs of villagers. The communities traditional norms and conventions have been formed slowly over many-many years. Approximately, more than three-fourth people survive in the villages and they are far behind socially and economically from grassroots level to the national level. Therefore, the development of the villages has become the need of the hour, while framing and formulating village development policies and planning for the remote under-developed villages and deprived of the common minimum necessities and amenities. It has been felt that the only conventional approaches cannot break the vicious circle of poverty, henceforth, we have to incorporate alternative views and methods of people's participatory need based village development planning. The village development policy, planning must be turned to the local available natural and human infrastructural resources, without much disturbing traditional system and it should be based on the increasing demand and needs of the local village people through ensuring sustained participation of the village people.

It has been argued that the faster development is required to bridge the gap between Rural to Rurban to Urban areas. The urban areas are comparatively more developed than the rurban to rural areas, while the rurban areas are more developed in comparison to the rural areas. Therefore, an appropriate and faster development of rural areas are required to fulfil the increasing demand of the ever growing cattle and human population, so that the disparities between rural to urban can be bridged to ensure integrated development of the villages.

It has been realized that the development should be participatory and it should be planned according to the local needs of deprived rural poor multitudes. The development should be planned through tapping the local talent and available natural and human infrastructural resources of the village in order to make the implemented rural development programme self-sustainable. Various rural development programmes are being implemented aiming at the sustainable development of the rural areas, with a focus on enhancing the livelihoods of weaker and vulnerable sections of the society. In conformity with the commitments to accord foremost priority to rural development a number of steps have been initiated to make the implementation of ongoing rural development programmes more effective and accelerated.

The implementation of various rural development programmes can be made more effective through ensuing sustained people participation. Thus, the rural development should be **for the rural people,** and development should be implemented **with the people** and it should be **maintained** and **sustained through the rural people**. The people's participatory planning and need based implementation of integrated rural development programmes should be initiated and implemented at grassroots/village level.

It has been mentioned in the Constitution of India that, **"Government should evolve methods to unite the Village Panchayats and provide such powers and rights, which can be helpful to work as an unit of Self-Government."**

It has been the vision of the Mahatma Gandhi Ji that, "In the Panchayati Raj System, each village should be self-sustained and independent, the implementation of welfare programmes of the rural masses, can be implemented in a better manner in the villages of vast rural India."

In view of the above, as per policy of the Government of India, the State Government of Uttar Pradesh established Self-Government in rural areas. The historical and revolutionary decisions has been made to allocate the work and allocate the financial resources for implementation of the village panchayats planned rural development programmes. The government allocated financial and administrative rights to provide the Self-Government of the Village Panchayats → Block Panchayat → District Panchayat.

The village has been the lowest unit of the development in the new system of the Panchayati Raj Institutions. In the decentralized Panchayati Raj System Village has been the central focal point for development. In reality, it has been meaningful step to transfer physical, financial and administrative rights and powers for integrated village development planning programmes, its control and management has been ensured through people's participation. The planning process has been done from bottom to top. After independence first of all revolutionary steps of decentralization like significant changes have been realized in the life of the rural poors and it has provided a new era for integrated development of the rural areas.

The real meaning of democracy is the importance of the people and Village Self-Government is the main sole of rural development. The Government of Uttar Pradesh allocated financial management and administrative control of the Village Panchayat to the elected representatives of the Village Panchayats with the view to establish Self-Government of the Village Panchayat and to ensure peoples participatory need base integrated village development planning and it's implementation, management and self-sustenance.

In view of the above, an attempt has been made in this volume of the study to analyse the Village Information System for development planning at village panchayat level in the Amethi Block. An effort has been made to analyse the progress of ongoing implementation of various rural development programmes at village panchayat level in the Amethi Block. It has been attempted to analyse the need based village development planning at village panchayat level for the socio-economic development of the village and self-sustenance of the village panchayat with the view to strengthen the Panchayati Raj Institutions.

2. OBJECTIVES

The main objective of this volume (Village Information System), of this study is as follow :

1. To explain this policy planning for village development programmes.
2. To critically examine and assess the ongoing implementation of various rural development programmese at village panchayat level in the Amethi Block.
3. To analyse the need based people's participatory development planning at village panchayat level in Amethi.

3. STUDY AREA

The selection of an area for analysing Village Information System for development planning especially in this volume of the study involving grassroots level or micro-level or village level is very important. In this study 377 Purwas/Tolas/Hamlet Villages and 82 revenue villages of the 44 village panchayats of Amethi have been selected to analyse the implementation of the various rural development programmes and need based people's participatory village development planning at the grassroots level of Amethi.

There are five Tehsils in the Amethi District.

1. Salon,
2. Tiloi,
3. Musafirkhana,
4. Gauriganj, and
5. Amethi.

It has been observed that there are 16 Blocks in different tehsils of Amethi.

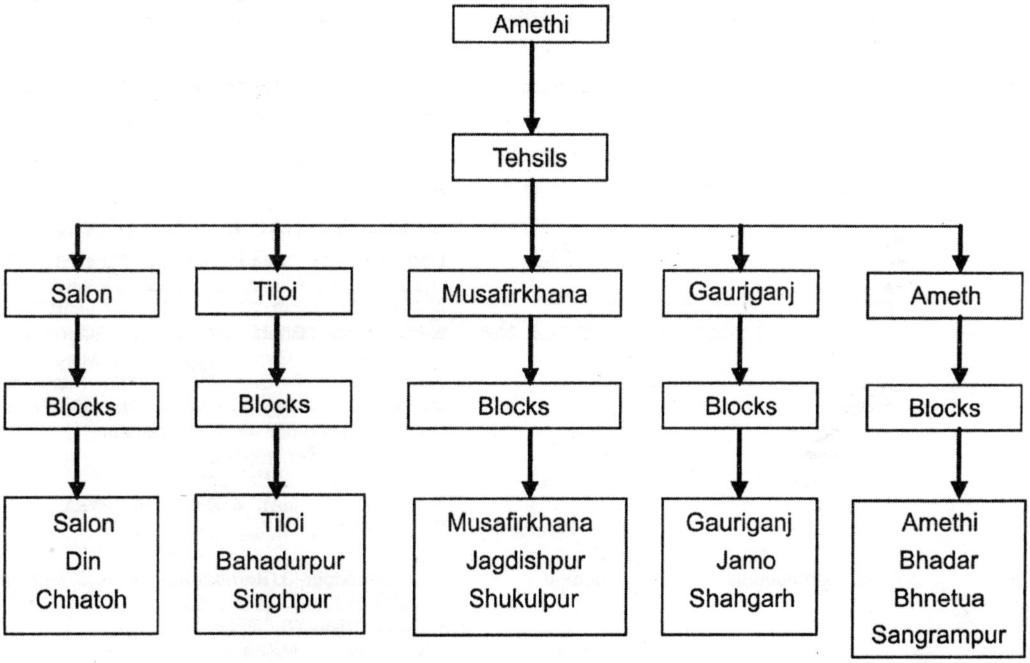

The Tehils and location of the Blocks of the Amethi District has been depicted in the **Map 1.1.**

It has been recorded that there are 44 village panchayats in the Amethi Block. The location of the various village panchayats of the Amethi Block has been shown in the **Map 1.2.**

It has been observed that there are 82 revenue villages in the Amethi Block and it has also been recorded that there are 377 Purwas/Tolas/Hamlet villages in Amethi Block. The detailed list of Purwas/Tolas/Hamlet villages including 82 revenue villages of Amethi Block has been mentioned in Table 1.1.

Table 1.1: Village Panchayat/Revenue/Hamlet Villages, Amethi Block

Sl. No.	*Village Panchayat*	*Revenue Villages*	*Hamlet Villages/ Purwa/Tola*
1.	Katra Maharani	1. Katara Maharani	1. Katara Maharani, 2. Munshiganj, 3. Chauraha, 4. Usarapur.
		2. Laukipur	1. Laukipur
		3. Matiyar Baghaura	1. Matiyar Baghaura
2.	Sarai Khema	1. Sarai Khema	1. Sarai Khema Khas, 2. Munshiganj, 3. Basuapur, 4. Halapur, 5. Beni Madhavpur, 6, Kutia, 7. Ahmad Nagar
		2. Dandupur	1. Dandupur Khas, 2. Pure Kutur, 3. Jagapur
		3. Ram Nagar Mafi	1. Pure Pandit, 2. Mainapur
3.	Trilokpur	1. Trilokpur	1. Pure Subedar, 2. Pure Bhagwandin, 3. Trilokpur, 4. Pure Darshan, 5. Dubepur.
		2. Teri	1. Teri, 2. Kutur Ka Purwa
4.	Ramdaipur	1. Ramdaipur	1. Ramdaipur, 2. Chhawani, 3. Punnapur
		2. Bhupatipur	1. Bhupatipur
		3. Naugnawa	1. Naugnawa
		4. Bahapur	1. Bahapur, 2. Sitarampur, 3. Rajan Ka Pura, 4. Gaudawa.

(Contd.)

Table 1.1 (*Contd.*)

Sl. No.	*Village Panchayat*	*Revenue Villages*	*Hamlet Villages/ Purwa/Tola*
5.	Jangal Ram Nagar	1. Jangal Ramnagar	1. Chhawani, 2. Pure Mannuram, 3. Pure Durga Pasi, 4. Ram Nagar, 5. Ram Nagar Pachhimi, 6. Katara, 7. Shiv Darshan Nagar, 8. Hanumat Nagar, 9. Amriti, 10. Uttari, 11. Van Satahi, 12. Pure Swayambar, 13. Pure Pathak, 14. Sitaram pur Usari, 15. Pure Jhilcai, 16. Pure Pandey, 17. Dhamrawa, 18. Pure Bodhan, 19. Derkha Chhatolia, 20. Pure Gayasi, 21. Baramati, 22. Pure Parsada, 23. Pure Bhwal, 24. Pure Digarihan, 25. Pure Sheetal, 26. Pure Hira Simar, 27. Pure Pandit, 28. Pure Belaura, 29. Semsahawa, 30. Pure Bhagan Ahir, 31. Bhusupar, 32. Pure Ram Prasad Kurmi, 33. Ranbir Nagar Uttari Bhag, 34. Ranbir Nagar Dakshini Bhag, 35. Gahari, 36. Gondwa, 37. Pure Murai, 38. Pure Mistri, 39. Karbala, 40. Devi Patam, 41. Kakarahi, 42. Amriti. 43. Mahua Tali. 44. Chhiwala Tali, 45. Walada. 46. Pure Dutta, 47. Usarahia, 48. Pure Banaha.
6.	Benipur	1. Benipur	1. Benipur, 2. Benipur New
7.	Parsawan	1. Parsanwa	1. Pure Bhatani, 2. Parsanwa, 3. Pasanwa Khalawa, 4. Parsanwa Dihwa.
		2. Ram Nathpur Chhota	1. Ram Nathpur Chhota.
8.	Mahmoodpur	1. Mahmudpur	1. Mahmoodpur, 3. Ramnathpur Bada, 3. Munshiganj Road, 4. Lakharia Khera Ke Pichhe, 5. Awaas Vikas Gopalpur.
		2. Marafapur	1. Marafapur, 2. Mainapur.
		3. Valipur	1. Valipur Khas, 2. Valipur Aam.
9.	Raipur Fulwari	1. Raipur Fulwari	1. Pure Ram Prasad Pandit, 2. Baniyani, 3. Salamat Ali Ka Purwa, 4. Ojha Ka Purwa, 5. Datta Ka Purwa, 6. Kakawa Mod.
		2. Katara Raja Himmat Singh	1. Katara Raja Himmat Singh
10.	Umapur Ganapatti	1. Umapur Ganapatti	1. Bhagwanpur, 2. Pure Guru Baksh, 3. Pure Prem, 4. Hati, 5. Pure Ichha, 6. Pure Nidhi, 7. Sri Rampur.
11.	Bhaganpur	1. Bhaganpur	1. Bhaganpur, 2. Durgapur, 3. Pure Lal, 4. Pure Nand, Mishra, 5. Sringarpur, 6. Pure Bhojai.
		2. Jangal Tikari	1. Jangal Tikari, 2. Dhamranwa.
12.	Tala	1. Tala	1. Tala, 2. Lodhani Patti, 3. Bhaisapur, 4. Pure Dina Mankata, 5 Baripur, 6. Mahadewan.
13.	Kushi Tali	1. Kushi Tali	1. Patakhapur, 2. Pure Nardutt, 3. Kushi Tali, 4. Pure Ram Lal.
		2. Haripur	1. Haripur
14.	Loharta	1. Loharata	1. Loharata, 2. Mali Ka Purwa.
		2. Sompur Mankanth	1. Pure Shiv Gulam, 2. Lala Ka Purwa, 3. Kalu Tewari Ka Purwa, 4. Chak Belan.
		3. Ahirawal.	1. Ahirawal, 2. Pure Mod.
15.	Darakha	1. Darakha	1. Pure Chandika, 2. Pure Shiv Lal, 3. Pure Bariyar, 4. Pure Dutta, 5. Darakha Diti, 6. Pure Jagannath, 7. Naya Purwa, 8. Pure Shital.
16.	Mochwa	1. Mochawa	1. Mochawa, 2. Maheshpur.
		2. Sarai Hirmati	1. Sarai Hirmati, 2. Barsati
		3. Jhaunei	1. Jhaunei, 2. Pure Daya Mishra
		4. Sultanpur	1. Sultanpur, 2. Pure Daljit, 3. Pure Dashrath, 4. Pure Galhin, 5. Pure Daya Mishra.
17.	Nuwawan	1. Nuwanwa	1. Nuwanwa Khas, 2. Dubepur, 3. Kodari, 4. Saidapur, 5. Teliyani, 6. Pure Gopal, 7. Pure Yamati.
18.	Loniapur	1. Loniapur	1. Mattha Shukul Ka Purwa, 2. Teliyani, 3. Badhai Ka Purwa, 4. Loniapur.
		2. Bharathipur	1. Bharathipur
19.	Kherauna	1. Kherauna	1. Kherauna, 2. Baramati, 3. Kewalapur, 4. Hardew Nagar.
		2. Sarai Raj Shah	1. Sarai Raj Shah
		3. Sarwanpur	1. Sarwanpur, 2. Keshawa Nagar, 3. Gayatri Nagar, 4. Gangaganj, 5. Sringarpur, 5. Pure Bhojai.

(*Contd.*)

Table 1.1 (*Contd.*)

Sl. No.	*Village Panchayat*	*Revenue Villages*	*Hamlet Villages/ Purwa/Tola*
20.	Katra Phulkunwar	1. Katara Phulkunwar	1. Katara Phulkunwar, 2. Bahorapur, 3. Tewaripur, 4. Kewalapur.
		2. Jagipatti	1. Jagapatti
		3. Baghwaria	1. Baghwaria
		4. Parsauli	1. Parsauli
21.	Hatli kila	1. Hathkila	1. Hathkila, 2. Dewaraka Tola, 3. Dewatar, 4. Baripur.
22.	Rebha	1. Rebha	1. Rebha, 2. Pure Pothi
		2. Mandharpatti	1. Mandharpatti
23.	Raidaipur	1. Raidaipur	1. Raidaipur
		2. Chachakapur	1. Chachakapur
		3. Birahimpur	1. Birahimpur Kundwa.
24.	Korari Girdhar Shah	1. Korari Girdhar Shah	1. Pure Matadin, 2. Ghatampur, 3. Pure Bhagwan, 4. Mahadewan, 5. Pure Roshani, 6. Baba Ka Purwa, 7. Pure Telin, 8. Pure Shoschiman.
		2. Mangalpur	1. Mangalpur
		3. Dariyapur	1. Tewari Ka Purwa, 2. Gohanwa, 3. Bariyapur, 4. Bikham Bharpur, 5. Manharia.
25.	Dedhpasar	1. Dedhpasar	1. Tulapur, 2. Parashuram, 3. Dedhpasar, 4. Sarai Kodha, 5. Pure Dakshin.
		2. Jamalpatti	1. Pure Uttar, 2. Jamalpatti
26.	Mahaso	1. Mahaso	1. Mahaso, 2. Basupur Tola, 3. Dewatar, 4. Paripar.
		2. Gyan Chandpur	1. Pandit Ka Pura, 2. Banktawa, 3. Pahia.
27.	Gangauli	1. Gangauli	1. Pandit Ka Purwa, 2. Subedar Ka Purwa, 3. Gangauli Matera, 4. Pure Diggaj Ka Purwa, 5. Bari Ka Pura, 6. Tulsi Pandey Ka Purwa, 7. Agaha, 8. Pure Kurai, 9. Dinaka Purwa, 10, Soiya.
28.	Dhandhudhar	1. Dhandhudhar	1. Dhandhudhar, 2. Pure Upadhyaya
		2. Pithipur	1. Pure Hanuman Tewari, 2. Pure Ojhan, 3. Pure Mishra.
29.	Gaderi	1. Gaderi	1. Gaderi, 2. Sadwa, 3. Banpurwa, 4. Pure Hardatt, 5. Pure Duban, 6. Pure Kalika, 7. Pure Tularam, 8. Rampur, 9. Pure Gangu, 10. Pure Bal, 11. Pure Bidhasia, 12. Samari, 13. Pure Bhagwandin, 14. Pure Hawaldar, 15. Pure Chandra Mani, 16. Bangarwa.
30.	Bhusahari	1. Bhusahari	1. Bhusahari Khas, 2. Barain Tola, 3. Pure Gaderian, 4. Karnaipur, 5. Makhdumpur, 6. Patipur, 7. Jham Singh Ka Purwa.
31.	Purabgaon	1. Purabgaon	1. Purabgaon
32.	Chaturbhujpur	1. Chaturbhujpur	1. Pure Shuklan, 2. Hanumanganj, 3. Jagat Gaon, 4. Chaurbhujpur, 5. Pure Harsahai, 5. Pilepur.
33.	Mahrajpur	1. Maharajpur	1. Maharajpur Khas, 2. Kurmiyan Ka Purwa, 3. Khusadi.
34.	Agahar	1. Agahar	1. Agahardih, 2. Pure Ram Sewak, 3. Pure Bhawani, 4. Pure Gosnai, 5. Pure Patoli.
35.	Saidpur	1. Saidpur	1. Pure Shivalal, 2. Pure Dala, 3. Pure Vir Singh, 4. Saidpur
		2. Dalshahpur	1. Dalshahpur, 2. Ram Nagar Pur, 3. Sadakpur.
36.	Kakawa	1. Kakawa	1. Kuwnarganj, 2. Kakawa, 3. Pure Ganesh Baksh Singh, 4. Pure Ram Sahai, 5. Pure Girdhari, 6. Shahadara, 7. Kakarahia, 8. Voda Nagar, 9. Pure Valdi Tewari.
		2. Vidhasiya	1. Pure Gadarian, 2. Vidhasiya, 3. Pure Dhandauia, 4. Pure Valdu, 5. Pure Tada Tewari.
37.	Saraiya Duban	1. Saraiya Duban	1. Saraiya Duban, 2. Jaggubari, 3. Pure Lal Ram Prasad, 4. Gudiyan Tola, 5. Pure Man Kunwar, 6. Pure Brahmachari, 7. Murarpur.
38.	Kohara	1. Kohara	1. Harakhpur, 2. Dodhai Ka Purwa, 2. Dihawan, 4. Vishyapur, 5. Devigarh, 6. Kohara Khas, 7. Ahiranki Saraiya, 8. Aditya Nagar (Chamrauti). 9. Pure Jogdhar, 10. Ulapur, 11. Pure Shivdas, 12. Pure Hanuman Mishra. 14. Bhawani Baksh (Chaubepur), 14. Pure Jagannath. 15. Baniyan Ka Purwa, 16. Ganga Mishra Ka Purwa, 17. Pure Shiv Bhikh, 18. Malin Ka Purwa, 19. Ojha Ka Purwa, 20. Murai Ka Purwa, 21. Pure Bhadosian, 22. Mukunpur, 23. Pure Ghisiya.
39.	Mahmadpur	1. Mahmadpur	1. Mahmadpur, 2. Shankarpur, 3. Dudhai Ka Purwa, 4. Kalu Ka Purwa, 5. Sitaram Nagar, 6. Chaubepur, 7. Kurmi Ka Purwa, 8. Pure Baksh Singh, 9. Hulasi Ka Purwa, 10. Bhawani Baksh Ka Purwa, 11. Pure Pandit Ka Purwa, 12. Pure Hari Baksh.

(*Contd.*)

Table 1.1 (*Contd.*)

Sl. No.	Village Panchayat	Revenue Villages	Hamlet Villages/ Purwa/Tola
40.	Naraini	1. Naraini	1. Narainidih, 2. Pure Pachhim, 3. Pure Matlu, 4. Pure Wakta, 5. Dadi, 6. Pure Gangeran, 7. Pure Ayodhya, 8. Pure Khojhwa.
41.	Nainaha	1. Nainaha	1. Nainaha Khas, 2. Pure Tewari, 3. Pure Bishen, 4. Dhanapur, 5. Pure Satya Shukul.
		2. Bartali	1. Bartali Khas, 2. Dhaksahiya
		3. Rajapur Kohara	1. Pure Jangali, 2. Damgarha, 3. Rajapur, 4. Ajyab Sinda, 5. Sadarpur.
42.	Ramgarh	1. Ramgarh	1. Badisoiya, 2. Chhoti Soiya, 3. Pure Bhoop, 4. Rampur, 5. Bahni, 6. Mahoka, 7. Saraiya Purwa, 8. Pure Kotwa, 9. Ramgarh Khas.
43.	Himmatgarh	1. Himmatgarh	1. Pure Bhoop, 2. Madaripur, 3. Pure Ajit, 4. Jhali, 5. Visheshganj, 6. Pure Upadhyaya.
44.	Dehra	1. Dehra	1. Dehra Khas, 2. Pure Darjiyan, 3. Pure Shivpal, 4. Pure Pandey, Shanichara, 6. Gulabgarh, 7. Shukla Ka Purwa.
		2. Kudawa Mohamadpur	1. Daya Garha, 2. Pure Jhingur, 3. Kudwa Mahmadpur.
Total	**44**	**82**	**377**

The village panchayat is the lowest unit of development followed by the Block Panchayats and District Panchayat are engaged in the implementation of various need based village development programmes through people's participation at the grassroots level. All 44 village panchayats of the Amethi Block has been selected as study area to analyse the development planning, rural development programmes and village development planning through developing Village Information System for development planning.

4. SOURCE OF DATA

This study is based on micro-level information, i.e. grassroots level or village level Information System for development planning. Due attention has been given for the collection of dependable data which can be used for propounding a theory. The data base vary from the theme to another according to the nature of the problem. The various sources of information/data base for this volume of the study on the Village Information System for development planning has been as follows :

1. *Records* — Land revenue records, Amethi Tehsil, Village Khasara Map, Khasara Register, and other land revenue records, economic register from the Block Development Office, Amethi.
2. **District Statistical Hand Book** of Sultanpur and Rae Bareli Districts.
3. **Primary Census Hand Book/District Census** of the District Rae Bareli and District Sultanpur, 2001-2011.
4. **Fieldwork** — Most of the information and data had been collected through field-work questionnaires involving revenue officials, Village Development Official, Block Development Official, Village Pradhan, Members of the Village Land Management Committee of the respective villages. Village Panchayat Secretary, Rojgar Mitra, Panchayat Mitra and other Government and Non-Government officials of the Amethi Block. Requisite data has been collected through field observation, primary field survey and grassroots level fieldwork has been carried out to collect the informations related to the on-going implementation of various rural development

programmes and need based village development planning at village panchayat level in the Amethi Block.

5. **National Atlas for Thematic Maps Organization** (NATMO) maps of the District Rae Bareli and District Sultanpur.
6. **Survey of India** — Topo-sheets : 63f/10, 11, 12, 14, 15, 16, 63J/3, 4, 7, 8, 11, 12 and 63 k/5, 9.
7. **Annual Report** of the development of Forest, Government of Uttar Pradesh.
8. **Action Fieldwork** at grassroots level to evaluate and assess the implementation of on-going rural development programmes at village panchayat level in Amethi.
9. **District Development Planning** of Amethi, Sultanpur and Rae Bareli districts.
10. **Block Development Planning of the Amethi.**
11. **Village Planning** of village panchayats.
12. **Performance Budget 2011-12**, Department of Rural Development, Government of Uttar Pradesh.
13. **District Plan Budget 2012-13**, District Amethi.
14. **Block Yojana** of Amethi 2012-13.
15. **Village Panchayat Yojana** 2012-13 (44 Village panchayats of Amethi).

5. EXPLANATORY SYSTEM

The study of the casual relationship among the dependent variables and independent variables are an essential concern of any scientific investigation. Precise quantitative measurement of the degree and direction of correlations and co-efficient variations of correlations have been computed to analyse the variable data. The correlation matrix has been prepared to workout the correlation of dependent variables and independent variables as per requirements of the data analysis. The stepwise regression analysis has also been carried out as per the needs to analyse the collected data, as the final step to study inter-relationship between the dependent and independent variables related to village development.

6. CHOICE OF THE TIME PERIOD

The choice of the time period has been very much, a matter of convenience, as the analysis is based on field observations, direct fieldwork and primary field survey at the grassroots level. The time period for this volume of study on Village Information System for development planning has been based on the year 2011-12 as a base year, for observation of temporal variations 2001 to 2011 has been decided for the needful indicators at village panchayat level in Amethi. The fieldwork, field observation and direct field survey at the grassroots, level has been carried out for the recent years as per availability of the requisite data.

7. CARTOGRAPHIC TECHNIQUES

Various cartographic techniques has been adopted to represent and depict the collected and collated data in a graphic form. The choroplething techniques have been adopted to show the various indicators to rural development and village development planning at the village panchayat level in the Amethi Block. The Geographic Information System (GIS) techniques have been adopted for appropriate analysis of available information at village panchayat level in Amethi. Various other techno-scientific approaches have been applied to depict the variations of the rural development programmes and need based village development planning at village panchayat level in the Amethi Block.

8. CHOICE OF INDICATORS

The selection of the indicators plays an important role in analysing the study at grass-roots level. Various indicators related to the implementation of rural development programmes at the village panchayat level in the Amethi Block have been mentioned in Table 1.2.

The indicators related to the need based village development planning at village panchayat level in Amethi has been mentioned in Table 1.3.

9. DEVELOPMENT

The development is after all a multifaceted phenomenon. It can neither be understood, nor promoted unless it is seen from interdisciplinary and holistic perspectives. Moreover, development is basically a human enterprise and therefore, it requires the combined efforts of all systems of knowledge, be they physical, biological, social or human to comprehend and articulate it. It is more so with respect to planned development. Planning must draw upon all relevant disciplines including physics on the extreme and linguistics on the other.

The development is one which is pursued with genuine concern for human values. Development means the evolution of people in which the people acquires better perception and best control over its natural and human resources. In the process of development, growth alone does not ensure development.

The development must ensure the betterment and welfare of all the local people. Thus the feel good of the development has not been realized from National, State and District level but also from Block and village panchayat level perspectives. The existing development of process is neither true, nor good, nor beautiful but it does not mean that everything is wrong. Really the development lies in the development of Science and Technology and its application by the common people. The progress of the people in the Socio-Economic front has made more destructive than constructive approach of development for all the people in an integrated manner.

Thus, it has become a arduous task to find out a well accepted definition of development. The Techno-scientific, academic scholars across communities differ on its meaning, objectives, goals, shaped by the individual and collective perception and experience of the micro and macro aspects of their environment.

The development has been fundamentally a process of change that involves the whole society—its socio-economic, politico-cultural and physical structure as well as the value system and way of life of the people even surviving in the remote rural areas. The tools of measuring the level of development ranges from accessing economic factors and other socio-cultural political indicators realized against an accepted standards, norms and aspirations. The goals of development planning is to replicate the level of achievements of others which have been perceived as superior in the echelon of the development.

Thus, the National → State → District → Block → Village panchayat level administrative machineries and communities can be comparatively studied and the empirical differences between them can be used to illustrate the appropriate meaning

Table 1.2: Rural Development Programme

Sl. No.	*Particulars*	*Purwas/tolas/ Hamlet Villages*	*Revenue Villages*	*Village Panchayats*
(1)	(2)	(3)	(4)	(5)
1.	Mahatma Gandhi National Rural Employment Guarantee Act (MNREGA)			
2.	Education			
	1. Primary and Junior			
	2. High School and Intermediate			
	3. Higher Education			
	4. Technical Education			
	5. Professional/Skill Development Training Programme			
3.	Irrigation			
	1. Canal			
	2. Tube-wells Private			
	3. Government Tube-well			
	4. Other Sources of Irrigation			
4.	Drinking water — India Mark II Hand pumps			
5.	Youth Welfare Programmes			
6.	Medical and Health			
7.	Women and Child Development			
8.	Animal Department			
9.	Food Supply Shops			
10.	Agricultural Work			
	— Hybrid Seeds			
	— Fertilizers			
	— Insecticides/Pesticides			
11.	Rural Development Programmes			
12.	Panchayati Raj Institutions			
13.	All types of Pension and scholarship — BPL/OBC/SC/Minorities			
14.	Horticulture Programmes			
15.	Social Forestry Programmes			
16.	Jal Nigam			
17.	Public Works Department Road Constructions			
18.	Small Scale Industries			
19.	Agro Industries			
20.	Fisheries Work			
21.	Non-Conventional Energy Sources			
22.	Electricity-Private and Commercial			
23.	Rural Housing/Indira Avas Yojana			
24.	Low Cost Sanitation			
25.	Welfare Programmes — BPL/OBC/SC/Minorities/Others			
26.	Rural Roads — Pucca Road/Kachha Road/Kharanja Road/Chackroad			
27.	Dairy Development			
28.	Integrated Rural Development Programme			
29.	Pradhan Mantri Gram Sadak Yojana			
30.	Rajiv Gandhi Grameen Vidyutikaran Yojana			
31.	Pradhan Mantri Rojgar Yojana			
32.	National Rural Health Mission Programmes			
33.	Watershed Development			
34.	Pradhan Mantri Grameen Jal Samvardhan Yojana			
35.	Other Rural Development Programmes			

and level of development. At the National Level or Macro Level the focus of development as always been priority issues like poverty elimination, social inequality, unemployment and the development means and perceived to achieve these Macro-level goals with the view to increase the GDP. The development planning at the Macro-level, focused largely on economic growth. It has been justified by the overwhelming belief that by increasing the Gross National Product the base of economy may expand directly or indirectly, the benefits of growth shall percolate down to the poorest of the poor living in the remote rural areas and thereby to help in the eradication of poverty, inequality and

Table 1.3: Need Based Village Development Planning

Sl. No.	*Particulars*	*Purwas/tolas/ Hamlet Villages*	*Revenue Villages*	*Village Panchayats*
1.	MNREGA			
2.	Education			
3.	Irrigation			
4.	Drinking Water			
5.	Youth Welfare Programme			
6.	Medical and Health			
7.	Women and Child Development			
8.	Social Welfare Programmes SC/BC/Minorities/BPL			
9.	Animal Husbandry			
10.	Food Supply/Public Distribution System			
11.	Agriculture Development			
12.	Horticulture Development			
13.	Social Forestry Development			
14.	Rural Development			
15.	Panchayati Raj Institutions			
16.	Pension/Scholarship			
17.	Jal Nigam — Drinking Water			
18.	Road and Rural Road			
19.	Small Scale Industries			
20.	Agro-Industries			
21.	Fisheries Programmes			
22.	Non-commercial societies of Energy			
23.	Electricity			
24.	Low Cost Rural Housing			
25.	Low Cost Sanitation			
26.	Dairy Development			
27.	Integrated Rural Development			
28.	Pradhan Mantri Grameen Sadak Yojana			
29.	Rajiv Gandhi Grameen Vidyutikaran Yojana			
30.	Pradhan Mantri Grameen Rojgar Yojana			
31.	Rural Halth Mission Programmes			
32.	Wastelands Development			

unemployment at the grassroots level. It has been assumed that the quantitative rise in the Gross National Product (GNP) may automatically percolate to lower level deprived sections of the society who has been perceived as deprived. It has been realized and experienced that this has not happened at any level.

It has been realized that more than 30 per cent of the population continues to survive in abject poverty, deprived of access to education, health, sanitation, and other basic common minimum amenities for the survival of life. One can also ascribe that the level of the deprivation has been the potent cause of their socio-political marginalization offering little or no space to live as dignified entities in the contemporary society.

The agriculture is the backbone of our economy. The agriculture continues to employ as high as more than 40 per cent of the National Workforce offering little or no respite to teeming millions to break free from shackles of subsistence farming, which has been a key contributor of poverty. It has been stated that the common programmes of the development in different sectors has been concerned with the continued growth in employment and productivity in the different sectors of economy. In view of the above, there has been development in the different sectors of economy, i.e. Agriculture, Industsry, Mining and Social-Sciences, showing islands of prosperity benefiting a select stratum of the society.

It has been noticed that one of the most contested elections of the 21st century has been organized and fought under the theme of **"India Shining"** and the political party in question believed that by selling a dream it could ensure its return to the portals of power. The end result has been indeed disastrous for the election campaign managers who have learned in the hard way that winning the elections is not similar for promoting sales for consumer durables based on the strength of creative advertisement campaign. The former campaign required public trust. The political party lost power as masses of the people did not believe that their India was truly shining, so as to mark a difference in their day-to-day life. It has been felt by the large section of the society that the poverty is real, in which, the growth in the selected segments of the economy could not ameliorate. Thus the political election campaign debacle reiterate that few islands of prosperity here and there does not connote integrated development but the development is meaningful when it supports concentrate efforts that aim to empower the majority in planning and building the development process of reflecting their aspirations and requirements. The reasons for the development clearly indicates that the lack of commitment of the all concerned to really empower people in materializing the development goals. In a welfare district the development has been believed to be the sole duty of the Government and identification of the means its prerogative. The peoples are considered to be its beneficiaries and bureaucrats its architects. What is overlooked in the process is the need and the importance of participation. The development plan formulation is accompanied by a lot of prescriptions rather than to adopt an in-depth analysis to assess its strength, weakness, opportunities and threats on which the integrated development shall stand help and support communities desirous of adding value to their existing life. It has been realized that such development plannings are as bureaucratic, arrogance oblivious of the requirements of the people and unable to address them by building people the importance of evolving and ensuing people's partnership *vis-à-vis* formulation of the policy planning for integrated sustainable village development at the grassroots level.

In view of the above, backdrops of the popular perceptions of the integrated village development, its goals, utility and experiences so far, the important basic question still remains open and unanswered, that is, defining development. There are some questions in this regard may be:

- Does development connote initiated changes under a top down approach?
- Is development directed towards matching the life styles of the other peoples?
- Can the mode of integrated development be uniform across societies?
- Does the integrated village development means westernization through enabling a process of rampant and random initiation?
- Does the development means urbanization, cross materialism, industrialization or establishing socio-economic and politico-cultural, hegemony overtly or tacitly?
- Is there one best way to initiate and integrated village development?
- If the response to the above questions is a big no, then we are back again at the basic question of what is development?

In view of the above, it has been realized that the answer of development lies in defining the society as a collection of creativity that is imbibed, learnt, transferred and sharpened by ones daily experiences obtained from the circumstances and unique conditions specific to ones social-economic-environment with little or no resemblance with other areas.

Thus, it has been reviewed that the integrated development has a range of meanings and definitions but it has been commonly regarded as immanent and desirable hints at the material progress and improved standard of living irrespective of whether initiated under capitalistic orientation. The integrated development has to be planned and formulated, structured and carried out to have maximum leverage regarding its performance and have utility for those whose lives it purports to change or more on the basis rather than replacement of the various developmental programmes.

Thus, the development is the primary goal and thinking begins, with the emergence of capitalism and it has been observed that most of the village communities have been shut off from the main streams of the integrated village development. The inequalities between rural to urban and the gap has been widening due to rapid industrialization and urbanization, marketing and urban centres and unidirectional, non-planned development at the grassroots level. The dynamics of the urban and marketing centres do not tend to penetrate deeply to the socio-economic structure of the peripheral area. The centre, in contrast, propagates and spread in the periphery its technology, forms of the consumption, life styles, institutions and ideologies. The peripheral capitalism increasingly draws its inspiration from the centres and tends to develop its image, likeness and preferences. The penetration of technologies and it takes place through capital accumulation, in terms of both of the physical means and the training for the local people. In most of the remote rural villages the communities have been facing challenges for declining the real wages, very high under-employment and increasing rates of income inequality due to the consequences of capitalism. It has been noticed that during the recent years despite the unprecedented growth which has occurred in the service and trade sectors of the economy the rural trade sector has steadily lost market shares in the remote rural villages.

The United Nations Development Programme (UNDP) has determined the Human Development Index (HDI) on the three main parameters :

- ***Per Capita Income*** (Sufficient resource to live decent life),
- ***Education*** (Adult Literacy and Primary Education and Schooling),
- ***Life Expectancy at Birth*** (Health Care, Good quality drinking water, nutrition etc.).

The Human Development Index takes into accounts the efficiency of social, political and cultural variables. It also calculates the Human Freedom Index (HFI) that measures level of political participation, the role of law, freedom of expression and non-discrimination because it has been commented by Streeten that "Life expectancy and literacy could be quite high in a well managed prison and basic physical needs are well met in a zoo."

The development in the today's system is the modern advances in sciences, technology, democracy, values, ethics and social organization fuse into the single humanitarian programme of producing a better quality of life for those people surviving in the remote rural areas. The most important thematic deficiency of the traditional developmental economics has been related to the concentration on rational products, aggregate income and total supply of the particular goods rather than on entitlements of people and the capabilities of such entitlements. The village development is not complete with some physical inputs it includes social system or the norms of the society and the village people. The development does not resemble a one way traffic where utilities flow from one end to another. The development is a participative exercise which involves the common strength, combined infrastructural resources at the grassroots level and collective wisdom to make it effective through peoples participatory planning process for the integrated village development. Anything which calls for the common strength, resources and wisdom has its source in the culture of the people and it has been nothing but a social capital. To cope with the modern development the village community has to adopt an alternative measures that take into account social variables more attuned to development than just the economic growth the remote rural area. The conventional views of development ignore the ability of indigenous communities to articulate and negotiate their local village level identity in the midst of the rurban and urban pressure of development. It has been generally assumed that the village people face cultural extinction when confronted with modernizing forces, which has been frequently given the level of "Progress" a symbol for integrated village development. The alternative views, for the integrated village development, not only encompass both the indigenous people and the local grassroots level environment with also challenge the linear, top to down approaches of main stream of development efforts, such as conventional conceptions of the sustainable development, that all too frequently ignore the cultural and social capital of the so-called traditional social systems of the society at village level. The norms of the traditional villages are also independent and such socio-economic backward villages are to be incorporated hand to hand with the conventional factors in designing the integrated village development model. An effort must be made to recognize that the so-called traditional norms and practices are not isolated, static or absolute artifacts that only have a place in museum and that so called grassroots level force of changes are not homogenously hegemonic. The role of social systems in the process of sustaining economic development has been examined and analysed by the various social scientist at the different levels. The social scientists attempted to seek to expand the understanding of the village level available local social infrastructure, structure and how it affects the welfare of the people on development places. The scientists and research scholars have diverted their attention from conventional models of the village development to the alternative, community based models that put to the interests of workers and the community sustainability over rurban and urban, marketing centers. It has been realized that the cultures play a significant role in the economic growth. It has also been advocated that in the peripheral development the science and technology accompanied through the continuous changes in their social structure play a fundamental role for the integrated village development.

10. DEVELOPMENT POLICY

The terms 'development' has been generally used in connection with the poor or under developed remote rural areas. The development differs from the economic growth. The development pays attention to the conditions of the production, for example, the environments especially affected by the various economic activities and also to the social consequences, for example, income distribution and human welfare. Stemming from enlightenment notions of the use of the modern, techno-scientific minds for improving existence, development entails the human emancipation in two senses :

- Liberation from the vicissitudes of the nature through advanced technology and self-emancipation.
- Control over social, relations, consciousness control over the conditions under which the human nature is formed.

In the both senses the development entails socio-economic-cultural progress including in the latter sense, the finer ethical ideals and higher moral values. The development means improvement in a complex of linked nature socio-economic, cultural and political conditions.

The social capital has been defined as the norms, networks and social trust that make society/community to function more smoothly. The social capital theory explains development from a structural rather than an economic perspectives. The emphasis in the social capital has been on the 'embeddedness' within which economic relations take place, based on the notions both individuals and group decisions are embedded in a particular social context that includes community traditions, norms, networks and the likeness of the people and society. The diversity of the village institution has been instrumental in how the government policies, planning and economy and environmental changes affect the economic activities and income of the village poors which has been responsible for the integrated village development.

The developmentalism is the belief in the visibility of this kind of socio-economic progress of the grassroots area. A resource rich region including Natural → Social → Economic → Institutional infrastructural resources can be developed only when it is exploited effectively, efficiently as per the common minimum needs of the people in the right direction. It has been realized that the three things are essential for rural development to succeed in a global environment.

- Human Capital,
- Physical Infrastructure, and
- Adequate Financing.

The human capital and infrastructure has been termed as public capital and it has critical components of the sustainable integrated development of the people living the remote villages. It has been felt that the third element should be social capital. The communities that have been thriving social networks, institutions and good human capital must have adequate financing as well. The another very much important component has been debated about today has been the social capital. The importance of infrastructure in the development of the village economy has been accepted by everyone, but the equally important factor which has not been noticed by everyone has been the social norms at grassroots level. It has been suggested by the various social scientists that the economics growth has been largely the result of the investment in the human capital. It has also been agreed that an increase in the capital-income ratio has been largely due human capital development, not material capital especially-reproducible and non-human capital, which has been originally thought to account for all increase in the income and subsequent economic growth. An investment in the human knowledge and skills has been the critical determinant of the economic growth and it has been necessary if the village lacking human capabilities ever expected to attract and fully benefit from infusions of new capital. The integrated village development policies and planning must be formulated as per the needs of the local villagers and through ensuring the peoples participation. The implementation of the people's participation planned village development programmes should be ensured through peoples participation and the maintenance of the implementation of village development programmes should be maintained and managed through the local level village beneficiaries for its sustenance.

11. HUMAN DEVELOPMENT

It has been noticed that, of late, the various economists have shifted their main focus from different development indicators to the human beings as one of the forceful catalysts for attaining all round integrated development at the village level at the grassroots level. The people have grown and become advanced, out perspectives towards life has also come under the dramatic transformations. One of the major factor, depending, for defining the economic development, i.e. income, has now been considered out of date. In real sense, it is not only the single factor for looking at a country's advancement. In spite of the income, there are other factors influence the integrated development of the remote rural area.

The human/population are one of the very precious and powerful resources which can tigger all-round development of a region— "diverse patterns of the development has been, of course, the product of a number of historical, cultural and various other circumstances peculiar to various countries involved. In view of these special circumstances, there has been certain forces which has been found, by the economists, to be central point for the process of economic growth at the micro-level. One of the above productive and valuable apparatuses has been human beings, which needs to be converted into human capital for all-round development of the area. The development of human beings has been one of the fore most criteria today, for the speedy economic growth and the integrated development of the village. The human development encompasses various spheres of life that have to be moulded in accordance to the needs of the local people for achieving the required economic growth rate at the village level. The levels and disparities of the human development at the micro-level plays an important role for the sustained integrated development at the grassroots level.

The human development has been a process of enlarging people's choices and need based preferences at the village level. Among other things the choices of the humans are to lead a long and healthy life, to be educated and to enjoy a decent standard of living.

Thus, the basic objectives of the human development has been to create an enabling environment in which the people can enjoy long life, healthy and creative lives. Still the vision of the United Nations Development Programme (UNDP) retains a powerful significance for the human development. If these essential choices are not available, many other opportunities remain inaccessible. The human development does not end here. The additional choices of the people has been highly valued by many economists, range from economic, political and social freedom to opportunities for being creative and productive and enjoying personal self-respect and guaranteed human values and rights at the village level. The human development has mainly two aspects :

I. **The formation of Human Capabilities** — such as improved health, knowledge and skills.
II. **The use of people's acquired capabilities** — for leisure, productive purpose or being active in the social, cultural and political affairs.

If the scales of human development do not finely balance the two sides, considerable human frustration may occur. Therefore, it is apparent that the human development does not only mean increasing one's income and accumulating the same, but sometimes more than that. The income has been just a means for the satisfaction of the people always provide happiness to the people — the happiness of common people sometimes look for. According to United Nations Development Programme (UNDP) the human development can be measured through including some variables as indicators of the human development infrastructural resources at the village level. The infrastructural indicators may together reflect the attainment of human development. In reality, there are various numbers of indicators for measuring human development which includes Natural-Social-Economic-Institutional Infrastructural resources available at the grassroots level or village level. The development is possible only when rural India or rural areas/ remote villages are developed. In spite of massive development efforts initiated and undertaken by the Government of India and State Governments in the different plan periods, the problems of malnutrition mass poverty, malignant growth of unemployed youth and large scale migration of the people to the urban areas persists in the remote rural villages. Unless we improve the rural economy, one cannot lessen the burden of poverty nor can we solve the problems of unemployment. It has been noticed that more than 40 per cent of our rural population still lives under the below poverty line (BPL). The problem of unemployment cannot be tackled by creating more jobs in the public sector and other government agencies and non-government organizations. The skill development, small scale entrepreneurship for self-employment and expansion of the job opportunities at the village level. The educated youth sat the village level must be trained and involved in the entrepreneurship oriented vocations through different Entrepreneurship Development Programmes (EDP) and Skill Development Training Programme through Science and Technology at the grassroots level or village level with the view to generate employment and increase the income of the deprived rural poor multitudes for the overall economic growth and human development.

12. PLANNING

The planning is an organized process by which the people achieves, its developmental goals or planning is a means to achieve the development. But, when, the intentions and objectives of the development are distorted, then planning also becomes a distorted exercise.

The planning is a systematic procedure which objects at the implementation of the several specific aims and objectives, therefore, it is necessary to :

- Specify quantified targets.
- Specify potential variants of reaching such targets, i.e. variants of utilization of various resources.
- Find out the available infrastructural resources reaching such targets.
- Provide the targets, if some of the resources are not fully utilized or proved insufficient for reaching the targets.
- Find out which variant is optimal in the sense of allowing the best set of targets to be reached with the available Natural-Social-Economic-Institutional infrastructural resources.
- Organize the instruments which may ensure operational implementation of the variant finally chose.
- Organize the instruments which may ensure operational implementation of the planned programmes as per the needs of the local level village people.
- Supervise the process of implementation in order to find out eventual discrepancies and set in motion the adaptive activities.
- Ensure need base formulations of the policy planning at the village level.
- People's participatory integrated village development planning at the grassroots level must be ensured.
- Participation of the village people in the implementation of the planned programmes for the integrated village development.
- Appropriate planning and policies must be ensured to maintain and manage the successfully implemented village development programmes for its further sustenance and optimal utilization of created and developed infrastructure at the grassroots level.

Presently, in our country planning is done without willing consent of the local village people. It has been noticed that in some cases the planners interpret people's need and aspirations for developing a plan for the people. Lastly, the planning is the task of the people in which the planners can provide back up support to achieve their planning goals. The government has been stressing very hard for the involvement of the people in the development, i.e. development planning from within.

Thus, the planners will have to provide developmental planning as per the needs of the local level village people. To provide techno-scientific backup support at the grassroots level, i.e. village level to the village peoples representatives, villagers, and officials involved in the implementation and maintenance of the integrated village development and in the formulation of the need based village development planning. The planners should not be only a technocrat to provide projections but they should assist villagers as a social scientists who can easily understand the basic grassroots level needs of the village people is planned and the development activities are carried out as per the need of the people, with the involvement of the village people, for the village people and the village development is achieved as per the planned target according to increasing demand of the ever increasing cattle and the human population.

13. DEVELOPMENT PLANNING

It has been noticed that in our country there is a quest for evolving a model for planning at various levels. Macro-level resource planning has been adopted in India and it did not yield the desired results due to inequities amongst people and disparities between one region and the another regions. The environmental conditions continued to degrade leading to severe stress on land and water (Natural) resources. Around late 1970s sustainable and integrated development the areas has been ensured. In this regard conceptual changes in the planning practice has been adopted in the micro-level or local level process of planning. The objectives of the decentralized process of planning area :

- To increase the productivity of the land.
- To increase the scope for employment generation with the focus on creation and development of assets.
- Poverty alleviation.
- Providing minimum amenities and infrastructural facilities at the grassroots level.

Institutional changes has been brought to implement the strategy of the development planning through the 73rd and 74th Constitutional Amendment Acts (1992 and 1993). The State Governments have been empowered through the institutions of local level self-governance right from the Village Level-Block Level-District Level and within the Municipal jurisdiction, i.e. Panchayats and Nagar Palikas in the context of rural and urban respectively. The Eleventh and Twelfth Schedules of the Constitution, while specifying the Sectors for the Panchayats and Nagar Palikas have also been defined and the role for the multi-level institutions of governance in planning and implementing the integrated rural development schemes. The State Governments have accordingly constituted such local level bodies with definite mandates to collect revenues, to draw need based plan and implement integrated rural development programmes the rough people participation. It requires the capacity building at the institutions of local self-governance to prepare and implement the need base area specific integrated village development programmes by assessing and utilizing the available Natural, Social,

Economic, Institutional and Human Infrastructural resources available at the grassroots level.

The formulation of the policy planning and implementation of the various integrated rural development programmes in the remote rural area is an information oriented intensive task. The Natural and Human Infrastructural Resources Data Management System, which are existing at the grassroots level or Village Level to Block Level and District Level are not properly arranged but such available information needs to be integrated for village development planning. The conventional methods of the data collection, collation and storage are not amenable for the quick updation, retrieval and holistic analysis and several problems which are existing in the conventional system has been follows :

(i) In compatible and non-standard data sets inhibiting integration of the available infrastructural resources.
(ii) In-efficient inter-sectoral data flow.
(iii) Lack of information on quality, completeness and lineage of the available data.
(iv) Integrated approach to the planning process requires a detailed knowledge of the interrelations and inter-dependencies between various sectors to resolve often conflicting demands. This lead to a requirement for appropriate data management and analysing tools and techniques and large matrix of sectoral indicators information, in a digital format related to Natural, Social, Economic- Institutional Infrastructural resources and invites for the specific scientific and technological interactions:

- Creation of the need base data.
- Development and improvement in the data handling and analysis tools.
- Efficient distribution of data and information to the use institutions and the integrated development planning and programme implementing agencies at the grassroots level.

In view of the above, requirements and the developments in the area of Information and Communication Technology (ICT) and Geo-spatial Data Management System and Analysing Techniques, like Remote Sensing and Geographical Information System (GIS) certain initiations awareness on the usefulness of these technologies amongst planners and the decision makers. The Natural Resources Data Management System (NRDMS) prograamme of the Department of Science and Technology, Government of India has been such pioneering efforts while the other programmes are as follows :

- National Natural Resources Informaiton System (NRIS), Department of Space.
- Integrated Mission for Sustainable Developmenet (IMSD) Department of Space.
- Geographic Information System (GIS), District Information System (DIS) of the National Informatics Centres (NIC).

The collection, collation, storage and analysis of the available National and Human (Economic, social, institutional) Infrastructural Resources Data at the grassroots level or at the village level will be an asset for the formulation of the policy planning according to the needs of the deprived rural poor multitudes and implementation of the planned rural development programmes through ensuring people participation and to ensure the maintenance and management of the created assets for the optimal utilization of the common village people.

14. INFRASTRUCTURAL RESOURCES DATA MANAGEMENT SYSTEM (IRDMS)

It is well-known fact that there is a longest tradition of systematic collection of spatial data through various organizations at the National Level in India. Different line departments are engaged in the collection of Non-spatial Data in a strong traditional system. Hanumantha Rao Committee (1984) has emphasized on the management of the spatial data for the efficient local level integrated village development planning.

In view of the above, requirements, the Department of Science and Technology, Government of India, during 1983, started a programme on the Natural Resources Data Management System (NRDMS). The Natural Resources Data Management System in a multi-interdisciplinary and multi-institutional Research Development Programme with a vision to provide appropriate scientific and technological inputs for operationalizing the concept of decentralized planning. The main objective of the Natural Resources Data Management System (NRDMS) is to develop scientific data base approach to support the local level planning. During the end of the first decade of the programme, the 73rd and 74th Constitutional Amendments came into being and with the entry of the computers at the District Level and Geographic Information System (GIS) in India, during the late 1980s the goals of Natural Resources Data Management System programmes has been evolved to develop spatial data management technologies for integrated rural development planning and its demonstration in the local decision making process in the context of the Natural Resources Data Management System. Many National Resources which are important for the local area development specially for the policy making, need based plan development through people's participations. The Natural Resources Data Management System (NRDMS) has been supporting various academic, Techno-scientific, Research and Development Programmes through Grants-in-Aid Projects at various levels.

The Natural Resources Data Management System has always been supporting and focusing on technological and institutional capacity building in a multi-level framework so that the local village level people can utilize the available Natural and Human Resources to meet their day-to-day increasing demands. In this regard Natural Resources Data Management System develops and provides scientific tools and techniques for assessing local level Natural Resources endowments and its appropriate utilization, potential and generating the alternative scenarios for the integrated village development planning.

It has been noticed that in spite of the national efforts, spanning several years large segments of end-users are yet to explore the full potential of the system and the natural Resources Data Management System created and generated data has been used for the planning activities. But due to the lack of the technical organizational and institutional capacity the NRDMS data has not been properly utilized for the policy decisions and need based plan formulations. To reduce the impediments in the widespread use of the technological and scientific applications and to make it an effective tool in the process of local level integrated development planning at the grassroots level. The Natural Resources Data Management System has been focusing its research on simplifying the methods and techniques of the data collection, collation, its organization, analysis, and to devise suitable strategies to transfer the techniques for adoption by the end user implementing institutions for the programme planning activities.

In view of the above, it has been noticed that the recent trends in the development of spatial data technologies and the emerging changes in the system of governance, planning, policies and its institutionalization to meet the aspirations of the users and in support of the transformation in the concept of information sharing and the felt need for refocusing the Research and Development programmes.

- The spatial Data Management and Analysis Techniques.
- Applications of advanced technologies in the large scale spatial data collection and collation.
- Natural (Land and Water) Resources Data Management.
- Transfer of Technology and institutional capacity building at the grassroots level.

The vision of the Natural Resources Data Management System has been to enable the people, communities and institutions of Self-Governance with Spatial Data Technologies through ensured peoples participation in the decision-making and need base formulation of the integrated village development planning to strengthen the three-tier Panchayati Raj Institutions.

The basic goals of the Natural Resources Data Management System has been to strengthen the Techno-scientific inputs for the integrated infrastructural resources management through development of appropriate tools and techniques for collection, collation of the data, and its analysis for the plan formulation.

The objectives of the Institutional Infrastructural Resources Data Management System (IRDMS) have demonstrated and promoted the use of Spatial Data Technologies for the micro-level planning.

- To provide software support for the management of the requisite formation for the research and development activities.
- To promote the Research and Development through application of the spatial Data Technologies.
- To promote the transfer of technology and the capacity, building of the potential users.
- To provide Techno-Scientific inputs for framing policies related to Spatial Data Techniques.
- To develop and demonstrate pilot level spatial infrastructure resources data management system.
- To provide appropriate support for research and development through Spatial Data Infrastructural Resources Data Management.
- To ensure proper documentation and the dissemination of the collected, collated data for appropriate use of the policy makers and need base people participatory integrated village development planning process at the grassroots level.

In order to implement at least some of the activities to realize the vision of the Infrastructural Resources Data Management System, support from a large segment of scientists and entrepreneurs are required. The Infrastructural Resources Data Management System is expected to stimulate the imagination of the research community to relate specific problems in the areas of their interest and to evolve suitable research programmes to pursue line of investigation to arrive at meaningful solution to the problems as well as in advancing the existing knowledge in certain spheres of activity thereby aiding the overall development at the grassroots level or village level and to strengthen the Panchayati Raj Institutions.

15. RURAL DEVELOPMENT

The Government of India has initiated several programmes to develop the rural areas and also trying to ensure the faster development to bridge the gap between rural to urban. An appropriate and faster development of rural areas are required to fulfil the even increasing demand of the growing population so that the disparities between rural and urban can be bridged through ensuring integrated rural development.

It has been realized that the development should be formulated according to the needs of the local rural people. The rural development must be planned through tapping the local talent and available Natural Resources and Human Infrastructural Resources available at the grassroots level.

The Government of India has launched following several rural developmental progrmmes for upliftment and proper development of the deprived and downtrodden vulnerable sections of the society :

- **National Social Assistance Programme (NSAP)** is a welfare programme being administered by the Ministry of Rural Development. These welfare programmes are meant for providing social assistance benefit to the ages, the BPL household in the case of death of the primary bread earner and for maternity.
- **Mahatma Gandhi National Rural Employment Guarantee Act (MNREGA)** has been launched to enhance the livelihood, security in rural areas by providing at least 100 days guaranteed wage employment in a financial year to every household whose adult members volunteer to do unskilled manual work.
- **Mahila Kisan Sashaktikaran Pariyojana (MKSP)** has been initiated for the rural women who form the most productive workforce in the economy of majority of the rural people. The basic objective of this programme is to empower women in agriculture by making systematic investments to enhance their participation and productivity, as also to create and sustain agriculture based livelihood of rural poor women.
- **Special Projects for Placement linked skill development of the Rural BPL Youth under Swaranjayanti Gram Swarojgar Yojana (SGSY)** is a special project for skill development to ensure a time-bound training and capacity building programme for bringing a specific number of Below Poverty Line families above the poverty line through placement ensuring regular wage employment to rural youth.
- **Swarnjayanti Gram Swarojgar Yojana (SGSY)** has been launched to bring the assisted poor families (*swarojgaris*) above the poverty line by ensuring appreciable sustained level of income over a period of time. The main objective of the programme is to achieve through *inter alia* organizing the rural poor into Self-Help Groups (SHGs) through the process of social mobilization, their training and capacity building and provision of income generating assets.
- **Pradhan Mantri Gram Sadak Yojana (PMGSY)** is launched to provide all weather road connectivity in the rural areas. The programme envisages connecting all habilitations with a population of 500 persons and above in the plain areas.
- **Hariyali** programme has been launched to harness every drop of rain water for purpose of irrigation and Integrated Wastelands Development Programmes (IWDP), Drought Prone Areas Programme (DPAP) and Desert Development Programme through involving Panchayati Raj Institutions (PRIs) more meaningfully in planning, implementation and management of economic development activities.

- **Rural Housing Programme** known as Indira Awaas Yojana (IAY) has been launched primarily to help construction/upgradation of dwelling units of members of scheduled castes, freed bonded labourers, minorities in the below poverty line category and other below poverty line non-scheduled caste rural households by providing them a lump sum financial assistance.
- **Computerization of Lands Records (CLRs)** scheme has been launched to provide computerized copies of Records of Rights (RORs). The ultimate objective of the scheme is on-line management of land records.
- **Watershed Development Programme (WDP)** has been launched for treating degraded lands with the help of low cost moisture conservation measures, afforestation, etc. and through a participatory approach to converse the wastelands and improve the degraded environment of the area.
- **Rural Drinking Water Supply (RDWS)** has been initiated to provide drinking water facilities to rural areas because water is an essential ingredient of people's daily ife.
- **Rural Sanitation Programme** is being implemented to remove the disposal of human excreta of cess-pools, open ditches, pit latrines, bucket system etc. The water, sanitation, health hazards and consumption of unsafe drinking water, improper disposal of human excreta, lack of personal and health hygiene have caused several diseases. High Infant Mortality Rate (IMR) has also been attributed to poor sanitation.
- **National Rural Health Mission (NRHM)** Programme has been launched to provide health feasibilities to all resourceless deprived rural poor multitudes living in the remote villages.
- **Rajeev Gandhi Grameen Vidyutikaran Yojana (RGGVY)** has been initiated to provide Electricity Connections to the people living in the remote village and surviving under the Below Poverty Line.
- **Pradhan Mantri Grameen Jal Samvardhan Yojana (RMGJSY)** is being implemented for water conservation, water storage technologies to mitigate the efforts of drought and improving ground water potential and augmenting water supply especially to meet the drinking water requirements through rain water harvesting of rainy water stressed villages.
- **National Biogas Programme** has been launched for appropriate utilization of cow-dung for developing bio-gas and bio-fertilizer to increase the fertility status of the soil for increasing agricultural productivity.
- **National Health Insurance Programme (NHIP)** has been initiated to facilitate the health Insurance Policy during hospitalization, Medical and health facilities and treatment of various diseases for the Below Poverty Line (BPL) families and to provide free medical health services to the downtrodden deprived resourceless rural poor people.

In spite of the above, there are various other welfare programmes for scheduled caste, minorities, tribals, old age persons, scholarships, pensions, Panchayati Raj Institutions and ***Bharat Nirman*** programme launched and implemented by the Government of India along with the Members of Parliament, Local Area Development Programmes to ensure sustainable integrated rural development.

The Government of Uttar Pradesh has also initiated various rural development programmes :-

- Swaranjayanti Gram Swarojgar Yojana (SGSY).
- Mahatma Gandhi National Rural Employment Guarantee Act (MNREGA).

- Indira Avas Yojana.
- Mahamaya Avas Yojana.
- Mahamaya Sarvjan Avas Yojana for Non-Scheduled Caste Avas Yojana.
- Pradhan Mantri Gram Sadak Yojana.
- Rural Drinking Water Supply.
- State Drinking Water and Sanitation Mission Swajaldhara Programme.
- Member of Legislative Assembly, Local Area Development Fund (MLA-LAD).
- Construction of Community Hall for scheduled caste dominant villages.
- Ambedkar Vishesh Rojgar Yojana (AVRY).
- National Bio-Gas Programme.
- Community Development Programme.
- National Health Insurance Scheme.
- District Rural Development Agency.
- Regional/District Rural Development Institutes/Extension Education Programmes.
- Deen Dayal Upadhyay State Rural Development Institute.
- Uttar Pradesh Grameen Avas Parisha.
- E-Governance Programme.
- Bhoomi Sena Programme.

Allocated Programmes of the District Panchayat

- Medical and Health.
- Development Programme.
- Education.
- Government Tube-wells.
- Youth Welfare Programme.
- Women and Child Development.
- Animal Husbandry.
- Food Supply Shops.
- Agriculture and Horticulture Department.
- Panchayati Raj.
- Jal Nigam.
- Food Supply.
- Forest Department.
- Public Works Department.
- Irrigation Department.
- Industries.
- Fisheries Department.
- Other Departments.

Programmes of the Block Panchayat

- Rural Development Programmes.
- Primary Health Centres.
- Animal Hospitals.
- Seed Centres.
- Marketing Stores.

- Care of Additional Villages.
- Maintenance of Assets.

Programmes of the Village Panchayats

- Education — Primary and Secondary Education.
- Government Tube-well.
- Hand Pumps.
- Youth Welfare.
- Medical and Health.
- Women and Child Development.
- Animal Husbandry.
- Food Supply Shops.
- Agriculture Work.
- Rural Development.
- Panchayati Raj Department.
- All types of Pensions and Scholarships.

In view of the above, it is evident that the Government of India → State Government of Uttar Pradesh → District Panchayat Amethi → Block Panchayat Amethi → Village Panchayat of Amethi have earmarked their action plan to ensure integrated village development to fulfil the ever increasing demand of growing population. An attempt has been made to analyse the policy planning, rural development programmes and need base village development planning at village panchayat level in Amethi.

16. CONCLUSION

Economic development has been realized at various levels and commendable advances have been made in the diversified rural development. It has been noticed that several implemented rural development programmes failed to translate into better and dignified life for the majority of the people living in the remote rural areas.

It is known fact that more than three-forth population live in the rural areas who are deprived of the basic common amenities and necessities required for the survival of the human being. It has been noticed that there is faster development of the rural areas followed by rurban areas while rural areas are socially, economically and educationally backward. The village people are isolated from the main streams and the villages are identified as an independent unit for implementation of rural development programmes.

In view of the above, an attempt has been made in this study to analyse the "Village Information System" — Development Planning at village panchayat level in Amethi, covering 377 Purwas/Tolas/Hamlet Villages and 82 Revenue Villages and 44 Village Panchayats of the Amethi Block.

The social structure of the village or gaon or gram is not just a physical space or settlement of a group of people. The social life in the village is organized through definite ritual and secular principles, such as those of castes, kinship, politics, economy and religion, etc.

The physical characteristics of the village have a definite pattern of social relations based on traditional principles of kinship and marriage ceremony such as those of village exogamy. The social relations extend the interactive network and social space of a village well beyond its boundaries into surrounding villages. The community institutions and organization are flexible and fail to adjust to the changing needs of villages. The communities' traditional norms and conventions have been formed slowly over many many years.

It has been realized that the development should be participatory and it should be planned according to the local needs of the deprived rural resourceless poor multitudes. The development should be planned through tapping the local level talent and available natural and human infrastructural resources. The planning process has been done from bottom to top. The real meaning of democracy is the importance of the people and village self-government is the main soul of the rural development. Governance—Management, Financial and Administrative control of the village panchayat, continued participation, cooperation of the people to establish the village panchayat for the Self-Governance to ensure people's participatory planning and the implementation integrated village development programmes are being ensured for the self-sustenance of the remote villages of Amethi Block.

The main objectives of this study is to analyse the policy, planning, programmes and to assess the implementation of rural development programmes and to explain the need based people's participatory development planning at village panchayat level in Amethi.

Effort has been made to explain the various policies, plannings initiated by the Government of India and State Government of Uttar Pradesh and the District Panchayat → Block Panchayat → Village Panchayat. Various indicators related to the rural development programmes and the need based village development planning of grassroots level has been selected and primary field survey at the field level has been carried out to collect the requisite data for an appropriate analysis and assessment of the implementation of various rural development programmes and also to explain the people's participatory need based village development planning at the village panchayat level in Amethi because the development is a multifaceted phenomenon. The development is basically a human enterprise and it requires the combined efforts of all the systems of knowledge, whether, they be physical, biological, social or human to comprehend and articulate it.

The development is one which is pursued with genuine concern for human values. The development means evolution of people in which the people acquires better perception and best control over its natural and human infrastructural resources.

The development has been fundamentally a process of change that involves the whole society its socio-economic, politico-cultural and physical structures as well as the value system and way of life of the people even living in the remote rural areas. The tools of measuring the levels of development ranges from assessing economic factors and other socio-cultural, political indicators realized against an accepted standards, norms and aspirations. The goals of development planning is to replicate the level of achievements of others which has been perceived as superior in the echelon of the development.

The development in the today's system is the modern advances in science, technology, democracy, values, ethics and social organization, fuse into the single humanitarian programme of producing a better quality of life for those people living in the remote villages.

The social scientists have attempted to seek to expand the understanding of the village level available social infrastructure and how it affects the welfare of the people and development of places. The scientists and research scholars have diverted their attention from conventional models of the village development to the alternative, community based models that put to the interest of works and the community sustainability over urban and rurban marketing centres. It has been realized that the clusters play a significant role in the economic growth. It has also been advocated that in the peripheral development, the science and technology accompanied through the continuous changes in their social structural play a fundamental role for the integrated village development.

The human development has been a process of enlarging people's choices and need based preferences at the village level. The basic objectives of the human development has been to create an enabling environment in which the people can enjoy long life, healthy and creative livelihood at village level. The infrastructural indicators may together may reflect the attainment of human development. In reality, there are various numbers of indicators for measuring human development which includes — Natural-Social-Economic-Institutions (Human) infrastructural resources available at the village level. The development is possible only when rural India or rural areas or remote rural villages are developed.

In spite of massive development efforts initiated, undertaken by the Government of India, Government of Uttar Pradesh in the different plan-periods, the problems of the malnutrition, mass poverty, malignment, growth of unemployed rural youth and large scale migration of people to the urban areas residing in the rural villages, unless we improve the rural economy, one cannot lesson the burden of poverty nor can we solve the problems unemployment. It has been noticed that more than 40 per cent of our rural population still lives under the below poverty line.

The problem of unemployment cannot be tackled by creating more jobs in the public sector and other government agencies and non-governmental organizations (NGOs). The skill development, small scale entrepreneurship for self-employment, and expansion of the job-opportunities at the village level. The educated youths at the village level must be trained and involved in the entrepreneurship oriented vocations through different Entrepreneurship Development Programmes (EDP) and Skill Development Training Programme through Science and Technology at the village level with the view to generate employment and increase the income of the deprived rural poor multitudes for the overall economic growth and integrated village development.

It has been realized that there is a quest for evolving a model for planning at various levels. The Constitutional and Institutional changes has been brought to implement. The State Government has been empowered through the institutions of local self-governance, right from the Village Level → Block Level → District Level. The State Governments have accordingly constituted such local level bodies with definite mandates to collect revenues, to draw need based plan and to implement integrated rural development programmes through peoples participation. It requires the capacity building at the institutions of local Self-Governance to prepare and implement the need base local area specific integrated village development programmes through assessing and utilizing the available Natural-Human (Social-Economic-Institutional) Infrastructural Resources available at the grassroots level.

The formulation of the policy, planning and implementation of the various integrated rural development programmes in the remote villages is an information oriented intensive tasks. The Government of India has initiated various programmes to develop the rural areas and also trying to ensure the faster development to bridge the gap between rural to urban. It has been realized that the development should be formulated according to the local needs of the villagers. The Government of India and State Government of Uttar Pradesh has launched various need based rural development programmes for upliftment and appropriate development of the deprived, downtrodden resourceless vulnerable sections of the society living in the remote villages.

The Panchayati Raj Institutions have been strengthened, financial and administrative powers have been allocated to the Village-Block-District Panchayat with the view to ensure people's participatory need based integrated village development. In view of the an attempt has been made in the third volume of the Village Information System to analyse the various policy, planning and programmes initiated by the Government of India and State Government and District Level three-tier Panchayati Raj Institutions, i.e. District-Block-Village Panchayat and to assess the implementation of various rural development programmes at village panchayat level in the Amethi Block and to explain the people's participatory need based village development planning at village panchayat level in Amethi Block, which will be a mile stone for the grassroots level policy planners, implementing agencies, research scholars and various government and non-government implementing institutions and local level villagers, Village Panchayat representatives, Village Pradhans, Block Development Committee Members and Block Pramukh and District Panchayat Committee Members and Chairman and the District Rural Development Agency, Amethi and others engaged in the implementation of various rural development programmes at grassroots level in Amethi.

2

Policy and Planning

1. INTRODUCTION

Integrated Development has been realized at various levels from top to bottom. Commendable advances have been made in the diverse field of rural development programme but it has been recorded incomplete in reality because such implemented rural development programmes failed to translate into better and dignified meaning for the life of the majority of the people who are surviving in the remote villages. It has been noticed that the rural areas are comparatively backward than the urban areas. Therefore, the appropriate planning and faster integrated development of the rural areas are required to fulfil the ever increasing demand of the growing population so that the disparities between urban to rural areas can be bridged to ensure the integrated village development.

It has been observed that the policy, planning for the various development programmes is being formulated without willing consent and need of the local level village people. In most of the cases the planners interpret people's requirements and aspirations for developing plan for the people but their continued participation in the programmes' implementation has been mostly ignored. Lastly, the planning is the task of the people in which the policy-makers can provide backup support to achieve their planning goals. The government is stressing hard for ensuring peoples involvement in the plan formulation and continued participation in the implementation of the integrated village development with the view to ensure the development planning from within.

The policy-makers and the planners must have to provide integrated development planning, scientific and technical backup support to the grassroots level, i.e. village level people's representatives including the villagers and involved officials of the village panchayats in the formulation of integrated village development planning. The policy, planners should not only be a technocrat to provide projections but they should assist the village panchayat's representatives and villagers as a social workers who can easily understand the basic requirements of the village peoples and also formulate the programmes policy, planning and ensure people's participation in the implementation of the planned integrated village development programmes. Thus, the policy, planning of the village development programmes must be carried out as per the needs and requirements of local village people, with the involvement of the village people, for the village people and with the participation of the village people to achieve formulated planned, integrated village development targets.

In view of the above, an attempt has been made in this part of the study to analyse the formulated policies, visions and the initiatives of the Government at various levels to strengthen the grassroots level, i.e. village panchayat level. Panchayati Raj Institutions with the view to bridge the gap between rural to rurban to urban through ensuring faster and rapid integrated development of the backward remote villages of the Amethi.

2. POLICIES

It has been noticed that there is a quest for evolving a model for planning. Mostly, macro-level resource management planning has been adopted in India. The approach for the macro-level planning in India did not yield the desired results due to inequities amongst people and disparities between one area to another area at various levels. The environmental conditions continued to degrade leading to severe stress on land, water and other natural resources.

After independence, various policies had been adopted by the government especially "*Adhik Ann Upjao*" or (Produce More Grains) "Poverty Alleviation Programmes", Development of Women and Children in Rural Areas (DWCRA), TRYSEM and Twenty-Point Programme to ensure the integrated village development and also to ensure appropriate implementation of the planned programmes at the grassroots level.

Around the late 1970s, sustainable and integrated development of the villages has been ensured. In this regard, conceptual changes in the policy, planning practices has been adopted at the micro-level or village level process of the planning.

Institutional changes were brought to implement this strategy through the 73rd and 74th Constitutional Amendment Acts (1992 and 1993).

The State Government were empowered from the institutions of Self-Governance right from the Village level → Block level → District level and also within the municipal jurisdiction.

The Eleventh and Twelfth Schedules of the Constitution, while specifying the sectors for the Panchayats and Nagar Palikas have also been defined the role for the multi-level institutions of governance in planning and implementing the integrated development schemes.

The State Government have accordingly constituted such local bodies with the definite mandates to collect revenues, draw up plans and implement integrated development programmes. It requires capacity building at institutions of local self-governance to prepare and implement local level areas specific integrated development programmes through assessing and utilizing the available Natural and Human (Socio-Economic-Institutional) infrastructural resources at the grassroots level.

The formulation of the policy and the process of programme implementation requires appropriate financial assistance for the successful implementation of the planned programmes at various levels. The Ministry of Programme Implementation has been consistently providing financial assistance to the District Rural Development Agency under the Members of Parliament (Lok Sabha and Rajya Sabha) Local Area Development (MP-LAD) fund and the State Government has also been providing financial assistance under the Member of Legislative Assembly (MLA) and Members of Legislative Council (MLC) Local Area Development founder for implementation of various need based programmes at the village level.

The financial support for District Development, Block Development and Village Development planning is being received from International agencies, Central

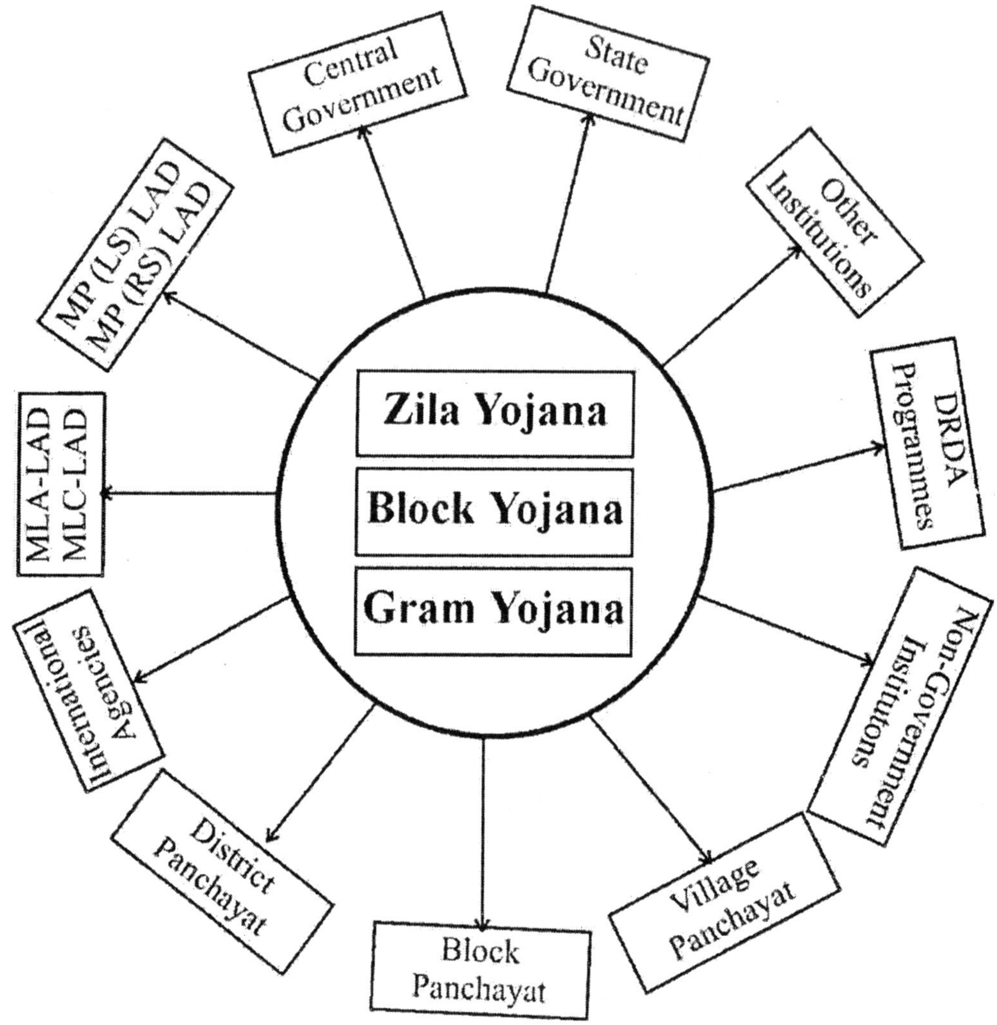

Fig. 2.1: Grassroots Level Financial Flow

Government, State Government, District Rural Development Agency, Non- Government Institutions and District Panchayat, Block Panchayat and Village Panchayat through Central and State Government for formulation of the need based people's participatory village development planning.

It has been realized that the integrated village development should be participatory and it should be formulated, planned according to the felt needs of the deprived, resource less poor multitudes living in the remote rural areas or villages. Various policies have been formulated and development programmes have been planned through tapping the available local talent and Natural and Human (Social-Economic-Institutional) Infrastructural Resources at the grassroots level, in order to make the implemented village development programmes self-sustainable. It has been noted that various rural development programmes are being implemented aiming at sustainable development of the backward villages, with a focus on enhancing the vulnerable sections of the society. In conformity with the commitments to accord foremost priority to integrated village development, a number of steps have been initiated to ensure the implementation of various on-going village development programmes more efficient, effective and accelerated.

In view of the above, as per the policy of the Government, the implementation of various village development programmes have been made more effective through ensuring people's participation at micro-level or village level. The Government has made policy to ensure the implementation and rural development programmes with the involvement of the villagers and the implemented programmes should be maintained and sustained through the village people/beneficiaries. The people's participatory need base formulation of the village plan and implementation of the village development programmes should be initiated at the field level/village level.

It has been mentioned in the Constitution of India that "The Government should evolve methods to unite the village panchayat and provide such powers and rights which can be helpful to work as an unit of Self-Government."

As per the policy of the Government, the Three-Tier Panchayati Raj System has been established and each village has been made self-sustainable and independent. The implementation of the need has village development and welfare programmes related to the village people and the rural masses, has been implemented through people's participation and in an appropriate manner in the interest of the village people.

As per the decisions and policy of the Government of India, the State Government of Uttar Pradesh established Self-Government in the rural areas. Historical and revolutionary decisions has been taken to allot the work and to allocate financial resources to implement the need based planned programmes and allocated the financial and administrative rights and powers to provide the Self-Governance of the Village Panchayat → Block Panchayat → District Panchayat,

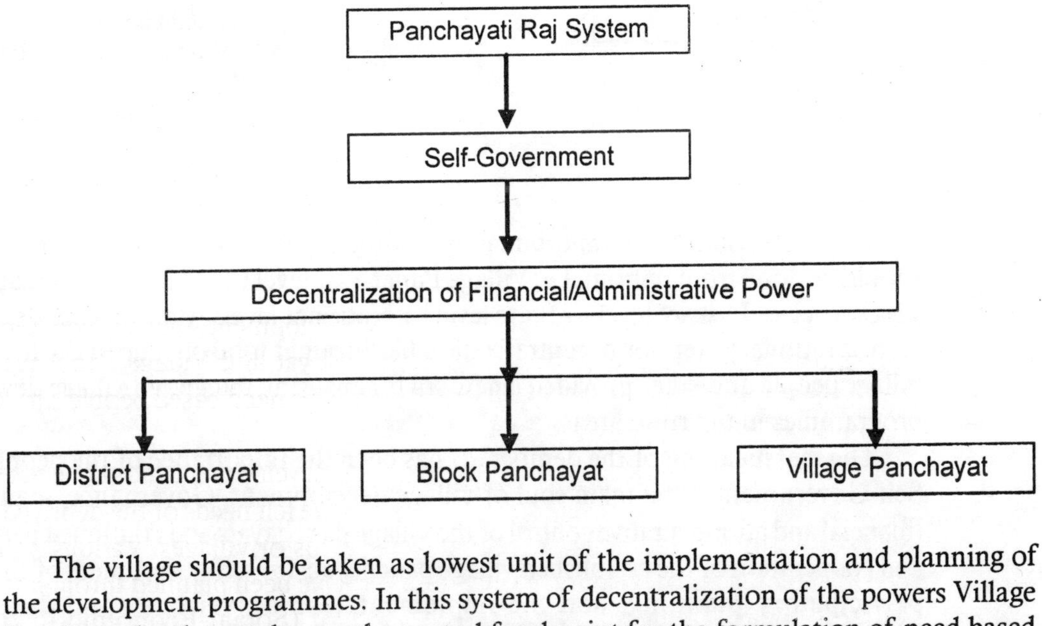

The village should be taken as lowest unit of the implementation and planning of the development programmes. In this system of decentralization of the powers Village Panchayat has been taken as the central focal point for the formulation of need based village development planning at grassroots level. It has been realized in reality that the transfer of the formulation of the planning and implementation powers to ensure integrated village development and its financial control and management of administrative powers to the village panchayats through ensuring sustained peoples participation has been an asset for the successful implementation of the need based integrated village development programmes.

Panchayati Raj Institutions

↓

Self-Government

↓

Allocated Work

↓

Village Panchayat	**Block Panchayat**	**District**
1. Education — Primary and Secondary. 2. Government Tube-wells. 3. Hand Pumps. 4. Youth Welfare. 5. Medical and Health 6. Women and Child Development. 7. Animal Husbandry. 8. Food Supply Shops. 9. Agriculture. 10. Rural Development. 11. Panchayati Raj. 12. All types of Pension/ Scholarships.	1. Rural Development Programmes. 2. Primary Health Centres. 3. Animal Hospitals. 4. Seed Centres. 5. Marketing Stores. 6. Management of Additional Villages. 7. Maintenance of Assets.	1. Medical Health. 2. Rural Development Programmes. 3. Education. 4. Government Tube-wells. 5. Youth Welfare. 6. Women and Child Development. 7. Animal Husbandry. 8. Food Supply Shops. 9. Agriculture Departmen. 10. Horticulture Department. 11. Panchayati Raj. 12. Food Supply. 13. Forest Department. 14. Public Works Department. 15. Jal Nigam. 16. Irrigation Department. 17. Industries. 18. Fisheries Department. 19. Prantiya Vikas Dal. 20. Other Departments.

It has been one of the important policy of the Government that the planning process should be done from bottom, i.e. Village Panchayat level to top level, i.e. Village level → Block level → District level → State level → National level. After independence first of all revolutionary steps of decentralization has brought total change in the life of rural/ village people and it has provided a new era for ensuring integrated village development programmes in the rural areas.

The real meaning of the democracy has been the importance of the people and the Self-Government is the main soul of village development. Governance, management, financial and administrative control of the village panchayats and continued participation and cooperation of the established village panchayats for self-government of the people's participatory planning, and the implementation of various rural development programmes for its sustenance and upgrading the living standard of the village people through generating employment and increasing the income of the deprived resource-less villagers living in the remote rural areas.

As per policy of the Government of India, the State Government of Uttar Pradesh has allocated Primary and Secondary education, Government Tube-wells, Hand Pumps, Youth Welfare, Medical and Health, Women and Child Development, Animal Husbandry, Food Supply shops, Agriculture Department, Rural Development,

Panchayati Raj Department and all types of Pensions and Scholarships, work and programmes to the Village Panchayat Committee has been made responsible for the formulation of need based village planning and implementation of the planned integrated village development programmes and its maintenance and sustenance for an appropriate, optimum utilization of the created assets by the villagers.

In the Panchayati Raj System the Block Panchayats have been allocated Rural Development, Primary Health Centre, animal hospital, seed centres, marketing centres, management of additional villages and maintenance of asset works. The Block Pramukh and Block Development Committee has been allocated physical, financial and administrative powers for the formulation of plans and its implementation at the village level.

As per the policy and decisions of the Government, District Panchayat's has been allocated medical health, rural development programmes, education Government Tube-wells, Youth Welfare, Women and Child Development, Animal Husbandry, Food Supply shops, Agriculture, Horticulture, Panchayati Raj, Jal Nigam, Food Supply, Forest, Public Works Department, Irrigation, Industries, Fisheries, Prantiya Vikas Dal and other Departments work. Chairman, Zila Panchayat and Members of the District Panchayat Committee has been allocated physical, financial and administrative process for the formulation of need based village development planning and also the successful implementation of the planned programmes and maintenance and management of the created assets for optimum utilization of the village peoples.

District Panchayat has formed five committees and elected one Member of the District Panchayat is being nominated as the Chairman of the Committee and other few members of the District Panchayat as its member to ensure the formulation of the plan as per decision of the District Panchayat and its implementation. The District Panchayat has formed Planning and Development, Education, Construction, Health Welfare and Administrative Committees has been constituted to prepare and formulate the need based plans and to ensure the successful implementation of the planned programmes as per the decisions of the Distsrict Panchayat Board.

As per policy of the Government District Rural Development Agency (DRDA) is functional. The Chairman, Zila Panchayat is as *Ex-Officio* Chairman of the District Rural Development Agency. In the Governing Body of the District Rural Development Agency 5 additional members are included, viz. Chairmen of 5 Standing Committees of the Zila Panchayat and District Magistrate as Co-Chairman, local level people's representatives including local members of Parliament and Members of the Legislative Assembly and Members of the Legislative Council and other nominated members.

The District Fisheries Agency is chaired by the Chairman, Zila Panchayat including 5 Chairmen of the Standing Committees of the Zila Panchayat. Chairman of the Sinchai Bandhu is the Chairman of the District Panchayat. Various Financial Schemes are being implemented by Chief Development Officer (DO), through the District, Rural Development Agency (DRDA) in which various District level implementing line departments are vested under the control of the Zila Panchayats.

District Planning Committee (Zila Yojana Samiti) has been formed as per policy of the Government. District Planning Committee is chaired by nominated Minister of the State Government of the Uttar Pradesh. The Chairman of the Zila Panchayat is the Vice-Chairman of the Zila Yojana Samiti. The meeting of the Zila Yojana Samiti is being held at District Headquarters. The Chairman of the local body used to be the Vice-Chairman of the Zila Yojana Samiti. The District Collector by virtue of Post is the Co-Chairman/Member and the Members of Parliament Lok Sabha and Rajya Sabha

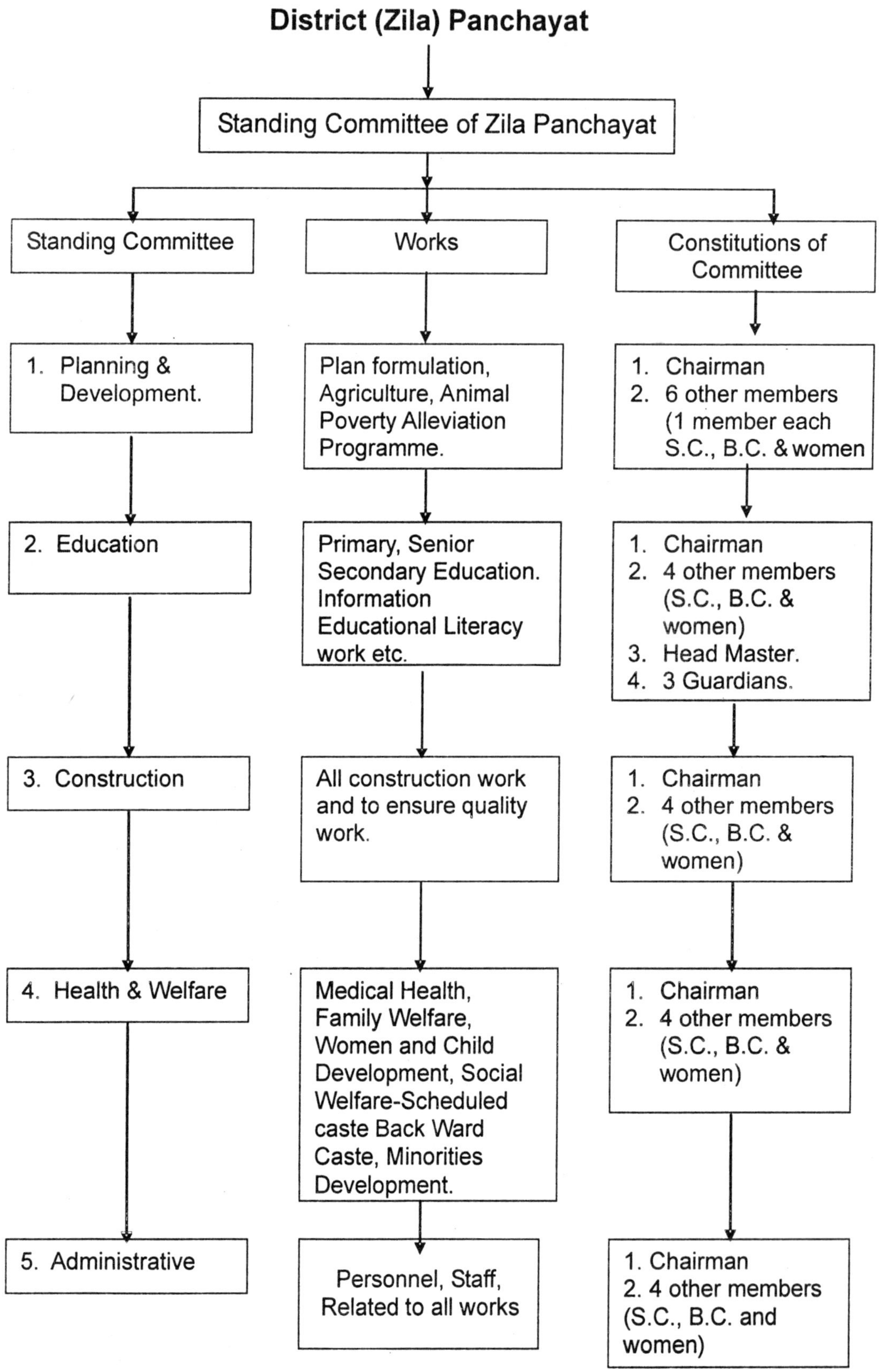
District (Zila) Panchayat
Standing Committee of Zila Panchayat
Standing Committee
Works
Constitutions of Committee
1. Planning & Development.
Plan formulation, Agriculture, Animal Poverty Alleviation Programme.
1. Chairman
2. 6 other members (1 member each S.C., B.C. & women
2. Education
Primary, Senior Secondary Education. Information Educational Literacy work etc.
1. Chairman
2. 4 other members (S.C., B.C. & women)
3. Head Master.
4. 3 Guardians.
3. Construction
All construction work and to ensure quality work.
1. Chairman
2. 4 other members (S.C., B.C. & women)
4. Health & Welfare
Medical Health, Family Welfare, Women and Child Development, Social Welfare-Scheduled caste Back Ward Caste, Minorities Development.
1. Chairman
2. 4 other members (S.C., B.C. & women)
5. Administrative
Personnel, Staff, Related to all works
1. Chairman
2. 4 other members (S.C., B.C. and women)

and Members of the Legislative Assembly and Members of Legislative Council are the permanent members of the Zila Yojana Samiti. The Chief Executive Officer of the Zila Panchayat is the Member Secretary and District Economic and Statistical Officer is the Joint Secretary of the District Planning Committee (DPC) and other Members are nominated by Government of Uttar Pradesh.

The Village Panchayat, Block Panchayat and District Panchayat and Zila Yojana Samiti-Plans are formulated annually. Thus, the decentralization of the Government policy, i.e. Self-Government from the Village Panchayat → Block Panchayat → District Panchayat has been ensured through allocating the physical, financial and administrative powers and rights for the formulation of the plans and its implementation with the people's involvement at the grassroots level. The Panchayati Raj Institutions are also responsible for the management, maintenance and the sustenance of the created assets for its optimum utilization of the Common Village People.

3. PLANNING

Planning is an organized process by which the people achieved its developmental goals. The planning is a means to achieve the development aims and objectives. It has been noticed that the planning is formulated without the willing consent of the local people. The aspiration and needs of the people are not appropriately incorporated in the process of planning. The planning is the task of the people by which the planners can provide techno-scientific back-up support to achieve their planning goals. As per the policy and priorities, the government is stressing hard for the peoples involvement in the plan formulation and in the implementation of the planned programmes through people's participation.

Thus the policy planners must have to provide techno-scientific back-up support at the grassroots level or village level with involvement of the people's representatives, villages and concerned officials involved in the formulation of the village plan for integrated village development. The planners should provide projections and they should assist villagers as a social workers so that they can make the villagers to understand basic grassroots level needs of the village peoples, so that the need of the villagers are planned and development activities are carried out as per the needs of the local people, with the involvement of the village people, for the village people and the integrated village development is achieved as per the planned target.

The "*Bharat Nirman*" a plan of the Government of India has been launched to strengthen the Infrastructures of Rural Areas has been prioritized. Construction of various infrastructural, resource management and employment generation programmes are planned with the view to generate employment and to increase the income of the deprived rural poor multitudes at the village level. The planning programmes initiated by the Government of India to ensure integrated village development are as follows :

3.1 Computerization of Land Records

The scheme of Computerization of Land Records (CLR) was started in 1988-89. It is a 100 per cent grant-in-aid scheme executed by the State Governments. The main objective of CLR scheme is that land owners should get computerized copies of Records of Rights (RORs) at a reasonable price. The ultimate objective of the scheme is 'on-line management' of land records in the country.

Under the scheme, 100 per cent financial assistance is provided to State for completion of data entry work, setting up computer centres at the tehsil or taluk or block and sub-divisional levels and monitoring cell at the State level. Funds are also provided under the scheme for imparting training on computer awareness and applications software to revenue officials for regular updation of records of rights and smooth operation of computer centres.

The main objectives of the computerization of land records are as follows :-

- Providing computerized copies of the Record of Rights (ROR) to the Land owners at nominal rates on demand.
- Ensuring speed, accuracy, transparency and dispute resolution.
- Information empowerment of land owners and freeing them from the clutches of colonial systems — paradigm shift from tax based approach to management of land administration.
- Providing fast and efficient retrieval of information for decision-making.
- Achieving low cost and easily reproducible basic and record data for reliable and durable preservation.
- Value addition and modernization in Land Administration.

Thus, the computerization of the Land Records has been ensured at the Tehsil level in the Uttar Pradesh and the land owners are able to obtain the computerized copies of the Land Records of Rights at a reasonable price at the Tehsil level.

3.2 Watershed Development

The approach of the watershed development has been conventionally aimed at treating degraded land with the help of low cost, moistures conservation measures, afforestation etc. through people's participatory approach. The main objective of the watershed development was the promotion of the overall economic development and improvement of the people in habiting in the programmes areas. The Drought Prone Area Programme (DPAP) and the Desert Development Programme (DDP) has been brought under the Integrated Wastelands Development Programmes (IWDP) launched in 1989 under the aegis of National Wastelands Development Programmes on the watershed basis.

National Watershed Development Project in the rain-fed areas has been initiated by the Ministry of Agriculture as per the guidelines and approach of the watershed development. Later on the watershed Development programmes has been implemented by the Department of Land Resources. The main focus of the programme may have differed, the common of them that under-printed their structure and management for sustainable development of natural resources and community empowerment. The implementation, in fact, of the Drought Prone Areas Programme has recommended a common set of operational guidelines, strategies and features of the Watershed Development Programmes have been initiated by the Department of Land Resources in April 1995.

An appropriate need has been felt to infuse a greater degree of flexibility into the needs of the local areas and the social structure. The watershed Development Programmes has greater flexibility in implementation, well defined role of State-District-Village level Panchayati Raj Institutions. The Watershed Development Programmes have greater role of women participation and effective role for the Panchayati Raj Institutions and to bring the Centre-State Self-Help Group (SHG's) comprising rural poor, especially those belonging to scheduled caste/scheduled tribe categories. The Watershed

Gram Panchayat, stating the time and duration for which work is sought. The minimum days of employment have to be at least fourteen.

(v) The Gram Panchayat will issue a dated receipt of the written application for employment, against which the guarantee of providing employment within 15 days operates.

(vi) Employment will be given within 15 days of application for work, if it is not then daily unemployment allowance as per the Act, has to be paid liability of payment of unemployment allowance is of the States.

(vii) Work should ordinarily be provided within 5 km radius of the village. In case work is provided beyond 5 km, extra wages of 10 per cent are payable to meet additional transportation and living expenses.

(viii) Wages are to be paid according to the Minimum Wages Act, 1948 for agricultural labourers in the State, unless the Centre notifies a wage rate which will not be less than Rs. 60 per day. Equal wages will be provided to both men and women.

(ix) Wages are to be paid according to piece rate or daily rate. Disbursement of wages has to be done on weekly basis and not beyond a fortnight in any case.

(x) At least one-third beneficiaries shall be women who have registered and requested work under the scheme.

(xi) Work site facilities such as creche, drinking water, shade have to be provided.

(xii) The shelf of projects for a village will be recommended by the gram sabha and approved by the zila panchayat.

(xiii) At least 50 per cent of works will be allotted to Gram Panchayats for execution.

(xiv) Permissible works predominantly include water and soil conservation, afforestation and land development works.

(xv) A 60:40 wage and material ratio has to be maintained. No contractors and machinery is allowed.

(xvi) The Central Government bears the 100 per cent wage cost of unskilled manual labour and 75 per cent of the material cost including the wages of skilled and semi-skilled workers.

(xvii) Social Audit has to be done by the Gram Sabha.

(xviii) Grievance redressal mechanisms have to be put in place for ensuring a responsive implementation process.

(xix) All accounts and records relating to the Scheme should be available for public scrutiny.

NREGA marks a paradigm shift from all precedent wage employment programmes. The significant aspects of this paradigm shift are captured below:

(i) NREGA provides a statutory guarantee of wage employment.

(ii) It provides a rights-based framework for wage employment. Employmentis dependent upon the worker exercising the choice to apply for registration, obtain a Job Card, and seek employment for the time and duration that the worker wants.

(iii) There is a 15 day time limit for fulfilling the legal guarantee of providing employment.

(iv) The legal mandate of providing employment in a time bound manner is underpinned by the provision of Unemployment Allowance.

(v) The Act is designed to offer an incentive structure to the States for providing employment as ninety per cent of the cost for employment provided is borne by the Centre. There is a concomitant disincentive for not providing employment as the States then bear the double indemnity of unemployment and the cost of unemployment allowance.

(vi) Unlike the earlier wage employment programmes that were allocation based. NREGA is demand driven. Resource transfer under NREGA is based on the demand for employment and this provides another critical incentive to States to leverage the Act to meet the employment needs of the poor.

(vii) NREGA has extensive inbuilt transparency safeguards:

(a) *Documents*: Job Cards recording entitlements (in the custody of workers) written application for employment, Muster-Rolls, Measurement Books and Asset Registers.

(b) *Processes*: Acceptance of employment application, issue of dated receipts, time bound work allocation and wage payment, Citizen Information Boards at worksites, Vigilance Monitoring Committees, regular block, district and state level inspections and social audits.

(viii) The public delivery system has been made accountable, as it envisages an Annual Report on the outcomes of NREGA to be presented by the Central Government to the Parliament and to the Legislature by the State Government. Specifically, personnel responsible for implementing the Act have been made legally responsible for delivering the guarantee under the Act.

Under Section 4 of the Act, the Scheme to be formulated by the State Government will conform to the legally non-negotiable parameters laid down in Schedules I and II of the Act. In addition, the Schemes will conform to the operational parameters delineated in the Guidelines. The Scheme so formulated will be called the National Rural Employment Guarantee Scheme (NREGS), followed by the name of the State. The National level name and logo is mandatory. This logo will be used for all IEC materials and activities.

The scheme is being implemented as a centrally sponsored scheme on a Cost-sharing basis between the Central Government and the State Government as determined by the Act.

3.7 Mahila Kisan Sashaktikaran Pariyojana (MKSP)

Rural women form the most productive workforce in the economy of majority of the developing nations including India. Agriculture, the single largest production endeavour in India, contributing to 16 per cent of the GDP is increasingly becoming a female activity. Agriculture sector employs 80 per cent of all economically active women; they comprise 33 per cent of the agricultural labour force and 48 per cent of self-employed farmers. About 18 per cent of the farm families in India, according to NSSO Reports are reported to be headed by women. Beyond the conventional market-oriented, narrower definition of 'productive workers', almost all women in rural India can be considered as 'farmers' in some sense, working as agricultural labourers, unpaid workers in the family farm enterprises or combination of the two.

Women in Agriculture are generally not able to access extension services and production assets like seed, water, credit, subsidy etc. As most of them are not recognized as farmers for want of ownership of land, they are not considered as beneficiaries of various government programmes/services. The wage differentials between men and women being adverse to them, the situation is further aggravated. Some of the tasks performed by the women are not valued adequately and considered less important economically.

Further, due to multiple roles that a woman has to perform within the family and the farm, her access to knowledge and information, is constrained and therefore, her opportunities get limited.

To improve the present status of women in Agriculture, and to enhance the opportunities for her empowerment, Government of India has announced "Mahila Kisan Sashaktikaran Pariyojana" (MKSP), as a sub-component of the National Rural Livelihood Mission (NRLM) and decided to provide support to the tune of Rs. 100 crore during 2010-11 budget.

The primary objective of the MKSP is to empower women in agriculture by making systematic investments to enhance their participation and productivity, as also create and sustain agriculture based livelihoods of rural women. By establishing efficient local resource based agriculture, wherein women in agriculture gain more control over the production resources and manage the support systems, the project seeks to enable them to gain better access to the inputs and services provided by the government and other agencies. Once the production capacities of women in agriculture improve, food security ensues for their families and communities.

Specific objectives of MKSP are as under:

- To enhance the productive participation of women in agriculture;
- To create sustainable agricultural livelihood opportunities for women in agriculture;
- To improve the skills and capabilities of women in agriculture to support farm and non-farm-based activities;
- To ensure food and nutrition security at the household and the community level;
- To enable women to have better access to inputs and services of the government and other agencies;
- To enhance the managerial capacities of women in agriculture for better management of bio-diversity; and
- To improve the capacities of women in agriculture to access the resources of other institutions and schemes within a convergence framework.

3.8 Placement Linked Skill Development of Rural BPL Youth under Swarnjayanti Gram Swarojgar Yojana (SGSY)

With a view to ensure inclusion of the rural poor in the growth process, the Ministry of Rural Development, Government of India, had formulated several schemes specifically targeted at rural BPL. Among these, the Swarnjayanti Gram Swarozgar Yojana (SGSY), launched on 1st April, 1999, aims to bring the assisted families (Swarozgaris) above the poverty line by ensuring appreciable sustained level of income over a period of time. This objective is to be achieved by *inter alia* organizing the rural poor into Self-Help Groups (SHGs) through the process of social mobilization, training and capacity building and provision of income generating assets. The SHG approach helps the poor to build their self-confidence through community action. This process would ultimately lead to the strengthening and socio-economic empowerment of the rural poor as well as their collective bargaining power.

Following the recommendations of an Inter-Ministerial Group (IMG) constituted to address the issue of capacity building and training, the Special Projects for Skill Development of Rural Youths under Swarnjayanti Gram Swarozgar Yojana (SGSY) was designed to equip the unemployed rural youths from the BPL Households with marketable skills, which would enable them to either secure placement in the industry or pursue sustainable self-employment opportunities through micro enterprise.

These programmes were aimed at delivery of training, largely through the government machinery, supported by some civil society participants. Under special project component of SGSY, placement linked skill development programme was taken up on pilot basis through Public Private Partnership (PPP). In view of success of the pilot projects, efforts have been made to up scale the skill development programme as it was felt that regular wage employment to at least one member of rural BPL family will enable it to come out of poverty. In this perspective, MORD has made concerted efforts in bringing about paradigm shifts in the delivery mechanism and in involving industry stakeholders, besides strengthening the process through output linked support. MORD has so far assisted several PPP or private sector led initiatives emanating from industry, civil society organizations etc.

The objective of each Special Projects for Skill Development1 would be to ensure a time-bound training and capacity building programme for bringing a specific number of Below Poverty Line (BPL) families above the poverty line through placement ensuring regular wage employment. Salient Features of this programme follow:

Strategy and Approach

- **Placement Linked:** Assured placement for at least 75 per cent of the trainees. This is a demand driven programme and one of the main prerequisite of the programme is the commitment of the PIA/industry to employ the trained persons.
- **Physical Infrastructure:** No new infrastructure creation is supported by MORD under the Programme. Leverage and utilization of existing infrastructure and facilities for operation of training centres is the fundamental principle. This enables appropriate use of underutilized infrastructure and helps immediate start of the training programme in decentralized locations.
- **Machinery and Equipment:** The PIA has to arrange for requisite machinery and equipments on its own or from the perspective employers to the extent possible on lease/rent or as contribution/participation of employer/PIA.

Training

- **Training Contents**: The PIA has to ensure innovative content development with inputs from the industry to ensure employability as per current industry practices. Course/curriculum should preferably be designed jointly with prospective employers/industry. Training and course content into local languages has to be ensured to enable better absorption by BPL youth who may not have exposure to English.
- **Skill Sets:** The objective of the programme is to impart skills necessary for regular employment, so that the initial wages are not less than the prescribed minimum wages. In addition to technical skills, Soft Skills are also to be imparted to beneficiaries to face transition challenges of moving from an agrarian backdrop to the industry environment.
- **Training Partners:** Partnership with training agencies and employers which have aptitude and capability to conduct training and placement of rural BPL youth after certification acceptable to the industry is solicited.

- **Course Duration:** Preferably short duration of up to three months so that the opportunity cost of being away from productive work opportunities during training period are minimized.
- **Certification and Assessment of Trainees**: Independent certification and assessment by third party agencies acceptable to the industry or employers is mandatory to ensure high quality standards and employment.
- **Trainee Accommodation:** Wherever, necessary, boarding and lodging facilities are to be provided to the trainees by the PIA so that BPL youth in remote locations can be covered. In other cases, trainees are to be provided with to and fro transport and food.

3.9 Swarnjayanti Gram Swarozgar Yojana (SGSY)

The objective of the Swarnjayanti Gram Swarozgar Yojana (SGSY) is to bring the assisted poor families (*Swarozgaris*) above the Poverty Line by ensuring appreciable sustained level of income over a period of time. This objective is to be achieved by *inter alia* organising the rural poor into Self-Help Groups (SHGs) through the process of social mobilization, their training and capacity building and provision of income generating assets. The SHG approach helps the poor to build their self-confidence through community action. Interactions in group meetings and collective decision-making enables them in identification and prioritization of their needs and resources. This process would ultimately lead to the strengthening and socio-economic empowerment of the rural poor as well as improve their collective bargaining power. The poverty line varies from State to State. As per the latest (1999-2000) estimates of the Planning Commission, the poverty line in terms of per capita consumption expenditure per month in the rural areas varies from Rs.262.94 in Andhra Pradesh to Rs.367.45 in Himachal Pradesh. Thus the poverty lines in terms of per capita expenditure per month varies specifically from one state to the another state.

SGSY lays stress on the cluster approach. What this means is that instead of funding diverse activities, each block should concentrate on a few select activities (key activities) and attend to all aspects of these activities, so that the Swarozgaris can draw sustainable incomes from their investments. These key activities should preferably be taken up in clusters so that the backward and forward linkages can be effectively established. This would facilitate not only monitoring but more importantly provision of various services required by the Swarozgaris.

The success of SGSY will therefore, depend, to start with, on the choice of activities. The key element is that the choice of activity should be based on the local resources, the aptitude as well as the skill of the people. It is also necessary that the products have ready market.

The choice of key activities should not be an arbitrary or an adhoc decision but should be a carefully thought out process. The Block SGSY committee has a very important role to play in it. For identifying the key activities that can be taken up, the committee should ensure that this selection takes place through a participative process. For selection of key activities, a profile of the poor families, as reflected in the BPL Census should be analyzed. There will be poor families with assets, such as land. Efforts should be made to see that those having a minimum extent of land are enabled to cross the poverty line by making additional investment on their lands, such as wells or other irrigation facilities, pump sets, etc. The experience over the years as well as Evaluation Studies have shown that investments on land based activities have resulted in generation of income on a more sustainable basis. The Block SGSY committee should, therefore, analyze the potential for farm activities on priority. Care must be taken to see that they also have access to short term credit and other inputs required in the farm sector to supplement the efforts under the Scheme. The next priority may be given to those who have an inherent skill. These would primarily be the rural artisans who significant segment of the rural society. Under the SGSY, rural artisans should be covered in a significant manner. Another category would be the unemployed educated youth. A number of them would have been trained under the erstwhile TRYSEM Programme. An inventory may be taken of such people to find out which activities are best suited for the area. Generally, the people who are assetless and skill-less are poorest of poor and get left out under the Programme. Such category of people may require small doses of multiple credit over a period of time coupled with emphasis on awareness creation, training and capacity building. The activities which are easier to handle and product is easily marketable could be identified for such category of people to ensure sustainable income, so that, they do not fall into debt trap.

"The Block SGSY Committee may also look at the potential link plans prepared by NABARD as well as any other survey carried out by various banks, industrial/technical organizations, etc. The local Khadi & Village Industry officials as well as the District Manager of District Industry Centre may also be consulted.

The Block SGSY Committee must interact with as many sarpanches as possible and also discuss with groups of the rural poor such as the landless labour, the educated unemployed, those rural poor with lands, the artisan groups etc. Where self-help groups are in position, they should also be consulted. In their discussions, the Committee should explore various opportunities that are available (provided credit, technology, skill up gradation and marketing are assured) to enable the poor to cross the poverty line. While conducting this dialogue, the Block SGSY committee should be equipped with information relating to the performance of various activities in the village whether such activities are taken up under government programmes or otherwise. The committee should use that knowledge to supplement the traditional knowledge of the poor households and to facilitate the identification of suitable activities. In this process, the traditional wisdom of the poor families acquires value and the Block Committee builds upon the traditional knowledge of the poor families with its knowledge base. It must be ensured that the consultation process is genuine and not perfunctory or token in nature.

In so far as on-farm activities are concerned, provision of irrigation facilities continues to be important. These facilities can be provided either in the form of open dug wells or bore/tube-wells or through lift irrigation or check dams etc. In other words, the nature of source is not important for providing irrigation facilities under SGSY. Effort may be made to bring in as much of the land of the rural poor as possible under irrigation so that they can have sustainable incomes. Minor irrigation investment will include cost of well, lifting device and land development — a composite investment. Working capital requirement can also be considered but would not be eligible for subsidy.

Minor irrigation projects may be group oriented or individual oriented. It is preferable to adopt as far as possible, a project approach under minor irrigation instead of spreading the investment in a scattered manner. Minor irrigation can also be the basis for activity clusters or formation of SHGs.

As regards the non-farm activities, care must be taken to identify only those activities which result in the production of goods/services that have a ready market.

Based on this consultation process, the committee may identify about 8-10 activities, which they may rank in the order of preference. This list should then be placed before the general body of the Panchayat Samiti (Block Panchayat). The Panchayat Samiti should be asked to give its recommendations. The list of selected key activities, along with the recommendations of the Panchayat Samiti, should then be forwarded by the

BDO to the District SGSY committee for consideration. Before sending the list to the District SGSY Committee, the Block Committee should prepare a brief project report, keeping in view of the guidelines.

The District SGSY committee will receive the block-wise proposals and will vet them. The committee will select about 10 activities per block. However, focus should be on 4-5 Key activities which are identified for training and micro-enterprise development in a cluster approach for larger number of Groups. In the process, scope for other potential activities should not be excluded with the District level SGSY Committee.

3.10 Pradhan Mantri Gram Sadak Yojana (PMGSY)

Pradhan Mantri Gram Sadak Yojana (PMGSY) was launched on 25th December, 2000 as a fully funded Centrally Sponsored Scheme to provide all weather road connectivity in rural areas of the country. The programme envisages connecting all habitations with a population of 500 persons and above in the plain areas and 250 persons and above in hill states, the tribal and the desert areas.

According to latest figures made available by the State Governments under a survey to identify Core Network as part of the PMGSY programme, about 1.67 lakh Unconnected Habitations are eligible for coverage under the programme. This involves construction of about 3.71 lakh km. of roads for New Connectivity and 3.68 lakh km. under upgradation.

3.11 Bharat Nirman

The President of India, in his address to Parliament on 25th February, 2005, announced a major business plan for rebuilding rural India called Bharat Nirman. The Finance Minister, in his Budget Speech of 28th February, 2005, identified Rural Roads as one of the six components of Bharat Nirman and has set a goal to provide connectivity to all habitations with a population of 1000 persons and above (500 persons and above in the case of hilly or tribal areas) with an all-weather road. A total of 59564 habitations are proposed to be provided new connectivity under Bharat Nirman. This would involve construction of 1,46,185 km of rural roads. In addition to new connectivity, Bharat Nirman envisages upgradation/renewal of 1,94,130 km of existing rural roads. This comprises 60 per cent upgradation from Government of India and 40 per cent renewal by the State Government.

3.12 National Bio-Gas Programme

National Bio-Gas programme has been launched to facilitate the cooking gas through cow dung and utilize the end product as fertilizer for increasing the agricultural productivity.

3.13 National Health Insurance Policy Scheme

National Health Insurance Policy Scheme has been launched to provide Insurance facilities to the village people to obtain suitable facilities during their medical treatment in the hospitals.

3.14 Sampoorna Grameen Rojgar Yojana (SGRY)

The Sampoorna Grameen Rojgar Yoajana has been implemented to provide additional wage employment in the rural areas as well as to provide food security along with the creation of durable community assets, social and economic infrastructure in the Rural Area. The programme is self-targeting in nature with special emphasis to provide wage employment to women scheduled caste and children's parents withdrawn from health hazards.

3.15 Rajiv Gandhi Grameen Vidyutikaran Yojana

Rajiv Gandhi Grameen Vidyutikaran Yojana has ben launched to facilitate the Electricity connection in the remote villages to the Below Poverty Line people and resourceless deprived rural poor multitudes.

3.16 Rural Drinking Water Supply

Drinking water supply programme is being implemented for providing drinking water facilities to rural areas because water is an essential ingredient of the people's daily life. The importance of safe drinking water cannot be underestimated. Poor quality and contaminated water cause many diseasese.

3.17 Rural Sanitation

Central rural sanitation programme is being implemented to remove the deposal of human excreta of cesspools open ditches, pit latrines, bucket system, etc. It is well-known fact that a direct relationship exists between water, sanitation, health, consumption of unsafe drinking water and improper disposal of human excreta, lack of personal and fod hygiene have been the major reasons of the several diseases. High Infant Mortality Rate (IMR) has also been attribute due to large scale poor sanitation.

3.18 Pradhan Mantri Grameen Jal Samvardhan Yojana

Pradhan Mantri Grameen Jal Samvardhan Yojana is being implemented with the objective of drought proofing in the identified dry and rainfed aress through location specific water conservation measures and water storage technologies to mitigate the adverse effects of drought. Improving groundwater potential and augmenting water supply especially for meeting drinking water requirements through harvesting of the rainwater in the Water Stressed villages. Better management of water domain especially in the over exploited areas for improving soil moisture availability and water security in a holistic approach in the long term of the planning process.

In spite of the above, various other rural Development Programmes are being implemented in the Amethi. Women empowerment programme through Women Self-Help Groups (SHGs) are also being implemented. The grants-in-aid Bank credit and micro-finance facilities are made available to the women Self-Help Groups (SHGs) through the local Lead Banks with the view to generate employment and increase the income of the deprived rural poor women beneficiaries.

The women empowerment programme has been launched by the Government of India through formation of Self-Help Groups (SHGs) through developing entrepreneurial and skill development to generate employment and increase their income for self-sustenance various other programmes related to women empowerment has also been initiated by the Government of India.

National Rural Health Mission (NRHM) is one of the pioneering programme of the Government of India with the view to provide rural health services especially in immunization, mother and child care and various problems related to health hazards, water borne diseases. There are more than three dozen disease which are covered under the National Rural Health Mission programme with the view to provide free of cost medical and health facilities to the patient and interest needy resource less deprived rural poor multitudes surviving in the remote villages.

4. GOVERNMENT OF UTTAR PRADESH

In the point of view of population, Uttar Pradesh is the largest State of our country. More than three-fourth population of the State is engaged in the agricultural activities. The establishment and construction of infrastructural resources and generation of employment has been the special priority to ensure the integrated development of the rural areas. During 1952 Community Development Programme was initiated and later on Department of Rural Development has been established. The Department of Rural Development has been engaged in the implementation and obtain the planned target of the programmes co-ordination and contribution of the implementing Departments is being obtained. The participation of the Panchayati Raj Institutions in the implementation of rural development programmes has been obtained with the view to provide direct benefit of the programme to the common people at every level. The effective planning of the programme, implementation, monitoring and follow up action and coordination is being ensured through commission or Rural Development. Hamd Pump has been installed in the settlement having 150 population and good quality drinking water facility is being provided to the downtrodden resourceless sections of the society in the remote villages.

The skill development and training programmes has been launched at wider level and the department of rural development has been giving especial emphasis the employment generation to the rural youths. State level and District Level Rural Development Training Institutes has been established. The skill Development Training Programmes are being organized for the Rural Development, and Panchayati Raj Department's related officers, staff, voluntary organizations, and grassroots level people's representatives with the view to provide appropriate benefit of the development programmes in the rural areas.

As per the Administrative Improvement Commission, the Rural Development Programmes related to the Central Government and Government of Uttar Pradesh work plan and performance budget has been prepared for successful implementation of the planned programmes at the grassroots level.

In view of the above, various rural Development Programmes are being implemented through different line departments at village level through the District Rural Development Agency with the involvement of Village Panchayat → Block Panchayat → District Panchayat. Various planned programmes are being implemented are as under:

- Swarnjayanti Gram Swarojgar Yojana.
- Sampoorna Grameen Rojgar Yojana.
- Mahatma Gandhi National Rural Employment Guarantee Act.
- Pradhan Mantri Gram Sadak Yojana.
- Indira Awaas Yojana.
- Rural Drinking Water Supply Scheme.

- Community Development Programmes.
- Member of Legislative Assembly and Member of Legislative Council. Local Area Development Fund.
- District Rural Development Agency.
- Ambedkar Vishesh Rojgar/Rojgar Chhatri Yojana.
- Bio-gas Programme.

In spite of the above various basic requirements other programmes have been initiated to fulfil the common needs of scheduled caste dominated settlements especially Rural Drinking Water Supply Scheme, Housing Scheme for Scheduled Castes and Scheduled Tribes, Construction of the Community Hall/Central programmes.

The employment generation and income increasing programme has been launched for the poor people living under the below poverty line with the view to bring them above poverty line and to improve their socio-economic conditions and also improve their quality of life.

5. DISTRICT PLAN OF AMETHI

Various plans are formulated for the integrated development of District Amethi. Amethi has been a newly created district taking Salon and Tiloi Tehsils of the Rae Bareli District and Amethi, Gauriganj and Musafirkhana Tehsils of the Sultanpur District. There are 16 blocks in the Amethi District, the detail of the Blocks and its locations has been discussed in the previous chapter of this study. The Amethi District is one of the most backward area of the Uttar Pradesh and Amethi is socially, economically and institutionally backward district. The fertility status of available natural land resources mostly has deteriorated and poor fertility status of the soil has caused poor agricultural productivity. The main important plans of the district are as follows :

1. ISOPAM
2. Bhoomi Sena.
3. State Horticultural Mission.
4. Horticulture Development for Scheduled Caste farmers.
5. Production and distribution of high yield variety sugarcane seed.
6. Seed and Land Development Programme.
7. Construction of inter-rural road.
8. Assistance for small and marginal farmers.
9. Animal, Health and Improvement in the disease cure and extension.
10. Artificial in seminization of cows and buffaloes improvement and extension facilities through BAIF.
11. Strengthening and extending the pig production areas.
12. Green Fodder and Development of green fodder scheme and strengthening the certified green fodder.
13. Fisheries Development Agency.
14. Accidental Community Insurance for fishermen.
15. Re-organization, extension and strengthening of the Milk Federation and Milk Societies.
16. Technical demonstrations for increasing milk production to the milk producers and milk societies.
17. Farmers Training.

18. Automatic Milk Collection Unit.
19. Social Forestry.
20. Interestless loan/grants for partial purchase to the Scheduled Caste and weaker sections.
21. Swarnjayanti Gram Swarojgar Yojana.
22. Integrated Watershed Development Programmes.
23. Mahatma Gandhi National Rural Employment Guarantee Act (MNREGA).
24. Financial Assistance for Patta Land Allottees.
25. Construction of concrete road and drain.
26. Construction of multi-purpose Panchayat Bhawan.
27. Hungerless and Life Safety Guarantee Yojana.
28. Building Construction for Block/District Development.
29. Deep Tube-well.
30. Boring Pumpset/Tube-well.
31. Blast Well/Deepening well.
32. Groundwater charging/check dam.
33. General Tube-well Programme (Construction of New Tube-well).
34. Modernization of Tube-well.
35. Construction of Government Tubewell under the Dr. Ram Manohar Lohia Tube-well Scheme.
36. Smaller Projects for Flood Control.
37. Street light — Additional Source of Energy.
38. Solar Lamp — Additional Source of Energy.
39. Solar Water Heater — Additional Source of Energy.
40. Village Industries Employment Scheme of the Chief Minister.
41. Vocational Training for entrepreneurs.
42. Catalytic Development Project financially supported by Central Silk Board.
43. Silk Worm Development Scheme.
44. Silk Development Progarmme.
45. Integrated Handloom Development Scheme.
46. Health Insurance Scheme for Weavers.
47. Renovation of New Rural Roads.
48. Construction of New Rural Roads.
49. Environment Education, Awareness, Training, and Extension Programmes.
50. Promotion and Propagation of Science and Technology.
51. Beautification and Development of Tourism.
52. Renovation of Tourist places and Monuments.
53. Local Tourism Development.
54. Sulabh Shauchalaya.
55. Shelters for Passengers.
56. Sarvashiksha Abhiyan.
57. Installation of Hand Pumps, Electrification, Construction of Boundary wall for the Primary and Higher Secondary Schools.
58. Mid-Day Meal Programme.
59. Purchase of Land, Building Construction, Electrification for Government Higher Secondary Schools.
60. Construction of Education Office and Houses at the District Level.

61. Remuneration for the subject matter specialist of vocational educational syllabus.
62. Establishment of Government Higher Secondary Schools and Government Girls Junior High Schools and High Schools at Block level.
63. Grants-in-Aid for opening girls schools through self-financing management
64. National Campaign for Higher Secondary Education.
65. Building Construction for Government District Library.
66. Renovation of Government Degree Colleges.
67. Building Construction for Government Degree College.
68. Equipment, furnishing, new professional education.
69. Building construction for polytechnic institutions.
70. Establishment of Government Polytechnic.
71. Construction of Hostels, Renovation and Extension of Government Polytechnic.
72. Organization of Rural Sports Competition.
73. Panchayat level Play campaign and youth sports.
74. Construction of sports building.
75. Construction of Patients shelter in the Allopathic Hospitals.
76. Establishment of Plastic Surgery and Burn Unit.
77. Radiology Unit.
78. Intensive Care Unit.
79. Construction of Mortuary House.
80. Construction of Primary Health Centres.
81. Construction and establishment of New Primary Health Centres.
82. Construction of Community Health Centres.
83. Building Construction of Community Centres.
84. Renovation of Hospitals, Extension and Arrangement of Electricity and Water.
85. Renovation of existing primary health centres and electricity and water arrangement.
86. State Share of National Rural Health Mission Programme.
87. Establishment of Government Homoeopathic Hospitals.
88. Construction of Homoeopathic Hospitals.
89. Establishment of Unani/Ayurvedic Hospital. Building construction of Unani/ Ayurvedic Hospital.
90. Rural Drinking Water.
91. Construction of Clean Latrines.
92. Pooled Housing.
93. Indira Avaas Yojana.
94. Lohai Grameen Avaas.
95. Grant-in-Aid for the marriage of the sick persons' daughters.
96. Scholarship up to 10th standard for the Scheduled Caste.
97. Establishment of Book Banks for the Scheduled Caste.
98. Financial support for exploited persons of Scheduled Caste.
99. Construction/establishment of Government Ashram Styled Schools for Scheduled Caste.
100. Scholarship for Backward Caste students up to 10th standard.
101. Grants-in-Aid for treatment of seriously ill and marriage of daughters for backward caste persons.
102. Scholarship for Minorities students.
103. Marriage for the daughters of Minorities.
104. Scholarship up to 10th standard for the general caste students.
105. Treatment and marriage for the daughters of general caste persons.

106. Financial Assistance for exploited and troubled.
107. Guideline and Training Centres for the applicants of Scheduled Caste.
108. Remuneration for unemployment.
109. Building Construction for industrial training institute.
110. Renovation of Industrial Training Institutes.
111. Upgradation and incorporation of new trades old age pension.
112. Family Benefit Scheme.
113. Rani Laxmi Bai Scheme.
114. Grants-in-aid for deaf and dumb physically incapable handicapped.
115. Financial assistance for resourceless widows after death of their husband.
116. Women and Child Development Programmes for the Nutritious Food.

The District Plan of Amethi has been formulated by the District Rural Development Agency (DRDA) in coordination with the various line departments of the Government of the District Level under the supervision of the Chief Development Officer and the District Magistrate Amethi. The Planned expenditure of the Amethi District has been approved by the District Planning Committee, chaired by the nominate Minister of the Government of Uttar Pradesh.

6. ZILA PANCHAYAT YOJANA

Zila Panchayat Yojana of Amethi has been formulated in coordination with Standing Committees of the Planning and Development, Education, Construction, Health Welfare and Administrative Standing Committee in coordination with the Chief Executive Officer of the Zila Panchayat of the Amethi District. District Panchayat Amethi has formulated following need based plans priorities by the members of the District Panchayat and other peoples representative :

- Medical and Health Programme.
- Rural Development Programme.
- Education.
- Government Tube-wells.
- Youth Welfare Programme.
- Women and Child Development Programme.
- Animal Husbandry.
- Food Supply Shops.
- Agriculture.
- Horticulture.
- Panchayati Raj.
- Jal Nigam.
- Food Supply.
- Social Forestry.
- Public Works Department.
- Irrigation.
- Industries.
- Village/Small Scale Industries (Gramodyog).
- Fisheries.
- Others line department.

7. BLOCK PANCHAYAT PLANNING

The planning of the Block Panchayat is being formulated by the Block Development Officer and Additional Block Development Officers, in coordination with the Village Pradhan and Block Development Committee, Members (BDC) under the Chairmanship of the Block Pramukh of the Amethi Block. The Block level planning of the Amethi has been formulated for the following programmes as per the prioritized needs of the local level village people.

- Rural Development Programmes.
- Primary Health Centres.
- Animal Hospitals.
- Seed Centres.
- Marketing Stores.
- Look after of the additional villages.
- Maintenance and Management of the created assets.

The Block Panchayat Planning has been formulated by the Block Level elected people's representatives and the planned programmes are being implemented under the supervision of the Block Panchayat.

8. VILLAGE PANCHAYAT PLANNING

State Government of Uttar Pradesh has allotted the work and allocated the financial resources to implement the planned programmes and administrative powers and rights has been given to the Village Panchayats with the view to strengthen the Self-Governance of the Village Panchayats. The Plan Programmes of the Village Panchayats are formulated by the Village Panchayat Secretary in coordination with the member of the Village Panchayat Committee under the Chairmanship of the Village Pradhan. The planned programmes of the Village Panchayats are as follows :

- Primary Education and Secondary.
- Junior High School and Secondary Education.
- Government Tube-wells.
- Hand Pumps.
- Youth Welfare Programme.
- Medical and Health Programme.
- Women and Child Development Programme.
- Animal Husbandry.
- Food Supply Shops.
- Agriculture.
- Horticulture.
- Social Forestry.
- Rural Development — Road Construction, Concrete Road, Kharanza Road, Kuchcha Road construction and repair and maintenance of the road.
- Panchayati Raj System.
- All types of pension.
- All types of scholarship, etc.

Thus it is evident that the Government of India has been supporting various centrally sponsored schemes to the State Government to strengthen and upgrade the existing Natural → Social → Economics → Institutional Infrastructural Resources at the village level. The most important programme of the Government of India has been the '*Bharat Nirman*' under which local level infrastructural resources are created to strengthen the institutional infrastructural resources to meet the common minimum needs of the ever increasing population. The appropriate conservation of our natural resources, reclamation of wastelands and watershed development programmes, employment generation to the deprived rural poor, upgrading the educational pattern at the grassroots level, rural health, women empowerment and various other welfare programmes are launched and implemented to benefit the deprived resourceless poor village people. Some of these programmes are very successful like construction of Rural roads under Pradhan Mantri Gram Sadak Yojana and Rajiv Gandhi Grameen Vidyutikaran Yojana but some of the programmes like women empowerment through Self-Help Groups and Rural Health Mission and various other programmes could not benefit the grassroots level village people, the way it has been targeted and planned initially.

State Government of Uttar Pradesh has also been making an effort to successful implementation of programmes as per the plan of the Government of India through contributing state share. Various other programmes like Bhoomi Sena for the reclamation of Banjar land. Dr. Ram Manohar Lohia Government Tube-wells, Mukhya Mantri Gramodyog Rojgar Yojana and various other programmes are launched and implemented by the State Government of Uttar Pradesh.

District Plan is being formulated by the Zila Yojana Samiti of the District and the District Plan is formulated in accordance with the State Plan and the financial support earmarked by the Government of Uttar Pradesh.

District Panchayat, Block Panchayat and Village Panchayat are also formulating their need based plans as per decisions and willingness of the elected Village-Block-District Panchayat level people's representatives. The vision of the Mahatma Gandhi has been ensured through implementing the three-tier Panchayati Raj System, i.e. Village Panchayat → Block Panchayat → District Panchayat through providing physical work, allocating financial powers and administrative powers. The Panchayati Raj System has been found successful on paper but at field level the related deprived village poor people are still awaiting to achieve the people's participatory planning goals to upgrade their living standard and fulfil their aspirations for the better quality of life.

9. CONCLUSION

It has been realized that the commendable advances have been made in the diverse field of the development but it has been noticed that such development has been found incomplete in reality because the implemented programmes failed to translate into better and dignified meaning for the life of the majority of the people surviving in the remote villages.

The policy-makers and the planners must provide integrated development planning techno-scientific backup support to the grassroots level people's representatives. Thus the policy planning for the integrated Development Programmes must be carried out as per the needs and requirements of local village people, with the involvement of the village people and with the sustained participation of the village people to achieve the formulated planned, integrated village developmental target.

It has been observed that there is a quest for evolving a model for the planning. The Macro-level resources management planning has been adopted in our country and it did not yield desired results due to inequities amongst the people and disparities from one area to another.

Initially the Government of India made policy for the poverty alleviation and "*Adhik Ann Upjao*" (Produce More Grain). Twenty-Point Programme, TRYSEM and Development of Women and Children in Rural Areas have been launched as per the policy of the Government of India.

Due emphasis has been given for strengthening the three-tier Panchayati Raj Institutions and Local bodies in the Eleventh and Twelfth Schedules of our Constitution.

It has been mentioned in the Constitution of India that, "The Government should evolve methods to unite the village panchayats and provide such powers and rights which can be helpful to work as a unit of self-governance."

In view of the above three-tier Panchayati Raj System has been established and administrative and financial powers have been allocated to the Panchayats. The village should be taken as lowest unit for planning and the implementation of the Development Programmes.

The planning is an organized process by which the people achieves their developmental goal. It has been noticed that the planning is formulated without the willing consent of the local people. The aspirations and the requirements of the people are not incorporated in the planning process. The planning is the task of the people by which the planners can provide techno-scientific back-up support to achieve their planning goals.

The Government of India has initiated various Rural Development Programmes like Computerization of Land Records, Watershed Development, Hariyali Rural Housing, National Social Assistance Programmes, Mahatma Gandhi National Rural Employment Guarantee Act (MNREGA), Mahila Kishan Sashaktikaran Pariyojana, Placement linked skill development of Rural B.P.L. youth under Swarnjayanti Swarojgar Yojana, Pradhan Mantri Gram Sadak Yojana, Rajiv Gandhi Grameen Vidyutikaran Yojana, Rural Housing, Drinking Water Supply, Rural Sanitation and Pradhan Mantri Grameen Jal Samvardhan Yojana, Women empowerment and Rural health mission programmes at the grassroots level, i.e village panchayat level.

The Department of Rural Development of the Government of Uttar Pradesh has been engaged in the implementation of various Rural Development Programmes like Swarnjayanti Gram Swarojgar Yojana, Mahatma Gandhi National Rural Employment Guarantee Act, Pradhan Mantri Gram Sadak Yojana, Rural drinking water supply and various other programmes for the deprived rural poor people.

It has been noticed that different rural Development Programmes are being implemented by the District Authorities through various line departments at various levels in Amethi.

The agriculture, horticulture, social-forestry, rural road, support to small and marginal farmers, animal husbandry, Mahatma Gandhi National Rural Employment Guarantee Act (MNREGA), Dairy Development, Drinking water, irrigation support, rural sanitation, employment generation, pension, scholarships, social welfare, rural health, Indira Awaas Yojana and various other programmes are being implemented through concerned district level line department.

Zila Panchayat Yojana, Block Panchayat Yojana and Village Panchayat Yojana have also been implemented through various implementing organizations. Zila Panchayat has been engaged in the implementation of the rural health, education, irrigation, women and child development, agriculture, horticulture, social forestry, drinking water, public works department and various other rural development programmes.

Block Panchayat has been engaged in the implementation of rural development, primary health centres, animal hospital, seeds and marketing centres, maintenance and management of the created assets.

Village Panchayat has also been engaged in the implementation of various rural Development Programmes including primary education, medical health, animal husbandry, agriculture, horticulture, social-forestry, rural development, panchayati raj system, all types of scholarships and pensions.

District Panchayat, Block Panchayat and Village Panchayat are engaged in the implementation of various need based policy plans as per the decisions and willing consent of the grassroots level village people. The visions and mission of the Mahatma Gandhi has been ensured through implementing Panchayati Raj System and to strengthen the concept of local self-government. The Panchayati Raj System has been found successful on paper but at the field level, the concerned deprived rural poor village beneficiaries are still awaiting to achieve the people participatory planning goals and to upgrade their living standards for the better quality of life through improving their socio-economic conditions of the resourceless deprived rural poor multitudes surviving in the remote villages of Amethi.

3

Rural Development

1. INTRODUCTION

The development means the evolution of the common people, in which the down trodden, deprived section of the society can acquire better perceptions and best control for optimum utilization of the available Natural and Human (Social-Economic-Institutional) infrastructural resources at the micro-level. The development is pursued with the genuine concern for human values their actions and aspirations for the better quality of life. In the process of development the growth alone does not ensure the integrated development, because the development is after all a multifaceted phenomenon.

Basically, the development is a human enterprise and it requires combined efforts of all systems of knowledge by they physical, biological, social, economic, institutional with the view to comprehend and articulate it. It is more, so with respect to the formulated planned and implemented Development Programmes.

Thus the development should ensure the betterment of deprived needy people and welfare of all the grassroots level, village people. The feel good of the development has not only been realized at the National Level → State Level → District Level → Block Level → Village panchayat level perspective and perception of the deprived resource less poor people.

The existing process of development whether urban or rural development has neither been true, nor good, nor beautiful but it does not mean that every thing is wrong. In the real sense, the development lies in the progress and development of latest Science and Technology and its application by the common people for their betterment. The progress of the people and economic growth along with the socio-economic-institutional, infrastructural development, man has made and adopted destructive approach than constructive approach of development without incorporating the willing consent, and interest of the deprived sections of the society and also ignoring the continued sustained participation of the grassroots level interested beneficiaries, for its sustenance to fulfill the increasing demand of the growing cattle and human population at micro-level.

Thus, an integrated economic development has been realized and commendable progress has been made in the different field of various Rural Development Programmes. But there is a great question, whether actually, would it in reality be in complete, if such Rural Development Programmes fail to translate, into better and dignified life for the majority of the people surviving in the remote backward villages.

It has been noted that urban areas are comparatively more developed than the rural area. Therefore, faster and appropriate integrated development of rural areas are required to fulfil the growing demand of the ever increasing population, so that the disparities between rural to urban and rurban areas can be bridged, to ensure an integrated development of the rural and neglected areas at the grassroots level.

It has been observed that the implementation of rural development should be people's participatory and it should be planned and formulated according to the willing consent and needs of the deprived rural poor multitudes. The development should be planned through optimum utilization of available natural and human resources at the village panchayat level in order to make the implemented rural development programmes self-sustained. It has been recorded that various village development programmes are being implemented aiming at sustainable integrated development of the remote rural areas, with a focus on enhancing the livelihood of the weaker and vulnerable sections of the society. In conformity with the commitment to accord foremost priority of the remote rural areas. Various steps have been initiated to make the implementation of ongoing rural development programmes more efficient, effective and accelerated at the local level.

2. PANCHAYATI RAJ SYSTEM

The implementation of the integrated rural development programmes can be made more effective through ensuring proper participation of the local people. The development should be for the village people and it should be maintained and sustained by the village people. Need based formulation of people's participatory planning and the implementation of development programmes should be initiated at the grassroots level or village panchayat level. The needs of the local village people and their priorities should be given due consideration in the plan formulation at the micro-level.

In view of the above, it has been stated in the Constitution of India that, "The Government should evolve methods to unite the village panchayat and provide such power and rights, which can be helpful to work as on unit of Self-Government."

The village should be made independent and self-sustained through village panchayat. The implementation of welfare programmes as per the needs of the rural poor, should be implemented in a better and systematic manner at the village panchayat level.

The State Government of Uttar Pradesh established self-government through strengthening Village Panchayat → Block Panchayat → District Panchayat level. Historical and revolutionary decisions have been taken by the Government of Uttar Pradesh to allot the works, to allocate the financial powers and resources to implement the need based formulated planned programme and administrative rights have also been allocated to provide self-government of the Village Panchayat → Block Panchayat → District Panchayat.

The village panchayat has been considered as the lowest unit of the development. In the Panchayati Raj System of the decentralization village panchayat has been taken as the central focal point for the integrated village development. It has been meaningful to transfer the physical, financial and administrative powers and rights to the village panchayats for the formulation of the need based plan and people participatory implementation of the integrated development programmes. The formulation of the need based planning process has been initiated from the bottom, i.e. village panchayat level to top level, i.e. Block Panchayat level to District Panchayat level. The initiated revolutionary steps of the decentralization have shown a drastic change in the life of the deprived rural poor multitudes and it has also provided a new era for the integrated village development through ensuing people's participation.

It has been realized that the real meaning of democracy has been the people's importance in the formulation of the need based planning and the implementation of integrated village development at the field level. The governance, management, financial powers and rights and administrative control of village panchayat and the continued participation and cooperation to establish the village panchayat for the self-government through ensuing the people's participatory need based planning, implementation of the integrated village development programmes for the its self-sustenance.

The Village Panchayat → Block Panchayat → District Panchayat have been allotted planning and development, education construction, social and health welfare and the administrative work and various other activities related to village development and financial and administrative powers, rights and financial control have been allocated under the Panchayati Raj System.

District Rural Development Agency (DRDA) — has been reconstituted, i.e. the Chairman-DRDA, at present is the Chairman of the District Panchayat. In the Governing Body of the DRDA—5 additional are included, viz. 5 Chairmen of the 5 Standing Committees of the District Panchayat.

District Fisheries Development Agency (DFDA) — has been chaired by the District Panchayat's Chairman along with 5 additional members of the 5 Chairmen of the Standing Committees of the District Panchayat.

The Chairman of the *Sinchai Bandhu* is the Chairman of the District Panchayat. It has been recorded that various schemes are being implemented under the supervision of the Chief Development Officer (CDO) through the District Rural Development Agency (DRDA) in co-ordination and in collaboration with various line departments and implemented agencies have also been transferred under the control of the District Panchayat to strengthen the Panchayati Raj Institutions.

3. RURAL DEVELOPMENT

The Zila Yojana Samiti (District Planning Committee) has been constituted and it is chaired by the nominated Minister of the State Government. The Chairman of the District Panchayat is the Vice-Chairman of the Zila Yojana Samiti. The Chairman of the local body and District Collector by post are the Vice-Chairman of the District Planning Committee. The members of the Parliament (Lok Sabha and Rajya Sabha) and Members of Legislative Assembly (MLA) and Members of the Legislative Council (MLC) are the permanent members of the Zila Yojana Samiti. The Chief Executive Officer of the Zila Panchayat is the Member Secretary and the District Economics and Statistical Officer is the Joint Secretary of the District Planning Committee, while other members are nominated by the State Government. The Village Panchayat level, Block panchayat level and District panchayat level plans are formulated annually. The decentralization system of the Government, i.e. Self-Government from Village Panchayat → Block Panchayat → District Panchayat has been established and implemented successfully. The Panchayats have been allotted working powers, allocated financial powers and administrative control for the formulation of the need based people's participatory integrated planning and implementation of the various village development programmes at the grassroots level, and to ensure the maintenance and sustenance of the implemented rural development programmes.

An effort has been made in this study to analyze the progress of the implementation of various rural development programmes being implemented at village-block-district level. The centrally sponsored programmes supported by the Government of India and the programmes supported by the State Government of Uttar Pradesh and the planned programmes supported by the District Planning Committee and Zila Panchayat, Block Panchayat and Village Panchayat and implemented by the various line departments and implementing institutions have been analyzed at village panchayat level in the Amethi Block. The progress of the on-going implementation of the various rural development programmes requisite information has been collected at the grassroots level, i.e. field level and interacting with the concerned officials of the implementing line departments at the village panchayat level. The assessment of the progress of the ongoing implementation of the various rural development programmes at village panchayat level, i.e. area specific at the grassroots level or field level has been analyzed in this study.

3.1 Job Card Holders under Mahatma Gandhi National Rural Employment Guarantee Act (MNREGA)

The Job Card holders and the beneficiaries of the Mahatma Gandhi National Rural Employment Guarantee Act (MNREGA) have been found 15520 beneficiaries belonging to the Below Poverty Line (BPL) category for the whole Amethi Block. The landless agricultural labourers, non-skilled workers and other workers belonging to the Below Poverty Line (BPL) has been provided MNREGA Job Cards and they have been given 100 Days Guarantee Job for the employment and income generation for their better livelihood within the village.

At village panchayat level, distribution of the MNREGA Job Card Holders or the Beneficiaries of the MNREGA at village panchayat level have been mentioned in Table 3.4. The proportionate distribution of the MNREGA beneficiaries at village panchayat level has been depicted in **Map 3.3**. It has been recorded that very high more than 600 MNREGA Job Card Holders have been recorded in the village panchayat Jangal Ram Nagar, Kakawa and Nuwawan Village Panchayats of the Amethi Block. Proportionately, medium number of the Job Card Holders between 400 and 600 beneficiaries has been noticed in the Ramdaipur, Tala, Umanpur Ganapatti, Raipur Phulwari, Korari Girdhar Shah, Bhusahari and Ramgarh village panchayats of the Amethi Block. It has been recorded that low number of beneficiaries belonging to the Mahatma Gandhi National Rural Employment Guarantee Act (MNREGA) varying between 200 and 400 beneficiaries has been found in the Katra Maharani, Trilokpur, Bhaganpur, Kushi Tali, Loharata, Darakha, Mochawa, Parsawan, Kherauna, Katra Phulkunwar, Hathkila, Dedhpasar, Rebha, Mahaso, Gangauli, Loniapur, Himmatgarh, Dehara, Nainaha, Gaderi, Dhandhudhar, Chaturbhujpur, Naraini, Saidpur, Saraiya Duban, Kohara and Mahmadpur Village Panchayats of the Amethi Block. Very low less than 200 beneficiaries/Job Card Holders of the Mahatma Gandhi National Rural Employment Guarantee Act (MNREGA) has been recorded in the Benipur, Mahmadpur, Raidaipur, Agahar, Purab Gaon and Maharajpur village panchayats of the Amethi Block.

3.2 Education

The details of the educational pattern especially the number of students studying in various classes has been explained in this study.

Table 3.4: Rural Development Programme, Amethi, 2011-12

Sl. No.	Village	MNREGA Beneficiaries	Education Profile No. of Students				Net Irrigated Area (in Hectare)			
			Primary & Junior	High School Intermediate	Higher Education	Technical Education	Canal	Private Tube-well	Government Tube-well	Other Sources of Irrigation
1	2	3	4	5	6	7	8	9	10	11
1.	Katra Maharani	314	200	25	5	1	15	46	10	5
2.	Sarai Khema	576	486	35	8	2	0	180	35	5
3.	Trilokpur	343	308	25	5	2	5	175	5	0
4.	Ramdaipur	573	413	40	5	1	5	40	5	0
5.	Jangal Ram Nagar	794	526	96	4	2	120	440	10	10
6.	Benipur	187	156	38	8	2	5	30	0	3
7.	Parsawan	212	208	15	3	1	10	135	1	0
8.	Mahmoodpur	190	129	20	4	1	15	130	0	5
9.	Raipur Fulwari	422	315	35	5	0	10	120	0	0
10.	Umapur Ganapatti	419	386	40	5	2	10	130	5	0
11.	Bhaganpur	344	201	30	2	0	5	65	0	0
12.	Tala	450	329	38	5	1	5	75	5	5
13.	Kushi Tali	302	218	35	8	2	15	150	5	10
14.	Loharta	267	186	22	5	1	2	24	0	0
15.	Darkha	233	186	22	2	0	5	140	3	5
16.	Mochwa	333	286	25	2	1	5	70	5	0
17.	Nuwawan	905	308	41	5	1	10	230	4	0
18.	Loniapur	267	218	38	5	1	2	40	1	2
19.	Kherauna	253	203	35	15	1	3	70	1	1
20.	Katra Phulkunwar	287	221	35	2	0	5	70	2	1
21.	Hathkila	288	155	17	5	0	15	105	5	0
22.	Rebha	248	235	32	6	2	2	40	1	0
23.	Raidaipur	197	203	15	4	0	10	90	5	0
24.	Korari Girdhar Shah	407	329	41	5	1	5	140	3	2
25.	Dedhpasar	294	190	20	10	0	5	20	130	3
26.	Mahaso	281	228	35	5	2	1	30	1	2
27.	Gangauli	356	201	16	2	0	3	170	2	0
28.	Dhadhudhar	364	186	13	2	0	5	40	3	2
29.	Gaderi	393	186	18	1	0	2	118	0	0
30.	Bhusahari	429	204	16	2	0	20	80	0	5
31.	Purabgaon	178	138	15	1	0	5	100	0	0
32.	Chaturbhujpur	346	146	21	1	0	5	45	3	2
33.	Maharajpur	165	148	25	2	1	4	80	0	1
34.	Aghar	186	127	23	3	1	10	100	2	0
35.	Saidpur	329	318	22	5	1	4	70	3	3
36.	Kakwa	614	203	55	4	1	3	45	2	0
37.	Saraiya Duban	329	308	25	8	2	5	123	1	1
38.	Kohra	375	229	35	8	2	15	260	0	0
39.	Mahmadpur	392	221	38	9	2	2	201	2	1
40.	Naraini	355	305	38	5	1	20	250	5	5
41.	Nainaha	300	252	21	8	2	5	80	2	1
42.	Ramgarh	521	402	41	5	1	10	270	10	5
43.	Himmatgarh	212	180	15	2	0	5	180	2	2
44.	Dehara	230	186	21	2	0	5	120	1	0
	Amethi Block	**15520**	**10763**	**1308**	**208**	**41**	**418**	**5109**	**280**	**87**

3.2.1 Primary and Junior School Students

The proportionate distribution of the primary and junior school students at village panchayat level in Amethi has been depicted in **Map 3.4**. Very high more than 100 students under primary and junior school has been recorded in the Ramdaipur, Sarai Khema, Jangal Ram Nagar and Ramgarh village panchayats of the Amethi Block. Medium number of students between 300 to 400 students belonging to the primary and junior school has been observed in the Trilokpur, Tala, Umapur Ganapatti, Nuwawan, Korari Girdhar Shah, Raipur Phulwari, Naraini, Saidpur, Saraiya Duban, village panchayats of the Amethi Block. Low number of students ranging between 200 to 300 students has been found in the Katra Maharani, Bhaganpur, Kushi Tali, Mochawa, Parsawan, Kherauna, Katra Phulkunwar, Loniapur, Raidaipur, Rebha, Mahaso, Gangauli, Bhusahari, Nainaha, Kakawa, Kohara and Mahmadpur village panchayats of the Amethi Block. It has been noticed that very low less than 200 number of the students belonging to primary and junior school students has been found in the Benipur, Mahmoodpur, Hathkila, Dedhpasar, Himmatgarh, Dehara, Gaderi, Purabgaon, Chaturbhujpur, Maharajpur, and Agahar village panchayats of the Amethi Block. It has also been noticed that there are 10763 number of students studying in the primary and junior school in the Amethi Block. It has been recorded that there are 10763 number of students studying in the primary and junior school in the Amethi Block.

3.2.2 High School and Intermediate Students

The progress of High School and Intermediate Students at village panchayat level has been mentioned in Table 3.4. The number of students studying in the High School and Intermediate classes had been depicted in **Map 3.5**. It has been observed that more than 60 number of students studying in the High School and Intermediate classes has been noticed in the village panchayat Jangal Ram Nagar of the Amethi Block while medium 40 to 60 students studying in the High School and Intermediate classes has been found in the Ramdaipur, Umapur Ganapatti, Nuwawan, Korari Girdhar Shah, Kakawa and Ramgarh village panchayats of the Amethi Block. It has been observed that low number of student ranging between 20 to 40 students has been found in the Katra Maharani, Trilokpur, Sarai Khema, Benipur, Mahmoodpur, Raipur Phulwari, Kherauna, Katra Phulkunwar, Loniapur, Rebha, Dedhpasar, Mahaso, Bhaganpur, Tala, Kushi Tali, Loharata, Darakha, Mochawa, Chaturbhujpur, Maharajpur, Agahar, Naraini, Dehara, Agahar, Saidpur, Saraiya Duban, Kohara and Mahmadpur village panchayats while very low less than 20 number of students studying in the High School and Intermediate classes has been found in the Parsawan, Hathkila, Raidaipur, Dhandhudhar, Gangauli, Himmatgarh, and Purabgaon village panchayats of the Amethi Block. It has been recorded that there are 1308 students studying in the High School and Intermediate classes in the Amethi Block.

3.2.3 Higher Education

It has been noticed that there are 208 number of students studying in Higher Education including Graduate and Post Graduate level courses. The proportionate distribution of Higher Education students at village panchayat level in Amethi Block has been depicted in **Map 3.6**. It has been observed that more than 12 number of students studying in the Higher Education programme has been noticed in the Kherauna village panchayat while medium number of students ranging between 8 to 12 students has been found in the Sarai Khema, Benipur, Dedhpasar, Kushi Tali, Nainaha, Saraiya Duban, Kohara and Mahmadpur village panchayats of the Amethi Block. It has been observed that low number of students between 4 to 8 students has been found in the Katra Maharani, Trilokpur, Ramdaipur, Jangal Ram Nagar, Mahmoodpur, Umapur Ganapatti, Nuwawan, Tala, Loharata, Korari Girdhar Shah, Loniapur, Raidaipur, Mahaso, Rebha, Hathkila, Raipur Phulwari, Ramgarh, Naraini, Kakawa and Saidpur village panchayats of the

Amethi. It has been observed that less than 4 number of students studying in the Higher Educational programmes has been found in the Bhaganpur, Parsawan, Katra Phulkunwar, Darakha, Mochawa, Agahar, Chaturbhujpur, Maharajpur, Purabgaon, Dhandhudhar, Gaderi, Gangauli, Bhusahari, Himmatgarh and Dehara village panchayats of the Amethi Block.

3.2.4 Technical Education

The distribution of the number of students studying in the technical and professional educational courses has been mentioned in Table 3.4. There are 41 number of students studying in the Technical education including professional education in the Amethi Block. It has been noted that there are two students studying the technical education has been found in Sarai Khema, Trilokpur, Kushitali, Rebha, Mahaso, Saraiya Duban, Kohara, Mahmadpur and Nainaha village panchayats of the Amethi Block. It has been recorded that there are only one student studying in the technical educational programmes has been found in the Korari Girdhar Shah, Maharajpur, Agahar, Saidpur, Kakawa, Naraini, Ramgarh, Katra Maharani, Ramdaipur, Parsawan, Mahmoodpur, Tala, Loharata, Mochawa, Nuwawan, Loniapur and Kherauna village panchayats of the Amethi Block.

It has been observed that there are 10763 number of students studying in the Primary and Junior School which has been reduced up to 1308 number of students in the High School and Intermediate classes in Amethi Block. Similarly, there is drastic dropout up to 208 number of students in the Higher Educational Courses including Graduate level and Post Graduate level educational programmes in the Amethi Block. Further, the education dropout has been drastically reduced up to only 41 students studying in the technical and professional educational programmes in the Amethi Block. Thus, it has been recorded that there is drastic dropout from Primary education → Junior → High School → Intermediate → Graduate → Post Graduate level → Professional educational programmes at the village panchayat level in Amethi Block.

3.3. Net Irrigated Area

The source of irrigation, irrigated area, plays an important role as an input to increase the agricultural productivity in Amethi has been canal, private tube-well, government tube-well and other sources of the irrigation. The details of the net irrigated area through various sources of irrigation at village panchayat level in Amethi has been mentioned in Table. 3.4.

3.3.1 Canal Irrigated Area

The village panchayat Jangal Ram Nagar has the highest canal irrigated area having 120 hectares of canal irrigated area in the Amethi Block. It has been noticed that 2.0 hectares canal irrigated area has been found in the Bhusahari, Naraini village panchayats while 10 to 15 hectares canal irrigated area has been found in the Ramgarh, Kohara, Agahar, Hathkila, Raidaipur, Nuwawan, Kushi Tali, Umapur Ganapatti, Raipur Phulwari, Mahmoodpur, Parsawan and Katra Maharani village panchayats of the Amethi Block. It has been observed that canal irrigated area between 5 to 10 hectares has been found in Trilokpur, Ramdaipur, Benipur, Bhaganpur, Tala, Darakha, Mochawa, Katra Phulkunwar, Korari Girdhar Shah, Dedhpasar, Dhandhudhar, Purabgaon,

Chaturbhujpur, Saraiya Duban, Nainaha, Himmatgarh and Dehara village panchayats of the Amethi Block. It has been recorded that very low less than 5 hectares canal irrigated area has been found in the Loharata, Loniapur, Kherauna, Rebha, Mahaso, Gangauli, Gaderi, Maharajpur, Saidpur, Kakawa, and Mahmadpur village panchayats of the Amethi Block. The total canal irrigated area has been recorded 418 hectares in the Amethi Block.

3.3.2 Private Tube-well Irrigated Area

The private tube-well irrigated area has been recorded 5109 hectares in the Amethi Block. Net irrigated area through private tube-well had been depicted in **Map 3.7**. It has been recorded that more than 300 hectares irrigated area through private tube-well source of irrigation has been noticed in the village panchayats Jangal Ram Nagar, while medium between 200 to 300 hectare irrigated area through private tube-well has been found in the Nuwawan, Naraini, Ramgarh, Kohara and Mahmadpur village panchayats of the Amethi Block. It has been noticed that low private tube-well irrigated area between 100 to 200 hectares has been seen in the Trilokpur, Sarai Khema, Parsawan, Raipur Phulwari, Darakha, Korari Girdhar Shah, Gangauli, Agahar and Saraiya Duban village panchayats of the Amethi Block. It has been observed that less than 100 hectares net irrigated area through private tube-well source of the irrigation has been found in the Katra Maharani, Ramdaipur, Bhaganpur, Tala, Loharata, Mochawan, Chaturbhujpur, Maharajpur, Dhandhudhar, Bhusahari, Nainaha, Saidpur, Kakawa, Mahaso, Dedhpasar, Rebha, Raidaipur, Benipur, Loniapur, Katra Maharani and Kherauna village panchayats of the Amethi Block.

3.3.3 Government Tube-well Irrigated Area

The government tube-well Irrigated Area has been recorded 280 hectares in the Amethi Block. The distribution of the government tube-well Irrigated Area in hectares has been mentioned in Table 3.4. It has been recorded that 130 hectares area being irrigated through the Government tube-well has been found in the Dedhpasar and 35 hectares government tube-well Irrigated Area has been seen in the village panchayats Sarai Khema of the Amethi Block. It has been recorded that 10 hectares irrigated area through government tube-well has been seen in the Katra Maharani, Jangal Ram Nagar, and Ramgarh village panchayats while 5 hectares irrigated area through Government tube-well has been noticed in the Naraini, Raidaipur, Hathkila, Mochawan, Kushi Tali, Tala, Umapur Ganapatti, Ramdaipur and Trilokpur village panchayats of the Amethi while less than 5 hectares irrigated area through Government tube-well has been found in the Parsawan, Darakha, Nuwawan, Loniapur, Kherauna, Katra Phul Kunwar, Rebha, Korari Girdhar Shah, Mochawa, Gangauli, Dhandhudhar, Chaturbhujpur, Agahar, Saidpur, Saraiya Duban, Mahmadpur, Nainaha and Himmatgarh village panchayats of the Amethi Block.

3.3.4 Other Sources of Irrigation

The other sources of irrigation like pond, etc. has been recorded 87 hectares in the Amethi Block. The distribution of the irrigation area through other sources of irrigation has been mentioned in Table. 3.4. It has been recorded that 10 hectares irrigated area through other sources of irrigation has been found in the Kushi Tali and Jangal Ram Nagar village panchayats while 5 hectares irrigated area through other sources of irrigation has been found in the Katra Maharani, Sarai Khema, Mahmoodpur, Tala, Darakha, Bhusahari, Naraini, Ramgarh village panchayats of the Amethi Block. It has been noticed that less than 5 hectares irrigated area through other sources of irrigation has been seen in the Himmatgarh, Nainaha, Mahmadpur, Saraiya Duban, Saidpur, Maharajpur, Chaturbhujpur, Dhandhudhar, Mahaso, Dedhpasar, Korari Girdhar Shah, Benipur, Loniapur, Kherauna and Katra Phulkunwar village panchayats of the Amethi Block.

In view of the above it has been recorded that canal irrigated area contributes 418 hectares and 5109 hectares irrigated area has been shared by the private tube-well Irrigation. The Government Tube-well area contributes only 280 hectares area while other sources of irrigation shares only 87 hectares irrigated area. The support of the Government as an irrigational input has been found very nominal while the farmers have developed their own source of irrigation through private tube-well. Therefore, the installation of more Government Tube-well in the remote villages must be initiated at larger extent to ensure good quality irrigation to increase the agricultural productivity of the villages of the Amethi Block.

3.4 Drinking Water (India Mark-II Hand Pumps)

Rural Drinking water supply or Accelerated Rural Drinking Water Supply Programme (ARWSP) has been launched by the Government of India and the State Government of Uttar Pradesh in coordination with District Planning Committee and District Rural Development Agency (DRDA) along with the District Panchayat-Block Panchayat and Village Panchayat. It has been recorded that there are 2380 India Mark-II Hand Pumps have been installed in the different village panchayats of the Amethi Block. The detailed distribution of the India Mark-II Hand Pump at village panchayat level has been mentioned in Table 3.5. The proportionate distribution of the India Mark-II Hand Pump at village panchayat level in Amethi has been depicted in **Map 3.8**. It has been recorded that more than 90 India Mark-II Hand Pump has been installed in the Sarai Khema and Jangal Ram Nagar village panchayats of the Amethi Block. It has been observed that medium installation of India Mark-II Hand Pumps between 60 to 90 India Mark-II Hand Pumps has been found in the Ramdaipur, Tala, Raipur Phulwari, Kherauna, Korari Girdhar Shah, Dhaduhdhar, Mochawa, Ramgarh, Dehara, Naraini, Kakawa, Kohara and Mahmadpur village panchayats of the Amethi Block. Proportionately low distribution of India Mark-II Hand Pumps between 30 to 60 India Mark-II Hand Pumps has been found in the Trilokpur, Mahmoodpur, Parsawan, Katra Phulkunwar, Hathkila, Dedhpasar, Rebha, Loniapur, Gangauli, Bhusahari, Himmatgarh, Nainaha, Purabgaon, Gaderi, Saraiya Duban, Saidpur, Agahar, Maharajpur, Chaturbhujpur, Nuwawan, Darakha, Umapur Ganapatti, Loharata, Kushi Tali, Bhaganpur and Trilokpur village panchayats of the Amethi Block. Very low less than 30 installations of the India Mark-II Hand Pumps has been recorded in the Katra Maharani, Benipur and Mahaso village panchayats of the Amethi Block.

The Rural Drinking Water Supply and Sanitation programmes are being implemented through Zila Yojana with the view to provide drinking water in the settlements of the rural areas. The rural drinking water supply programme is being implemented under the financial support of the Government of India. In spite of the above Central and State financially supported drinking water supply programme are being implemented at the grassroots level to ensure the availability of good quality drinking water to the villagers. Currently, the installation of New India Mark-II Hand Pumps and New pipe line for

Table 3.5: Rural Development Programme, Amethi, 2011-12

Sl. No.	*Villages*	*No. of India Mark-II Hand pumps*	*Sports & Youth Welfare*	*Primary Health Care Centres*	*No. of Women & Child Development Programmes*	*Animal health Care Centre*	*No. of A.P.L. Card Holders*	*No of B.P.L. Card Holders*
1	2	3	4	5	6	7	8	9
1.	Katra Maharani	25	—	2	3	—	126	86
2.	Sarai Khema	145	1	2	4	—	208	125
3.	Trilokpur	55	—	2	4	—	138	96
4.	Ramdaipur	60	1	2	4	—	165	105
5.	Jangal Ram Nagar	125	2	2	3	1	413	203
6.	Benipur	15	—	1	1	—	98	51
7.	Parsawan	45	—	2	4	—	125	80
8.	Mahmoodpur	50	—	2	3	—	105	80
9.	Raipur Fulwari	65	1	2	3	—	140	90
10.	Umapur Ganapatti	55	1	2	4	—	180	105
11.	Bhaganpur	45	—	—	1	—	70	40
12.	Tala	80	—	2	4	—	175	103
13.	Kushi Tali	55	—	2	3	—	146	100
14.	Loharta	25	—	2	3	—	96	68
15.	Darkha	55	1	1	3	1	175	86
16.	Mochwa	65	—	2	4	—	121	86
17.	Nuwawan	35	1	2	4	—	130	96
18.	Loniapur	40	—	2	3	—	95	68
19.	Kherauna	65	1	2	3	—	129	95
20.	Katra Phulkunwar	35	—	2	3	—	138	91
21.	Hathkila	40	—	2	3	—	101	78
22.	Rebha	45	1	2	1	—	105	86
23.	Raidaipur	105	1	2	4	—	102	80
24.	Korari Girdhar Shah	70	1	3	3	1	156	102
25.	Dedhpasar	35	1	2	2	1	102	65
26.	Mahaso	15	—	2	3	—	108	76
27.	Gangauli	45	1	2	3	1	138	76
28.	Dhadhudhar	60	—	2	3	—	96	58
29.	Gaderi	55	1	2		1	138	92
30.	Bhusahari	40	2	—	1	—	112	75
31.	Purabgaon	40	—	2	3	—	102	65
32.	Chaturbhujpur	40	—	3	3	—	126	68
33.	Mahrajpur	35	—	2	3	—	98	65
34.	Aghar	45	—	—	1	—	110	76
35.	Saidpur	40	1	2	4	—	138	102
36.	Kakwa	60	1	1	2	1	125	96
37.	Saraiya Duban	35	1	2	2	1	139	102
38.	Kohra	65	—	2	3	—	146	101
39.	Mahmadpur	60	—	2	3	—	129	76
40.	Naraini	80	1	3	2	1	138	95
41.	Nainaha	45	1	2	3	—	108	75
42.	Ramgarh	65	1	3	4	—	165	105
43.	Himmatgarh	35	1	2	3	1	121	86
44.	Dehara	65	1	2	3	—	138	65
	Amethi Block	**2380**	**24**	**83**	**129**	**11**	**5914**	**3819**

drinking water supply programmes has been implemented through the participation of the community. As per the policy of the Government of India 10 per cent cost of the installation is being shared by the community, where the community is not agreed to contribute the 10 per cent share for the installation of the Drinking Water Supply, in such cases the State Government has taken the responsibility to share the community's contribution as per the policy of the Government of India.

3.5. Sports and Youth Welfare

Sports and youth welfare programmes have been launched in various village panchayats of Amethi. It has been noticed that the two sports and youth welfare centres or units have been found in the Jangal Ram Nagar and Bhusahari village panchayats of Amethi, while the sports and youth welfare units have been found in Sarai Khema, Ramdaipur, Raipur Phulwari, Umapur Ganapatti, Darakha, Nuwawan, Kherauna, Rebha Raidaipur, Korari Girdhar Shah, Dedhpasar, Gangaui, Gaderi, Saidpur, Kakawa, Saraiya Duban, Naraini, Nainaha, Ramgarh, Himmatgarh and village panchayats of Amethi.

3.6. Primary Health Care Centres

The Primary Health Care Centres have been established covering all the village panchayats of Amethi. The distribution of the Primary Health Care Centres at village panchayat level has been mentioned in Table 3.5. It has been observed that three Primary Health Care Centres have been established in Ramgarh, Naraini, Chaturbhujpur, and Raidaipur village panchayats while two Primary Health Care Centres are established and functional in Katra Maharani, Sarai Khema, Trilokpur, Ramdaipur, Jangal Ram Nagar, Parsawan, Raipur Phulwari, Mahmoodpur, Umapur Ganapatii, Tala, Kushi Tali, Loharata, Mochawa, Nuwawan, Loniapur, Kherauna, Katra Phulkunwar, Rebha, Hathkila, Korari Girdhar Shah, Dedhpasar, Mahaso, Gangauli, Dhandhudhar, Bhusahari, Gaderi, Purabgaon, Maharajpur, Saidpur, Saraiya Duban, Kohara, Mahamadpur, Nainaha, Himmatgarh and Dehara Village panchayats of the Amethi Block. One Primary Health Care Centre has been established and functional in the Kakawa, Benipur and Darakha village panchayats while there is no Primary Health Care Centre in the village panchayats Bhusahari and Agahar, the needy patients are forced to visit the nearby village panchayat's Primary Health Care Centres.

3.7 Women and Child Development Programmes

Women and Child Development Programmes are functional in most of the village panchayats of Amethi. The Women and Child Development Programmes include Anganbadi Kendra and other associated health care services to the interested below poverty line village beneficiaries. It has been noticed four Anganbadi Kendra that have been found in Sarai Khema, Trilokpur, Ramdaipur, Parsawan, Umapur Ganapatti, Tala, Mochawa, Nuwawan, Raidaipur, Saidpur and Ramgarh village panchayats of the Amethi Block. It has been recorded that three Anganbadi Kendras have been established in Katra Maharani, Jangal Ram Nagar, Mahmoodpur, Raipur Phulwari, Kushi Tali, Loharta, Darakha, Loniapur, Kherauna, Katra Phulkunwar, Hathkila, Korari Girdhar Shah, Mahaso, Gangauli, Dhadhudhar, Gaderi, Purabgaon, Chaturbhujpur, Maharajpur, Mahmadput, Nainaha, Himmatgarh and Dehara village panchayats of the Amethi Block. It has been recorded that one Anganbadi Kendra under Women and Child Development Programmes has been found in the Agahar, Bhusahari, Rebha, Benipur and Bhaganpur village panchayats of the Amethi Block.

3.8 Animal Health Care Centres

The Animal Health Care Centres or veterinary hospitals have been established in the village panchayats of Jangal Ram Nagar, Darakha, Korari Girdhar Shah, Dedhpasar

Gangauli, Gaderi, Kakawa, Naraini, Nainaha, Saraiya Duban village panchayats of the Amethi Block. The rest of the village panchayat's Animal Husbandry beneficiaries are forced to visit in the limited veterinary hospitals. In view of the ever increasing cattle it is necessary to establish more veterinary hospitals and animal health care centres in the various village panchayats of the Amethi Block.

3.9 Above Poverty Line Card Holders

Above poverty line card holders are significantly distributed in Amethi. There are 5914 Above Poverty Line Card Holders in the Amethi Block. The distribution of above poverty line card holders at village panchayat level in Amethi has been depicted in **Map 3.9.** It has been noticed that highest more than 300 above poverty line card holders are found in the village panchayat Jangal Ram Nagar. It has been recorded that medium between 200 to 300 above poverty line card holders has been seen in the Sarai Khema, village panchayat while low between 100 to 200 above poverty line card holders are noticed in Katra Maharani, Trilokpur, Ramdaipur, Mahmoodput, Parsawan, Raipur Phulwari, Kherauna, Hathkila, Katra Phulkunwar, Dedhpasar, Mahaso, Rebha, Raidaipur, Korari Girdhar Shah, Gangauli, Bhusahari, Himmatgarh, Dehara, Nainaha, Naraini, Purab Gaon, Chaturbhujpur, Mochawa, Nuwawan, Darakha, Kushi Tali, Tala, Agahar, Kakawa, Saidpur, Saraiya Duban, Kohara and Mahmadpur village panchayats of the Amethi Block. Very low less than 100 above poverty line card holders are found in Bhaganpur, Loharata, Loniapur, Dhandhudhar and Maharajpur village panchayats of the Amethi Block.

3.10 Below Poverty Line Card Holders

It has been recorded that there are 3819 Below Poverty Line Card Holders in the Amethi Block. The distribution of the Below Poverty Line Card Holders at village panchayat level in Amethi has been depicted in **Map 3.10**. It has been recorded that highest more than 150 Below Poverty Line Card Holders are found in the village panchayat Jangal Ram Nagar of the Amethi Block, while medium between 100 to 150 Below Poverty Line Card Holders are recorded in Ramdaipur, Sarai Khema, Tala, Kushi Tali, Umapur Ganapatti, Korari Girdhar Shah, Ramgarh, Saraiya Duban and Kohara village panchayats of the Amethi Block. It has been observed that low between 50 to 100 Below Poverty Line Card Holders are found in Katra Maharani, Trilokpur, Benipur, Mahmoodpur, Parsawan, Raipur Phulwari, Kherauna, Loniapur, Raidaipur, Rebha, Katra Phulkunwar, Hathkila, Dedhpasar, Mahaso, Gangauli, Himmatgarh, Dehara, Gaderi, Purabgaon, Nainaha, Mochawa, Nuwawan, Darkha, Loharata, Maharajpur, Chaturbhujpur, Agahar, Naraini, Kakawa, Saidpur and Mahmadpur village panchayats of the Amethi Block. It has been recorded that very low less than 50 Below Poverty Line Card Holders are found in Bhaganpur village panchayat of Amethi. It has been observed that the Below Poverty Line Card Holders are significantly distributed at village panchayat level in Amethi Block.

3.11 Rural Development

Various rural development programmes are implemented financially supported by the Central Government and State Government of U.P. The rural development programmes include cleaning, sanitation, individual hand pumps and drinking water under Swajaldhara and low cost rural housing programmes planned through Zila Yojana Samiti and implemented through various line departments and the implementing institutions at village level in Amethi.

3.11.1 Cleaning and Sanitation

Sanitation and cleaning programmes have been launched under the financially supported programmes of the Government of India. The construction of low cost latrines and construction of Nali's and maintenance of the village has been launched at village panchayat level under the supervision of the village panchayat. The implementation of sanitation programmes including low cost latrines, Nali's and cleaning programmes has been mentioned in Table 3.6. It has been noticed that implementation of 5 sanitation programmes have been ensured in the village panchayat Jangal Ram Nagar followed by two sanitation programmes in Katra Maharani, Sarai Khema, Trilokpur, Ramdaipur, Parsawan, Raipur Phulwari, Umapur Ganapatti, Tala, Darakha, Nuwawan, Hathkila, Raidaipur, Korari Girdhar Shah, Dedhpasar, Gangauli, Dhadhudhar, Gaderi, Purabgaon, Maharajpur, Agahar, Saidpur, Kakawa, Saraiya Duban, Kohara, Mahmadpur, Naraini, Nainaha, Ramgarh and Dehara village panchayats. The implementation of the sanitation programmes has been launched in Himmatgarh, Chaturbhujpur, Bhusahari, Mahaso, Benipur, Bhaganpur, Kushi Tali, Loharata, Mochawa, Loniapur, Kherauna and Katra Phulkunwar village panchayats of the Amethi Block.

3.11.2 Hand Pumps

Individual and private hand pumps have been installed to fulfil the ever increasing demand of drinking water at the household level. The distribution of hand pumps at village panchayat level has been mentioned in Table 3.6. The proportionate distribution of private hand pumps has been depicted in **Map 3.11**. It has been observed that more than 100 hand pumps has been installed in the village panchayats Sarai Khema, Jangal Ram Nagar and Raidaipur village panchayats. Medium between 70 to 100 hand pumps has been installed in Tala, Naraini, and Korari Girdhar Shah village panchayats of the Amethi Block. Proportionate low distribution between 40 to 70 hand pumps has been noticed in Trilokpur, Ramdaipur, Bhaganpur, Kushi Tali, Umapur Ganapatti, Mochawa, Darakha, Mahmoodpur, Parsawan, Raipur Phulwari, Kherauna, Katra Phulkunwar, Hathkila, Rebha, Lonaipur, Dhadhudhar, Chaturbhujpur, Purabgaon, Gaderi, Nainaha, Ramgarh, Dehara, Bhusahari, Gangauli, Agahar, Saidpur, Kakawa, Kohara and Mahmadpur village panchayats of the Amethi Block. Very low less than 40 individual hand pumps are recorded in Katra Maharani, Benipur, Loharata, Nuwawan, Maharajpur, Saraiya Duban, Himmatgarh, Mahaso and Dedhpasar village panchayats of the Amethi Block. It has been recorded that there are 2380 hand pumps individually installed to fulfil the increasing demand of good quality drinking water of the growing population in the Amethi Block.

3.11.3 Rural Housing

It has been recorded that there are 42 rural houses constructed in the Amethi Block. The distribution of rural houses has been mentioned in Table 3.6. The proportionate distribution of rural housing facilities at village panchayat level has been depicted in

Map 3.12. It has been noticed that highest more than 15 number of rural houses has been constructed in Gadri, Bhusahari and Korari Girdhar Shah village panchayats of the Amethi Block. It has been observed that medium between 10 to 15 number of low cost rural houses has been constructed in Tala, Bhaganpur, Loharata, Mochawa, Ramdaipur, Jangal Ram Nagar, Mahmoodpur, Raipur Phulwari, Parsawan, Kherauna, Dhadhudhar, Ramgarh, Nainaha, Naraini, Maharajpur, Agahar, Kakawa, Saraiya Duban, Kohara and Mahmadpur village panchayats of the Amethi Block. Low distribution between 5 to 10 number of low cost houses has been constructed in Katra Maharani, Trilokpur, Sarai Khema, Kushi Tali, Umapur Ganapatti, Nuwawan, Loniapur, Katra Phul Kunwar, Rebha, Dedhpasar, Chaturbhujpur and Saidpur village panchayats of the Amethi Block. Very low less than 5 number of low cost houses has been constructed in the Hathkila, Mahaso and Raidaipur village panchayats of the Amethi Block.

3.12 Pension and Scholarship

The old age pension and widow's pension have been distributed at village panchayat level and financial assistance to support Handicapped people and Scholarship to scheduled caste, backward caste, minorities student's scholarship has been distributed at village panchayat level in Amethi. The distribution of Pension and scholarship at village panchayat level have been mentioned in Table 3.6.

3.12.1 Old Age Pension

It has been recorded that there are 643 old age pensions has been distributed in the Amethi Block. The proportionate number of old age pensions at village panchayat level in Amethi has been depicted in **Map 3.13**. It has been observed that more than 20 numbers of the old age pension beneficiaries have been recorded in Jangal Ram Nagar village panchayats while medium between 15 to 20 number of the old age pension beneficiaries has been found in Katra Maharani, Ramdaipur, Sarai Khema, Parsawan, Kushi Tali, Nuwawan, Korari Girdhar Shah, Raipur Phulwari, Kherauna, Katra Phulkunwar, Rebha, Mahaso, Dedhpasar, Gangauli, Bhusahari, Ramgarh, Dehara, Naraini, Kohara, Saraiya Duban and Saidpur village panchayats of Amethi. Low between 10 to 15 number of old age pension beneficiaries has been recorded in Trilokpur, Mahmoodpur, Hathkila, Loniapur, Raidaipur, Umapur Ganapatti, Dhadhudhar, Gaderi, Himmatgarh, Nainaha, Purabgaon, Chaturbhujpur, Maharajpur, Mochawa, Darakha, Loharata, Tala, Bhaganpur, Agahar, Kakawa and Mahmadpur village panchayats of the Amethi Block. Very low less than 10 number of old age pension beneficiaries has been found in Benipur village panchayat of the Amethi Block.

3.12.2 Handicapped

It has been recorded that in the Amethi Block 143 handicapped persons have been provided financial assistance under the Handicapped special assistance programme. It has been observed that highest 18 handicapped has been financially supported in Mahaso village panchayat followed by 7 handicapped persons in Sarai Khema while six handicapped persons have been assisted in the Ramgarh, Saraiya Duban, Dhadhudhar, Korari Girdhar Shah, Nuwawan, Jangal Ram Nagar and Katra Maharani village panchayats of the Amethi Block. It has been noticed that 5 handicapped persons have been financially supported in Parsawan, Raipur Phulwari, Umapur Ganapatti, Kushi

Table 3.6: Rural Development Programme, Amethi, 2011-12

Sl. No.	*Villages*	*Rural Development Programmes*			*Pension and Scholarship in No.*			
		Sanitation	*No. of Hand Pump for drinking water*	*Rural Housing No.*	*Old age pension*	*Handicapped*	*Scholarship*	*Widow Pension*
1	2	3	4	5	6	7	8	9
1.	Katra Maharani	2	25	6	16	6	128	—
2.	Sarai Khema	2	145	8	20	7	378	6
3.	Trilokpur	2	55	8	13	4	213	—
4.	Ramdaipur	2	60	10	15	4	225	—
5.	Jangal Ram Nagar	5	125	15	22	6	465	5
6.	Benipur	1	15	3	7	0	80	—
7.	Parsawan	2	45	10	15	5	180	—
8.	Mahmoodpur	2	50	10	13	2	88	—
9.	Raipur Fulwari	2	65	10	15	5	225	—
10.	Umapur Ganapatti	2	55	8	13	5	302	3
11.	Bhaganpur	1	45	10	12	0	70	—
12.	Tala	2	80	10	10	4	248	5
13.	Kushi Tali	1	55	5	18	5	108	—
14.	Loharta	1	25	10	13	0	70	—
15.	Darkha	2	55	15	12	5	90	—
16.	Mochwa	1	65	10	14	3	168	—
17.	Nuwawan	2	35	8	18	6	206	—
18.	Loniapur	1	40	8	14	0	146	—
19.	Kherauna	1	65	10	16	0	126	5
20.	Katra Phulkunwar	1	55	9	18	5	165	3
21.	Hathkila	2	40	4	13	0	88	3
22.	Rebha	2	45	8	15	5	260	4
23.	Raidaipur	2	105	1	12	5	150	—
24.	Korari Girdhar Shah	2	70	20	20	6	102	—
25.	Dedhpasar	2	35	7	16	3	90	—
26.	Mahaso	1	15	3	18	18	20	—
27.	Gangauli	2	45	8	16	4	98	—
28.	Dhadhudhar	2	60	10	12	6	30	—
29.	Gaderi	2	55	20	12	3	112	—
30.	Bhusahari	1	40	20	15	0	130	—
31.	Purabgaon	2	40	8	10	0	105	—
32.	Chaturbhujpur	1	40	5	12	0	80	—
33.	Mahrajpur	2	35	10	13	0	102	—
34.	Aghar	2	45	10	10	0	70	—
35.	Saidpur	2	40	7	15	4	26	6
36.	Kakwa	2	60	15	12	0	108	—
37.	Saraiya Duban	2	35	10	18	6	203	—
38.	Kohra	2	65	10	18	0	108	—
39.	Mahmadpur	2	60	15	13	5	60	—
40.	Naraini	2	80	15	16	5	203	3
41.	Nainaha	2	45	10	12	0	138	4
42.	Ramgarh	2	65	10	20	6	308	—
43.	Himmatgarh	1	35	7	13	0	108	2
44.	Dehara	2	65	6	18	5	90	—
	Amethi Block	**79**	**2380**	**422**	**643**	**143**	**4270**	**49**

Tali, Darakha, Katra Phulkunwar, Rebha, Raidaipur, Naraini, Mahmadpur, and Rebha village panchayats while 4 handicapped persons have been given financial assistance in the Saidpur, Gangauli, Tala, Ramdaipur and Trilokpur, village panchayats. It has been observed that 3 handicapped persons have been financially supported in Dedhpasar, Gaderi, Mochawa village panchayats and 2 handicapped persons have been financially supported in the village panchayat Mahmadpur of the Amethi Block.

3.12.3 Scholarship

It has been recorded that there are 6470 scholarship holders in the Amethi Block which includes scholarship starting from Primary Education → Junior School → High School → Intermediate → Graduate → Post Graduate level and Professional/Vocational educations. The distribution of scholarship at village panchayat level has been mentioned in the Table 3.6. The proportionate distribution of scholarships at village panchayat level in Amethi has been depicted in **Map 3.14**. It has been recorded that more than 300 number of students availing scholarship has been found in the Sarai Khema, Jangal Ram Nagar, Umapur Ganapatti, and Ramgarh village panchayats while 200 to 300 number of students obtaining scholarship at various educational levels has been found in Trilokpur, Ramdaipur, Tala Nuwawan, Rebha, Raipur Phulwari, Naraini and Saraiya Duban village panchayats of the Amethi Block. It has been observed that low between 100 to 200 number of students who have been provided scholarship has been noticed in Katra Maharani, Kushi Tali, Mochawa, Parsawan, Katra Phulkunwar, Kherauna, Loniapur, Ramdaipur, Korari Girdhar Shah, Bhusahari, Himmatgarh, Nainaha, Purabgaon, Gaderi, Maharajpur, Kakawa and Kohara village panchayats of the Amethi Block. Very low less than 100 number of students receiving scholarships has been found in Benipur, Mahmoodpur, Hathkila, Dedhpasar, Mahaso, Gangauli, Dhadhudhar, Dehara, Darakha, Loharata, Chaturbhujpur, Agahar, Saidpur and Mahmoodpur village panchayats of the Amethi Block.

3.12.4 Widows Pension

It has been recorded that 49 widows have been given widow pension in different village panchayats of the Amethi Block. It has been observed that 6 widow pension have been distributed in Sarai Khema and Saidpur village panchayats and 5 widows have been provided pensions in Jangal Ram Nagar, Tala, Kherauna village panchayats while 4 number of widows received pensions in Nainaha, Rebha village panchayats. It has been noticed that three widows received pension in Umapur Ganapatti, Katra Phulkunwar, Hathkila, Naraini and 2 widows have received pension in Himmatgarh village panchayat of the Amethi while rest of 32 village widows could not received widow pensions in the Amethi Block.

3.13 Agro-Afforestation

Agro-afforestation programmes have been launched by the Agriculture-Horticulture-Social-Forestry Departments of Amethi. It has been recorded that 2453 number of beneficiaries have been provided agro-afforestation facilities in the Amethi Block. The detailed number of agro-afforestation beneficiaries has been mentioned in Table 3.7. The proportionate number of Agro-afforestation beneficiaries at village panchayat level has been depicted in **Map 3.15**. It has been recorded that more that 80 agro-afforestation beneficiaries have been found in Mahmoodpur and Jangal Ram Nagar village panchayats. Medium between 60 to 80 number of the agro-afforestation beneficiaries has been found in Ramdaipur, Katra Phulkunwar, Hathkila, Raipur Phulwari, Mahaso, Gangauli, Bhusahari, Dehara, Ramgarh, Nainaha, Gaderi, Dhadhudhar, Nuwawan, Darakha, Chaturbhujpur, Naraini, and Kakawa village panchayats of the Amethi Block. It has been noticed that low between 40 to 60 agro-afforestation beneficiaries has been found in the Rebha, Dedhpasar, Kherauna, Purabgaon, Benipur Loniapur, Raidaipur, Korari

Table 3.7: Rural Development Programme, Amethi, 2011-12

Sl. No.	*Villages*	*Agro-Afforestation No. of Beneficiaries*	*Social Forestry No. of Plants*	*Constructed Pakka Road kms.*	*No. of Small Scale Industries*	*No. of Agro-Industries*	*No. of Low cost Sanitation*
1	2	3	4	5	6	7	8
1.	Katra Maharani	55	225	3	2	2	2
2.	Sarai Khema	55	350	4	3	8	2
3.	Trilokpur	35	350	2	1	2	2
4.	Ramdaipur	75	400	2	4	7	2
5.	Jangal Ram Nagar	85	300	5	5	10	5
6.	Benipur	40	156	3	2	2	2
7.	Parsawan	60	300	2	2	5	2
8.	Mahmoodpur	86	212	2	2	4	2
9.	Raipur Fulwari	65	350	2	4	4	2
10.	Umapur Ganapatti	35	425	3	2	4	2
11.	Bhaganpur	50	156	7	4	6	1
12.	Tala	35	300	3	2	3	2
13.	Kushi Tali	40	300	2	2	4	1
14.	Loharta	25	200	3	1	3	1
15.	Darkha	70	200	5	4	6	2
16.	Mochwa	46	300	1	3	7	1
17.	Nuwawan	65	300	2	2	4	2
18.	Loniapur	60	215	2	2	4	1
19.	Kherauna	60	250	3	2	3	2
20.	Katra Phulkunwar	70	300	2	4	5	1
21.	Hathkila	75	200	3	1	2	2
22.	Rebha	40	230	—	2	3	2
23.	Raidaipur	40	230	—	—	1	2
24.	Korari Girdhar Shah	45	250	3	5	10	2
25.	Dedhpasar	60	180	4	5	18	2
26.	Mahaso	70	250	—	—	1	1
27.	Gangauli	65	250	5	5	7	2
28.	Dhadhudhar	65	185	5	4	5	2
29.	Gaderi	65	225	4	4	7	2
30.	Bhusahari	80	158	2	4	7	1
31.	Purabgaon	35	200	—	2	4	2
32.	Chaturbhujpur	68	200	6	3	4	1
33.	Mahrajpur	45	200	1	—	3	2
34.	Aghar	60	170	10	4	5	2
35.	Saidpur	40	250	2	1	5	2
36.	Kakwa	75	243	13	6	6	2
37.	Saraiya Duban	43	265	2	3	7	2
38.	Kohra	45	235	2	3	7	2
39.	Mahmadpur	40	215	3	4	10	2
40.	Naraini	65	300	2	4	5	2
41.	Nainaha	65	285	1	3	12	2
42.	Ramgarh	65	300	—	5	4	2
43.	Himmatgarh	30	200	4	3	5	1
44.	Dehara	70	213	2	4	5	1
	Amethi Block	**2453**	**11023**	**132**	**132**	**226**	**81**

Girdhar Shah, Kushi Tali, Bhaganpur, Mochawa, Maharajpur, Agahar, Saidpr, Saraiya Duban, Kohara and Mahmadpur village panchayats of the Amethi Block while very low less than 40 number of agro-afforestation beneficiaries has been recorded in Trilokpur, Umapur Ganapatti, Tala, Loharata, Himmatgarh and Purabgaon village panchayats of the Amethi Block.

3.14 Social-Forestry

The Department of Social Forestry in Amethi has distributed 11023 number of plants through village panchayats in the Amethi Block. The distribution of the social forestry plants in Amethi has been mentioned in Table 3.7. The proportionate distribution of social forestry plants at village panchayat level in Amethi has been depicted in **Map 3.16**. It has been observed that more than 400 number of social forestry plants has been distributed and planted in Umapur Ganapatti village panchayat. Medium between 300 to 400 number of social forestry plants has been distributed in the Katra Phulkunwar, Parsawan, Raipur Phulwari, Sarai Khema, Trilokpur, Ramdaipur, Tala, Kushi Tali, Nuwawan, Mochawa, Ramgarh and Naraini village panchayats of the Amethi Block. Low between 200 to 300 number of the social forestry plants has been distributed in Hathkila, Rebha, Kherauna, Mahmoodpur, Katra Maharani, Jangal Ram Nagar, Loniapur, Raidaipur, Mahaso, Gangauli, Korari Girdhar Shah, Himmatgarh, Dehara, Nainaha, Purabgaon, Gaderi, Maharajpur, Chaturbhujpur, Darakha, Loharata, Saidpur, Kakawa, Saraiya Duban, Kohara and Mahmadpur village panchayats of the Amethi Block. Very low less than 200 number of the social forestry plants has been distributed in the Benipur, Bhusahari, Dedhpasar, Dhadhudhar, Agahar and Bhaganpur village panchayats of the Amethi Block.

3.15 Pucca Road

It has been noticed that 123 km. Pucca Road has been constructed during 2011-12 in Amethi. The Pucca Road has been constructed under the various schemes of the government to provide better network from the village to another. The details of the constructed Pucca Road in kilometres have been mentioned in Table 3.7. It has been observed that 13 km Pucca Road has been constructed in Kakawa, 10 km in Agahar, 6 km in Chaturbhujpur and 5 km Pucca Road have been constructed in Darakha, Gangauli, Dhadhudhar village panchayats of the Amethi Block. It has been observed that 4 km Pucca Road has been constructed in Himmatgarh, Naraini, Mahmadpur, Agahar, Bhusahari, Gaderi, Dhadhudhar and Sarai Khema village panchayats of Amethi. It has been noticed that 3 km Pucca Road have been constructed in Katra Maharani, Benipur, Umapur Ganapatti, Tala, Loharata, Kherauna, Korari Girdhar Shah, Hathkila and Maharajpur village panchayats while two km Pucca Road have been constructed in Dehara, Naraini, Saraiya Duban, Kohara, Saidpur, Bhusahari, Katra Phulkunwar, Nuwawan, Loniapur, Kushi Tali, Raipur Phulwari, Mahmoodpur, Parsawan, Ramdaipur and Trilokpur village panchayats. It has been recorded that one km Pucca Road has been constructed in Mochawa, Maharajpur and Nainaha village panchayats of the Amethi Block through the State Government and Zila Yojana including Pradhan Mantri Gram Sadak Yojana (PMGSY) of the Government of India.

3.16 Small Scale Industries

There are 132 small scale industries established at the village panchayat level in Amethi. It has been noticed that 6 small scale industries at the household level have been established in Kakawa and 5 small scale industries have been established in Jangal Ram Nagar, Korari Girdhar Shah, Dedhpasar, Gangauli and Ramgarh village panchayats of the Amethi Block while 4 small scale industries have been established in Ramdaipur, Raipur Phulwri, Bhaganpur, Darakha, Katra Phulkunwar, Dhandhudhar, Bhusahari,

Gaderi, Agahar, Mahmadpur, Naraini, and Dehara village panchayats of Amethi. It has been observed that three small scale industries have been established in Sarai Khema, Mochawa, Chaturbhujpur, Saraiya Duban, Kohara, Nainaha and Himmatgarh village panchayats of Amethi, while 2 small scale industries have been established in Rebha, Purabgaon, Katra Maharani, Benipur, Parsawan, Mahmoodpur, Umapur Ganapatti, Tala, Kushi Tali, Loniapur, Nuwawan, Kherauna village panchayats. It has been recorded that one small scale industry has been established in Trilokpur, Loharata, Hathkila and Saidpur village panchayats of the Amethi Block.

3.17 Agro-industries

Various agro-industries have been established in Amethi. The agro-industries include Masala Chakki, Sarso Tel Ghani, Aata Chakki (Flour Mill), Rice Mill and other agro-processing units to fulfil the growing demand of ever increasing population at village level. The agro-industries has been established at household level or very low level unit to process the agri-products at village panchayat level. It has been recorded that 225 low level, i.e. household level, agro-industries has been established in the Amethi. It has been noticed that 12 agro-industries has been established in Nainaha and 10 agro-industries have been established in the Korari Girdhar Shah, Mahmadpur and Jangal Ram Nagar village panchayats of Amethi. It has been observed that 8 agro-industries have been established in Sarai Khema, Dedhpasar and 7 agro-industries have been established in Saraiya Duban, Kohara, Bhusahari, Gangauli, Gaderi, Mochawa and Ramdaipur village panchayats of Amethi. It has been observed that 6 agro-industries have been established in Bhaganpur, Darakha, Kakawa village panchayats and 5 agro-industries have been established in Parsawan, Katra Phulkunwar, Saidpur, Dhandhudhar, Agahar, Naraini, Himmatgarh and Dehara village panchayats of the Amethi Block. It has been recorded that 4 agro-industries have been established in Mahmoodpur, Raipur Phulwari, Umapur Ganaptti, Kushi Tali, Nuwawan, Loniapur, Purabgaon, Chaturbhujpur and Ramgarh village panchayats while 3 agro-industries have been established in Tala, Loharata, Kherauna, Rebha, Maharajpur village panchayats and two agro-industries have been established in Katra Maharani, Trilokpur, Benipur and Hathkila village panchayats of the Amethi Block. It has been observed that one agro-industry has been established in Mahaso village panchayat and Raidaipr village panchayat of the Amethi Block.

3.18 Low Costs Sanitation

The low cost latrines have been constructed under the centrally assisted scheme of Sanitation and Cleaning Programme of the Government of India. The construction of low cost latrines and sanitation support has been facilitated in most of the village panchayats of the Amethi Block. The distribution of the number of low cost sanitation has been depicted in Table 3.7. It has been recorded that 5 low cost latrines/sanitaion have been constructed in Jangal Ram Nagar and two low cost latrines have been constructed in Katra Maharani, Sarai Khema, Ramdaipur, Trilokpur, Benipur, Parsawan, Mahmoodpur, Raipur Phulwari, Umapur Ganapatti, Tala, Darakha, Nuwawan, Kherauna, Hathkila, Rebha, Raidaipur, Korari Girdhar Shah, Dedhpasar, Gangauli, Dhadhudhar, Gaderi, Purabgaon, Maharajpur, Agahar, Saidpur, Kakawa, Kohara, Saraiya Duban, Mahmoodpur, Naraini, Nainaha, Ramgarh and Dehara village panchayats of Amethi. Construction of one low cost latrine/sanitation has been ensured in Bhaganpur, Kushi Tali, Loharata, Mochawa, Loniapur, Katra Phulkunwar, Mahaso, Bhusahari, Chaturbhujpur and Himmatgarh village panchayat of the Amethi Block.

3.19 Dairy Development

It has been recorded that 6 dairy development or mini dairy programmes have been launched in Amethi. Mini dairy of low level or at the household level dairy programmes have been established in Jangal Ram Nagar, Darakha, Korari Girdhar Shah, Gangauli, Himmatgarh and Dehara village panchayats of the Amethi Block. It has been noticed that some of the animal husbandry workers are having nominal cows/buffaloes and their milk is being marketed in the local level village market within the village level. The dairy programme contributes very nominal income of the village people.

3.20 Integrated Rural Development

Integrated Rural Development includes cleaning/sanitation, women and child development programmes, rural health, Kishori Yojana, Pulse-Polio, immunization and other welfare programmes are being implemented in Amethi. There are 74 number of programmes related to integrated development has been implemented in the village panchayat level in Amethi. The details of the number of integrated rural development programmes at village panchayat level has been mentioned in Table 3.8. It has been noticed that three integrated rural development programmes are being implemented in Sarai Khema, Trilokpur, Ramdaipur, Raipur Phulwari, Umapur Ganapatti, Tala, Mochawa, Nuwawan, Rebha, Purabgaon, Saidpur, Saraiya Duban and Ramgarh village panchayats of the Amethi Block. It has been recorded that two integrated rural development programmes are being implemented in Katra Maharani, Jangal Ram Nagar, Parsawan, Mahmoodput, Kushi Tali, Loharata, Kherauna, Raidaipr, Korari Girdhar Shah, Mahaso, Maharajpur, Kohara, Mahmadpur, Naraini, Nainaha, and Himmatgarh village panchayats of the Amethi Block. It has been observed that one integrated rural development programmes are being implemented in Loniapur and Katra Phulkunwar village panchayats of the Amethi Block.

3.21 Pradhan Mantri Gram Sadak Yojana

Pradhan Mantri Gram Sadak Yojana (PMGSY) has been implemented in most of the village panchayats of the Amethi Block. Pradhan Mantri Gram Sadak Yojana is totally supported by the Government of India as per norms with the Government of Uttar Pradesh through its implementing agencies. The details of the constructed road in kilometres under the Pradhan Mantri Gram Sadak Yojana have been mentioned in Table 3.8. It has been observed that more than 10 km Pradhan Mantri Gram Sadak Yojana has been constructed in Ramdaipur, Jangal Ram Nagar, Raipur Phulwari, Darakha, Mochawa, Katra Phulkunwar, Raidaipur, Chaturbhujpur, Maharajpur, Agahar, Saidpur, Kakawa village panchayats of the Amethi Block. The construction of the road between 5 and 10 km under the Pradhan Mantri Gram Sadak Yojana has been recorded in Katra Maharani, Sarai Khema, Trilokpur, Parsawan, Mahmoodpur, Umapur Ganapatti, Bhaganpur, Tala, Kushi Tali, Loharata, Nuwawan, Lonaipur, Rebha, Hathkila, Dhadhudhar, Gaderi, Saraiya Duban, Kohara, Mahmadpur, Naraini, Nainaha, Ramgarh, Himmatgarh and Dehara village panchayats of the Amethi Block. Very low less than 5 kms. construction of road Pradhan Mantri Gram Sadak Yojana has been

Table 3.8: Rural Development Programme, Amethi, 2011-12

Sl. No.	Villages	Integrated Rural Development No. of Programmes	PMGSY Constructed Road in kms.	No. of Beneficiaries under PMGSY	N.R.H.M. Programmes	Rajiv Gandhi Vidyutikaran Yojana No. of Houses
1	2	3	4	5	6	7
1.	Katra Maharani	2	8	50	2	–
2.	Sarai Khema	3	6	35	2	–
3.	Trilokpur	3	9	20	2	–
4.	Ramdaipur	3	12	45	2	–
5.	Jangal Ram Nagar	2	10	100	2	–
6.	Benipur	–	3	–	–	–
7.	Parsawan	2	5	40	2	–
8.	Mahmoodpur	2	6	35	2	80
9.	Raipur Fulwari	3	10	35	2	–
10.	Umapur Ganapatti	3	8	35	2	–
11.	Bhaganpur	–	5	–	–	30
12.	Tala	3	6	38	2	65
13.	Kushi Tali	2	5	40	2	80
14.	Loharta	2	7		2	–
15.	Darkha	–	10	35	3	50
16.	Mochwa	3	10	40	2	–
17.	Nuwawan	3	7	25	2	–
18.	Loniapur	1	6	20	2	–
19.	Kherauna	2	–	–	–	–
20.	Katra Phulkunwar	1	10	20	2	–
21.	Hathkila		6	20	3	–
22.	Rebha	3	7	20	2	–
23.	Raidaipur	2	10	50	2	–
24.	Korari Girdhar Shah	2	10	50	2	–
25.	Dedhpasar	–	10	25	2	60
26.	Mahaso	1	3	20	2	–
27.	Gangauli	–	10	35	2	50
28.	Dhadhudhar	–	5	35	2	–
29.	Gaderi	–	9	35	2	–
30.	Bhusahari	–	4	30	3	–
31.	Purabgaon	3	4	20	2	–
32.	Chaturbhujpur	–	10	30	3	50
33.	Mahrajpur	2	10	35	2	–
34.	Aghar	–	12	–	–	–
35.	Saidpur	3	11	40	2	–
36.	Kakwa	–	13	–	1	112
37.	Saraiya Duban	3	9	35	2	–
38.	Kohra	2	7	25	2	–
39.	Mahmadpur	2	6	25	2	–
40.	Naraini	2	8	30	2	–
41.	Nainaha	2	8	25	2	–
42.	Ramgarh	3	7	40	2	65
43.	Himmatgarh	2	4	–	2	–
44.	Dehara		8	40	2	50
	Amethi Block	73	344	1423	85	847

recorded in Benipur, Mahaso, Purabgaon, Bhusahari, and Himmatgarh, village panchayats of Amethi Block.

3.22 Number of Beneficiaries of the Pradhan Mantri Gram Sadak Yojana

The Pradhan Mantri Gram Sadak Yojana has benefited most of the villagers of the Amethi. It has been recorded that 1423 villagers have been facilitated through the Pradhan Mantri

Gram Sadak Yojana. The proportionate distribution of the number of beneficiaries facilitated through Pradhan Mantri Gram Sadak Yojana has been depicted in Table 3.8. It has been observed that approximately 100 beneficiaries in Jangal Ram Nagar, 45 beneficiaries in Ramdaipur village panchayat and 50 beneficiaries in Raidaipur, Korari Girdhar Shah village panchayats and 40 beneficiaries have been facilitated under the Pradhan Mantri Gram Sadak Yojana has been noticed in the Dehara, Ramgarh, Saidpur, Mochawa, Kushi Tali and Parsawan village panchayats of the Amethi Block. It has been noticed that 30 to 40 number of the beneficiaries benefited out of the constructed Pradhan Mantri Gram Sadak Yojana has been found in Sarai Khema, Mahmoodpur, Raipur Phulwari, Umapur Ganapatti, Tala, Darakha, Gangauli, Dhadhudhar, Gaderi, Bhusahari, Chaturbhujpur, Maharajpur, Saraiya Duban and Naraini village panchayats of the Amethi. It has been recorded that 20 to 30 number of beneficiaries facilitated out of the constructed Pradhan Mantri Gram Sadak Yojana has been found in Trilokpur, Bhaganpur, Nuwawan, Loniapur, Katra Phul Kunwar, Hathkila, Rebha, Dedhpasar, Mahaso, Purabgaon, Agahar, Kakawa, Kohara, Mahmadpur and Nainaha village panchayats of the Amehti Block. Very low less than 20 number of beneficiaries benefited from constructed Pradhan Mantri Gram Sadak Yojana has been found in Benipur and Himmatgarh village panchayats of the Amethi Block.

3.23 National Rural Health Mission (NRHM)

National Rural Health Mission Programmes have been launched in the various village panchayats with the view to provide health care facilities to the women and child and ensure immunization programmes, maternity and other health care facilities to the resourceless poor, downtrodden deprived rural poor beneficiaries surviving in the remote villages. The National Rural Health Mission Programme centres have been established in the various village panchayats of the Amethi Block. It has been recorded that three National Rural Health Mission Programme centres have been established in Darakha, Hathkila, Bhusahari, Chaturbhujpr village panchayats while two National Rural Health Mission Programme centres has been recorded in Katra Maharani, Sarai Khema, Trilokpur, Ramdaipur, Jangal Ram Nagar, Parsawan, Raipur Phulwari, Mahmoodpur, Umapur Ganapatti, Tala, Kushi Tali, Loharata, Mochawan, Nuwawan, Loniapur, Katra Phulkunwar, Rebha, Raidaipur, Korari Girdhar Shah, Dedhpasar, Mahaso, Gangauli, Gaderi, Dhadhudhar, Purabgaon, Maharajpur, Saidpur, Saraiya Duban, Kohara, Mahmadpur, Naraini, Nainaha, Ramgarh, Himmatgarh, and Dehara village panchayats while one National Rural Health Mission Programme centre has been found in the Kakawa village panchayat of the Amethi Block.

3.24 Rajiv Gandhi Grameen Vidyutikaran Yojana

Rajiv Gandhi Grameen Vidyutikaran Yojana has been launched in some of the village panchayats of Amethi. It has been recorded that 847 number of houses have been facilitated under the Rajiv Gandhi Grameen Vidyutikaran Yojana in Amethi. It has been recorded that 112 households in Kakawa, 80 households in Mahmoodpur and Kushi Tali village panchayats, 65 households in Tala and Ramgarh, 60 households in Dedhpasar, 50 households in Darakha, Gangauli, Chaturbhujpur, Agahar and Dehara village panchayats and 30 households have been provided electricity connections free of cost under the Rajiv Gandhi Grameen Vidyutikaran Yojana in the Amethi Block.

4. PROGRESS OF MAHATMA GANDHI NATIONAL RURAL EMPLOYMENT GUARANTEE ACT (MNREGA)

The status of the Mahatma Gandhi National Rural Employment Guarantee Act has been prepared by the Block Development Office of Amethi. The progress report of the

Table 3.9: Mahatma Gandhi National Rural Employment Guarantee Act (MNREGA) Progress Report, 2011-2012, Amethi Block

(Amount in Lakh Rupees)

Sl. No.	*Name of the Village Panchayat*				*Work Progress*			*Expended Amount*				
		Initial Balance	*Release Amount During 2011-2012*	*Total Available Amount*	*Allocated Work*	*Completed Work*	*Work in Progress*	*Non Skilled Labour*	*Semi/Full Skilled Labour*	*Material*	*Temporary Administrative*	*Total Expenses*
1	2	3	4	5	6	7	8	9	10	11	12	13
1.	Aghar	0.70	7.50	8.20	9	1	8	4.50	0.13	2.61	0.225	7.465
2.	Benipur	0.60	7.40	8.00	9	1	8	4.54	0.12	2.43	0.225	7.318
3.	Bhaganpur	0.65	9.30	9.95	9	1	8	4.55	0.14	2.48	0.125	7.299
4.	Bhusahari	0.13	12.50	12.63	8	2	6	7.82	0.12	1.39	0.225	3.894
5.	Chaturbhujpur	0.11	6.50	6.61	9	1	8	2.20	0.08	1.39	0.225	3.894
6.	Darkha	0.11	3.60	3.71	5	1	4	3.20	0.08	1.39	0.225	4.894
7.	Dedhpasar	0.65	8.40	9.05	6	1	5	3.72	0.12	1.99	0.225	6.055
8.	Dehara	0.60	8.50	9.10	11	2	9	6.90	0.05	3.43	0.225	10.599
9.	Dhadhudhar	0.88	5.60	6.48	4	2	2	3.88	0.12	1.76	0.225	5.987
10.	Gaderi	0.89	8.00	8.89	6	1	5	3.14	0.11	1.85	0.075	5.173
11.	Gangauli	0.95	7.00	7.95	8	2	6	2.28	0.18	1.43	0.075	3.959
12.	Hathkila	0.60	6.40	7.00	9	2	7	2.84	0.07	1.19	0.225	4.329
13.	Himmatgarh	0.58	8.50	9.08	9	2	7	2.58	0.02	1.41	0.000	4.011
14.	Jangal Ram Nagar	0.89	6.30	7.19	15	2	13	7.82	0.18	3.72	0.225	11.951
15.	Kakwa	0.49	7.00	7.49	5	1	4	3.77	0.15	1.61	0.000	5.528
16.	Katra Maharani	0.46	8.40	8.86	6	2	4	4.09	0.18	2.78	0.225	7.272
17.	Katra Phulkunwar	0.14	7.20	7.34	5	1	4	4.69	0.20	2.56	0.000	7.444
18.	Kherauna	0.39	7.50	7.89	8	1	7	4.30	0.14	2.90	0.000	7.341
19.	Kohra	1.02	7.00	8.02	6	2	4	3.02	0.15	1.29	0.225	4.677
20.	Korari Girdhar Shah	0.60	4.60	5.20	5	1	4	2.10	0.14	1.88	0.000	4.117
21.	Kushi Tali	0.95	6.40	7.35	9	2	7	2.08	0.12	1.77	0.225	4.192
22.	Loharta	0.60	6.50	7.10	5	1	4	3.48	0.15	2.99	0.225	6.844
23.	Loniapur	0.62	5.10	5.72	9	1	8	3.83	0.18	1.73	0.000	5.745
24.	Mahaso	1.25	7.80	9.05	9	1	8	6.28	0.08	6.43	0.000	9.794
25.	Mahmadpur	1.20	9.20	10.40	5	1	4	2.07	0.10	1.32	0.000	3.488
26.	Mahmoodpur	1.05	7.00	8.05	9	1	8	3.73	0.08	2.03	0.000	5.841
27.	Mahrajpur	1.15	6.00	7.15	8	1	7	3.51	0.05	1.55	0.225	5.333
28.	Mochwa	0.85	5.80	6.65	5	1	4	3.53	0.15	1.93	0.000	5.595
29.	Nainaha	0.95	7.30	8.25	12	2	10	2.61	0.15	1.06	0.000	3.820
30.	Naraini	0.35	11.10	11.45	20	1	19	5.27	0.12	2.88	0.225	8.489
31.	Nuwawan	0.45	7.00	7.45	8	2	6	2.13	0.16	1.35	0.000	3.644
32.	Parsawan	0.65	7.50	8.15	6	1	5	4.78	0.15	3.61	0.225	8.773
33.	Purabgaon	0.65	5.80	6.45	11	1	10	1.12	0.18	0.89	0.000	2.195
34.	Raidaipur	0.85	7.80	8.65	9	1	8	5.52	0.22	3.01	0.000	8.756
35.	Raipur Fulwari	0.25	6.60	6.85	5	1	4	6.51	0.05	3.55	0.225	10.333
36.	Ramdaipur	0.45	8.50	8.95	7	1	6	4.28	0.08	3.43	0.225	8.019
37.	Ramgarh	0.35	9.30	9.65	8	1	7	5.53	0.14	1.93	0.225	7.820
38.	Rebha	0.23	7.40	7.63	2	1	1	4.40	0.15	3.06	0.225	7.839
39.	Saidpur	0.35	7.60	7.95	5	1	4	5.19	0.12	2.88	0.125	8.309
40.	Sarai Khema	0.35	7.00	7.35	8	2	6	3.13	0.16	2.35	0.225	5.569
41.	Saraiya Duban	0.65	6.20	6.85	8	1	7	4.78	0.15	2.61	0.000	7.548
42.	Tala	0.48	6.70	7.18	5	1	4	5.12	0.18	3.89	0.000	9.195
43.	Trilokpur	0.15	3.00	3.15	5	1	4	2.22	0.22	1.01	0.225	3.685
44.	Umapur Ganapatti	0.09	5.60	5.69	7	2	5	6.50	0.18	3.67	0.225	10.583
	Amethi Block	**26.36**	**315.40**	**341.76**	**337**	**58**	**279**	**179.57**	**5.79**	**101.21**	**5.80**	**292.36**

MNREGA at village panchayat level has been mentioned in Table 3.9. The MNREGA Programmes are being implemented through Block Panchayat and Village Panchayat.

4.1 Initial Balance Under MNREGA

The initial balance of the Mahatma Gandhi National Rural Employment Guarantee Act (MNREGA), of the previous year has been Rs. 26.36 lakh. More than one lakh initial balance of MNREGA programme has been found in Kohara, Mahaso, Mahmoodpur, Mahmadpur, Maharajpur village panchayats. Initial balance between 0.50 lakh to 1.00 lakh has been recorded in Agahar, Benipur, Bhaganpur, Dedhpasar, Dehara, Dhadhudhar, Gaderi, Gangauli, Hathkila, Himmatgarh, Jangal Ram Nagar, Korari Girdhar Shah, Kushi Tali, Loharata, Loniapur, Mochawan, Nainaha, Parsawan, Purabgaon, Raidaipur, Saraiya Duban village panchayats of the Amethi Block. It has been recorded that less than Rs. 0.50 lakh initial balance of the MNREGA scheme has been found in Umapur Ganapatti, Trilokpur, Tala, Sarai Khema, Saidpur, Rebha, Ramgarh, Ramdaipur, Raipur Phulwari, Nuwawan, Naraini, Kherauna, Katra Phul Kunwar, Katra Maharani, Kakawa, Darakha, Chaturbhujpur and Bhusahari village panchayats of the Amethi Block.

4.2. MNREGA Release Amount (2011-12)

It has been recorded that a sum of Rs. 315.40 lakh amount has been released under the Mahatma Gandhi National Rural Employment Guarantee Act (MNREGA) programmes in the Amethi Block. It has been observed that more than Rs. 10.00 Lakh amount has released for Bhusahari and Naraini village panchayats and Rs. 8.00 to 10.00 lakh has been released for Bhaganpur, Dedhpasar, Dehara, Gaderi, Himmatgarh, Katra Maharani, Mahmadpur, Ramdaipur, Ramgarh village panchayats of Amethi. It has been seen that Rs. 6.00 to 8.00 lakh has been released for Agahar, Benipur, Chaturbhujpur, Gangauli, Hathkila, Jangal Ram Nagar, Kakawan, Katra Phulkunwar, Kherauna, Kohara, Kushi Tali, Loharata, Mahaso, Mahmoodpur, Mahrajpur, Nainaha, Nuwawan, Parsawana, Raidaipur, Raipur Phulwari, Rebha, Saidpur, Sarai Khema, Saraiya Duban and Tala village panchayats of the Amethi. It has been observed that an amount of Rs. 4.00 to 6.00 lakh has been released for Dhadhudhar, Korari Girdhar Shah, Loniapur, Mochawa, Purab Gaon and Umapur Ganapatti village panchayats while less than 4.0 lakh amount has been released for the Trilokpur village panchayat of the Amethi Block.

4.3. Total Amount Available for MNREGA

Total amount of Rs. 341.76 lakh has been made available for the implementation of the planned programmes under the Mahatma Gandhi National Rural Employment Guarantee Act (MNREGA) in the Amethi Block. It has been observed that an amount of more than Rs. 10.00 lakh has been released for Agahar, Benipur, Bhaganpur, Chaturbhujpur, Dedhpasar, Dhadhudhar, Dehara, Gaderi, Gangauli, Hathkila, Himmatgarh, Jangal Ram Nagar, Kakawa, Katra Maharani, Katra Phulkunwar, Kherauna, Kohara, Kushi Tali, Loharata, Mahaso, Mahmoodpur, Maharajpur, Mochawa, Nainaha, Purabgaon, Raidaipur, Raipur Phulwari, Ramdaipur, Ramgarh, Rebha, Saidpur, Sarai Khema, Saraiya Duban and Tala village panchayats. It has been found that less than Rs. 6.00 lakh amount under the MNREGA has been released for the Trilokpur, Umapur Ganapatti, Loniapur, Korari Girdhar Shah, and Darakha village panchayats of the Amethi Block.

4.4 Work Progress

The progress of the Mahatma Gandhi National Rural Employment Guarantee Act (MNREGA) has been assessed through analyzing the total allocated work, completed work and under progress of the MNREGA programmes at village panchayat level in Amethi Block.

4.4.1 MNREGA Allocated Work

It has been recorded that highest 20 MNREGA works have been allocated and planned in the village panchayat Naraini, followed by 12 works in Nainaha, 15 works in Jangal Ram Nagar and 11 works in Purabgaon and Dehara village panchayats of the Amethi Block. It has been recorded that 6 to 10 MNREGA works have been allocated in Agahar, Benipur, Bhaganpur, Bhusahari, Chaturbhujpur, Dedhpasar, Gaderi, Gangauli, Hathkila, Himmatgarh, Kherauna, Kohara Kushi Tali, Loniapur, Mahaso, Mahmoodpur, Maharajpur, Nuwawan, Parsawan, Raidaipur, Ramgarh, Ramdaipur, Sarai Khema, Saraiya Duban and Umapur Ganapatti village panchayats of Amethi. It has been observed that less than 6 allocated works under MNREGA have been found in Trilokpur, Tala, Saidpur, Rebha, Mochawa, Mahmadpur, Loharata, Korari Girdhar Shah, Katra Phul Kunwar, Kakawa, Dhadhudhar and Darakha village panchayats of the Amethi Block.

4.2.2. MNREGA Completed Work

Planned, allocated and completed work under the Mahatma Gandhi National Rural Employment Guarantee Act (MNREGA) during the year 2011 to 2012 at village panchayat level has been mentioned in Table 3.9. It has been recorded that planned two works have been completed in Bhusahari, Dehara, Dhadhudhar, Gangauli, Hathkila, Himmatgarh, Jangal Ram Nagar, Katra Maharani, Kohara, Kushi Tali, Nainaha, Nuwawan, Sarai Khema, and Umpur Ganapatti village panchayats of Amethi. It has been noticed that one work has been completed in Agahar, Benipur, Bhaganpur, Chaturbhujpur, Darakha, Dedhpasar, Gaderi, Kakawa, Katra Phulkunwar, Korari Girdhar Shah, Loharata, Loniapur, Mahaso, Mahmadpur, Mahmoodpur, Maharajpur, Mochawan, Naraini, Parsawan, Purabgaon, Raidaipur, Raipur Phulwari, Ramdaipur, Ramgarh, Rebha, Saidpur, Saraiya Duban, Tala and Trilokpur village panchayats of the Amethi Block.

4.4.3. MNREGA Work in Progress

Mahatma Gandhi National Rural Employment Guarantee Act (MNREGA) planned and allocated work to the village panchayats are still in progress and in the process of its implementation in most of the village panchayats of the Amethi Block. It has been noticed that 19 works in Naraini, 14 works in Jangal Ram Nagar and 10 works in Nainaha and Purabgaon village panchayats under the Mahatma Gandhi National Rural Employment Guarantee Act (MNREGA) are in the process and progress of implementation of the planned work. It has been recorded that more than 8 MNREGA works are in the progress and process of its implementation in Agahar, Benipur, Bhaganpur, Dehara, Loniapur, Mahaso, Mahmoodpur, Raidaipur village panchayats, while 6 to 8 works under MNREGA are in progress in Bhusahari, Gangauli, Hathkila, Himmatgarh, Kherauna, Kushi Tali, Maharajpur, Nuwawan, Ramdaipur, Ramgarh, Sarai Khema and Saraiya Duban village panchayats of the Amethi Block. It has been recorded that less than 6 MNREGA works are still in the progress in Darakha, Dedhpasar, Dhadhudhar, Gaderi, Kakawa, Katra Maharani, Katra Phul Kunwar, Kohara, Korari Girdhar Shah, Loharata, Mahmadpur, Mochawan, Parsawan, Raipur Phulwari, Rebha, Saidpur, Tala, Trilokpur and Umapur Ganapatti village panchayats of the Amethi Block.

4.5 Financial Progress of MNREGA

The financial progress of the Mahatma Gandhi National Rural Employment Guarantee Act (MNREGA) has been assessed for the financial expenditure on account of the non-skilled labour, semi/full skilled labour, material cost and temporary administrative expenses at village panchayat level in Amethi. The details of the financial expenditure under the MNREGA programme at village panchayat level in Amethi has been mentioned in Table. 3.9.

4.5.1 Expenditure on Non-Skilled Labour

The expenditure on non-skilled labour in the various programmes of MNREGA has been recorded Rs. 179.67 lakh in Amethi. It has been recorded that more than Rs. 6.00 lakh for non-skilled labour expenditure under MNREGA has been done in Bhusahari, Dehara, Jangal Ram Nagar, Mahaso, Raipur Phulwari and Umpur Ganapatti village panchayats while expenditure from Rs. 4.00 to 6.00 lakh for the non-skilled labour in the MNREGA programme has been done in Agahar, Benipur, Bhaganpur, Katra Maharani, Katra Phulkunwar, Kherauna, Naraini, Parsawan, Raidaipur, Ramdaipur, Ramgarh, Rebha, Saidpur, Saraiya Duban and Tala village panchayats of the Amethi Block. It has been recorded that less than Rs. 4.00 lakh amount has been spent on account of the Non-skilled labour of the MNREGA programme in the Chaturbhujpur Darakha, Dedhpasar, Dhandhudhar, Gaderi, Gangauli, Hathkila, Himmatgarh, Kakawa, Kohara, Korari Girdhar Shah, Kushi Tali, Loharata, Loniapur, Mahmadpur, Mahmoodpur, Maharajpur, Mochawan, Nainaha, Nuwawan, Purabgaon, Sarai Khema and Trilokpur village panchayats of the Amethi Block.

4.5.2 Expenditure on Skilled Labour

The expenditure account of skilled labour under the Mahatma Gandhi National Rural Emplopyment Guarantee Act (MNREGA) has been seen Rs. 5.79 lakh in Amethi Block. As per the policy of the Government of India, the employment generation for 100 days is being created for the non-skilled labour belonging to the below poverty line (BPL) accordingly the preference has been given to the non-skilled labourers in the MNREGA programmes. It has been recorded that more than 0.20 lakh amount has been spent for the skilled labourers in Trilokpur, Raidaipur, Katra Phulkunwar village panchayats while Rs. 0.15 to 0.20 lakh amount has been expended for the skilled labourers in Gangauli, Jangal Ram Nagar, Kakawa, Loharata, Loniapur, Mochawan, Nainaha, Nuwawan, Parsawan, Raidaipur, Rebha, Sarai Khema, Saraiya Duban, Tala, Trilokpur and Umapur Ganapatti village panchayats of Amethi. The expenditure for the skilled labour under MNREGA Rs. 0.10 to 0.15 lakh has been found in Agahar, Benipur, Bhaganpur,

Bhusahari, Dedhpasar, Dhandhudhar, Gaderi, Kherauna, Korari Girdhar Shah, Kushi Tali, Mahmadpur, Naraini, Ramgarh, Saidpur village panchayats while less than Rs. 0.10 lakh expenditure for the skilled labour under the MNREGA programmes has been recorded in the Ramdaipur, Raipur Phulwari, Maharajpur, Mahmoodpur, Mahaso, Darakha, Chaturbhujpur, Dehara, Hathkila, Himmatgarh village panchayats of the Amethi Block.

4.5.3 MNREGA Material Expenditure

The material expenditure in the Mahatma Gandhi National Rural Employpment Guarantee Act (MNREGA) has been recorded Rs. 101.21 lakh in the Amethi Block. It has been noticed that Rs. 6.43 lakh amount has been expended for the material cost in the Mahaso village panchayat and Rs. 3 to 6 lakh expenditure on material cost has been recorded in Dehara, Jangal Ram Nagar, Parsawan, Raidaipur, Raipur Phulwari, Rebha, Ramdaipur, Tala and Umapur Ganapatti village panchayats of the Amethi Block. It has been observed that less than Rs. 3 lakh has been expended for the skilled labour under MNREGA programmes in Agahar, Benipur, Bhaganpur, Bhusahari, Chaturbhujpur, Darakha, Dedhpasar, Dhadhudhar, Gaderi, Gangauli, Hathkila, Himmatgarh, Kakawa, Katra Maharani, Katra Phulkunwar, Kherauna, Kohara, Korari Girdhar Shah, Kushi Tali, Loharata, Loniapur, Mahmadpur, Mahmoodpur, Maharajpur, Mochawa, Nainaha, Naraini, Nuwawan, Purabgaon, Ramgarh, Saidpur, Sarai Khema, Saraiya Duban and Trilokpur village panchayats of the Amethi Block.

4.5.4 Temporary Administrative Expenditure under MNREGA Programme

Temporary administrative expenditure under the Mahatma Gandhi National Rural Employpment Guarantee Act (MNREGA) a sum of Rs. 5.80 lakh amount has been increased in the Amethi Block. It has been recorded that more than Rs. 0.20 lakh amount expenditure under the MNREGA Programme has been made in the Agahar, Benipur, Bhusahari, Chaturbhujpur, Darakha, Dedhpasar, Dhandhudhar, Dehara, Hathkila, Jangal Ram Nagar, Katra Maharani, Kohara, Kushi Tali, Loharata, Maharajpur, Naraini, Parsawan, Raipur Phulwari, Ramdaipur, Ramgarh, Rebha, Sarai Khema, Trilokpur and Umapur Ganapatti village panchayats of Amethi. It has been noticed that between Rs. 0.10 to 0.20 lakh temporary administrative expenditure under the MNREGA programmes has been recorded in Bhaganpur, Saidpur and less than Rs. 0.10 lakh expenditure on temporary administrative head has been incurred in the MNREGA Scheme in Gaderi, Gangauli village panchayats of Amethi.

4.5.5 Total Expenditure under MNREGA Programme

Total expenditure under the Mahatma Gandhi National Rural Employpment Guarantee Act (MNREGA) programme has been recorded Rs. 292.36 lakh in the Amethi Block. It has been noticed that more than Rs. 10.00 lakh total expenditure under MNREGA Programme has been incurred in the Umapur Ganapatti, Raipur Phulwari, Jangal Ram Nagar, Dehara village panchayats while total expenditure under MNREGA scheme between Rs. 8.00 and 10.00 lakh has been noticed in the Naraini, Parsawan, Mahaso, Raidaipur, Ramdaipur Saidpur, Tala village panchayats and total incurred expenditure between Rs. 6.00 and 8.00 lakh under the MNREGA programme has been observed in Agahar, Benipur, Bhaganpur, Dedhpasar, Katra Maharani, Katra Phulkunwar, Kherauna,

Loharata, Ramgarh, Rebha and Saraiya Duban village panchayats of Amethi. It has been observed that total expenditure between Rs. 4.00 and Rs. 6.00 lakh has been incurred in the MNREGA Scheme in the Darakha, Gaderi, Dhadhudhar, Hathkila, Himmatgarh, Kakawa, Kohara, Korari Girdhar Shah, Mochawa, and Sarai Khema village panchayats while less than Rs. 4.00 lakh total expenditure incurred under the MNREGA programme has been incurred in Bhusahari, Chaturbhujpur, Gangauli, Mahmadpur, Nainaha, Nuwawan, Purabgaon and Trilokpur village panchayats of the Amethi Block.

It has been observed that the physical and financial planned targets of the Mahatma Gandhi National Rural Employpyment Guarantee Act (MNREGA) has been implemented at village panchayat level in Amethi. It has been noticed that mismanagement, malpractices in the actual implementation of the MNREGA work has not been appropriately implemented like fake wage payment, poor quality work and ignoring the needs of the local village people beneficiaries with people's participation in the maintenance management and sustenance of the implementation and created assets under the MNREGA programmes at village panchayat level in Amethi. People's participatory need base formulated planned programmes under the MNREGA and proper wage payment and appropriate creation of job to the needy and interested below poverty line land less labourers and quality MNREGA work and other planned targets and its successful implementation at village panchayat level in Amethi Block may be a mile stone for the ensuring the integrated development of the Amethi.

4.6 Self-Help Groups

The Self-Help Groups (SHGs) are fast emerging powerful tool of socio-economic empowerment of the rural poor people in the villages. The Self-Help Groups are a small body formed by the people for meeting their specific, objectives, particularly credit. The Self-Help Groups are managed by the rules and regulations formed by them and it functions on a democratic principles. The Self-Help Groups are extremely useful in generating saving, employment generation and increasing the income and ensuring successful delivery of credit to individual women and effecting recovery and also gradually moving the exploitation by local money lenders. Self-Help Groups serve as an ideal mechanism for bringing women out of their homes, making them more articulate and enhancing their leadership qualities and their skills upgradation as motivators.

Self-Help Groups (SHGs) are usually informal groups whose members have a common perception of need and importance of collective action. These groups promote savings among members and use the pooled resources to meet the emergent needs of their members, including the consumption needs. The number of members in Self-Help Groups normally range from 10 to 20. It is expected that, within the group, there should be a true democratic culture in which all the members must participate actively in the decision-making process by taking part in the debate or discussion. The basic objective of Self-Help Groups is to develop saving capability among the poorest sections of the society which in turn reduces dependence on financial institutions and develop self-reliance for the involved women beneficiaries.

The Self-Help Groups benefits of the SHGs have a multi-dimensional approach. Through group a beggar on the street can also avail the benefit; poor people who do not have collateral guarantees can also get loan from the bank through the group; the members have access to large quantum of resources; provide a window for better technology and skill upgradation; have access to various promotion assistance and assurance of freedom; experience self-reliance and empowerment. All these benefits can be attained through

Table 3.10: Self-Help Groups (SHGs), 2011-2012, Amethi

Sl. No.	Name of Branch	Total No. of SHGs	No. of Inactive	No. of Active SHGs	No. Active Self Help	Better than Grade I No.	No. of SHGs,	No. of SHGs received	No. of SHGs received	No. of SHGs Crossed.	Processed Files	Sanctioned Files	Financial Assistance	Rejected Files
1	2	3	4	5	6	7	8	9	10	11	12	13	14	15
1.	BPUPGB, Amethi	90	18	75	57	53	53	53	44	42	42	42	42	0.00
2.	BPUPGB, Maharajpur	190	60	130	103	96	96	96	94	64	64	64	62	0.00
3.	BPUPGB, Tala	51	13	38	30	28	28	28	27	23	23	23	20	1
4.	BPUPGB, Darapipur	21	5	16	14	12	12	12	11	11	11	11	11	0.00
5.	BPUPGB, Visheshergani	68	15	53	4	44	44	44	25	24	24	24	21	1
6.	SBI, Amethi	17	13	4	4	3	3	3	3	1	1	1	1	0.00
7.	BOB Amethi	41	8	33	26	26	26	26	20	18	18	18	16	1
8.	BOB, Munshiganj	11	1	10	8	8	8	8	5	4	4	4	4	0.00
9.	PNB, Amethi	11	3	8	8	6	6	6	3	1	1	1	1	0.00
10.	Allahabad Bank, Amethi	29	3	26	26	26	26	26	26	26	26	26	25	0.00
11.	OBC, Amethi	4	3	1	0.00	0.00	0.00	0.00	0.00	0.00	0.00	0.00	0.00	0.00
12.	DCB Amethi	4	3	1	0.00	0.00	0.00	0.00	0.00	0.00	0.00	0.00	0.00	0.00
13.	Central Bank of India, Amethi	1	0.00	1	0.00	0.00	0.00	0.00	0.00	0.00	0.00	0.00	0.00	0.00
	Total	**538**	**145**	**393**	**325**	**302**	**302**	**302**	**225**	**214**	**214**	**214**	**203**	**3**

* Baroda Purvi Uttar Pradesh Grameen Bank (BPUPGB)
* State Bank of India (SBI)
* Bank of Baroda (BOB)
* Punjab National Bank (PNB)
* Oriental Bank of Commerce (OBC)
* District Cooperative Bank (DCB)

collectively. Little drop of water make an ocean to generate employment and increase the income of deprived rural poor women to ensure their socio-economic development in the remote villages of the Amethi. An attempt has been made in this study to asses the progress of the implementation of the women Self-Help Groups (SHGs), activities received grants and Cash Credit Limits (CCL) and various trades which has been supported by the different Banks at village panchayats level in Amethi.

4.6.1 Status of the Self-Help Groups

It has been recorded that there are 538 women Self-Help Groups in Amethi, which have been financially supported and provided cash credit limits by the nearest service Bank. The highest 190 Self-Help Groups (SHGs) are functioning in the village panchayats Maharajpur, supported by Baroda Purvi Uttar Pradesh Grameen Bank. Thus the Baroda Purvi Uttar Pradesh Grameen Bank Branch at Amethi supported 90 SHGs, Tala—51 SHGs, Darapipur—21 SHGs and Vishesharganj Branch supported 68 women Self-Help Groups in Amethi. The State Bank of India, Amethi financially supported 41 SHGs and Munshiganj Branch supported 11 women SHGs. The Punjab National Bank, Amehti supported 11 SHGs, Allahabad Bank, Amethi supported 29 SHGs and Oriental Bank of Commerce financially supported 4 women SHGs in Amethi. It has been recorded that the District Co-operative Bank, Amethi supported 4 women SHGs and Central Bank of India, Amethi has supported to one women Self-Help Groups in Amethi.

It has been recorded that there are 145 inactive women Self-Help Groups in Amethi out of 538 formed Self-Help Groups, Baroda Purvi Uttar Pradesh Grameen Bank, Maharajpur has 60 inactive women Self-Help Groups followed by 18 inactive Self-Help Groups at Amethi Branch and 15 inactive SHGs in the Vishesharganj while State Bank of India has 13 inactive Self-Help Groups.

It has been found that there are 393 active Self-Help Groups in Amethi, which have been mentioned in Table 3.10. The highest 130 active SHGs are found in the Baroda Purvi Uttar Pradesh Grameen Bank and followed by 75 active SHGs at its Amethi Branch and 53 active SHGs in the Vishesharganj Branch and 38 active SHGs in Tala Branch while Bank of Baroda, Amethi has 33 active SHGs and 26 active SHGs has been found in the Allahabad Bank, Amethi. The Bank of Baroda, Munshiganj have 10 active SHGs and Baroda Purvi Uttar Pradesh Grameen Bank Darapipur has 16 active Self-Help Groups while other Banks have nominal active Self-Help Groups in Amethi.

The active Self-Help Groups have been assessed and it has been found that from more than 6 months among the active SHGs 325 Women Self-Help Groups have been found active and functional as per the norms. It has been noticed that 103 SHGs are active even after six months in the Baroda Purvi Uttar Pradesh Grameen Bank, Maharajpur followed by 57 active SHGs at its Amethi Branch and 30 active SHGs are functional from more than 6 months at its Tala Branch in Amethi.

The grading of the functional women Self-Help Groups are assessed and it has been noticed that better than the Grade-I Number of Women Self-Help Groups has been found 302 Women SHGs in Amethi, out of which 96 better active women SHGs has been found in the Baroda Purvi Uttar Pradesh Grameen Bank at Maharajpur followed by 53 SHGs at Amethi, and 44 SHTs at its Branch at Darapipur and 28 better active SHGs at its Branch at Tala and 26 better active women SHGs has been found in the Bank of Baroda, Amethi while other local service providing Bank branches are having nominal better active operation women Self-Help Groups in Amethi.

It has also been recorded that 302 Women Self-Help Groups have received the refund of the financial assistance and 302 women Self-Help Groups have also received Cash Credit Limits (CCL) assistance from their respective Banks in Amethi.

It has been noticed that 225 active Self-Help Groups have received Cash Credit Limits and functional successfully from more than 6 months in the various branches of the Banks in Amethi.

It has been recorded that there are 214 women Self-Help Groups which have crossed Grade-II and such active women Self-Help Groups have been graded even better than Grade-II Self-Help Groups in Amethi. Therefore, it can be said that out of 538 formed Self-Help Groups only 214 women Self-Help Groups in Amethi has successfully functional and has been graded better than Grade-II in the various Bank Branches in Amethi. It has been noted that there are 214 process files in different branches of the Bank related to the Women Self-Help Groups in Amethi and 214 active women Self-Help Groups financial assistance files have been sanctioned by the different Branchs of the Banks in the Amethi. There are 203 women Self-Help Groups filed in the respective branches of the Bank for which financial assistance has been sanctioned and it has also been recorded that 3 Self-Help Groups files for financial assistance has been rejected by the Baroda Purvi Uttar Pradesh Grameen Bank at Tala and Vishesharganj and one Self-Help Group file for financial assistance has been rejected by the Bank of Baroda, Amethi respectively.

4.6.2 Financial Status of Self-Help Groups

It has been noticed that the Bhagirathi SHGs, Kakawa and Jai Bajrang SHGs, Kakawa has been sanctioned Goat's project Rs. 1.00 lakh and Rs. 1.10 lakh respectively by the Baroda Purvi Uttar Pradesh Grameen Bank, Maharajpur which comprises the loan and grants component as well. Similarly, Jai Kali SHGs Chaturbhujpur, Prem Pujari SHGs Kushi Tali, Mother SHGs Kakawa, Dhan Laxmi Self-Help Groups, Raidaipur and Jai Basanti SHGs Mochawa have been supported for the Dairy project for which the concerned Service Bank has provided grants-in-aid and loan component of the financial assistance. The details of the grant number of the members of SHGs, Bank's name etc. has been mentioned in detail in Table 3.11. Dhan Nirankar SHGs Kakawa, Maha Kali SHGs Gaderi, Kiran SHGs, Naraini, Jai Maa Ambey SHGs, Mochawa, Gulab SHGs, Gaderi, Raj SHGs and Saroj SHGs, Gaderi. Gareeb Mahila SHGs, Maharajpur and Neelam SHGs, Agahar has been financially supported for the goat project as per the requirement of the proposal and these Self-Help Groups are functioning successfully as per the norms. Malati SHGs, Agahar has also been sanctioned Dairy Project supported by the Baroda Purvi Uttar Pradesh Grameen Bank, Maharajpur and Jagriti Self-Help Groups, Raidaipur has been supported Branch Bank project by the Baroda Purvi Uttar Pradesh Grameen Bank, Darapipur. It has been observed that the above discussed Self-Help Groups are operational and functional as per the norms and these Self-Help Groups have been graded better than Grade-II. It has been noticed that very nominal Self-Help

Table 3.11: Financial Support Self-Help Groups (SHGs), 2011-2012, Amethi Block

Sl. No.	*Name of SHGs*	*Village*	*Mem-bers of SHGs*	*Project Name*	*Grants in Aid*		*Name of Bank*
					Loan	*Grant*	
1	2	3	4	5	6	7	8
1.	Bhagirathi SHGs.	Kakawa	10	Goat	1.00	1.00	BPUPGB Maharajpur
2.	Jai Basanti SHGs	Mochawa	12	Dairy	3.60	1.20	BPUPGB Maharajpur
3.	Jai Bajranj SHGs	Kakawa	11	Goat	1.10	1.10	BPUPGB Maharajpur
4.	Dhan Laxmi SHGs	Raidaipur	10	Dairy	2.00	1.00	Allahabad Bank, Amethi
5.	Mother SHGs	Kakawa	10	Dairy	2.00	1.00	BPUPGB Maharajpur
6.	Prem Pujari SHGs	Kushi Tali	10	Dairy	2.00	1.00	BPUPGB Tala
7.	Jai Kali SHGs	Chaturbhujpur	11	Dairy	2.20	1.10	BPUPGB Maharajpur
8.	Dhan Nirankar SHGs	Kakawa	12	Goat	1.20	1.20	BPUPGB Maharajpur
9.	Mahakali SHGs	Gaderi	11	Goat	1.10	1.10	BPUPGB Amethi
10.	Kiran SHGs	Naraini	13	Goat	1.35	1.25	BPUPGB Mahrajpur
11.	Malti SHGs	Agahar	11	Diary	2.20	1.10	BPUPGB Maharajpur
12.	Jai Maa Ambey SHGs	Mochawa	10	Goat	2.00	1.00	BPUPGB Maharajpur
13.	Gulab SHGs	Gaderi	11	Goat	1.10	1.10	BPUPGB Amethi
14.	Raj SHGs	Gaderi	12	Goat	1.20	1.20	BPUPGB Amethi
15.	Saroj SHGs	Gaderi	12	Goat	1.20	1.20	BPUPGB Amethi
16.	Gareeb Mahila SHGs	Majarajpur	11	Goat	1.10	1.10	BPUPGB Maharajpur
17.	Grih Laxmi SHGs	Ramgarh	11	Dairy	2.20	1.10	BPUPGB Vishesharganj
18.	Neelam SHGs	Agahar	11	Goat	1.10	1.10	BPUPGB Maharajpur
19.	Jagriti SHGs	Raidaipur	11	Brass Band	2.20	1.10	BPUPGB Darpipur
20.	Vikas Self-Help Groups	Trilokpur	13	Shop	2.60	1.25	BPUPGB Darpipur.
21.	Bheem Self-Help Groups	Jangal Ram Nagar	10	Goat	1.00	1.00	BPUPGB Amethi
22.	Aarti Self-Help Groups	Parsawan	12	Goat	1.20	1.20	BPUPGB Amethi
23.	Jai Self-Help Groups	Kudwa Mahmadpur	11	Dairy	2.20	1.10	BPUPGB Vishesharganj
24.	Mishra Self-Help Groups	Dedhpasar	12	Tent House	2.40	1.20	BOB Amethi
25.	Kamal Self-Help Groups	Gaderi	13	Tent House	2.00	1.00	BPUPGB Amethi
26.	Ramdhar Self-Help Groups	Mahmadpur	10	Goat	1.00	1.00	BPUPGB Maharajpur
	Total		**291**		**44.25**	**28.70**	

Groups are successfully implementing the sanctioned project by the Bank but unfortunately most of the Self-Help Groups are inactive due to ignorance and their willingness. It is necessary to generate awareness and impart skill development training programme at larger extent among the weaker section women beneficiarires to accept and adopt the micro credit support system through Self-Help Groups at village panchayat level in Amethi.

4.7 Status of Swarnjayanti Gram Swarojgar Yojana (SGSY)

Swarnjayanti Gram Swarojgar Yojana has been launched to facilitate implementation of various programmes to generate the employment for the weaker section of the society. The Swarnjayanti Gram Swarojgar Yojana has been launched to facilitate self-sustenance of the households living below the poverty line through establishing small scale industrial units at larger extent, so that the supported families can develop up to the above poverty line.

The supported families may be an individual or groups even Self-Help Groups although focus has been given for the group system. Through this scheme 4-5 main activities has been identified in each Development Block. The identified activities related projects are formulated through clusters for the people living below the poverty line and provide benefit for the self-employment.

The Government of India shares and contributes 75 per cent cost of the project and 25 per cent project cost is being supported by the State Government.

In this programme 30 per cent cost of the project and maximum grant of Rs. 7500 is being sanctioned for the individual self-employee belonging to non-scheduled caste/ scheduled tribe. The scheduled caste/scheduled tribe or handicapped beneficiaries are being granted maximum 50 per cent grant to the total cost of the project or Rs. 1000 grant is sanctioned to the self-employee interested beneficiaries.

In the case of Self-Help Groups the 50 per cent of the total cost of the project or maximum Rs. 1.25 lakh (Rs. 1000 per person or Rs. 1.25 lakh which ever is lower) limit grants-in-aid are sanctioned.

There is no limit for the maximum grants related to the irrigation project.

In this programme much emphasis has been focused for the most poorest persons out of the rural poor. In view of the above it has been targeted to facilitate 50 per cent scheduled caste/scheduled tribe, 40 per cent women and 3 per cent handicapped persons out of the total beneficiaries under the Swarnjayanti Gram Swarojgar Yojana.

In this scheme interested below poverty line, rural poor, weaker section 155 beneficiaries have been selected in the Amethi Block during the year 2011-12. The detail list of the Swarnjayanti Gram Swarojgar Yojana is mentioned in Table 3.12.

It has been recorded that our of the total selected 155 scheduled caste, general 55 and 2 minorities Swarnjayanti Gram Swarojgar Yojana beneficiaries have been selected which has been mentioned in Table 3.12.

As per the norms, policies and plans laid by the Government of India the Grants-in-aid and loan component of the proposed cost of the project has been sanctioned by the concerned service Banks.

It has been recorded that Baroda Purvi Uttar Pradesh Grameen Bank financially supported and granted 98 self-employee beneficiaries under the Swarnjayanti Gram Swarojgar Yojana in the Amethi Block. The Allahabad Bank supported 21 beneficiaries, Oriental Bank of Commerce supported 17 beneficiaries and Central Bank supported 6 beneficiaries Banking financial support under the Swarnjayanti Gram Swarojgar Yojana in the Amethi.

Table 3.12: Swarnjayanti Gram Swarojgar Yojana List of Beneficiaries, Amethi Block

Sl. No.	*Name of Beneficiaries*	*Father's name*	*Village*	*Caste*	*Project*	*Loan*	*Grants*	*Name of Bank*
1	2	3	4	5	6	7	8	9
1.	Mohd. Jaheer	Najim	Chachakapur	Minority	Buffallo	25000.00	7500.00	OBC Amethi
2.	Mohd. Shabbir	Abir Khan		Minority	Buffallo	25000.00	7500.00	OBC Amethi
3.	Devmani	Ram Sewak	Rebha	Gen.	Shop	25000.00	7500.00	OBC Amethi
4.	Satyadeo	Ram Sewak	Rebha	Gen.	Buffalo	25000.00	7500.00	OBC Amethi
5.	Dilip Kumar	Keshaw Ram	Rebha	Gen.	Buffalo	25000.00	7500.00	OBC Amethi
6.	Shyam Milan	Gayatri	Rebha	Gen.	Buffalo	25000.00	7500.00	OBC Amethi
7.	Rekha	Ram Sumare	Rebha	Gen.	Buffalo	25000.00	7500.00	OBC Amethi
8.	Shyamkali	Budhiram	Kohara	S.C.	Goat	20000.00	10000.00	BPUPG Bank Maharajpur
9.	Reena	Kallu	Mahmadpur	S.C.	Goat	20000.00	10000.00	BPUPG Bank Maharajpur
10.	Kalawati	Raj Kumar	Agahar	S.C.	Goat	20000.00	10000.00	BPUPG Bank Maharajpur
11.	Ram Tirath	Mathura	Puramgaon	S.C.	Buffalo	20000.00	10000.00	BPUPG Bank Maharajpur
12.	Shesh Nath	Ram Lal	Mahmadpur	S.C.	Buffalo	20000.00	10000.00	BPUPG Bank Maharajpur
13.	Shripal	Ram Ajor	Kohara	S.C.	Buffalo	20000.00	10000.00	BPUPG Bank Maharajpur
14.	Ram Kishore	Mohan	Kohara	S.C.	Buffalo	20000.00	10000.00	BPUPG Bank Maharajpur
15.	Suryabali	Ramdeen	Kohara	S.C.	Buffalo	20000.00	10000.00	BPUPG Bank Maharajpur
16.	Dilip	Ramdhani	Kohara	S.C.	Buffalo	20000.00	10000.00	BPUPG Bank Maharajpur
17.	Ram Kushun	Dujai	Kohara	S.C.	Buffalo	20000.00	10000.00	BPUPG Bank Maharajpur
18.	Tara Devi	Pawan Kumar	Gaderi	S.C.	Goat	25000.00	10000.00	BPUPG Bank Maharajpur
19.	Rangeela	Matai	Kudawa	S.C.	Goat	25000.00	10000.00	BPUPG Bank Maharajpur
20.	Ram Chander	Bhagole	Kudawa	S.C.	Buffalo	25000.00	10000.00	BPUPG Bank Maharajpur
21.	Sarita	Sitaram	Bartali	S.C.	Goat	25000.00	10000.00	BPUPG Bank Maharajpur
22.	Uma	Mahesh	Bartali	S.C.	Goat	25000.00	10000.00	BPUPG Bank Maharajpur
23.	Raju	Ram Lal	Ramgarh	S.C.	Shop	25000.00	10000.00	BPUPG Bank Visheshargani
24.	Ram Sundar	Rajaram	Kudawa	S.C.	Buffalo	25000.00	10000.00	BPUPG Bank Visheshargani
25.	Lilawati	Rajesh	Kudawa	S.C.	Goat	25000.00	10000.00	BPUPG Bank Visheshargani
26.	Sita	Rajesh	Bartai	S.C.	Goat	25000.00	10000.00	BPUPG Bank Visheshargani
27.	Kailashi	Mewalal	Gaderi	S.C.	Goat	25000.00	10000.00	BPUPG Bank Visheshargani
28.	Shivkumari	Ram Sajiwan	Dhanapur	S.C.	Goat	20000.00	10000.00	BPUPG Bank Visheshargani
29.	Rajiv	Ram Chander	Gaderi	S.C.	Buffalo	20000.00	10000.00	BPUPG Bank Visheshargani
30.	Babu Lal	Ram Anjor	Himmatgarh	S.C.	Buffalo	20000.00	10000.00	BPUPG Bank Visheshargani
31.	Nanhey	Sher Ali	Himmatgarh	Gen.	Buffalo	20000.00	10000.00	BPUPG Bank Visheshargani
32.	Jairam	Jang Bahadur	Ramgarh	Gen.	Buffalo	20000.00	10000.00	BPUPG Bank Visheshargani
33.	Akhilesh	Daya Ram	Dhanapur	Gen.	Shop	20000.00	10000.00	BPUPG Bank Visheshargani
34.	Pitardin	Suratdin	Ramgarh	Gen.	Shop	20000.00	10000.00	BPUPG Bank Visheshargani

(Contd.)

Table 3.12 (*Contd.*)

1	2	3	4	5	6	7	8	9
35.	Virendra	Shobh Nath	Ramgarh	Gen.	Buffalo	20000.00	10000.00	BPUPG Bank Visheshargani
36.	Lalji	Ram Lakhan	Ramgarh	Gen.	Buffalo	20000.00	10000.00	BPUPG Bank Visheshargani
37.	Shiv Prasad	Ram Sundar	Nuwawan	Gen.	Shop	25000.00	10000.00	Central Bank Amethi
38.	Lalmati	Daddan	Nuwawan	Gen.	Goat	25000.00	10000.00	Central Bank Amethi
39.	Ranjan Kumar	Laxmi Narayan	Sarwanpur	Gen.	Shop	25000.00	10000.00	Central Bank Amethi
40.	Dharm Singh	Sri Nath Singh	Nuwawan	Gen.	Shop	25000.00	10000.00	Central Bank Amethi
41.	Rambodh	Satan	Darkha	Gen.	Buffalo	25000.00	10000.00	BPUPG Bank Tala
42.	Sunil Kumar	Daya Shankar	Katara Maharani	Gen.	Buffalo	20000.00	10000.00	BOB, Munshiganj
43.	Rakesh	Brij Bihari	Katara Maharani	Gen.	Shop	25000.00	10000.00	BOB, Munshiganj
44.	Radhey Shyam	Babu Lal	Tala	Gen.	Shop	20000.00	10000.00	BPUPG Bank Tala
45.	Hira Lal	Ram Adhar	Tala	Gen.	Buffalo	20000.00	10000.00	BPUPG Bank Tala
46.	Jyoti	Pradeep	Katara Maharani	Gen.	Goat	20000.00	10000.00	BOB, Munshiganj
47.	Sheetla Prasad	Babu Lal	Katara Phulkunwar	Gen.	Shop	20000.00	10000.00	BOB, Amethi
48.	Mukesh Chandra	Ram Saran	Katara Phulkunwar	Gen.	Buffalo	20000.00	7500.00	BOB, Amethi
49.	Jagdish Prasad	Bhawani Singh	Lokipur	Gen.	Buffalo	20000.00	7500.00	BOB, Munshiganj
50.	Ajit Kumar	Shyam Lal	Tala	Gen.	Buffalo	20000.00	7500.00	BPUPG Bank Tala
51.	Kasim Khan	Sattar	Chachakapur	Gen.	Shop	20000.00	7500.00	Allahabad Bank, Amethi
52.	Dinesh Kumar	Hariram	Mahmoodpur	Gen.	Shop	25000.00	7500.00	OBC, Amethi
53.	Shyam Sundar	Satya Narayan	Jamal Patti	Gen.	Buffalo	25000.00	7500.00	OBC, Amethi
54.	Shyam Lal	Panch	Dehara	S.C.	Buffalo	25000.00	10000.00	BPUPG Bank Vishesnarganj
55.	Budhram	Ram Sumer	Dehara	S.C.	Shop	25000.00	10000.00	BPUPG Bank Visheshargani
56.	Sursati	Ram Kumar	Dehara	S.C.	Goat	25000.00	10000.00	BPUPG Bank Visheshargani
57.	Kalpana	Mahadeo	Dehara	S.C.	Goat	25000.00	10000.00	BPUPG Bank Visheshargani
58.	Kanhaiya	Mathura	Dehara	S.C.	Buffalo	25000.00	10000.00	BPUPG Bank Visheshargani
59.	Jagdish	Bhagauti	Dehara	S.C.	Buffalo	25000.00	10000.00	BPUPG Bank Visheshargani
60.	Santlal	Ram Dulare	Dehara	Gen.	Buffalo	25000.00	7500.00	BPUPG Bank Visheshargani
61.	Harikesh	Dhanau	Dehara	S.C.	Shop	25000.00	10000.00	BPUPG Bank Visheshargani
62.	Santram	Ramdas	Dehara	S.C.	Shop	25000.00	10000.00	BPUPG Bank Visheshargani
63.	Prema Devi	Hari Prasad	Dehara	S.C.	Goat	20000.00	10000.00	BPUPG Bank Visheshargani
64.	Ram Piyare	Pudunram	Dehara	S.C.	Buffalo	20000.00	10000.00	BPUPG Bank Visheshargani
65.	Ashish Kumar	Ram Sundar	Dehara	S.C.	Shop	20000.00	10000.00	BPUPG Bank Visheshargani
66.	Dilip Kumar	Radhey Shyam	Dehara	Gen.	Shop	20000.00	7500.00	BPUPG Bank Visheshargani
67.	Jiya Lal	Mathura Prasad	Dehara	S.C.	Buffalo	20000.00	10000.00	BPUPG Bank Visheshargani

(*Contd.*)

Table 3.12 *(Contd.)*

1	2	3	4	5	6	7	8	9
68.	Shobh Nath	Ram Sumer	Dehara	S.C.	Buffalo	20000.00	10000.00	BPUPG Bank Vishesharganj
69.	Ram Sumer	Ramai	Dehara	S.C.	Buffalo	20000.00	10000.00	BPUPG Bank Vishesharganj
70.	Ram Ganesh	Ramdas	Ramgarh	Gen.	Buffalo	20000.00	7500.00	BPUPG Bank Vishesharganj
71.	Diwakar	Ramesh Chandra	Gaderi	Gen.	Shop	20000.00	7500.00	BPUPG Bank Vishesharganj
72.	Ram Chandra	Ram Prakash		S.C.	Shop	20000.00	10000.00	BPUPG Bank Vishesharganj
73.	Ram Khelawan	Girdhari		S.C.	Shop	20000.00	10000.00	BPUPG Bank Maharajpur
74.	Radha	Ram Palat		S.C.	Goat	20000.00	10000.00	BPUPG Bank Maharajpur
75.	Sahdei	Santu		S.C.	Buffalo	20000.00	10000.00	BPUPG Bank Maharajpur
76.	Neetu	Ajai Kumar	Rebha	Gen.	Goat	20000.00	7500.00	OBC, Amethi
77.	Mohd. Haleem	Mohd. Ali	Chachakapur	Gen.	Shop	20000.00	7500.00	OBC, Amethi
78.	Shiv Kumar	Badri Prasad	Rebha	Gen.	Shop	25000.00	7500.00	OBC, Amethi
79.	Vinod Kumar	Ram Chander	Rebha	Gen.	Shop	25000.00	7500.00	OBC, Amethi
80.	Sheetala Prasad	Surya Narayan	Rebha	Gen.	Buffalo	25000.00	7500.00	OBC, Amethi
81.	Krishna Kumar	Onkar Nath	Sarai Khema	Gen.	Buffalo	25000.00	7500.00	OBC, Munshiganj
82.	Ashok Kumar	Ram Anjor	Jamalpatti	Gen.	Shop	25000.00	10000.00	BOB, Amethi
83.	Raj Kumari	Sushil Tiwari	Tiwaripur	Gen.	Shop	25000.00	7500.00	BOB, Amethi
84.	Girjesh Tiwari	Sushil Tiwari	Tiwaripur	Gen.	Shop	25000.00	7500.00	BOB, Amethi
85.	Vinod Kumar	Mahadeo	Trilokpur	S.C.	Shop	25000.00	10000.00	BPUPG Bank Darpipur
86.	Raj Kumari	Saroj Panch	Kohara	S.C.	Goat	25000.00	10000.00	BPUPG Bank Maharajpur
87.	Badaka	Sheetla Prasad	Kohara	S.C.	Goat	25000.00	10000.00	BPUPG Bank Maharajpur
88.	Santuram	Ram Prasad	Kohara	S.C.	Buffalo	25000.00	10000.00	BPUPG Bank Maharajpur
89.	Sudha	Ramesh	Puramgaon	S.C.	Goat	25000.00	10000.00	BPUPG Bank Maharajpur
90.	Santram	Pherai	Kohara	S.C.	Buffalo	25000.00	10000.00	BPUPG Bank Maharajpur
91.	Parvati	Ramsukh	Kohara	S.C.	Goat	25000.00	10000.00	BPUPG Bank Maharajpur
92.	Ram Sundar	Dujai	Loharata	Gen.	Buffalo	25000.00	7500.00	BPUPG Bank Tala
93.	Ashok Kumar	Lal Saheb	Tiwaripur	Gen.	Shop	25000.00	7500.00	BOB, Amethi
94.	Parveen	Wasim	Sarwanpur	Gen.	Goat	20000.00	7500.00	BOB, Amethi
95.	Sheetala Prasad	Gaya Prasad	Kherauna	Gen.	Buffalo	20000.00	7500.00	BOB, Amethi
96.	Nirmala	Ram Piyare	Haripur	S.C.	Goat	20000.00	10000.00	BPUPG Bank Tala
97.	Srimati	Kallram	Haripur	S.C.	Goat	20000.00	10000.00	BPUPG Bank Tala
98.	Jayara Devi	Ram Prasad	Haripur	S.C.	Goat	20000.00	10000.00	BPUPG Bank Tala
99.	Gyan Prakash	Ram Asare	Kundwa	Gen.	Shop	20000.00	7500.00	Allahabad Bank, Amethi
100.	Lal Bahadur	Baijnath	Mahaso	Gen.	Shop	20000.00	7500.00	Allahabad Bank, Amethi
101.	Suraj Kumar	Brijlal	Ramnagar	S.C.	Shop	25000.00	10000.00	Allahabad Bank, Amethi
102.	Dev Narain	Ram Piyare	Kherauna	Gen.	Buffalo	25000.00	7500.00	Allahabad Bank, Amethi
103.	Manisha Singh	Narendra Singh	Birahimpur	Gen.	Goat	25000.00	7500.00	Allahabad Bank, Amethi
104.	Tahira	Mohd. Raseed	Sarai Kandh	Gen.	Goat	25000.00	7500.00	Allahabad Bank, Amethi

(Contd.)

Table 3.12 (*Contd.*)

1	2	3	4	5	6	7	8	9
105.	Sandip Singh	Kashi Nath	Kherauna	Gen.	Shop	25000.00	7500.00	Allahabad Bank, Amethi
106.	Dukhiram	Doodh Nath	Ahagar	S.C.	Buffalo	25000.00	10000.00	BPUPG Bank Maharajpur
107.	Kallu	Jhari	Dalshahpur	S.C.	Buffalo	25000.00	10000.00	BPUPG Bank Maharajpur
108.	Badri Prasad	Chhitanu	Mahrajpur	Gen.	Shop	25000.00	7500.00	BPUPG Bank Maharajpur
109.	Ramraj	Durga	Kohara	S.C.	Buffalo	25000.00	10000.00	BPUPG Bank Maharajpur
110.	Surendra	Nankau	Naraini	Gen.	Shop	25000.00	7500.00	BPUPG Bank Maharajpur
111.	Kashi Naresh	Jagannath	Darakha	Gen.	Shop	25000.00	7500.00	BPUPG Bank Tala
112.	Jai Narain	Sangam Prasad	Raidaipur	Gen.	Shop	25000.00	7500.00	OBC Amethi
113.	Ramraj	Chhedi Lal	Ramnagar	S.C.	Goat	10000.00	10000.00	Central Bank Amethi
114.	Ausan	Lallan Prasad	Liniapur	S.C.	Dairy	20000.00	10000.00	Central Bank Amethi
115.	Ram Sunder	Barsati	Sarai Khema	S.C.	Goat	10000.00	10000.00	PNB Amethi
116.	Gurucharan	Ramau	Sarai Khema	S.C.	Goat	10000.00	10000.00	PNB Amethi
117.	Roop Chandra	Ram Adhar	Sarai Khema	S.C.	Dairy	20000.00	10000.00	BOB, Amethi
118.	Lallan	Ram Dayal	Trilokpur	S.C.	Goat	10000.00	10000.00	Allahabad Bank, Amethi
119.	Gudda	Shi Charan	Birahimpur	S.C.	Dairy	20000.00	10000.00	Allahabad Bank, Amethi
120.	Sanjay Kumar	Ram Piyare	Birahimpur	S.C.	Dairy	20000.00	10000.00	Allahabad Bank, Amethi
121.	Devmati	Sukhram	Birahimpur	S.C.	Goat	10000.00	10000.00	Allahabad Bank, Amethi
122.	Ram Piyare	Maharaj Deen	Birahimpur	S.C.	Dairy	20000.00	10000.00	Allahabad Bank, Amethi
123.	Purvin	Jokhuram	Raidaipur	S.C.	Dairy	20000.00	10000.00	Allahabad Bank, Amethi
124.	Ramjash	Girdhari	Raidaipur	S.C.	Goat	10000.00	10000.00	Allahabad Bank, Amethi
125.	Parana	Kalluram	Raidaipur	S.C.	Shop	20000.00	10000.00	Allahabad Bank, Amethi
126.	Kamlesh	Ram Baran	Raidaipur	S.C.	Shop	20000.00	10000.00	Allahabad Bank, Amethi
127.	Budhram	Shiv Raj	Raidaipur	S.C.	Goat	10000.00	10000.00	Allahabad Bank, Amethi
128.	Sampati	Durjan	Raidaipur	S.C.	Dairy	20000.00	10000.00	Allahabad Bank, Amethi
129.	Kamlesh	Jamuna Prasad	Raidaipur	S.C.	Dairy	20000.00	10000.00	Allahabad Bank, Amethi
130.	Shiv Kumar	Bhagwan	Ramgarh	S.C.	Goat	10000.00	10000.00	BPUPG Bank Vishesharganj
131.	Vijay Shyam	Bhagauti	Ramgarh	S.C.	Goat	10000.00	10000.00	BPUPG Bank Vishesharganj
132.	Lallu	Maniram	Ramgarh	S.C.	Goat	10000.00	10000.00	BPUPG Bank Vishesharganj
133.	Phuladevi	Mata Prasad	Ramgarh	S.C.	Goat	10000.00	10000.00	BPUPG Bank Vishesharganj
134.	Sunita	Tribhuwan	Ramgarh	S.C.	Goat	10000.00	10000.00	BPUPG Bank Vishesharganj
135.	Jaggi Devi	Badri Prasad	Ramgarh	S.C.	Goat	10000.00	10000.00	BPUPG Bank Vishesharganj
136.	Ram Kumar	Ram Bahadur	Ramgarh	S.C.	Goat	10000.00	10000.00	BPUPG Bank Vishesharganj
137.	Nirmala	Panchu	Ramgarh	S.C.	Goat	10000.00	10000.00	BPUPG Bank Vishesharganj
138.	Ram Samujh	Ram Bahadur	Ramgarh	S.C.	Goat	10000.00	10000.00	BPUPG Bank Vishesharganj

(*Contd.*)

Table 3.12 (*Contd.*)

1	2	3	4	5	6	7	8	9
139.	Rama Devi	Shiv Prasad	Ramgarh	S.C.	Goat	10000.00	10000.00	BPUPG Bank Visheshargani
140.	Anita	Sushil	Ramgarh	S.C.	Dairy	20000.00	10000.00	BPUPG Bank Visheshargani
141.	Gajadhar	Pandohi	Ramgarh	S.C.	Goat	10000.00	10000.00	BPUPG Bank Visheshargani
142.	Ram Aasre	Pandohi	Ramgarh	S.C.	Goat	10000.00	10000.00	BPUPG Bank Visheshargani
143.	Rekha Devi	Ram Kewal	Gaderi	S.C.	Goat	10000.00	10000.00	BPUPG Bank Visheshargani
144.	Ram Naresh	Mengaru	Gaderi	S.C.	Goat	10000.00	10000.00	BPUPG Bank Visheshargani
145.	Purwadin	Ramraj	Gaderi	S.C.	Goat	10000.00	10000.00	BPUPG Bank Visheshargani
146.	Badaka	Rampal	Gaderi	S.C.	Goat	10000.00	10000.00	BPUPG Bank Visheshargani
147.	Ram Kupal	Mengaru	Gaderi	S.C.	Goat	10000.00	10000.00	BPUPG Bank Visheshargani
148.	Nirmala	Ramakant	Gaderi	S.C.	Goat	10000.00	10000.00	BPUPG Bank Visheshargani
149.	Suresh	Rakesh Kumar	Gaderi	S.C.	Goat	10000.00	10000.00	BPUPG Bank Visheshargani
150.	Bhagana	Shyamlal	Gaderi	S.C.	Goat	10000.00	10000.00	BPUPG Bank Visheshargani
151.	Ram Kishun	Shobh Nath	Gaderi	S.C.	Goat	10000.00	10000.00	BPUPG Bank Visheshargani
152.	Sitapati	Ram Lal	Gaderi	S.C.	Goat	10000.00	10000.00	BPUPG Bank Visheshargani
153.	Ayodhya	Ram Harakh	Gaderi	S.C.	Goat	10000.00	10000.00	BPUPG Bank Visheshargani
154.	Ram Prasad	Girdhari	Gaderi	S.C.	Goat	10000.00	10000.00	BPUPG Bank Visheshargani
155.	Ramdeo	Harilal	Gaderi	S.C.	Goat	10000.00	10000.00	BPUPG Bank Visheshargani

The selected, financially supported 155 swarojgaris under the Swarnjayanti Gram Swarojgar Yojana, 48 swarojgari's have been supported for the Buffalo project, 60 beneficiaries have been facilitated for the goat project, 38 beneficiaries have been supported for shop and 9 beneficiaries have been financially supported for the Dairy project under the Swarnjayanti Gram Swarojgar Yojana in the Amethi.

It has been observed that the number of selected beneficiaries under the Swarnjayanti Gram Swarojgar Yojana is very nominal and insignificant against the constantly very increasing population and sustained growth of the unemployed rural youth belonging to the downtrodden, resourcesless, surviving under the Below Poverty Line (BPL) in the remote villages of Amethi. It requires large scale propagation and motivation for the facilities related to the Swarnjayanti Gram Swarojgar Yojana in the remote villages and skill development training programmes must be organized at village level to create techno-scientific awareness among the interested rural youth at village level in the Amethi Block.

4.8 Progress of Indira Awaas Yojana

Indira Awaas Yojana (IAY) has been launched during 1985-86 as sub-scheme of the Landless Rural Employment Guarantee Programme (LREGP). This programme has been implemented as sub-scheme of the Jawahar Rojgar Yojana (JRY) during 1989-90.

Indira Awaas Yojana (IAY) has been launched as an autonomous programme from 1st April, 1996. Previously this programme has been launched especially for the scheduled caste/scheduled tribe families but during 1994-95 this programme has also been launched for other categories belonging to the people living below poverty line. An important condition of the programme has been that at least 60 per cent beneficiaries must belong to the scheduled caste/scheduled tribe families.

The important objective of this scheme has been to provide construction support for concrete houses, for the houseless people living below poverty line, through providing financial support in the form of grants-in-aid. The selection of the beneficiaries is done by the District level permanent waiting list based on the earmarked denial priority. The construction of houses is being done by the beneficiaries themselves in their own land. Appropriate instructions has been ensured to transfer the grant-in-aid in two installments directly to the Bank Accounts of the concerned beneficiaries. There is no proper design for the construction of house except the plinth area of the constructed house must be 20 sq.metre.

Presently, this scheme has been implemented through financial support having 75 per cent from Government of India and 25 per cent share from the State Government. The construction of Indira Awaas has been estimated Rs. 35,000 in the plain area from 1.4.2008.

The Government has planned to construct 25 lakh Indira Awaas to provide shelter for the houseless deprived rural people living under the below poverty line.

In view of the above, during the year 2011-12 it has been planned to construct 221 Indira Awaas Yojana in different village panchayats of Amethi. The progress report of the Indira Awaas Yojana at village panchayat level in Amethi has been mentioned in Table 3.13.

It has been recorded that 15 houses in Ramdaipur, 12 houses in Ramgarh and Mahmadpur and 10 houses in Kohara village panchayats has been planned and its construction has been successfully completed. It has been recorded that 9 houses has been constructed in Kakawa, Himmatgarh and 8 houses in Sarai Khema, Umapur Ganapatti, and 7 houses in Jangal Ram Nagar, Parsawan and 6 houses in Bhaganpur, Gaderi, Katra Phulkunwar, Naraini, Tala and 5 houses in Chaturbhujpur, Dhandhudhar, Korari Girdhar Shah, Loniapur and 4 houses in Dehara, Darakha, Katra Maharani, Nainia, Rebha, Saraiya Duban and 3 houses in Mahaso, Agahar, Benipur, Bhusahari, Dedhpasar, Gangauli, Kherauna, Nuwawan, Saidpur and 2 hosues in Hathkila, Kushi Tali, Loharata, Purabgaon, Raipur Phulwari, Raidaipur and one Indira Awaas has been constructed in Maharajpur and Trilokpur village panchayats of Amethi. As per the planned target for constructing Indira Awaas Yojana financial support has been released and the planned target has been successfully completed at village panchayat level in Amethi.

4.9 Progress of Mahamaya Awaas Yojana

The Mahamaya Awaas Yojana (MAY) has been launched by the State Government of Uttar Pradesh from 2007-08. The Mahamaya Awaas Yojana has been initiated for the scheduled caste/scheduled tribe families belonging to the Below Poverty Line (BPL) household living without houses as per the norms and standards of the Indira Awaas Yojana. Mahamaya Awaas Yojana is a cent-per-cent financially supported programme of the State Government of Uttar Pradesh. The per house construction cost of the Mahamaya Awaas Yojana has been estimated Rs. 35000 in the plain area on 10.4.2008.

Table 3.13: Indira Awaas Yojana Progress Report, 2011-12, Amethi

Sl. No.	*Year of Selection*	*Name of Village*	*No. of Houses*	*Financial Status*	*Comments*
1.	2011-12	Agahar	3	Fund received	Completed
2.	2011-12	Benipur	3	Fund received	Completed
3.	2011-12	Bhaganpur	6	Fund received	Completed
4.	2011-12	Bhusahari	3	Fund received	Completed
5.	2011-12	Chaturbhujpur	5	Fund received	Completed
6.	2011-12	Dehara	4	Fund received	Completed
7.	2011-12	Dedhpasar	3	Fund received	Completed
8.	2011-12	Darakha	4	Fund received	Completed
9.	2011-12	Gangauli	3	Fund received	Completed
10.	2011-12	Gaderi	6	Fund received	Completed
11.	2011-12	Dhadhudhar	5	Fund received	Completed
12.	2011-12	Hathkila	2	Fund received	Completed
13.	2011-12	Himmatgarh	9	Fund received	Completed
14.	2011-12	Jangal Ram Nagar	7	Fund received	Completed
15.	2011-12	Kakawa	9	Fund received	Completed
16.	2011-12	Katra Maharani	4	Fund received	Completed
17.	2011-12	Katra Phulkunwar	6	Fund received	Completed
18.	2011-12	Kherauna	3	Fund received	Completed
19.	2011-12	Kohara	10	Fund received	Completed
20.	2011-12	Korari Girdhar Shah	5	Fund received	Completed
21.	2011-12	Kushi Tali	2	Fund received	Completed
22.	2011-12	Loharata	2	Fund received	Completed
23.	2011-12	Loniapur	5	Fund received	Completed
24.	2011-12	Maharajpur	1	Fund received	Completed
25.	2011-12	Mahmadpur	12	Fund received	Completed
26.	2011-12	Mahmoodpur	4	Fund received	Completed
27.	2011-12	Mahaso	3	Fund received	Completed
28.	2011-12	Mochawa	5	Fund received	Completed
29.	2011-12	Nainaha	4	Fund received	Completed
30.	2011-12	Naraini	6	Fund received	Completed
31.	2011-12	Nuwawan	3	Fund received	Completed
32.	2011-12	Parsawan	7	Fund received	Completed
33.	2011-12	Purabgaon	2	Fund received	Completed
34.	2011-12	Raipur Phulwari	2	Fund received	Completed
35.	2011-12	Ramdaipur	15	Fund received	Completed
36.	2011-12	Ramgarh	12	Fund received	Completed
37.	2011-12	Raidaipur	2	Fund received	Completed
38.	2011-12	Rebha	4	Fund received	Completed
39.	2011-12	Saidpur	3	Fund received	Completed
40.	2011-12	Saraiya Duban	4	Fund received	Completed
41.	2011-12	Sarai Khema	8	Fund received	Completed
42.	2011-12	Tala	6	Fund received	Completed
43.	2011-12	Trolokpur	1	Fund received	Completed
44.	2011-12	Umapur Ganapatti	8	Fund received	Completed
		Total	**221**		

The implementation of Mahamaya Awaas Yojana is being implemented as per the norms and standards of the Indira Awaas Yojana through District Development Officer of the District Amethi.

It has been recorded that 6 houses under Mahamaya Awaas Yojana has been planned during 2011-12 in Bhusahari, 3 houses in Gaderi, Mahaso and two houses in Hathkila, Sarai Khema, Umapur Ganapatti, Agahar and one house has been planned and constructed in Dhadhudhar, Kushi Tali, Maharajpur, Himmatgarh, Ramgarh, Raipur Phulwari, Gangauli, Dehara and Loniapur village panchayats of Amethi. The detailed planned target and achievement for construction of Mahamaya Awaas Yojana at village panchayat level in Amethi has been mentioned in Table 3.14.

State Government of Uttar Pradesh has launched Mahamaya Sarvjan Awaas Yojana for scheduled castes/tribes. The Mahamaya Sarvjan Awaas Yojana has been implemented

Table 3.14: Maha Maya Awaas Yojana Progress Report, 2011-12, Amethi

Sl. No.	Year of Selection	Name of Village	Target	Achievement
1.	2011-12	Dhadhudhar	1	1
2.	2011-12	Kushi Tali	1	1
3.	2011-12	Maharajpur	1	1
4.	2011-12	Mahaso	3	3
5.	2011-12	Himmatgarh	1	1
6.	2011-12	Hathkila	2	2
7.	2011-12	Ramgarh	1	1
8.	2011-12	Bhusahari	5	5
9.	2011-12	Raipur Phulwari	1	1
10.	2011-12	Sarai Khema	2	2
11.	2011-12	Umapur Ganapatti	2	2
12.	2011-12	Saidpur	2	2
13.	2011-12	Gangauli	1	1
14.	2011-12	Dehara	1	1
15.	2011-12	Agahar	2	2
16.	2011-12	Loniapur	1	1
17.	2011-12	Gaderi	3	3
		Total	**31**	**31**

in the selected Dr. Ambedkar Village panchayats for the non-scheduled caste/tribe families belong to Below Poverty Line living without houses. The Mahamaya Sarvjan Awaas Yojana is a cent-per-cent financially supported programme of the State Government of Uttar Pradesh. The Mahamaya Sarvjan Awaas Yojana has been initiated from 2008-09. The unit cost of the Mahamaya Sarvjan Awaas Yojana has been estimated Rs. 35,000 for the plain area. The implementation of Mahamaya Sarvjan Awaas Yojana is being implemented as per the guidelines of the Indira Awaas Yojana through District Development Officer of the Amethi District.

4.10. Progress of India Mark-II Hand Pumps

It has been recorded that 2352 India Mark-II Hand Pumps have been installed in the Amethi Block. There are 143 defective India Mark-II Hand Pumps in Amethi. It has been noticed that 28 defective India Mark-II Hand Pumps have been repaired and maintained. It has been observed that 10 India Mark-II Hand Pumps have common defects and 18 India Mark-II Hand Pumps had defects in the G.I. Pipe and 115 defected India Mark-II Hand Pumps have been re-bored and these repaired and maintained India Mark-II Hand Pumps have been functional for the use of village people.

In the integrated Sanitation Programme it has been planned to construct 388 low cost latrines and sanitation. The planned target for construction of sanitation programme has been successfully completed village panchayat level in Amethi.

4.10. Progress of Other Rural Development Programmes

It has been planned to construct 3 Bio-gas but 2 Bio-gas has been constructed in the Amethi Block.

It has been recorded that there are 31 installed Government Tube-wells covering 26 village panchayats in Amethi. There are 26 functional Government Tube-wells in Amethi and 3 Government Tube-wells are out of order, while there are 7 defective Government Tube-wells out of which 5 tube-wells have mechanical fault and 2 Government Tube-wells have electricity fault which have been located in different village panchayats of the Amethi Block.

It has been noticed that there are 21165 families having Ration Cards and 19572 families belong to the Below Poverty Line and 4679 Antyodaya Card Holders and 5914 families are Above Poverty Line Card Holders in the various village panchayats of the Amethi Block.

It has been recorded that 171 Kisan Credit Cards have been issued in Amethi and 158 Kisan Credit Cards have been distributed among the farmers in different village panchayats in the Amethi Block.

It has been observed that Rs. 90.10 lakh crop loan has been sanctioned out of which Rs. 75.50 lakh crop loan has been distributed by various banks at village panchayat level in Amethi.

Installation of Free of Cost Tube-well for irrigation has been ensured for 151 borings out of which 126 Tube-wells boring has been done by the General Caste farmers and 25 Tube-wells boring has been ensured by the scheduled caste farmers in different village panchayats of the Amethi Block.

It has been recorded that there is one Community Health Centre (CHC) in Amethi and Homoeopathic Hospital at Amethi and Tala Village panchayats and there are Ayurvedic Hospitals at Himmatgarh, Amethi, Maharajpur and Mahmoodpur village panchayats in the Amethi Block. It has been observed that there are 17 Sub-Primary Health Centres in different village panchayats of the Amethi Block to provide medical and health facilities to the needy and interested village people of Amethi.

5. CONCLUSION

The development is a human enterprise and it requires combined efforts of the all systems of knowledge, by the physical, biological, social, economic, institutional efforts with the view to comprehend and articulate it. The development is pursued with the genuine concern for human values, their actions and aspirations for the better quality of life. In the process of development the growth alone does not ensure the integrated development, because the development is after all a multifaceted phenomenon.

The existing process of development whether urban or rural development has neither been true nor good, nor beautify but it does not mean that everything is wrong. The progress of people and economic growth along with the socio-economic-institutional, infrastructural development, man has made and adopted destructive approach than constructive approach of development without incorporating the willing consent and interest of the deprived sections of the society and also ignoring the continued sustained participation of the grassroots level interested beneficiaries for its sustenance to fulfil the increasing demand of the growing cattle and human population at the grassroots level.

It has been realized that commendable advances has been made in the diverse field of economic development. But there is a great question, whether, it would in reality be incomplete if such rural development programmes fail to translate into better and dignified life for the majority of the people living in the remote villages.

The implementation of the Integrated Rural Development Programmes (IRDP) can be made more effective through ensuring proper participation of the local village people. Need based people's participatory planning and the implementation of development programmes should be implemented at the grassroots level. The willingness, consent and needs of the local village people and their priorities should be given due consideration in the plan formulation at the grassroots level.

In view of the above an effort has been made in this study to analyze the progress of the implementation of various rural development programmes being implemented at Village-Block-District-Panchayat level.

The centrally sponsored programmes supported by the Government of India and the programmes supported by the State Government of Uttar Pradesh and the planned programmes supported by the District Planning Committee and Zila Panchayat-Block Panchayat-Village Panchayat and implemented by the various line departments and implementing institutions have been analyzed at village panchayat level.

It has been noticed that the job card holders and the beneficiaries of the Mahatma Gandhi National Rural Employment Guarantee Act (MNREGA) has been recorded 15520 beneficiaries, belonging to the Below Poverty Line (BPL) category in Amethi. The landless agricultural labourers, skilled and non-skilled labourers and other labourers have been provided MNREGA Job Cards and they are provided 100 days guaranteed job for the employment and to increase the income for their better livelihood.

It has been recorded that there are 10763 number of students studying in the Primary[1] Junior Schools at village panchayat level in Amethi. The High School and Intrermediate school students has been found 1308 in various villages of Amethi. It has been observed that 208 students are studying in the Higher Education including Graduate and Post Gradaute level education at village panchayat level in Amethi. The technical, engineering, management, medical and other vocational/professional education students are found very insignificant having only 41 students at village panchayat level in the Amethi Block.

It has been observed that the canal irrigated area has been found 418 hectares and the Private Tube-well irrigated area has been noticed 5109 hectares in the Amethi Block. The Government Tube-well irrigated area has been recorded 280 hectares while other sources of irrigation have been recorded 87 hectares in the Amethi Block.

The India Mark-II Hand Pumps are an important source of drinking water for the village people. It has been noticed that 2380 India Mark-II Hand Pumps have been installed in Amethi. The rural drinking water supply and sanitation programmes have been implemented at village panchayat level in Amethi and *Swajaldhara* drinking water yojana has been successfully implemented at village panchayat level in Amethi.

The Sports and Youth Welfare Programmes are implemented at village level. The Sports and Youth Welfare Centres and units at village panchayat level have been established at village panchayat level in Amethi.

The Community Health Care Centres, Primary Health Care Centres and Sub-Primary Health Centres have been established with the view to provide medical and health services to the needy and interested patients and villagers in the Amethi Block.

Various women and Child Development Programmes have been launched in Amethi including Anganwadi Kendras and other women and child health care supporting programmes at village panchayat level in Amehti.

Animal Health Care Centres and Veterinary Hospitals have been established and promoted the animal husbandry programmes at village level in Amethi.

It has been noticed that there are 5914 Above Poverty Line (APL) Card Holders and 3819 Below Poverty Line (BPL) Card Holders at village panchayat level in the Amethi Block.

Various other rural development programmes have been launched which include cleaning and sanitation programmes supported by the Government of India. The individual Hand Pumps have been installed due to insufficient installation of the India Mark-II Hand Pumps in Amethi.

The rural housing programmes have been initiated with the view to provide shelters for the houseless downtrodden deprived rural poor multitudes in Amethi. It has been recorded that 422 rural houses have been constructed at village panchayat level in Amethi.

The old age pension, widow pension and handicapped pension and the scholarship for the scheduled caste, backward caste and minorities students have been distributed at village panchayat level in Amethi. It has been observed that 643 old age pensions, 143 handicapped persons, 49 widow pensions and 6470 student's scholarships have been distributed at village panchayat level in Amethi.

Various agro-afforestation programmes have been launched by the Agriculture-Horticulture-Social Forestry Departments in Amethi. It has been noticed that 2453 people have been benefited under the Agro-afforestation programmes at village panchayat level in Amethi. It has been recorded that 11023 number of plants have been planted at village panchayat level to fulfil the increasing demand of the fuelwood, fodder and wood for the cattle and human population at village panchayat level in Amethi.

It has been noticed that 132 km. pucca road has been constructed in Amethi and 132 small scale industries have been installed at village panchayat level in Amethi. There are 225 agro-industries established in the Amethi Block.

The low cost latrines/low cost sanitation programmes have been launched at village panchayat level to facilitate clean environment and proper sanitation to control the health hazards at the grassroots level in Amethi.

It has been recorded that 6 dairy development programmes have been launched in the Jangal Ram Nagar, Darakha, Korari Girdhar Shah, Gangauli, Himmatgarh and Dehara village panchayats of Amethi.

Various integrated rural development programmes including cleaning/sanitation, women and child development, rural health, Kishori Shakti Yojana, Immunization and other welfare programmes have been launched in Amethi. There are 74 number of integrated rural development programmes which have been implemented at village panchayat level in Amethi.

Roods under Pradhan Mantri Gram Sadak Yojana have been constructed at village panchayat level in Amethi to provide accessibility and movement from one village to another village including Block and District Headquarters of Amethi. It has been recorded that 1423 number of villagers has been facilitated under the Pradhan Mantri Gram Sadak Yojana at village panchayat level in Amethi.

National Rural Health Mission (NRHM) Programmes have been successfully launched and implemented at village panchayats in Amethi. Rajiv Gandhi Grameen Vidyutikaran Yojana has been implemented and 847 households have been provided electricity connections in the various village panchayats of the Amethi Block.

Mahatma Gandhi National Rural Employment Guarantee Act (MNREGA) has been launched with Rs. 341.76 amount released for implementation of various programmes to generate guaranteed employment for the below poverty line to MNREGA Job Card Holders at village panchayat level in Amethi.

It has been recorded that a sum of Rs. 179.59 lakh has been incurred for non-skilled labour in Amethi while Rs. 5.79 lakh has been expended for the skilled labour work and a sum of Rs. 101.21 lakh has been spent on account of material cost for the various planned activities at village panchayat level in Amethi, and a sum of Rs. 5.80 lakh amount has been spent for the temporary administrative expenses for successful implementation of MNREGA programmes. It has been recorded that total amount of Rs. 292.36 lakh expenditure has been expended for the implementation of various planned programmes under Mahatma Gandhi National Rural Employment Guarantee Act (MNREGA) at village panchayat level in Amethi.

It has been noticed that the Self-Help Groups are fast emerging powerful tool of socio-economic empowerment of the rural people at village level. The Self-Help Groups are a small body formed by the people for meeting their specific, objectives particularly credit. There are 538 Self-Help Groups (SHGs) formed in Amethi out of which 393 SHGs are active Self-Help Groups in Amethi. There are 214 Self-Help Groups crossed Grade-II and financial files have been processed by the concerned service providing banks and financial assistance for 214 SHG have been sanctioned by the Banks. Out of which 203 Self-Help Groups have been distributed financial assistance by the respective Banks at village panchayat level in Amethi and three Self-Help Groups' financial assistance has been rejected by the concerned Bank.

It has been recorded that 26 Self-Help Groups (SHGs) covering 281 Members have been sanctioned 44.25 lakhs loan and 28.70 Grants Components sanctioned for the various projects implementation by the different service Banks in Amethi.

Swarnjayanti Gram Swarojgar Yojana (SGSY) has been launched to generate employment and increase the income of the deprived weaker people. In this scheme 155 beneficiaries have been supported out of which 48 buffaloes, 60 goats, 38 shops and 9 Dairy projects have been sanctioned to the selected under the Swarnjayanti Gram Swarojgar Yojana in Amethi. There are 2 minority, 55 general category and 98 scheduled caste beneficiaries selected and financially supported under the Swarnjayanti Gram Swarojgar Yojana in Amethi. It has been noticed that Baroda Purvi Uttar Pradesh Grameen Bank supported 98 beneficiaries, Oriental Bank of Commerce supported 17 beneficiaries, Central Bank supported 21 beneficiaries, and Bank of Baroda supported 13 beneficiaries under the Swarnjayanti Gram Swarojgar Yojana at village panchayat level in the Amethi Block.

It has been recorded that 221 number of houses under Indira Awaas Yojana (IAY) has been planned and financial assistance has been sanctioned as per the norms of the Government and such low cast houses have been constructed as per planned target in the selected villages of the Amethi Block.

It has been observed that 31 low cost houses under the Mahamaya Awaas Yojana of the State Government of Uttar Pradesh have been planned and sanctioned and the houses have been constructed as per guidelines and norms of the Government of Uttar Pradesh at village panchayat level in Amethi.

It has been noticed that 2352 India Mark-II Hand Pumps have been installed out of which 143 India Mark-II Hand Pumps are out of order and defective.

It has been recorded that 2 Bio-Gas Plants has been installed out of sanctioned 3 Bio-Gas Plants in Amethi and 31 Government Tube-wells have been installed covering 26 village panchayats of the Amethi Block and 3 Government Tube-wells are out of order in the Amethi Block.

It has been recorded that 171 Kisan Credit Cards have been issued out of which 158 Kisan Credit Cards have been distributed at village panchayat level in Amethi.

It has been noticed that Rs. 90.10 lakh crop loans have been sanctioned out which Rs. 75.50 lakh crop loans have been distributed at village level in Amethi. It has been recorded that 151 free of cost Tube-well borings have been sanctioned out of which 126 Tube-well borings have been successfully implemented at village level in Amethi and 25 Tube-well boring beneficiaries are at village panchayat level in Amethi.

It has been observed that various rural development programmes have been launched at village panchayat level especially improvement, betterment and upgradation of the available infrastructure at village panchayat level in Amethi. Various employment generating and income increasing programmes have been launched without willing consent and needs of the deprived resourceless, weaker and poor section of the society because social infrastructure of Amethi is inter-woven with social fabric of the caste, religion, etc. The caste system of Amethi has been based on their occupational structure, and the successful implementation of the employment generation must be based on the needs, willing consent and interest of their caste based occupation structure and agriculture development and its productivity should be ensured through application of better agricultural implements, appropriate irrigational system, use of High Yielding Variety (HYV) seeds, proper application of the organic and inorganic amendments and techno-scientific application of Post Harvest and Agro-processing technology for value addition of the Agricultural production and generating employment and increasing the income of the resourceless deprived downtrodden weaker section of the society. Appropriate quality education, including occupational/vocational/professional education must be ensured at grassroots level. Proper utilization of available infrastructural resources must be tapped and optimally utilized to meet the ever increasing demand of growing cattle and human population for the Food-Cloth-Shelter and Fuel Wood, Fodder, Fibre, Fruits, Foodgrains, Fisheries (F_6) and vegetable at village panchayat level in Amethi.

4

Development Planning

1. INTRODUCTION

The planning is an organized process by which the people achieve its developmental goals, aims and targets. The planning is a means to achieve the development for better quality of life. It has been noticed that the planning in our country is planned and formulated without the willing consent and interest of the local people. In most of the cases the planners interpret people's need, their actions and aspiration for developing a plan for the people. The planning is a task of the people in which the planners can provide backup support to achieve their planning goals. It has been noticed that the Government has been stressing hard for the involvement and people's participation in the implementation of the development or development planning from within.

The planners will have to provide development planning, techno-scientific backup support to the grassroots village level people's representative, villagers, and involved officials in the village development and formulation of the policy planning. The planners should not only be technocrat to provide projections but the planners should assist the Village Panchayats → Block Panchayats → District Panchayats and the Panchayati Raj Institution as a social scientist who can easily understand the basic grassroots level needs and requirements of the local village people so that the common minimum requirements of the village people are planned and the development activities are implemented as per the needs of the village people with the involvement of the villagers, and the programmes are planned for the villagers and the development is achieved as per the planned targets at the grassroots level in the remote villages.

It has been realized that the development is after all a multifaceted phenomenon, it can neither be understood nor promoted unless it is visualized from interdisciplinary and holistic approach. The development is basically a human enterprise and, therefore, it requires, the combined efforts of all system of knowledge to comprehend and articulate it. The development should ensure the betterment and welfare of all the local level village people. The feel good perception of the development has to be not only from National → State → District level but also from Tehsil → Block → Village level perspectives. It has been realized that the present process of development is neither true nor good, nor beautiful but it does not mean that everything is wrong. In a real sense the development lies in the development and adoption of related required development of science and technology and its application by the common village people.

In view of the above, an attempt has been made in this study to analyze the various development planning programmes from National Level → State Level → District Panchayat Level → Block Panchayat Level → Village Panchayat Level. The priorities, visions, missions and the goals of the Government for the formulation of the planning and the implementation of the planned programmes has been described in this study. An effort has been made to analyze the various developmental planned programmes of the Government of India and to explain the performance rural development planning budget of the Government of Uttar Pradesh. It has been attempted to explain the district level planning and the work plan of the Zila Yojana for the year 2012-13. An attempt has also been made to analyze the formulated plans and programmes planned by the Block Panchayat Amethi. An effort has been made to explain the priorities common minimum need based development planning programmes at the village panchayat level in Amethi Block and to develop Village Information System for the need based development planning at the grassroots level, i.e. village panchayat level in Amethi.

2. DEVELOPMENT PLANNING

It has been noted that there is a quest for evolving a model for the development planning. It has been observed that the macro-level or National level has been planned and adopted in our country. It has been realized that the approach of the Macro-level planning in India did not yield the requisite results due to inequities amongst people and disparities between one village to another village, i.e. at the macro level or micro level. The environment conditions continued to degrade which has led to severe stress on land, forest and water (Jal-Jangal-Zameen) natural resources. Around seventies sustainable and integrated development planning at various level has been ensured. In this regard conceptual changes in the planning process has been adopted at the micro-level or grassroots level process of planning. The main important objectives of the decentralized planning has been as follows :

- To increase the agricultural productivity.
- To generate the employment.
- To focus on the development of infrastructure.
- To ensure poverty alleviation.
- To provide common minimum infrastructural facilities amenities at the grassroots level.

The institutional changes has been ensured to implement this strategy through Constitutional Amendment Acts. The State Government has been empowered for the institutions of local self-governance right from the village panchayat level → Block Panchayat level → District panchayat level. The Eleventh and Twelfth Schedule of the Constitution while specifying the sectors for the Panchayat, have also defined the role for multi-level institutions of the governance in the planning and the implementation of the integrated development programmes.

The State Government of Uttar Pradesh has accordingly constituted such local level bodies with a definite mandate to collect revenues, formulate and draw up plans and implement integrated village development programmes. It needs capacity building at institutions of local self-governance to prepare and implement local level area specific integrated development schemes through assessing and optimum utilization of the available natural and human resources at the grassroots level.

The need based plan formulation and the implementation of integrated development programmes at the grassroots level is an information oriented intensive task. The innovation of available natural and human infrastructural resources at the grassroots level and developing Village Information System has not been yet properly arranged but such available information related to the planning and implementation of the development activities, such available information needs to be integrated, collected, collated and appropriately analyzed. The conventional methods of the data collection, collation, storage, are not amendable for quick updation, retrieval and holistic analyzing. Several problems have been faced in the existing conventional systems of the data collection at the grassroots level. It is known fact that the planned work and progress of the implementation of various rural development programmes at grassroots level are implemented but proper generation, creation of information and data have not been properly arranged. In view of the above, an attempt has been made in this study to analyze the development planning programmes from bottom, i.e. Village-Block-District-State and to top level, i.e. National level.

The need based people's participatory process of planning at village level and the implementation of the integrated developmental activities must be implemented with the continued involvement of the local people with the view to achieve the planned targets of the development.

The development should be participatory tapping the local talent and resources in order to make the created assets self-sustained and maintained for optimum use of the village level beneficiaries. An effort is being made to implement various rural development programmes with a focus on enhancing the livelihood of weaker and vulnerable sections of the society with the view to ensure sustainable development of the remote villages. The Government of India and the State Government of Uttar Pradesh has given fore-most priority to the integrated rural development for which a number of the steps have been initiated to make the implementation of on going programmes more effective, sustainable and accelerated.

In view of the above, the Government has been stressing hard to organize the village panchayats as a sole unit of developmental activities and decentralization of the village panchayats have been organized. Three-tier Panchayati Raj System, i.e. District Panchayat → Block Panchayat → Village Panchayat has been planned and the administrative and financial powers and rights have been allocated to the Panchayats. The Self-Government in the Rural areas and full autonomy to the local bodies, administrative financial resources allocation, transfer of related implementing line departments and their staff to the Village Panchayat → Block Panchayat → District Panchayat with the hope to achieve the goals and positive results at the grassroots level.

Village has been considered as the lowest unit of the plan formulation and implementation of people's participatory rural development activities. The village has been taken as the lowest unit of development in the new system decentralization local level village development has been ensured by the village panchayats. The faster development has been ensured assuming village as a centre and lowest unit for the integrated rural development. The local level administrative machinery has been transferred local level Panchayat Bodies in which the planning, development works, its management and control have been ensured through people's participatory Panchayati Raj System.

The planning has been done from bottom to top. The revolutionary step of decentralization has left an everlasting impact of complete change in the mind of the village life and it has created a new era of integrated rural development in the remote villages.

In view of the above, decentralization of administrative and financial powers of the

Village Panchayat → Block Panchayat → District Panchayat has been ensured in Amethi. The Village-Block-District Panchayat has been given requisite responsibilities administrative control, physical and financial powers and concerned line departments have also been handed over to the panchayats to ensure self-government.

The Self-Government of Panchayats at village panchayat level in Amethi Block and at Block level in Amethi District and need based people's participatory action plan has been formulated to fulfil the dream of the **Self-Government**, i.e. **Panchayati Raj → Lok Raj → Gram Raj** with the view to establish **Ram Raj** which has been the dream of the Father of Nation Mahatma Gandhi Ji.

3. NATIONAL DEVELOPMENT PLANNING

The Government of India has launched various programmes to ensure an integrated development of remote rural areas. The construction of infrastructural resources at the grassroots level has been launched under the '*Bharat Nirman*'. The development of common minimum amenities and upgradation of the available infrastructural resources have been initiated. The basic fundamental requirements of the common villagers have been strengthended through the various programmes launched by the Government of India. The *Roti-Kapada-Makan* (Food-Cloth-Shelter) the basic needs of the villagers has been incorporated in the plan formulation. The rights of the village people for *Jal-Jangal-Zameen* (Water-Forest-Land) have been ensured and an appropriate step has been initiated. The road network, education, rural health, agricultural development and various other need based programme have been launched by the Government of India through State Government of Uttar Pradesh.

3.1 Computerization of Land Records

The computerization of land records has been initiated to provide computerized copies of Records of Rights (RORs) at a reasonable price and to ensure on-line management of land records.

3.2 Watershed Development

The approach of watershed development has been conventionally aimed at treating degraded land with the help of low cost moisture conservation, afforestation, etc. through people's participation.

3.3 Hariyali

Hariyali programme has been initiated with the view to involve village communities in the implementation of watershed projects under the Integrated Watershed Development Programmes (IWDP), Drought Prone Areas Programme (DPAP) and Dessert Development Programme (DDP).

3.4 Rural Housing

Housing is one of the basic requirement for human survival. The Indira Awaas Yojana has been launched to help construction/upgradation of dwelling units of members of scheduled caste/tribes, freed bonded labourers, minorities belonging to the below poverty line category and other below poverty line Non-SC/ST rural households by providing them a lumpsum financial assistance.

3.5 National Social Assistance Programme (NSAP)

National Social Assistance Programme is being implemented to fulfil the directive principles of State Policy ensuring in the institutions of India to undertake within its means a number of welfare measures.

3.6 Mahatma Gandhi National Rural Employment Guarantee Act (MNREGA)

Mahatma Gandhi National Rural Employment Guarantee Act has been initiated to enhance livelihood security in rural areas by providing at least 100 days guaranteed wage employment during the financial year to every household whose adult members volunteer to do unskilled manual work.

3.7 Mahila Kisan Sashaktikaran Pariyojana (MKSP)

Mahila Kisan Sashaktikaran Pariyojana has been initiated to empower women in agriculture by making systematic investment to enhance thier participation and increase agricultural productivity; as also to create and sustain agriculture based livelihood of rural women.

3.8 Placement Linked Skill Development of Rural Below Poverty Line under Swarnjayanti Gram Swarojgar Yojana (SGSY)

The main objective of each special projects for skill development would be to ensure a time-bound training and the capacity building prorgramme for bringing a specific number of Below Poverty Line (BPL) families above the poverty through placement ensuring regular wage employment for those unemployed youth in remote locations at the grassroots level.

3.9 Swarnjayanti Gram Swarojgar Yojana

Swarnjayanti Gram Swarojgar Yojana has been initiated to bring the assisted poor families (Swarojgaris) Above Poverty Line by ensuring appreciable sustained level of income over a period of time.

3.10 Pradhan Mantri Gram Sadak Yojana (PMGSY)

Pradhan Mantri Gram Sadak Yojana has been launched to provide all weather road connectivity in rural areas. This programme envisages connecting all habitants with a population of 500 persons and above in the plain areas.

3.11 Bharat Nirman

The Government of India announced a major business plan for rebuilding rural India called "*Bharat Nirman*". The rural road is one of the six components of the Bharat Nirman and it has a set of goals to provide connectivity to all habitants with a population of 1000 persons with an all weather road.

3.12 National Bio-Gas

National Bio-Gas project has been launched to facilitate the cooking gas through cow dung and utilize the end product as fertilizer.

3.13 National Health Insurance Police Scheme

National Health Insurance Policy Scheme has been launched to provide insurance facilities for the medical health support during hospitalization and ill health and for their medial treatment in the hospitals.

3.14 Sampoorna Grameen Rojgar Yojana (SGRY)

Sampoorna Grameen Rojgar Yojana has been launched to provide additional wage employment in the rural areas as well as to provide food security along with the creation of durable community assets, social and economic infrastructure in the rural areas.

3.15 Rajiv Gandhi Grameen Vidyutikaran Yojana

Rajiv Gandhi Grameen Vidyutikaran Yojana has been initiated with the view to facilitate electricity connections in the remote villages to the Below Poverty Line households in the rural areas.

3.16 Rural Drinking Water Supply

Drinking Water Supply programme is being implemented with the view to provide good quality drinking water to the resourceless deprived rural poor people in the remote villages because the poor quality and contaminated water causes many diseases and leads to health hazards.

3.17 Rural Sanitation

Centrally sponsored rural sanitation programme has been launched to remove the disposal of human excreta of cesspools, open ditches, pits latrines, bucket system etc. in the remote rural areas.

3.18 Pradhan Mantri Grameen Jal Samvardhan Yojana

Pradhan Mantri Grameen Jal Samvardhan Yojana has been launched with the objective of drought proofing in the identified dry and rainfed areas through location specific water conservation measures and water technoloies to mitigate the adverse effects of drought.

In spite of the above, various other programmes like women empowerment through Self-Help Groups and National Rural Health Mission programme has been launched by the Government of India to improve socio-economic conditions of the deprived rural poor multitudes.

4. STATE DEVELOPMENT PLANNING

The Government of Uttar Pradesh has also initiated various rural development programmes through incorporating 25 per cent State's share in a ratio of 75 per cent from the Government of India, i.e. 75 : 25. The Government of Uttar Pradesh has not only launched the programmes of the Central Government but State Government has also initiated various other rural development programmes of the State with the view to fulfil the ever increasing demand of the growing cattle and human population proportionately three fourth population of the State of Uttar Pradesh has been engaged in the agricultural activity. State of Uttar Pradesh is having an agrarian economy. The construction of infrastructural resources and employment generation has been given top priority under the integrated development of rural area. The Community Development Programmes have been launched during 1952 and later on Department of Rural Development has been established. The Department of Rural Development has been engaged in the implementation of the schemes financially supported by the Central Government in collaboration with State Government of Uttar Pradesh. The successful effective implementation of the planned targets of the programmes has been ensured through sustained contribution of the related implementing line departments to ensure direct benefit of the programmes to the common people at every level. The participation of the Panchayati Raj Institutions has been obtained for the implementation of rural development programmes. The effective planning of the programmes, its implementation, monitoring and evaluation and co-ordination, has been ensured at the various levels.

To achieve the targeted goals, the different programmes have been launched by the Department of Rural Development Government of Uttar Pradesh, viz.—

- Swarnjayanti Gram Swarojgar Yojana.
- Sampoorn Grameen Rojgar Yojana.
- Mahatma Gandhi National Rural Employment Guarantee Act.
- Pradhan Mantri Gram Sadak Yojana.
- Indira Awaas Yajana.
- Rural Drinking Water Supply Programme.
- Community Development Programme.
- Members of Legislative Assembly Local Area Development Fund (MLA-LAD)
- Member of Legislative Council Local Area Development Fund (MLC-LAD)
- District Rural Development Agency.
- Ambedkar Vishesh Rojgar/Rojgar Chhatri Yojana.
- Bio-Gas Yojana.
- Bhoomi Sena.

In spite of the above commitment towards basic needs some of the programmes have been launched by the State Government of Uttar Pradesh for the scheduled caste dominated settlements especially for the rural drinking water, scheduled caste housing scheme and construction of the Community Hall/Centres have been initiated from 2006-07.

The skill upgradation development training programmes for the beneficiaries and the concerned officials of the implementing Institutions have been emphasized at wider level by the Department of Rural Development, Government of Uttar Pradesh.

To ensure appropriate benefit of the various rural development programmes in the rural areas, the related officials/staff, voluntary organizations, related to the rural development and Panchayati Raj and people's representatives has been launched by the Department of Rural Development, Government of Uttar Pradesh.

4.1 Swarnjayanti Gram Swarojgar Yojana

The aim of the Swarnjayanti Gram Swarojgar Yojana is to provide economic self-sustenance for the people living Below Poverty Line (BPL), with the view to establish large level/small scale industries with the view to uplift each supported family living below the poverty line.

The supported families may be individual or groups (Self-Help Groups) while emphasis has been given for the group system. Through this scheme, 4-5 main trades have been initiated and the implementation and establishment of the selected trade's activities, the selected *swarojgaris* clusters people living below poverty line is being benefited. In this scheme non-scheduled caste individual swarojgari is being supported 30 per cent cost of the project and maximum Rs. 7500 grants-in-aid is permissible, while the scheduled castes/tribes or physically handicapped persons are granted 50 per cent cost of the project or maximum Rs. 10,000 grants-in-aid is permissible.

In the case of the Self-Help Groups or Groups 50 per cent cost of project or maximum Rs. 1.25 lakh (Rs. 1000 per individual or Rs. 1.25 lakh whichever is lower) limit grants-in-aid is permissible is this scheme.

In this scheme out of the rural poor extremely poor persons, selection has been emphasized. Out of the total beneficiaries of swarojgaris 50 per cent scheduled castes/ tribes, 40 per cent women and 3 per cent physical handicapped persons target have been earmarked in the Swarnjayanti Gram Swarojgar Yojana. In this scheme 3.25 lakh groups have been formed out of which 1.80 lakh 1st grade groups and 2nd graded passed 97834 groups has been graded and 91344 groups has been provided loan and grants as per the norms of the scheme.

4.2 Mahatma Gandhi National Rural Employment Guarantee Act (MNREGA)

This scheme has been launched from 2nd February, 2006. The main aim of the programme is to provide 100 days guaranteed job creation for the interested households in the rural areas.

The Government of India contributes 100 per cent grants for the cost of non-skilled labour and 75 per cent material cost and 25 per cent material cost is shared by the State Government. The major points of the MNREGA programmes is:

- Since this scheme is demand base, therefore, the registration of the households has been done by the Gram Panchayat.
- Village Panchayat will issue group photograph Job Card to the related family, based on which a family will be provided 100 days minimum job during the financial year.
- As per the demand within the 15 days of MNREGA Job Card Holder will be provided at last 14 days job.
- Village Panchayat/Programme officer will allot the employment and maintain its records.

- Job will be provided within the 5 km. distance from the residence of labour and if the distance is more than 10 per cent additional labour payment will be given.
- If the employment is not given within the 15 days, then the unemployment allowance will be paid which will be one-fourth for the 1st 30 days of the financial year and for the rest of days it will be one and half of the wages.
- The provision of unemployment allowance will be sole responsibility of the State Government.
- The labour rate will be fixed as per the agricultural labour's minimum labour wage decided by the State Government. The State of Uttar Pradesh has fixed Rs. 100.00 per man day wage labour.
- Contract and machinery work has been prohibited.
- Important works of the MNREGA are as follows :

  — Water Conservation and Storage.
  — Drought Prone-afforestation.
  — Canal irrigation — minor and small irrigation.
  — Land Development — Agri-Horti-Afforestation.
  — Maintenance and Management of Ponds.
  — Land Development.
  — Flood Control and Construction of Drainage System.
  — Other activities as per the advice of State Government and Government of India.

4.3 Indira Awaas Yojana

Indira Awaas Yojana has been launched from 1985-86 and from 1996 Indira Awaas Yojana has become an independent scheme for the scheduled caste/tribe families.

The main aim of the Indira Awaas Yojana is to provide pucca houses for the household families living below poverty line. The beneficiaries selection is done as per serial number by the District Level temporary wait list. The construction of houses has been done in the own land by the selected beneficiaries. The grants-in-aid is directly transferred to the Bank in the two installments. The plinth area of the house construction is 20 sq.metre. Presently, the Indira Awaas Yojana is financially supported at the 75:25 ratio by the Government of India and State Government respectively. The estimated cost of Indira Awaas Yojana is Rs. 35,000 for the plain.

4.4 Mahamaya Awaas Yojana

Mahamaya Awaas Yojana has been launched for the below poverty line scheduled caste families as per the guidelines and norms of the Indira Awaas Yojana.

4.5 Mahamaya Sarvjan Awaas Yojana

Mahamaya Sarvjan Awaas Yojana has been launched for the non-scheduled caste families living below poverty line as per the norms and guidelines of the Indira Awaas Yojana.

4.6 Pradhan Mantri Gram Sadak Yojana

The implementation of Pradhan Mantri Gram Sadak Yojana is totally financially supported scheme of the Central Government. Initially 500 populated or more settlements have been connected by the Pradhan Mantri Gram Sadak Yojana. In view of the large number of non-connected settlements the target has been again divided up to 1000 populated or more than this settlement has been targeted to connect under the Pradhan Mantri Gram Sadak Yojana. The targets have been revised according to the '*Bharat Nirman*' Yojana to connect 1000 population or more settlements.

The Public Works Department and Rural Engineering Services have been identified as implementing agency for the construction of roads.

To ensure the proper implementation of the project Uttar Pradesh Grameen Sadak Vikas Abhikaran (Uttar Pradesh Rural Road Development Agency) has been registered under the Societies Registration Act, 1860. This agency is working as an independent agency.

Initially 40 Districts of Uttar Pradesh have been allotted to Public Works Department and 30 Districts have been allotted to the Rural Engineering Services Department.

Two new implementing agencies have been included, i.e. Uttar Pradesh Rajkiya Nirman Nigam Ltd. and Uttar Pradesh Rajya Setu Nigam Ltd. for quick disposal of the construction of roads.

To maintain the quality work, its maintenance and construction of the road three-tier quality control arrangements have been made :

I. National Quality Control Monitor.
II. State Quality Control Monitor.
III. Senior Officials of the Line Departments.

The constructed and under construction roads' quality is being checked and if there is poor quality road, that is improved as per the guidelines, norms and standards of the Government.

4.7 Rural Drinking Water Supply

Rural drinking water supply and sanitation programmes have been launched to provide drinking water for the settlement colonies in the Rural areas. This programme is being implemented through *Zila Yojana* under the Accelerated Rural Drinking Water Supply Programme financially supported by the Central Government.

Presently, the installation of the new Hand Pumps and the construction of new pipe line drinking water scheme is being implemented through community participation. As per policy of the Government of India 10 per cent cost of the programme is being contributed by the community, in case the community is not capable to bear the expenditure, the State Government takes the responsibility to contribute the share of the community.

Rajiv Gandhi National Drinking Water Mission Programme has been launched by the Government of India to survey in detail to know the real condition of the drinking water in the rural areas. The settlements/purwas/tolas/hamlet village has been considered as an unit in place of the revenue villages to facilitate the drinking water based on the survey. There are 243508 populated settlements in the Uttar Pradesh during 2001-02. The actual status of the Drinking Water has been re-surveyed in detail and there are 26010 populated settlements during 2004 in Uttar Pradesh. It has been recorded that 142736 new hand pumps have been installed and 84192 Rebore Hand Pumps have been installed in Uttar Pradesh.

4.8 State Drinking Water and Sanitation Mission (Swajaldhara Programme)

Rural drinking water and environment maintenance programme or sanitation (Swajaldhara Yojana) has been launched on 25 December, 2002 by the State Government of Uttar Pradesh. The principles of the Swajaldhara Yojana are as follows :

- The role of government will be of the policy planner, monitoring and evaluation.
- To strengthen the community to take decisions during the programme implementation.
- Total ownership responsibility will be of Panchayat and its sub-committee of the Water Management Committee.
- Cash contribution of the community or in the form of labour and 50 per cent share will be taken in the cash in advance.
- Implementation and maintenance of the scheme will be the responsibility of the village panchayat in coordination with the user groups.
- Total cost of the project will be contributed by the Government of India except the share of community under the Swajaldhara Programme.
- Government of India releases amount under the Swajaldhara in two installments to the District Drinking Water and Sanitation Committee.

4.9 Members of the Legislation Assembly and Member of Legislative Council Local Area Development Fund (MLA & MLC-LAD)

Members of the Legislation Assembly (MLA) and Member of Legislative Council (MLC) Local Area Development (LAD) has been launched to construct infrastructure facilities/ generation of assets as per the recommendations of the Member of the both houses of the State of Uttar Pradesh.

4.10 Construction of Community Hall in the Scheduled Caste Dominated Villages

This programme has been launched to facilitate common meeting place and organization of different programmes for the rural community. In this programme scheduled caste dominant settlement/villages community hall has been constructed. The construction cost and its rate has been fixed according to the schedule rates of the Public Works Department. The construction of the Community Hall/Centre is being ensured on the village panchayat land nearer to the settlement. Later on the constructed community hall/centre should be handed over to the Panchayat.

4.11 Ambedkar Vishesh Rojgar Yojana

The growing population has caused population growth in the rural areas of the State of Uttar Pradesh. Three-fourth population of the Uttar Pradesh is dependent on Agricultural activities. There is great demand of employment multifaceted and multipurpose self-employment generation programme based on the available infrastructure resources, much emphasis has been given by Uttar Pradesh Government. A Special Employment Programme according to the concept of the project has been launched in September 1991 which is known as Ambedkar Vishesh Rojgar Yojana.

In view of the local level available infrastructural resources and requirements in the rural areas, the implementation of the mutli-dimensional programmes at local level self-employment generation should be created so that the migration from rural areas to urban areas are controlled, through generating employment facilities in the rural areas.

- Implementation of employment generating programmes based on the geographical-natural-socio-economic infrastructural resources.
- To generate employment and increase the income through Agricultural and Non-Agricultural activities.
- Any unemployed and semi-employed individual can be beneficiary of the project who is interested to initiate the self-employment.
- The beneficiary must belong to the rural area.
- Collaboration and participation of established non-government organizations may be availed for successful implementation of the programme.
- To provide necessary infrastructural resources to the selected beneficiaries.

In this programme the scheduled caste beneficiaries will get 33 per cent grants of the total cost of the project unit or maximum Rs. 10,000 and other beneficiaries will be given 25 per cent or maximum Rs. 7,500 as government grant. In spite of the above financial support up to a certain limit will be arranged for the administrative expenses for implementation of this scheme. The Government will look after regular motivation, physical verification evaluation and follow up action to achieve the desired target for the employment generation.

Rojgar Chhatari Yojana

Rojgar Chhatari Yojana has been launched to provide suitable employment. In this scheme unemployed youth, landless labourers, small and marginal farmers, rural handicraft persons and other interested youths especially surviving below the poverty line has been given priority for their selection as beneficiary of the programme. The monitoring and evaluation of the Rojgar Chhatari Yojana is being ensured through three-tier committee, i.e. State Level, Division Level, District Level Monitoring and Evaluation Committee.

4.12 National Bio-Gas Programme

National Bio-Gas Programme has been launched during 1981-82, through 100 per cent financial support from the Government of India. Bio-Gas Programme is being implemented regularly from 1981-82. This programme is being implemented as per the guidelines and norms of the Government of India. The training of the Mason workers and proper implementation of Bio-Gas Plants and construction of the Bio-Gas plants has been arranged for which the Government of India provides required financial support for the successful implementation of the National Bio-Gas Programme at village level.

4.13 Community Development Programme

Community Development Programme has been launched for the construction of residential and non-residential buildings at the Block.

4.14 National Health Insurance Programme

National Health Insurance Programme has been launched to provide health support facilities during hospitalization and medical health services for the treatment of disease for the families living Below Poverty Line (BPL). National Health Insurance Scheme will facilitate for the hospitalized, health services and medical facilities for the Insurance Policy holders. The maternity benefit has been included in the health services.

4.15 Farmers Extension Training Programme

Latest research are being carried out by different Agricultural Universities/Research Centres in the field of Agriculture, Horticulture and Animal Husbandry. The important aim of the scheme is to transfer the latest development technologies through extension and training for the farmers/rural people/female farmers for agriculture, horticulture, animal husbandry, agricultural implements and various other training programmes. The training programmes are being organized for the beneficiaries of the Swarnjayanti Gram Swarojgar Yojana, Anganwadi Workers, Supervisors of the Women and Child Development Programmes.

4.16 Uttar Pradesh Grameen Awaas Parishad

Uttar Pradesh Grameen Awaas Parishad has been established to fulfil the basic needs of rural housing in the rural area. Uttar Pradesh Grameen Awaas Parishad has also been nominated as implementing agency for the construction of water recharging project under the Zila Yojana.

4.17 E-Governance

To ensure an appropriate monitoring and evaluation of rural development programmes are being ensured through E-Governance. The implementation of the various rural development programmes, its progress, pension, monitoring and evaluation and disposal of various other programmes can be easily completed through E-Governance. The revenue records, i.e. Khatauni, Ration Card, Pension and Scholarship, Food Supply, Social Welfare, Scheduled Caste, Backward Caste, Physically Handicapped persons, minority welfare and other necessary departments work related to the day-to-day needs of the common village people facilities are made available for the Income Certificate, Birth Certificate, Death Certificate, Caste Certificate, Land Records—Khatauni, Old Age Pension, Widow's Pension, Scholarship, etc. facilities are made available through the E-Governance facility.

Uttar Pradesh Rural Road Development Agency has been entrusted financial management and monitoring through on line Financial Management and Monitoring system to share the needful information among other implementing agencies at various levels.

The comprehensive new connectivity priority list is being prepared based on the population and the comprehensive upgradation priority list is also being prepared to ensure on line share of the informations at various levels.

In view of the above, Performance Budget of the Department of Rural Development, Government of Uttar Pradesh is being prepared for each financial year which clearly indicates the development planning of the Government of Uttar Pradesh to fulfil the vision, mission, intensions and priorities of the Government.

5. DISTRICT DEVELOPMENT PLANNING AMETHI

Development planning of the District Amethi has been formulated and planned and approved through District Planning Committee, i.e. Zila Yojana Samiti of the Amethi under the Chairmanship of Nominated Incharge, Minister of the Government of Uttar Pradesh. The Planwise Budget in the Form-2 of the Amethi District has been mentioned in Table 4.15. It has been observed that the total approved Budget of the Amethi District has been a sum of Rs. 23,692 lakhs for the financial year 2012-13. The Department-wise detailed sanction budget of the Amethi District has been analyzed.

5.1 Agriculture

The ISOPAM and Bhoomi Sena are two important programmes of the District for which Rs. 60.00 lakh has been earmarked in Zila Yojana of Amethi.

5.2 Horticulture

State Horticulture Mission and Horticultural Development Programme for scheduled caste farmers has been included in the Zila Yojana for which Rs. 11.70 lakh budget has been allocated.

5.3 Sugarcane

Sugarcane is not an important crop of Amethi except farmers cultivate for their personal family use due to which there is least demand for sugarcane allocation has been ensured in Zila Yojana of Amethi.

5.4 Assistance for Small and Marginal Farmers

Assistance for Small and Marginal Farmers scheme has been launched for providing agricultural cropping support to increase agricultural productivity for which Rs. 169.16 lakh budget has been earmarked in the Zila Yojana of Amethi.

5.5 Animal Husbandry

Animal Husbandry is an important programme in which artificial inseminization of cows and buffaloes, their improvement, and extension facilities through Bhartiya Agro-Industries Foundation (BAIF), for which a sum of Rs. 100.00 lakh has been allocated in the District Plan of Amethi.

5.6. Fisheries Development

District Fisheries Development Agency and Accidental Community Insurance programme for fisherman has been an important programme of the District Amethi for which Rs. 0.79 lakh budget has been earmarked in the Zila Yojana.

Table 4.15: District Plan 2012-2013, Amethi

(Amount in Lakh Rs.)

Sl. No.	*Line Department/ Sector/Progrmme*	*Proposed Budget from State Resources*			*Proposed Budget from Resource of District Panchayat*	*Proposed Budget from Resources of Local Bodies*	*Total Budget*
		Total	*Total Budget*				
			Capital	*SCP*			
1	2	3	4	5	6	7	8
1.	**Agriculture**						
	ISOPAM	10.00	0.00	2.50	0.00	0.00	10.00
	Bhoomi Sena	50.00	0.00	12.50	0.00	0.00	50.00
	Total	**60.00**	**0.00**	**15.00**	**0.00**	**0.00**	**60.00**
2.	**Horticulture**						
	State Horticulture Mission	0.00	0.00	0.00	0.00	0.00	0.00
	Horticulture Development for SC farmers	11.70	0.00	11.70	0.00	0.00	11.70
	Total	**11.70**	**0.00**	**11.70**	**0.00**	**0.00**	**11.70**
3.	**Sugarcane**						
	Production/Distribution of High Yield variety sugarcane seed	0.00	0.00	0.00	0.00	0.00	0.00
	Seed and Land Development Programe	0.00	0.00	0.00	0.00	0.00	0.00
	Paddy Management Programme	0.00	0.00	0.00	0.00	0.00	0.00
	Construction of Inter Rural road	0.00	0.00	0.00	0.00	0.00	0.00
	Total	**0.00**	**0.00**	**0.00**	**0.00**	**0.00**	**0.00**
4.	**Assistance for small and marginal farmers**						
	Assistance for Small & marginal farmers	169.16	0.00	59.16	0.00	0.00	169.16
	Total	**169.16**	**0.00**	**59.16**	**0.00**	**0.00**	**169.16**
5.	**Animal Husbandry**						
	Animal Health and improvement in the disease cure and extension.	80.00	0.00	15.00	0.00	0.00	80.00
	Artificial in seminization of cows and Buffaloes improvement and extension facilities through BAIF	20.00	0.00	7.30	0.00	0.00	20.00
	Strengthen and extending the pig production areas	0.00	0.00	0.00	0.00	0.00	0.00
	Green fodder and development of green fodder scheme and strengthening the certified green fodder	0.00	0.00	0.00	0.00	0.00	0.00
	Total	**100.00**	**0.00**	**22.30**	**0.00**	**0.00**	**100.00**
6.	**Deptt. of Fisheries Development**						
	Fisheries Development Agency	0.50	0.00		0.00	0.00	0.50
	Accidental community insurance for fisherman	0.29	0.00	0.29	0.00	0.00	0.29
	Total	**0.79**	**0.00**	**0.29**	**0.00**	**0.00**	**0.79**
7.	**Development of Milk**						
	Reorganization, extension and strengthening the Milk Federations and Milk Societies	100.00	0.00	21.60	0.00	0.00	100.00
	Technical demonstration for increasing milk production for the Milk produces and Milk Societies	19.57	0.00	4.07	0.00	0.00	19.57
	Farmers Training	5.00	0.00	2.00	0.00	0.00	5.00

(Contd.)

Table 4.15 *(Contd.)*

1	2	3	4	5	6	7	8
	Automatic Milk Collection Unit	7.50	0.00		0.00	0.00	7.50
	Total	**132.07**	**0.00**	**27.67**	**0.00**	**0.00**	**132.07**
8.	**Department of Forest**						
	Buildings	20.00	0.00	0.00	0.00	0.00	20.00
	Social Forestry	150.00	0.00	80.00	0.00	0.00	150.00
	Social Forestry in Urban area	150.00	0.00	75.00	0.00	0.00	150.00
	Total	**320.00**	**0.00**	**155.00**	**0.00**	**0.00**	**320.00**
9.	**Sahkarita**						
	Interestless loan/grants for partial purchase to the SC and weaker section	1.00	0.00	1.00	0.00	0.00	1.00
	Total	**1.00**	**0.00**	**1.00**	**0.00**	**0.00**	**1.00**
10.	**Special Programme for Village Development**						
	Swaranjayanti Gram Swarajgar Yojana.	291.00	0.00	145.50	0.00	0.00	291.00
	Administration & Direction.	22.50	0.00	0.00	0.00	0.00	22.50
	Total	**313.50**	**0.00**	**145.50**	**0.00**	**0.00**	**313.50**
11.	**Land Development and Water Resources**						
	Integrated watershed Development Programme	0.00	0.00	0.00	0.00	0.00	0.00
	Total	**0.00**	**0.00**	**0.00**	**0.00**	**0.00**	**0.00**
12.	**Employment Programmes (Village Development)**						
	Mahatma Gandhi National Rural Employment Guarantee Act (MNREGA)	1320.97	0.00	0.00	0.00	0.00	1320.97
	Total	**1329.97**	**0.00**	**0.00**	**0.00**	**0.00**	**1329.97**
13.	**Reclamation of Land**						
	Financial Assistance for Patta Land Allottees	0.00	0.00	0.00	0.00	0.00	0.00
	Total	**0.00**	**0.00**	**0.00**	**0.00**	**0.00**	**0.00**
14.	**Panchayati Raj**						
	Construction of CC Road and KC Drain	1314.47	0.00	394.34	0.00	0.00	1314.47
	Construction of multipurpose Panchayat Bhawan	296.80	0.00	74.20	0.00	0.00	296.80
	Hungerless and life safety guarantee yojana	580.00	0.00	120.00	0.00	0.00	580.00
	Total	**2191.27**	**0.00**	**588.54**	**0.00**	**0.00**	**2191.27**
15.	**Community Development**						
	Building Construction for Block/District Development	805.00	0.00	0.00	0.00	0.00	805.00
	Total	**805.00**	**0.00**	**0.00**	**0.00**	**0.00**	**805.00**
16.	**Individual Minor Irrigation**						
	Deep Tubewell	0.00	0.00	0.00	0.00	0.00	0.00
	Boring/Pump set/Tube-well	0.00	0.00	0.00	0.00	0.00	0.00
	Deepening of well	0.00	0.00	0.00	0.00	0.00	0.00
	Groundwater Charging/ Check Dam	135.00	0.00	0.00	0.00	0.00	135.00
	Construction of Boring/Storage.	20.00	0.00	0.00	0.00	0.00	20.00
	Medium Tubewell	918.00	0.00	45.90	0.00	0.00	918.00
	Total	**1073.00**	**0.00**	**45.90**	**0.00**	**0.00**	**1073.00**
17.	**Government Minor Irrigation**						
	General Tube-well Programme (Construction of New Tube-well)	80.00	0.00	20.00	0.00	0.00	80.00
	Modernization of Tube-well	0.00	0.00	0.00	0.00	0.00	0.00
	Dr. Ram Manohar Lohia Tube-well Scheme	180.00	0.00	40.00	0.00	0.00	180.00
	Total	**260.00**	**0.00**	**60.00**	**0.00**	**0.00**	**260.00**

(Contd.)

Table 4.15 (*Contd.*)

1	2	3	4	5	6	7	8
18.	**Flood Control**						
	Smaller Projects for Flood Control	0.00	0.00	0.00	0.00	0.00	0.00
	Total	**0.00**	**0.00**	**0.00**	**0.00**	**0.00**	**0.00**
19.	**Additional Sources of Energy (NEDA)**						
	Street Light	31.24	0.00	6.53	0.00	0.00	31.24
	Solar Pump	0.00	0.00	0.00	0.00	0.00	0.00
	Water Heater	0.00	0.00	0.00	0.00	0.00	0.00
	Total	**31.27**	**0.00**	**6.53**	**0.00**	**0.00**	**31.27**
20.	**Khadi Evam Gramodyog**						
	Village Industries Employment Scheme of Chief Minister	25.00	0.00	5.00	0.00	0.00	25.00
	Vocational Training for entrepreneur	0.00	0.00	0.00	0.00	0.00	00.00
	Total	**25.00**	**0.00**	**5.00**	**0.00**	**0.00**	**25.00**
21.	**Silk Industries**						
	Catalytic Development Project financially supported by Central Silk Board	0.00	0.00	0.00	0.00	0.00	0.00
	Silk Worm Development Scheme	0.00	0.00	0.00	0.00	0.00	0.00
	Silk Development Programme	0.00	0.00	0.00	0.00	0.00	0.00
	Eri Silk Development	0.00	0.00	0.00	0.00	0.00	0.00
	Total	**0.00**	**0.00**	**0.00**	**0.00**	**0.00**	**0.00**
22.	**Handloom Industries**						
	Integrated Handloom Development Scheme	0.00	0.00	0.00	0.00	0.00	0.00
	Health Insurance Scheme for weavers	0.00	0.00	0.00	0.00	0.00	0.00
	Total	**0.00**	**0.00**	**0.00**	**0.00**	**0.00**	**0.00**
23.	**Road and Bridges**						
	Renovation of Rural Roads	1000.00	0.00	600.00	0.00	0.00	1000 00
	Construction of New Rural Roads	5500.00	0.00	2000.00	0.00	0.00	5500.00
	Total	**6500.00**	**0.00**	**2600.00**	**0.00**	**0.00**	**6500.00**
24.	**Environment**						
	Environment education, awareness, training and extension program	4.00	0.00	1.00	0.00	0.00	4.00
	Total	**4.00**	**0.00**	**1.00**	**0.00**	**0.00**	**4.00**
25.	**Science and Technology**						
	Promotion and Propagation of Science and Technology	1.00	0.00	0.00	0.00	0.00	1.00
	Total	**1.00**	**0.00**	**0.00**	**0.00**	**0.00**	**1.00**
26.	**Tourism**						
	Beautification and Development of Tourism	0.00	0.00	0.00	0.00	0.00	0.00
	Renovation of Tourist places and Monuments	20.00	0.00	0.00	0.00	0.00	20.00
	Local Tourism Development	20.00	0.00	0.00	0.00	0.00	20.00
	Sulabh Sauchalaya	16.00	0.00	0.00	0.00	0.00	16.00
	Shelters for Passengers	9.00	0.00	0.00	0.00	0.00	9.00
	Total	**65.00**	**0.00**	**0.00**	**0.00**	**0.00**	**65.00**
27.	**Primary Education**						
	Sarva Shiksha Abhiyan	70.00	0.00	0.00	0.00	0.00	70.00
	Construction of B.S.A. Office in Districts	35.00	0.00	0.00	0.00	0.00	35.00

(*Contd.*)

Table 4.15 (*Contd.*)

1	2	3	4	5	6	7	8
	Installation of Handpumps, Electrification, construction of boundary wall for the primary and Higher secondary schools	79.00	0.00	0.00	0.00	0.00	79.00
	Mid-day-meal program	238.00	0.00	0.00	0.00	0.00	238.00
	Total	**422.35**	**0.00**	**0.00**	**0.00**	**0.00**	**422.35**
28.	**Intermediate Education**						
	Purchase of land, building construction, electrification, for Govt. Higher Secondary Schools	200.00	0.00	0.00	0.00	0.00	200.00
	Construction of Education Office and Houses at the District Level	0.00	0.00	0.00	0.00	0.00	0.00
	Remuneration for the subject matter specialist of vocational educational syllabus	28.00	0.00	0.00	0.00	0.00	28.00
	Establishment of Government Higher Secondary Schools and Government Girls Junior Schools and High Schools at Block level	0.00	0.00	0.00	0.00	0.00	0.00
	Grants-in-Aid for opening girls schools from one village panchayat to another village panchayat through self-financing management	10.00	0.00	0.00	0.00	0.00	10.00
	National campaign for higher secondary education	800.00	0.00	0.00	0.00	0.00	800.00
	Building Construction for Government District Library	0.00	0.00	0.00	0.00	0.00	0.00
	Total	**1038.00**	**0.00**	**0.00**	**0.00**	**0.00**	**1038.00**
29.	**Higher Education**						
	Renovation of Govt. Degree College	0.00	0.00	0.00	0.00	0.00	0.00
	Building Construction of Govt. Degree College	0.00	0.00	0.00	0.00	0.00	0.00
	Total	**0.00**	**0.00**	**0.00**	**0.00**	**0.00**	**0.00**
30.	**Technical Education**						
	Equipment, Furnishing New Professional Education	53.00	0.00	0.00	0.00	0.00	53.00
	Building Construction for Polytechnic Institutions	47.00	0.00	0.00	0.00	0.00	47.00
	Establishment of Govt. Polytechnic	0.00	0.00	0.00	0.00	0.00	0.00
	Construction of Hostels, Renovation and extension of Govt. Polytechnic	240.00	0.00	0.00	0.00	0.00	240.00
	Total	**340.00**	**0.00**	**0.00**	**0.00**	**0.00**	**340.00**
31.	**Pradeshik Vikas Dal**						
	Organization of Rural Sports Competition	2.80	0.00	0.70	0.00	0.00	2.80
	Panchayat youth sports and sports campaign	9.40	0.00	2.25	0.00	0.00	9.40
	Total	**12.20**	**0.00**	**2.95**	**0.00**	**0.00**	**12.20**
32.	**Sports**						
	Construction of Sports Buildings	100.00	0.00	0.00	0.00	0.00	100.00
	Total	**100.00**	**0.00**	**0.00**	**0.00**	**0.00**	**100.00**

(*Contd.*)

Table 4.15 (*Contd.*)

1	2	3	4	5	6	7	8
33.	**Medical (Allopathy)**						
	Construction of patient shelter in the Allopathic Hospital	0.00	0.00	0.00	0.00	0.00	0.00
	Plastic Surgery and Burn Unit	0.00	0.00	0.00	0.00	0.00	0.00
	Radiology Unit	0.00	0.00	0.00	0.00	0.00	0.00
	Incentive Care Unit	0.00	0.00	0.00	0.00	0.00	0.00
	Construction of Mortuary House	50.00	0.00	0.00	0.00	0.00	50.00
	Construction of Primary Health Centre	200.00	0.00	0.00	0.00	0.00	200.00
	Establishment of New Primary Health Centre	40.00	0.00	0.00	0.00	0.00	40.00
	Establishment of Community Centre	50.00	0.00	0.00	0.00	0.00	50.00
	Rennovation of Hospitals, Extension and provision of Electricity and water	84.00	0.00	0.00	0.00	0.00	84.00
	Rennovation of existing primary health centre and electricity and water	60.00	0.00	0.00	0.00	0.00	60.00
	Total	**484.00**	**0.00**	**0.00**	**0.00**	**0.00**	**484.00**
34.	**Family Planning**						
	State share of National Rural Health Mission Programme	300.00	0.00	0.00	0.00	0.00	300.00
	Total	**300.00**	**0.00**	**0.00**	**0.00**	**0.00**	**300.00**
35.	**Medical (Homeopathy)**						
	Establishment of Govt. Homeopathic Hospitals (Urban)	9.00	0.00	0.00	0.00	0.00	9.00
	Establishment of Govt. Homeopathic Hospitals (Rural)	18.00	0.00	0.00	0.00	0.00	18.00
	Construction of Homeopathic Hospitals	0.00	0.00	0.00	0.00	0.00	0.00
	Total	**27.00**	**0.00**	**0.00**	**0.00**	**0.00**	**27.00**
36.	**Ayurvedic**						
	Establishment of Unani/Ayurvedic Hospital in Urban Area	6.00	0.00	0.00	0.00	0.00	6.00
	Establishment of Unani/ Ayurvedic Hospital in Rural Area	12.00	0.00	0.00	0.00	0.00	12.00
	Building construction of Unani/Ayurvedic Hospital	0.00	0.00	0.00	0.00	0.00	0.00
	Total	**18.00**	**0.00**	**0.00**	**0.00**	**0.00**	**18.00**
37.	**Rural Drinking Water (Jal Nigam)**						
	Rural Drinking water (Deptt. of Rural Development)	1011.73	0.00	280.00	0.00	0.00	1011.73
	Total	**1011.73**	**0.00**	**280.00**	**0.00**	**0.00**	**1011.73**
38.	**Rural Sanitation Programme (Panchayati Raj)**						
	Construction of Sanitation	42.00	0.00	7.00	0.00	0.00	42.00
	Total	**42.00**	**0.00**	**7.00**	**0.00**	**0.00**	**42.00**
39.	**Pooled Housing (PWD)**						
	Pooled Housing	875.00	0.00	0.00	0.00	0.00	875.00
	Total	**875.00**	**0.00**	**0.00**	**0.00**	**0.00**	**875.00**
40.	**Rural Housing**						
	Indira Awaas Yojana	969.98	0.00	484.00	0.00	0.00	969.98
	Lohia Grameen Awaas	720.00	0.00	54.00	0.00	0.00	720.00
	Total	**969.98**	**0.00**	**484.00**	**0.00**	**0.00**	**969.98**
41.	**Urban Drinking Water Scheme**						
	Urban Drinking Water	493.00	0.00	260.40	0.00	0.00	493.00
	Total	**493.00**	**0.00**	**260.40**	**0.00**	**0.00**	**493.00**

(*Contd.*)

Table 4.15 (*Contd.*)

1	2	3	4	5	6	7	8
42.	**Welfare Programmes (Schedule Caste)**						
	Grants-in-Aid for the marriage of Sick persons' daughter	132.00	0.00	132.00	0.00	0.00	132.00
	Scholarships upto 10th Class for Schedule Caste	216.00	0.00	216.00	0.00	0.00	216.00
	Establishment of Book Bank for SC	10.00	0.00	10.00	0.00	0.00	10.00
	Financial support for exploited persons of SC	20.00	0.00	20.00	0.00	0.00	20.00
	Construction/ Establishment of Ashram based Govt. Schools for Schedule Caste	0.00	0.00	0.00	0.00	0.00	0.00
	Total	**378.10**	**0.00**	**378.10**	**0.00**	**0.00**	**378.10**
43.	**Backward Caste Welfare**						
	Scholarship for Backward Class students upto 10th Class	127.25	0.00	0.00	0.00	0.00	127.25
	Grants-in-aid for treatment of seriously ill and marriage for daughters of backward caste people	132.00	0.00	0.00	0.00	0.00	132.00
	Total	**259.25**	**0.00**	**0.00**	**0.00**	**0.00**	**259.25**
44.	**Minority Welfare**						
	Scholarship for Minority Students	3.18	0.00	0.00	0.00	0.00	3.18
	Marriage of daughters of minorities	15.00	0.00	0.00	0.00	0.00	15.00
	Total	**18.18**	**0.00**	**0.00**	**0.00**	**0.00**	**18.18**
45.	**Social Welfare (General Category)**						
	Scholarship upto 10th class for the general caste students	80.00	0.00	0.00	0.00	0.00	80.00
	Scholarship above 10th class for the general caste students	180.00	0.00	0.00	0.00	0.00	180.00
	Financial Assistance for the treatment and daughter's marriage	30.00	0.00	0.00	0.00	0.00	30.00
	Total	**290.00**	**0.00**	**0.00**	**0.00**	**0.00**	**290.00**
46.	**Schedule Tribes Welfare**						
	Class 9 to 10	0.00	0.00	0.00	0.00	0.00	0.00
	Class 6 to 8	0.00	0.00	0.00	0.00	0.00	0.00
	Class 1 to 5	0.00	0.00	0.00	0.00	0.00	0.00
	Grants-in-aid for daughter's marriage of schedule tribes	0.00	0.00	0.00	0.00	0.00	0.00
	Financial Assistance for exploited and troubled.	0.00	0.00	0.00	0.00	0.00	0.00
	Total	**0.00**	**0.00**	**0.00**	**0.00**	**0.00**	**0.00**
47.	**Employment**						
	Guideline and training centre for the applicants of Schedule caste	0.00	0.00	0.00	0.00	0.00	0.00
	Remuneration for unemployment	1100.00	0.00	0.00	0.00	0.00	1100.00
	Total	**1100.00**	**0.00**	**0.00**	**0.00**	**0.00**	**1100.00**
48.	**Artisans Training**						
	Building Construction for ITI	150.00	0.00	0.00	0.00	0.00	150.00
	Rennovation of Industrial Training Institutes	30.00	0.00	0.00	0.00	0.00	30.00
	Upgradation and incorporation of new trades	60.00	0.00	0.00	0.00	0.00	60.00
	Total	**240.00**	**0.00**	**0.00**	**0.00**	**0.00**	**240.00**

(*Contd.*)

Table 4.15 (*Contd.*)

1	2	3	4	5	6	7	8
49.	**Social Welfare - Pension for Old age person**						
	Pension for old age person	180.00	0.00	90.00	0.00	0.00	180.00
	National Family Benefit Scheme	160.00	0.00	80.00	0.00	0.00	160.00
	Rani Laxmi Bai Pension Scheme	1200.00	0.00	600.00	0.00	0.00	1200.00
	Total	**1540.00**	**0.00**	**770.00**	**0.00**	**0.00**	**1540.00**
50.	**Handicapped Welfare**						
	Grants-in-aid for deaf and dumb physically incapable/ handicapped	49.22	0.00	11.32	0.00	0.00	49.22
	Total	**49.00**	**0.00**	**11.32**	**0.00**	**0.00**	**49.00**
51.	**Family Welfare**						
	Financial Assistance for resourceless widows after death of their husband	275.29	0.00	76.15	0.00	0.00	275.29
	Total	**279.29**	**0.00**	**76.15**	**0.00**	**0.00**	**279.29**
52.	**Women and Child Development**						
	Women and Child Development and Nutritious Food Programme	15.00	0.00	0.00	0.00	0.00	15.00
	Total	**15.00**	**0.00**	**0.00**	**0.00**	**0.00**	**15.00**

5.7 Development of Milk

Development of Milk, re-organization, extension and strengthening the Milk Federations and Milk Societies, Technical demonstration for increasing milk production for the Milk Producers and Milk Societies, Farmers Training and establishment of Automatic Milk Collection Unit programmes has been launched for which Rs. 132.07 lakh budgetary provisions has been made in the District Plan.

5.8 Forest

A sum of Rs. 320.00 lakh has been earmarked for the various programmes of the Department of Forest in Amethi.

5.9 Sahkarita (Co-operative)

Interest less loan/grants-in-aid for the partial purchase of necessary items for scheduled caste and weaker sections of the society etc. has been incorporated in the Zila Yojana for which Rs. 10.00 lakh has been allocated in the District Plan of Amethi.

5.10 Special Programmes for Village Development

Special Programmes for village development especially employment generation through Swarnjayanti Gram Swarojgar Yojana and administration and guidance to the unemployed youth has been an important programmes of the District for which Rs. 313.00 lakh has been earmarked in the District Plan.

5.11 Land Development and Water Resources

Integrated watershed development programmes, land development and water resources management has been incorporated in the Zila Yojana but budgetary provisions has not been made during the year 2012-13 in the Zila Yojana of Amethi.

5.12 Employment and Village Development

Mahatma Gandhi National Rural Employment Guarantee Act (MNREGA) has been an important scheme under the Employment and Village Development programme of Amethi for which Rs. 1329.27 lakh has been allocated in the District Plan Amethi.

5.13 Panchayati Raj

Construction of C.C. Road and K.C. Drain, multipurpose Panchayat Bhawan, Hungerless and Life Safety Guarantee Yojana has been launched under the Panchayati Raj Department for which a sum of Rs. 2191.27 lakh has been earmarked in the Zila Yojana of Amethi.

5.14 Community Development

The construction of building and other community development programmes has been planned for which Rs. 805.00 lakh has been allocated in the District Plan of Amethi.

5.15 Individual Minor Irrigation

Deep Tube-well, Boring, Pumping set, Tube-well, deepening of wells, groundwater charging, check dam, construction of boring, storage and medium tube-well work has been planned under the individual minor irrigation for which Rs. 1073.00 lakh has been allocated in the District Plan of Amethi.

5.16 Government Minor Irrigation

General Tube-well, construction of New Tubewell and Dr. Ram Manohar Lohia Tube-well Scheme have been planned for which a sum of Rs. 260.00 lakh has been earmarked in the Zila Yojana.

4.17 Flood Control

Amethi is not affected by the flood, therefore, budgetary provisions have not been made for flood control in the District Plan for the financial year 2012-13.

5.18 Additional Sources of Energy

Street light, solar pump, water heater through Non-conventional sources of Energy has been planned for which a sum of Rs. 31.27 lakh has been allocated in the Zila Yojana of Amethi.

5.19 Khadi and Gramodyog

The Village Industries Employment Scheme of the Chief Minister has been planned to generate employment at village level for which Rs. 25.00 lakh has been earmarked in the District Plan of Amethi.

5.20 Silk Industries

Tussar Silk and Mulberry rearing is not done in Amethi and there is no favourable agro-climatic conditions for the Tussar and Mulberry worm rearing in Amethi due to which budgetary provisions has not been made in the District Plan of Amethi.

5.21 Handloom Industries

The budgetary provisions has not been made for integrated handloom development and health insurance scheme for weavers in the handloom sector in the Budget Plan of Amethi for year 2012-13.

5.22 Road and Bridges

The renovation of rural roads and construction of rural roads under the road and bridges budget heads a sum of Rs. 650.00 lakh has been allocated in the District Plan of Amethi.

5.23 Environment

Environment education, awareness, training and extension programmes for environment head a sum of Rs. 4.00 lakh has been earmarked in the District Plan of Amethi.

5.24 Science and Technology

To promote and propagate science and technology a sum of Rs. 1.00 lakh has been allocated in the District Plan of Amethi.

5.25 Tourism

Renovation of tourist places and monuments, local tourism development, Sulabh Sauchalaya and shelters for Passengers has been planned for which a sum of Rs. 65.00 lakh has been earmarked in the District Plan of Amethi.

5.26 Primary Education

Sarva Shiksha Abhiyan, construction of offices, installation of hand pumps, electrification, construction of boundary wall for the primary and higher secondary schools and mid-day-meal programmes has been incorporated in the Zila Yojana for which Rs. 423.35 lakh has been earmarked in the District Plan of the Amethi.

5.27 Intermediate Education

The purchase of land building construction, electrification for Government Higher Secondary School, Construction of Education Office, Remuneration for the Subject matter specialist of vocational educational syllabus, establishment of Government Higher Secondary Schools, Government Girls Junior Schools and High Schools at block level, Grants-in-aid for opening girls school from one village panchayat to another village panchayat through Self-Financing management, National Campaign for Higher Secondary education etc. have been planned in the District plan of Amethi for which a sum of Rs. 1038.00 lakh has been allocated in the district plan for the year 2012-13.

5.28 Higher Education

Renovation of Government Degree College and Building Construction of Government Degree College in the Higher Education Sector has not been considered in the work plan for the year 2012-13 for which no budgetary allocation has been earmarked in the Zila Yojana of Amethi.

5.29 Professional Education

Furnishing of equipment of new professional education, building construction for Polytechnic Institutions, Establishment of Polytechnic, Construction of Hostels, renovation and extension of the Government Polytechnic in the professional/Technical education sector a sum of Rs. 340.00 lakh budgetary allocations has been earmarked in the Zila Yojana of Amethi.

5.30 Pradeshik Vikas Dal

Organisation of Rural Sports, Panchayat Youth Sports and Sports Campaign programme being organized by Pradeshik Vikas Dal Rs. 12.20 lakhs budget has been allocated in the District Plan of Amethi.

5.31 Sports

A sum of Rs. 100.00 lakh budget has been allocated in the Zila Yojana for the construction of sports building in Amethi.

5.32 Medical (Allopathy)

Construction of Mortuary Houses and construction of Primary Health Centre, establishment of new Primary Health Centre, establishment of community centre, renovation of hospitals, extension and provision of electricity, water, renovation of existing primary health centres, water and electricity provisions have been made in the District plan for which Rs. 484.00 lakh amount has been allocated in the Zila Yojana of Amethi.

5.33 Family Planning

A sum of Rs. 300.00 lakh state share of National Rural Health Mission (NRHM) programme has been allocated in the Zila Yojana of Amethi.

5.34 Medical Homoeopathy

Establishment of the Government Homoeopathic Hospitals in the Rural and Urban areas and construction of Homoeopathic Hospitals has been incorporated in the District Plan for which Rs. 27.00 lakh has been allocated in the District Plan of Amethi.

5.35 Ayurvedic

Establishment of Unani/Ayurvedi Hospitals in urban and rural areas and construction of building for Unani/Ayurvedi Hospitals has been incorporated in the Zila Yojana for which Rs. 18.00 lakh has been allocated in the District Plan of Amethi.

5.36 Rural Drinking Water (Jal Nigam)

Rural Drinking Water (Department of Rural Development) has been included as an important programmes for which a sum of Rs. 1011.73 lakh budget has been allocated in the District Plan of Amethi.

5.37 Rural Sanitation Programme

Construction of latrine/sanitation under the Rural Sanitation Programme has been included in the Zila Yojana for which Rs. 42.00 lakh amount has been allocated in the Zila Yojana.

5.38 Pooled Housing (PWD)

A sum of Rs. 875.00 lakh budget has been earmarked for the construction of pooled houses through public works department in the District Plan of Amethi.

5.39 Rural Housing

An important programme for providing shelter to the shelterless people has been launched under the Indira Awaas Yojana and Lohia Grameen Awaas Yojana has been initiated for which Rs. 869.00 lakh budget has been allocated in the District Plan of Amethi.

5.40 Urban Drinking Water

A sum of Rs. 493.00 has been allocated for the construction of urban drinking water scheme in the Zila Yojana of Amethi.

5.41 Welfare Programmes (Scheduled Caste)

Grants for the marriage of sick person's daughter, scholarship up to 10th class scheduled caste students, establishment of Book Bank for scheduled caste, construction/ establishment of Ashram based Government Schools for scheduled caste students has been incorporated in the District Plan for which Rs. 378.00 lakh budget has been allocated in the Zila Yojana of Amethi.

5.42 Welfare Programmes of Backward Caste

Scholarship for backward caste students up to 10th class and Grants-in-aid for treatment of seriously ill and marriage of daughters of backward caste people has been incorporated in the Zila Yojana for which a sum of Rs. 259.25 lakhs budget has been allocated in the District Plan.

5.43 Minority Welfare

Scholarships for the Minority students and marriage of daughters of minorities has been included under the Minority Welfare Programme for which Rs. 18.18 lakh has been allocated in the Zila Yojana of Amethi.

5.44 Social Welfare (General Caste)

The scholarship up to 10th class for the general caste students, scholarships above 10th class for the general caste students. Financial Assistance for the treatment, daughter's marriage of general caste people has been included in the District Plan for which Rs. 290.00 lakh budget has been allocated in the Zila Yojana of Amethi.

5.45 Scheduled Tribes

As such there is no scheduled tribe population and settlement in Amethi due to which budgetary provisions has not been made under the welfare programme for scheduled tribe peoles in Zila Yoajana of Amethi.

5.46 Employment

Guidelines and training centre for the scheduled caste and remuneration for the unemployment allowance (*Berojgari Bhatta*) has been incorporated in the Zila Yojana for which Rs. 1100.00 lakh budget has been allocated in the District Plan.

5.47 Artisans Training

Construction of building for Industrial Training Industries, and renovation of Industrial Training Industries, upgradation and incorporation of new trade has been included in the Zila Yojana for which Rs. 240.00 lakh amount has been allocated in the District Plan of Amethi.

5.48 Social Welfare Programme for old age persons

Pension for old age persons, National Family Benefit Scheme and Rani Laxmi Bai Pension Scheme under the social welfare programme has been incorporated in the Zila Yojana for which Rs. 1540.00 lakh has been allocated in the District Plan of Amethi.

5.49 Handicapped Welfare

Gants-in-aid for deaf and dumb, physically incapable and handicapped persons budgetary provisions has been made in the District Plan for which Rs. 49.00 lakh budget has been allocated in the Zila Yojana of Amethi.

5.50 Family Welfare

Financial assistance for resourceless widows after death of their husbands has been included in the District Plan of Amethi for which Rs. 279.29 lakh budget has been allocated in the Zila Yojana of Amethi.

5.51 Women Level and Child Development Programmes

Women and Child Development Programmes and Nutritious Food Programmes have been incorporated in the Women and Child Development Programmes in the Zila Yojana of Amethi for which a sum of Rs. 15.00 lakh budget has been allocated in the Zila Yojana of Amethi.

In view of the above, descriptions a sum of Rs. 23692.00 lakh budget for the financial year 2012-13 has been allocated and approved for the District Plan of Amethi. The details of the proposed budget as per the plan of the District has been mentioned in details in Table 4.15.

6. BLOCK LEVEL DEVELOPMENT PLANNING — AMETHI

Block level development planning of the Amethi has been only planned for the road construction/renovation of the constructed roads at village level in Amethi. Need based planning for the construction of road or link road including earth work from Tolas/ Purwas/Hamlet villages and revenue villages. The plan formulation for the construction of the road has been based on the recommendations and proposals of the members of the Block Development Committee (BDC) and Block Pramukh of Amethi.

The details of the Mahatma Gandhi National Rural Employment Guarantee Act (MNREGA) proposed work plan for the year 2012-13 for the Amethi Block has been mentioned in Table 4.16. It has been recorded that soling work from Tewari's Garden to Hanuman Pandey's house has been proposed covering 200 metres distance for which estimated cost has been proposed Rs. 1.30 lakh out of which Rs. 0.26 lakh is the labour and Rs. 1.04 lakh is the material cost and there will be 208 man-days employment generation for the MNREGA Job Card Holders. The link road has been proposed fiom Tube-well of Ram Samujh to Ram Naresh's Garden and Kallu's field to Ram Chandra's machines, Dhanapur road to Benchu Babo School etc. the proposed six link road may generate an employment of 4880 man-days and it is estimated to extend Rs. 8.60 lakh.

Table 4.16: Mahatma Gandhi National Rural Employment Guarantee Act (MNREGA) Work Plan 2012-13, Amethi

(Amount in lakh Rs.)

Sl. No.	*Construction of Work*	*Measurement in Mtr.*	*Estimated Cost*	*Labour Cost*	*Material Cost*	*Total*	*Man-days*
1	2	3	4	5	6	7	8
1.	Soling Work from Tiwari's Garden to Hanuman Pandey's House.	200	1.30	0.26	1.04	1.30	208
2.	Link Road from Kallu's Field to Ramchander's Machine.	350 × 3	1.10	0.88	0.22	1.10	704
3.	Link Road from Old Barban Purwa to New Barban Purwa.	500	1.50	1.20	0.30	1.50	960
4.	Link Road from Anuj Pratap's house to Chhawani Pakki Road.	600	1.60	1.28	0.32	1.60	1024
5.	Link Road from Amarnath's house to Kiln.	570 × 4	1.50	1.20	0.30	1.50	960
6.	Link Road from Ram Samujh's Tubewell to Ram Naresh's Garden.	650	1.60	1.28	0.32	1.60	1024
7.	Soling Work from Purabgaon Link Road to Lavkush's house.	300	1.60	1.28	0.32	1.60	1024
8.	Soling Work from Pithipur Link Road to centre of Gaderi road.	200	1.20	0.96	0.24	1.20	768
9.	Link Road from Dhanapur Road to Baltu Baba School.	300	1.30	0.26	1.04	1.30	208
10.	Link Road from Babaganj Bazar to Baltu Baba School.	410	1.25	0.25	1.00	1.25	200
11.	Link Road from Sarai Hirmati P.M. Road to Datta Bariyar Junior High School Road.	1390	2.57	0.51	2.06	2.57	411
12.	Soling work from Kakawa-Amethi Road to Fakir's house.	195	2.00	0.40	1.60	2.00	320
13.	Drain construction work from Ram Sahai Pal's house to Ram Lakhan Pal's house.	100	1.11	0.22	0.89	1.11	178
14.	Link Road from Amethi Pratapgarh Road to Railway Line.	450	1.00	0.80	0.20	1.00	640
15.	Nala digging work from Amethi-Kakawa Road to Sultanpur Village.	1100	0.75	0.60	0.15	0.75	480
16.	Drain construction work from Ramdeen's well to Kakawa-Kohara Link Road.	150	2.00	0.40	1.60	2.00	320
17.	Link Road from Ram Laut's field to Lalji Mishra's field.	600	1.60	1.28	0.32	1.60	1024
18.	Link Road from from Maharaj's pond to Dada's garden.	800	1.80	1.44	0.36	1.80	1152
19.	Soling work from Prakash Singh's house to Daddu Mishra's house.	1000	8.20	1.64	6.56	8.20	1312
20.	Pond digging work of Purakhi Ji Pond.	50 × 50	3.90	3.12	0.78	3.90	2496
21.	Pond digging work in Vaishan's Tara and Hulasi's purwa.	50 × 50	3.75	3.00	0.72	3.75	2400
22.	Link Road from Canal border to Ghuraha border.	600	1.60	1.28	0.32	1.60	1024
23.	Link Road from Shankargarh Bazar to Manbodh's House.	800	1.80	1.44	0.36	1.80	1152
24.	Drain work from Kandhu Shukla's House to Gadahi.	900	6.90	1.38	5.52	6.90	1104
25.	Soling work from Haribaksh Ka Purwa School to Haribaksh's Purwa.	500	3.99	0.80	3.19	3.99	638
26.	Link Road from Bhawani Bux's Purwa to Hulasi's Purwa.	700	1.70	1.36	0.34	1.70	1088
27.	Link Road from Haribax's Purwa to Old Pandit's Purwa.	900	1.90	1.52	0.38	1.90	1216
28.	Link Road from Chaubepur Canal culvert to Kharanja of Barban's Purwa.	750	1.75	1.40	0.35	1.75	1120
29.	Cleaning of drain from Ram Nagar Mafi to Kuturu Bundh.	2000	1.50	1.20	0.30	1.50	960
30.	Cleaning of drain from Kuturu Bundh to River.	2000	1.50	1.20	0.30	1.50	960

(Contd.)

Table 4.16 (*Contd.*)

1	2	3	4	5	6	7	8
31.	Link Road from Dandupur pakki road to Bhupatipur pakki road.	1500 × 3	1.85	1.48	0.37	1.85	1184
32.	Link Road from Badaicha pond to Dandupur Charagaah.	1500 × 3	1.60	1.28	0.32	1.60	1024
33.	Digging work of Malle Tara Pond.	50 × 50	3.80	3.04	0.76	3.80	2432
34.	Soil work from Amethi-Durgapur Pitch road to Triyugi Narain's Machine.	1000	1.90	1.52	0.38	1.90	1216
35.	Link Road from Vinod Singh's tubewell to Rafik's tubewell.	1200	3.60	2.88	0.72	3.60	2304
36.	Soling work from Pintoo's house to Teri pakki road.	1200	3.60	2.88	0.72	3.60	2304
37.	Soling work from Chhawai pakki road to Kedar Shukla's house.	250	1.95	0.39	1.56	1.95	312
38.	Link Road from Milan's chakki to Harijan basti.	1500 × 4	1.90	1.52	0.38	1.90	1216
39.	Kharanja work from Radhey Shyam's house to Nanda's house.	500	1.20	0.96	0.24	1.20	768
40.	Digging work of Barai pond.	50 × 50	3.90	3.12	0.78	3.90	2496
41.	Link Road from Kewalapur to Saraiya village.	3000 × 4	3.60	2.88	0.72	3.60	2304
42.	Road construction work from Place of Baltu Baba to Naraini border/Mukut's field.	1000	1.90	1.52	0.38	1.90	1216
43.	Link Road from Dhrubraj Singh's Machine to Chhedi Maurya's hosue.	500	1.50	1.20	0.30	1.50	960
44.	Drain construction work from Swami Nath's house to Ram Tahal Maurya's house.	300	2.60	0.52	2.08	2.60	416
45.	Kharanja work from Nahar to Sharda Devi Balika Inter College.	300	2.60	2.08	0.52	2.60	1664
46.	Kachcha work from Chhawani Link Road to Ambedkar Park.	220	1.20	0.96	0.24	1.20	768
47.	Link Road from Yunus's shop to Chhawani Masjid.	250	1.20	0.96	0.24	1.20	768
48.	Link Road from Angad Flour mill to door of Ram Kumar Maurya.	500	1.50	1.20	0.30	1.50	960
49.	Link Road from Ram Kishore's water tank to Bharhawan Ram Saran's house.	800	1.80	1.44	0.36	1.80	1152
50.	Link Road from Kodari Link Road to Sri Ram's field.	700 × 4	1.70	1.36	0.34	1.70	1088
51.	Link Road from Nuwawan Link Road to Daya Ram Chauhan's house.	300 × 6	1.30	1.04	0.26	1.30	832
52.	Pond digging in Gata No. 537	40 × 60	2.60	2.08	0.52	2.60	1664
53.	Link Road from Jagdish's hosue to Kodari link road.	750	1.75	1.40	0.35	1.75	1120
54.	Link Road from Kodari link road to Bairagi's field.	550 × 3	1.50	1.20	0.30	1.50	960
55.	Link Road from Dubepur Pakka Link Road to Brijlal's house.	200 × 3	1.10	0.88	0.22	1.10	704
56.	Drain construction from Rajendra Dubey's well to pond.	300	2.60	2.08	0.52	2.60	1664
57.	Drain cleaning work from Ram Nagar Mafi to Kutur Bandh.	2000	1.80	1.44	0.36	1.80	1152
58.	Link Road from Sarai Khema-Dandupur Pakki Road to Bhupatipur Pakki Road.	1500	3.20	2.56	0.64	3.20	2048
59.	Link Road from Badaicha pond in Sarai Khema Village Panchayat to Dandupur Charagaah.	1000	2.60	2.08	0.52	2.60	1664
60.	Drain digging work from Pure Kalwaran to Malati River.	1500	2.30	1.84	0.46	2.30	1472
61.	Cleaning & digging work of minor from Kakawa road to Sultanpur Lalati River.	3000	3.60	2.88	0.72	3.60	2304
62.	Link Road from Ram Sundar Yadav's house to Shambhu Nath's house.	190	0.64	0.51	0.13	0.64	411

(*Contd.*)

Table 4.16 *(Contd.)*

1	2	3	4	5	6	7	8
63.	Link Road from Pratapgarh road to Sanjay Sharma's field.	290	0.53	0.42	0.11	0.53	339
64.	Link Road from Jagdish Pandey's field to Saheb Bux Singh's field.	90	0.21	0.17	0.04	0.21	134
65.	Link Road from Gurubax's Purwa to Ranjeet's field.	1250 × 6	3.60	2.88	0.72	3.60	2304
66.	Link Road from Amethi-Suiya Road to Kithawar Road.	1000	3.00	2.40	0.60	3.00	1920
67.	Link Road from Canal culvert to Ram Baran Singh's house.	300	1.30	1.04	0.26	1.30	832
68.	Soling work from Munna Bhujwa's house to Pramukh Ram Shankar's field.	150	1.50	0.30	1.20	1.50	240
69.	Soling work from Baijnath Yadav's house to Purabgaon pitch road.	500	4.60	0.92	3.68	4.60	736
70.	Drain construction work from Ram Sundar Yadav's house to Chhedi Yadav's house.	250	2.90	0.58	2.32	2.90	464
71.	Drain construction work in Bisheshargani market just near of Interlocking.	235	2.60	0.52	2.08	2.60	416
72.	Drain construction work from Shivram Singh's house to Ramgarh Saraiya road.	100	0.95	0.19	0.76	0.95	152
	Total		**158.95**	**96.97**	**61.98**	**158.95**	**77576**
	Additional Amended Work Plan						
73.	Soling work from Ram Sajiwan Kori's house to Daya Ram Gupta's house.	250	2.00	0.40	1.60	2.00	320
74.	Soling and soil work from Padari Link Road to Bhawni's house.	200	3.00	0.60	2.40	3.00	480
75.	Soil work Kakawa Jr. High School to Chahandara Village.	400	4.00	0.80	3.20	4.00	640
76.	Soling work from Padari road to Ram Samujh's house.	230	2.00	0.40	1.60	2.00	320
77.	Soil work from Viysia School pitch road to Pure Dhanau.	250	4.00	0.80	3.20	4.00	640
78.	Link road from Bhagwandeen Road to Bodanaar.	400	1.00	0.80	0.20	1.00	640
79.	Soil work from Kakawa Bazar to Ram Shankar Tiwari's house.	600	6.00	2.40	3.60	6.00	1920
80.	Soil and Kharanza work from Gangauli link road to Ram Sumer Mali's house.	450	5.00	4.00	1.00	5.00	3200
81.	Kharanza and soil work from Amethi Vishesharganj road to Jokhu Prajapati's house.	500	5.50	4.40	1.10	5.50	3520
82.	Link road from Amaha Kharanza to Jokhu's house.	450	2.00	1.60	0.40	2.00	1280
83.	Soil and soling work from Amethi Pratapgarh road to Ram Harakh's and Shiv Lal's house.	160	1.20	0.96	0.24	1.20	768
84.	Soling work from Amehti Pratapgarh road to Primary School.	150	1.70	1.36	0.34	1.70	1088
85.	Soling work from Paware Harijan Basti to Nanda's field.	400	4.00	3.20	0.80	4.00	2560
86.	Link road from Amethi Badhani Vishesharganj pitch road to Mahaso village.	1200	3.00	2.40	0.60	3.00	1920
87.	Link road from Ram Prasad's House to Vasupur mod.	1100	2.75	2.20	0.55	2.75	1760
88.	Link road from Panchayat Bhawan to Transformer.	500	1.50	1.20	0.30	1.50	960
89.	Link road from Antipur Pitch Road to Dewhaar Mata Sthan.	600	1.75	1.40	0.35	1.75	1120
90.	Link road from Ram Lal's house to Antipur.	1000	2.70	2.16	0.54	2.70	1728
91.	Link road from Pandit purwa to Gyanchandrapur.	350	0.90	0.72	0.18	0.90	576

(Contd.)

Table 4.16 (*Contd.*)

1	2	3	4	5	6	7	8
92.	Link road from Antipur Link Road to Kadedeen's field.	1000	2.50	2.00	0.50	2.50	1600
93.	Link road in village Mahaso to Devideen's house.	1000	2.50	2.00	0.50	2.50	1600
94.	Link road from Ramdaipur BRO Road to pitch road.	1500	3.25	2.60	0.65	3.25	2080
95.	Kharanja work from Ram Khelawan's house to old bridge.	200	2.00	1.60	0.40	2.00	1280
96.	Link road from Maksood's house Mauhariya link road.	1000	2.50	2.00	0.50	2.50	1600
97.	Link road from Amilaina to Pawan's house.	200	50.00	40.00	10.0	50.00	32000
98.	Drain construction from Nai Abadi to Kudi pond.	100	1.00	0.80	0.20	1.00	640
99.	Link road from Rebha pitch road to Manipur village.	1500	3.50	2.80	0.70	3.50	2240
100.	Link road from Bhagwanpur pitch road to Gurdwara.	100	1.00	0.80	0.20	1.00	640
101.	Soling and soil work from Barban Purwa to Ramdhan Baba.	750	7.50	3.00	4.50	7.50	2400
102.	Soling and soil work from Pandit Purwa to Pratapgarh border.	340	3.50	1.40	2.10	3.50	1120
103.	Soling and soil work from Ramdhan Baba to Kohara Border.	800	8.00	3.20	4.80	8.00	2560
104.	Link road from Old Barban Purwa to Udairaj's house.	200	0.85	0.34	0.51	0.85	272
105.	Link road from Madhav Raj Vaid's house to Pandit Purwa border.	100	1.20	0.48	0.72	1.20	384
106.	Link road from Mahmadpur Sangipur pakki road to Baba's Kuti.	900	2.10	1.68	0.42	2.10	1344
107.	Link road from Haribux Tiwari's Purwa to Pandit's Purwa.	900	2.10	1.68	0.42	2.10	1344
108.	Link road from Baramasi Crossing centre of Ram Nagar Road before Ramkishore Shastri to Ram Saran Maurya's house.	700	1.70	1.36	0.34	1.70	1088
109.	Link road from Ram Sundar Yadav's house to Murali Yadav's field	600	1.60	1.28	0.32	1.60	1024
110.	Soil and Soling work from Mahadev Maurya's House to Chandrabhan Maurya's house.	700	2.90	2.32	0.58	2.90	1856
111.	Soling work from Swami Nath's house to Ram Tahal's house.	400	2.40	0.48	1.92	2.40	384
112.	Kharanza work from Nagar Bridge of Patakhapur in village Patakhapur Kushitali to Anawasiya village.	800	5.60	1.12	4.48	5.60	896
113.	Soil and soling work from Ojha Ka Purwa to Madunpur PWD Road.	500	2.50	1.00	1.50	2.50	800
114.	Soil and soling work from Kohara-II Primary School to Khatri Ramraj Pasi's house.	600	2.60	1.04	1.56	2.60	832
115.	Soil and soling work from Shiv Darshan Maurya's house to Brijendra Maurya's house.	200	1.30	0.52	0.78	1.30	416
116.	Soil and soling work from P.M. Road Dhana Devi Sthan to Ratan Yadav's house.	200	1.30	0.52	0.78	1.30	416
117.	Soil and soling work from Dewri Springi PWD road, Near Badalu Singh's house to PWD road.	800	4.50	1.80	2.70	4.50	1440
118.	Soling work from Ram Pratap's house to Kundawa border.	500	3.60	1.44	2.16	3.60	1152
119.	Link Road from Primary School to Katara.	500	1.50	0.60	0.90	1.50	480
120.	Drain construction from Ram Sajiwan's house to Bhawni's house.	500	4.50	1.80	2.70	4.50	1440

(*Contd.*)

Table 4.16 *(Contd.)*

1	2	3	4	5	6	7	8
121.	Drain Construction from Jagatpal's house to Karamveer's house.	500	4.50	1.80	2.70	4.50	1440
122.	Soling work from Jairam master's house Nanhe Singh's door and Nandu Bhuj's house to Shyam Lal's house.	145	1.40	0.28	1.12	1.40	224
123.	Soling work from Ramgarh Pitch road to Sanjay Singh's house.	50	0.95	0.19	0.76	0.95	152
124.	Soling work from Ram Pratap's house to Jang Bahadur's field.	500	3.99	0.80	3.19	3.99	638
125.	Soling work from Wood Cutting Machine to Gokul Prasad's door.	100	1.00	0.40	0.60	1.00	320
126.	Soling and soil work from Sai Dham Katara to Neeraj's house.	150	1.50	0.60	0.90	1.50	480
127.	Drian construction Pawan Kumar Singh's house Mahmadpur Tiraha pond.	0.00	0.00	0.00	0.00	0.00	000
128.	Link road from Kakawa Sangipur to Vodanar.	1000	2.00	0.80	1.20	2.00	640
129.	Link road from Teliyani to Lalji's Chak.	250	0.50	0.20	0.30	0.50	160
130.	Link road from Loniapur to Lalji's Chak.	200	0.50	0.20	0.30	0.50	160
131.	Drain cleaning work from Badhni Pond to Vasupur village.	2000	2.00	0.80	1.20	2.00	640
132.	Soling work from Bansatti P.M. Road to Mamunnu Tiwari's house.	250	3.00	1.20	1.80	3.00	960
133.	Soling and soil work from Daddu Mishra's house to Ram Dayal's house.	500	5.00	2.00	3.00	5.00	1600
134.	Link Road from Ram Gareeb's house to Damgara Link road.	200	0.75	0.30	0.45	0.75	240
135.	Link Road from Nainaha Link road to Ram Narain's field.	700	1.80	0.72	1.08	1.80	576
136.	Link Road from Ram Narain's field to Ram Pratap's house.	800	2.00	0.80	1.20	2.00	640
137.	Dressing work of Miyadeen's Field.	0.00	0.00	0.00	0.00	0.00	000
138.	Link Road from Ram Prasad and Asha Devi etc.'s field to Munshiganj Gauriganj Road.	250	0.60	0.24	0.36	0.60	192
139.	Link Road from Bhagauti's field to Asha Devi's house.	150	0.40	0.16	0.24	0.40	128
140.	Link Road from Nuwawan Gate to Baba's Kuti.	150	0.45	0.18	0.27	0.45	144
141.	Link Road from Sahdev Maurya's house to Harijan Basti.	300	0.60	0.24	0.36	0.60	191
142.	Link Road from Kodari link road Ramdeo's field to Ram Naresh's field.	600	1.50	0.60	0.90	1.50	480
143.	Link Road from Loniapur link road to Mewalal's field.	500	1.00	0.40	0.60	1.00	320
144.	Link Road from Panna Lal Maurya's house to Shiv Karan Sharma's house.	200	0.45	0.18	0.27	0.45	144
145.	Link Road from Bhusupur to Bhagnahir Ka purwa.	400	1.00	0.40	0.60	1.00	320
146.	Drain digging work from Bhagwanpur Road to Samdatal.	800	2.00	0.80	1.20	2.00	640
147.	Link Road from Koredar's house to R.P. Rai Mod.	300	1.30	0.52	0.78	1.30	416
148.	Kharanja work from Mangalpur tube-well to Paras Nath's tube-well.	300	3.00	1.20	1.80	3.00	960
149.	Drain construction work from Vijay Mishra's house to Bypass turn.	325	3.50	1.40	2.10	3.50	1120
150.	Drain construction work from Daya Shankar Gupta's house to Ramesh Singh's karkhana.	500	5.00	2.00	3.00	5.00	1600
151.	Link Road from Rajesh Maurya's field to Amethi Durgapur.	300	3.00	1.20	1.80	3.00	960
152.	Link Road from Shiv Pujan's house to Santosh's House.	100	0.20	0.08	0.12	0.20	64

(Contd.)

Table 4.16 *(Contd.)*

1	2	3	4	5	6	7	8
153.	Link Road from Bypass to Kewalapur.	1000	2.00	0.80	1.20	2.00	640
154.	Drain digging work from Ram Kewal Kalwaran's purwa to river.	1000	3.00	1.20	1.80	3.00	960
155.	From Madhav Dube's purwa to Shiwala.	500	1.00	0.40	0.60	1.00	320
156.	Driai digging work from Dharmalaya School to Shiv Ji's Kiln.	2 km	2.00	0.80	1.20	2.00	640
157.	Road from Primary School to Jamuna's house.	150	0.50	0.20	0.30	0.50	160
158.	Link Road from Shiv Poojan Singh's field to Lalji Mishra's field.	600	0.75	0.30	0.45	0.75	240
159.	Link Road from Maharaj's pond to Dada's pond.	800	1.00	0.40	0.60	1.00	320
160.	Soling work from Shankarji's Temple to Daddu Mishra house.	300	3.00	1.20	1.80	3.00	960
161.	Link Road from Raj Narain Singh's field to Kartal Singh's field.	900	1.00	0.40	0.60	1.00	320
162.	Link Road from Bypass to Virendra's field.	1000	1.50	0.60	0.90	1.50	480
163.	Link Road from Verma's field to Saraiyan Gaon.	1000	1.50	0.60	0.90	1.50	480
164.	Soling work from Kodari link road to Vanshi Lal's field.	400	4.00	1.60	2.40	4.00	1280
165.	Soling work from Kodari link road to Yadav's Field.	250	2.50	1.00	1.50	2.50	800
166.	Digging work of Bandhwa Baba pond.	40 × 50	4.00	1.60	2.40	4.00	1280
167.	Soling work from Pintu's house to Teri Pakki road.	1000	10.00	4.00	6.00	10.00	3200
168.	Link Road from Ram Naresh's field to bypass.	600	1.00	0.40	0.60	1.00	320
169.	Drain digging work from Raipur Phulwari to Samada Pond.	1500	1.50	0.60	0.90	1.50	480
170.	Drain digging work from Nuwawan Canal to Shri's field.	1200	1.20	0.48	0.72	1.20	384
171.	Drain digging work from Palokhari pond to Malati river.	1000	2.00	0.80	1.20	2.00	640
172.	Soling work from Gopalpur Road to Chhedi Verma's house.	250	2.00	0.80	1.20	2.00	640
173.	Drain construction from Ram Chandra's house to Kundwa pond.	250	3.50	1.40	2.10	3.50	1120
174.	Link road from Gopalpur to Parsauli village.	800	1.00	0.40	0.60	1.00	320
175.	Link road from Gopalpur Sri Datt Tiwari's house to Bypass.	600	0.75	0.30	0.45	0.75	240
176.	Link road from Amethi Dhammaur Road to Valipur Village.	500	0.75	0.30	0.45	0.75	240
177.	Soling work from Gopalpur link road to Pasi basti.	200	2.00	0.80	1.20	2.00	640
178.	Drain construction from Amethi Dhammaur Rod to Mother Gita School	200	2.00	0.80	1.20	2.00	640
179.	Drain construction from Ajay's house.	500	1.50	0.60	0.90	1.50	480
180.	Soling work from Pure Prem to Gurubux's Purwa.	500	3.00	1.20	1.80	3.00	960
181.	Drain construction from road bank.	400	2.00	0.80	1.20	2.00	640
182.	Drain construction from Tej Bahadur Saroj's house to Arjun Singh's house.	300	4.00	1.60	2.40	4.00	1280
183.	Link road from P.M. Road in Village Panchayat Darakha to Arjun Singh's house.	350	1.30	0.52	0.78	1.30	416
184.	Soling work from Mahuwa Bojhi to Kallu link road.	400	4.00	1.60	2.40	4.00	1280
185.	Soling work from Sarai Hirmati P.M. Road to Datta Bariyar J.H. School road.	750	6.00	2.40	3.60	6.00	1920
186.	Link road from Pure Shiv Gulam to Pure Modi link road.	1000	2.00	0.80	1.20	2.00	640

(Contd.)

Table 4.16 (*Contd.*)

1	2	3	4	5	6	7	8
187.	Link road from Darakha Deeh to Pure Dulla pond.	600	1.60	0.64	0.96	1.60	512
188.	From Ganga Ram Pandey's house to Primary School.	500	0.00	0.00	0.00	0.00	000
189.	Drain construction work from Ganga Ram Pandey house to Ram Chandra's house.	200	0.00	0.00	0.00	0.00	000
190.	Link road from Shambhu Nath's Machine to Garden.	500	1.50	0.60	0.90	1.50	480
191.	Kharanza work from Kanta Yadav's house to west.	300	0.00	0.00	0.00	0.00	000
192.	Link road from Kakawa road via 8 AG Tube-well to Ismail's house.	0.00	0.00	0.00	0.00	0.00	000
193.	Link road from Naugawan Pitch road to Ramdev's field.	1500	2.50	1.00	1.50	2.50	800
194.	Link road from Santosh Tiwari's house to Dablu Doctor's house.	110	0.85	0.34	0.51	0.85	272
195.	Digging and cleaning of drain from Dewata Tiwari's field to Ram Sagara Taal.	500	0.50	0.20	0.30	0.50	160
196.	Link road from from Gayadeen Yadav's Tube-welll to Banduveer Baba.	700	1.50	0.60	0.90	1.50	480

The soling work from Prabgaon to Lavkush House and Pithipur link road to centre of Gaderi Road and Kakawa Amethi road to Fakir's house and Prakash Singh's house to Dabbu Mishra house has been proposed and a sum of Rs. 13.0 lakh and there will be 656 man-days employment generation to the MNREGA Job Card Holders in Amethi.

The construction of link road from Babaganj Bazar to Baltu Baba School Sarai Hirmati to Datta Bariyar School, Amethi Road to Railway line, Ram Laut to Lalji Mishra's field, Ram Deen's well to Kakawa-Kohara road, Maharaj's pond to Data's garden etc. for which Rs. 8.20 lakh amount expenditures has been proposed and it will generate 3427 man-days job generation under the MNREGA programe in Amethi.

Nala digging, drain construction, and Pond digging work has been proposed for which a sum of Rs. 11.51 lakh and construction of it will generate 5874 man-days employment in the respective village panchayat.

It has been proposed to construct link road from canal border to Chauraha, Shakkargarh Bazar to Maboth's house, Bhawani Bax Purwa to Hulasi Purwa, Hari Bux Purwa to Old Pandit Purwa, Chaubeypur to Barban's Purwa, Dandupur to Bhupatipur, Badaicha Pond to Dandupur Charagaah, Vindo Singh's Tube-well to Rafiq's Tube-well, Milan's Chakki to Harijan Basti, Kharanza Work from Rebha Shyam's house to Nanda's house, link road from Dhrubraj Machine to Chhedi Maurya's house, Baltu Baba to Naraini Border, Nahar to Sharda Devi School, Chhawani Link Road to Ambedkar Park, Yunus Shop to Chhawani Masjid and Angad Flour Mill to Ram Kumar Maurya's door for which a sum of Rs. 33.10 lakh budget has been allocated with the view to generate 21184 man-days employment generation of the MNREGA Job card holders.

The drain work from Kandhu's house to Gadai, soling work from Hari Bux Purwa to school, drain cleaning from Ram Nagar Mafi to Kutur Bandha and to river, digging of Malli Tara Pond, digging work Barai Pond, drain construction from Swami Nath's house to Ram Tahal Maurya's House has been incorporated in the work plan of the Amethi Block for which a sum of Rs. 24.19 lakh has been earmarked from the Block Yojana and it is proposed to generate 6448 man-days employment generation for the MNREGA Job Card Holders at village level.

The soling work from Hari Bux Purwa to school, Pintu's hosue to Teri road, Chhawai road to Kedar Shukla's house, Munna Bhujwa's house to Pramukh Ram Shanker's field and Baij Nath house to Pitch road for which Rs. 15.64 lakh budget has been allocated and it has also been planned to generate 4230 man-days employment generation to the MNREGA Job card Holders of the respective village panchayat.

It has been proposed in the Block Development Planning to construct link road from Ram Kishore's water tank to Ram Saran's house, Kodari Road to Sri Ram's field Nuwawan road to Dayaram's House, Jagdish's house to Kodari Link road and up to Bairagi's field, Dubepur Link Road to Brijlal's house, Sarai Khema-Dandupur road to Bhupatipur road, Bacaich Pond to Sarai Khema to Dandupur Charagaah, Ram Sunder's house to Shambhu Nath's house, Pratapgarh road to Sanjay Sharma's house, Jagdish Pandey's field to Saheb Bux Singh's field, Gurbux Purwa to Ranjeet's field, Amethi-Suiya Road to Kithawar road, canal culvert to Ram Baran's House, etc. has been planned for which a sum of Rs. 24.29 lakh budget has been earmarked with the view to generate 16340 man-days employment to the MNREGA Job card holders belonging to the respective village panchayats of the Amethi Block.

It has also been planned to dig pond in the land plot No. 537 and drain construction from Rajendra Dube's well to pond, cleaning of drain from Ram Nagar Mafi to Kutur Bandh, Drain digging from Pure Kalwaran to Malati River, cleaning and digging of minor from Kakawa road to Lalati river, drain construction from Ram Sunder's house to Chhedi Yadav's house, Bishesharganj Market to Interlocking and Shivram Singh's house to Ram Garh Saraiya Road has been incorporated in the Block development planning for which a sum of Rs. 13.35 lakh budget has been allocated and it is planned to create 5512 man-days employment generation to the MNREGA Job card Holders of the respective village panchayats of the Amethi Block.

Thus, it has been recorded that the Block Development planning of the Amethi Block has proposed work plan and allocated Rs. 158.95 lakh budget for the different programmes under the Mahatma Gandhi National Rural Employment Guarantee Act (MNREGA) with the view to generate 77576 man-days employment to the Below Poverty Line (BPL) MNREGA Job Card Holders of the Amethi Block.

In spite of the above Block Panchayat of Amethi Block has incorporated additional work plan through necessary amendments in the work plan. The Block Panchayat has incorporated 124 additional work plan and a sum of Rs. 326.09 lakh budget has been allocated in the work plan of the Block Panchayat Amethi with the view to generate 135389 man-days employment for the Mahatma Gandhi National Rural Employment Guarantee Act Job Card Holders belonging to different villages of the Amethi Block with the view to not only generate 100 days guaranteed jobs but also to increase their income to improve their socio-economic conditions. The details of the construction work under Mahatma Gandhi National Rural Employment Guarantee Act (MNREGA) for the Amethi Block planned by Block Panchayat has been mentioned in Table 4.16.

7. VILLAGE DEVELOPMENT PLANNING

Village Development planning has been planned formulated at village panchayat level. The village panchayat and members of the village Panchayat Committee in open meeting decides the needs and requirements of the villagers under the Chairmanship of the elected Village Pradhans of the village panchayats. The need based people's participatory village development planning is being formulated as per the policy, guidelines of the Government. The top most important priority of the Government has been to ensure

Table 4.17: Mahatma Gandhi National Rural Employment Guarantee Act (MNREGA) Work Plan 2012-13

Sl.No.	Village Panchayat	Cost	Labour	Materials	Total	Man-days
1	2	3	4	5	6	7
1.	Nuwawan	48.05	38.44	9.61	48.05	30752
2.	Ramgarh	20.20	11.12	9.08	20.20	8896
3.	Jangal Ram Nagar	40.95	32.76	8.19	40.95	26208
4.	Dehara	83.85	62.06	21.79	83.85	49648
5.	Himmatgarh	62.70	48.84	13.86	62.70	39072
6.	Chaturbhujpur	20.60	12.22	8.38	20.60	9776
7.	Benipur	27.20	19.42	7.78	27.20	15536
8.	Parsawan	41.35	33.08	8.27	41.35	26464
9.	Katara Maharani	50.40	34.62	15.78	50.40	27696
10	Katara Phulkunwar	63.90	51.12	12.78	63.90	40896
11.	Dedhpasar	74.83	46.83	28.00	74.83	37461
12.	Raipur Phulwari	41.45	30.88	10.57	41.45	24704
13.	Hathkila	36.65	19.78	16.87	36.65	15824
14.	Mahaso	63.10	48.56	14.54	63.10	38848
15.	Loniapur	85.50	41.46	44.04	85.50	33168
16.	Korari Girdharshah	58.00	32.51	25.49	58.00	26008
17.	Umapur Ganapatti	46.50	32.03	14.47	46.50	26808
18.	Naraini	78.92	50.51	28.41	78.92	40405
19.	Gaderi	44.66	34.59	10.08	44.66	28857
20	Maharajpur	26.59	15.78	10.81	26.59	17415
21.	Mahmoodpur	126.21	100.97	25.24	126.21	80774
22.	Nainaha	43.55	34.84	8.71	43.55	27872
23.	Purab Gaon	59.62	47.70	11.92	59.62	38157
24.	Rebha	91.80	63.60	28.20	91.80	50880
25.	Kherauna	48.65	27.22	21.43	48.65	20368
26.	Sarai Khema	42.40	23.18	19.22	42.40	18416
27.	Trilokpur	27.08	16.47	11.21	27.08	13179
28.	Ramdaipur	31.85	12.19	19.66	31.85	9752
29.	Gangauli	17.45	9.46	7.99	17.45	7568
30	Raidaipur	35.60	28.48	7.12	35.60	22784
31.	Kakawa	84.80	53.59	31.21	84.80	42872
32.	Mahmadpur	50.93	40.74	10.19	50.93	32595
33.	Agahar	28.90	18.44	10.46	28.90	14752
34.	Saidpur	72.33	42.77	29.56	72.33	34219
35.	Bhusahari	54.84	42.97	11.87	54.84	34378
36.	Bhaganpur	100.95	51.74	49.21	100.95	41392
37.	Darakha	26.29	10.35	15.94	26.29	8282
38.	Loharata	70.25	47.20	23.05	70.25	37760
39.	Mochawa	69.44	40.24	29.20	69.44	32194
40.	Tala	52.00	36.38	15.62	52.00	29104
41.	Saraiya Duban	33.65	21.31	12.34	33.65	17048
42.	Kushi Tali	19.70	13.00	6.70	19.70	10400
43.	Kohara	63.03	43.20	19.83	63.03	34560
44.	Dhadhudhar	82.29	53.62	28.67	82.29	42898
	Total	**2349.62**	**1576.27**	**773.34**	**2349.62**	**1266645**

100 days guaranteed job for the Below Poverty Line of the Amethi Block. Various village panchayats of the Amethi Block have formulated their need based village development planning for the implementation of various priority works under the Mahatma Gandhi National Rural Employment Guarantee Act to generate job and increase the income of the deprived rural poor multitudes in Amethi. An effort has been made in this study to analyze the various activities planned by the respective village panchayats for the year 2012-13 in Amethi. The details of the Mahatma Gandhi National Rural Employment Guarantee Act (MNREGA) Work Plan for the Financial Year 2012-13 at village panchayat level has been mentioned in detail in Table 4.17.

7.1 Village Panchayat Nuwawan

Flood Control and digging of ponds, nala, digging and cleaning of drains, construction of link road, soling and kharanza work has been planned in the village panchayat Nuwawan for which Rs. 48.05 lakh budget has been allocated with the view generate 30752 man-days employment for MNREGA Job Card Holders.

7.2 Village Panchayat Ramgarh

Water storage, water conservation, levelling and land development, flood control, minor irrigation and rural link road work has been identified for which Rs. 20.20 lakh amount has been allocated with the view to generate 8896 man-days employment for the interested MNREGA Job card holders in the village panchayat Ramgarh.

7.3 Village Panchayat Jangal Ram Nagar

Renovation and construction of the Rural link road, land development, land levelling, cleaning of drainage and construction of *Nalis* etc. has been planned in the village panchayat Jangal Ram Nagar for which a sum of Rs. 40.95 lakh has been allocated with the view to generate 26208 man-days ensured job to the MNREGA Job card holders in the village panchayats Jangal Ram Nagar of Amethi.

7.4 Village Panchayat Dehara

Minor Irrigation, water conservation and storage of water, rural link road, land levelling and afforestation programme has been planned in the village panchayat Dehara for which Rs., 83.85 lakh has been allocated with the view to generate 49648 man-days employment for the MNREGA Job card holders in village panchayat Dehara.

7.5 Village Panchayat Himmatgarh

Land development, land levelling, water conservation and water storage, minor irrigation, flood control, construction of rural link road has been planned and Rs. 62.70 lakhs budget has been allocated with the view to generate 39072 man-days employment for the MNREGA Job card holders in the village panchayat Himmatgarh.

7.6 Village Panchayat Chaturbhujpur

Land levelling, land development, flood control, construction of rural link road activities has been planned and Rs. 20.60 lakh budget has been allocated with the view to generate 9776 man-days employment in the village panchayat Chaturbhujpur.

7.7 Village Panchayat Benipur

Construction of rural link road, water conservation, water storage, minor irrigation and construction drain has been planned and Rs. 27.90 lakh budget has been allocated with the view to generate employment of 15536 man-days for MNREGA Job card holders in the village panchayat Benipur.

7.8 Village Panchayat Parsawan

Water conservation, water storage, construction of rural link road, minor irrigation work has been planned and Rs. 41.35 lakh budget has been allocated with the view to generate employment of 26464 man-days for MNREGA Job card holders in the village panchayat Parsawan of Amethi Block.

7.9 Village Panchayat Katra Maharani

Minor irrigation, water storage, water conservation, flood control and construction of rural link road etc. work has been planned and Rs. 50.40 lakh budget has been allocated with the view to generate employment of 27696 man-days for MNREGA Job card holders in the village panchayat Katra Maharani of the Amethi Block.

7.10 Village Panchayat Katra Phulkunwar

Land development, land levelling, construction of rural link road, renovation of traditional water resources, drought prone and afforestation, flood control, water conservation and water storage work has been planned and Rs. 63.90 lakh budget has been allocated with the view to generate employment of 40896 man-days for MNREGA Job card holders in the village panchayat Katra Phulkunwar to Amethi Block.

7.11 Village Panchayat Dedhpasar

Water conservation, water storage, land development, land levelling, renovation of traditional water resources, construction of rural link road has been planned and a sum of Rs. 74.83 lakh budget has been allocated with the view to generate 37461 man-days employment for MNREGA Job card holders in Dedhpasar village panchayat.

7.12 Village Panchayat Raipur Phulwari

Construction of rural link road, water conservation, water storage, drought prone and afforestation, Flood Control, renovation of traditional water resources programme has been planned for which Rs. 41.45 lakh budget has been allocated with the view to generate 24704 man-days employment for MNREGA Job card holders in Raipur Phulwari village panchayat.

7.13 Village Panchayat Hathkila

Drought prone and afforestation, water storage, water conservation, flood control, land development, land levelling, construction of rural link road has been planned for which a sum of Rs. 36.65 lakh budget has been allocated with the view to generate 15824 man-days employment for MNREGA Job card holders in the village panchayat Hathkila.

7.14 Village Panchayat Mahaso

Construction of Rural link road, drought prone, afforestation, flood control, land development, land levelling, constsruction of Nali work has been planned and Rs. 63.105

lakh budget has been allocated with the view to generate 38848 man-days employment for MNREGA Job card holders in village panchayat Mahaso.

7.15 Village Panchayat Loniapur

Water conservation, storage, drought prone and afforestation, minor irrigation, land development, land levelling, construction of rural link road programmes have been planned for which Rs. 85.50 lakh budget has been allocated with the view to generate 33168 man-days employment for MNREGA Job card holders in village panchayat Loniapur of Amethi.

7.16 Village Panchayat Korari Girdhar Shah

Water conservation, water storage, drought prone and afforestation, minor irrigation, land development and land levelling, renovation of water resources, construction of rural link road work has been planned and a sum of Rs. 58.00 lakh budget has been allocated with the view to generate 26008 man-days employment for MNREGA Job card holders in the village panchayat Korari Girdhar Shah.

7.17 Village Panchayat Umapur Ganapatti

Construction of rural link road, water conservation, water storage, land development, land levelling work has been planned for which a sum of Rs. 46.66 lakh budget has been allocated with the view to generate 25912 man-days employment for MNREGA Job card holders in village panchayat Umapur Ganapatti.

7.18 Village Panchayat Naraini

Water conservation, water storage, drought prone, afforestation, minor irrigation, renovation of traditional water resources construction of rural road and construction of *Nali* and *kharanza*, road work have been planned and a sum of Rs. 78.92 lakh budget has been allocated with the view to generate 40405 man-days employment for MNREGA Job card holders in village panchayat Naraini of Amethi Block.

7.19 Village Panchayat Gaderi

Construction of rural link road, drought prone and afforestation, water conservation and water storage, land levelling land development and flood control work have been planned for which a sum of Rs. 44.66 lakh budget has been allocated with the view to generate 28857 man-days employment for MNREGA Job card holders in village panchayat Gaderi.

7.20 Village Panchayat Maharajpur

Drought prone, afforestation, water conservation, water storage, construction of rural link road, land development, land levelling work have been planned for which a sum of Rs. 26.56 lakh budget has been allocated with the view to generate 17415 man-days employment for MNREGA Job card holders in village panchayat Maharajpur.

7.21 Village Panchayat Mahmoodpur

Water conservation, water storage, drought prone, afforestation, construction of rural link road, flood control, land development and land levelling work have been planned for which a sum of Rs. 126.21 lakh budget has been allocated with the view to generate 80774 man-days employment for MNREGA Job card holders in village panchayat Mahmoodpur.

7.22 Village Panchayat Nainaha

Water conservation, water storage, drought prone, afforestation, minor irrigation, flood control, land development, land levelling, construction of rural link road work have been planned for which a sum of Rs. 43.55 lakh budget has been allocated with the view to generate 27872 man-days employment for MNREGA Job card holders in village panchayat Nainaha.

7.23 Village Panchayat Purabgaon

Land Development, land levelling, water conservation, water storage, minor irrigation, construction of rural link road work have been planned for which a sum of Rs. 59.62 lakh budget has been allocated with the view to generate 38157 man-days employment for MNREGA Job card holders in village panchayat Purabgaon of the Amethi Block.

7.24 Village Panchayat Rebha

Water conservation, construction of rural link road, minor irrigation, drought prone and afforestation work have been planned for which a sum of Rs. 91.80 lakh budget has been allocated with the view to generate 50880 man-days employment for MNREGA Job card holders in village panchayat Rebha.

7.25 Village Panchayat Kherauna

Construction of rural link road, minor irrigation, land development, land levelling, flood control, renovation of traditional water resources, etc. have been planned for which a sum of Rs. 48.65 lakh budget has been allocated with the view to generate 20368 man days employment for MNREGA Job card holders in the village panchayat Kherauna of Amethi.

7.26 Village Panchayat Sarai Khema

Water conservation, flood control, construction of rural link road, land development, land levelling, minor irrigation etc. work have been planned for which a sum of Rs. 42.40 lakh budget has been allocated with the view to generate 18416 man-days employment to the MNREGA Job card holders in the village panchayat Sarai Khema.

7.27 Village Panchayat Trilokpur

Construction of rural link road, water conservation, water storage, land development and land levelling work have been planned for which a sum of Rs. 27.08 lakh budget has been allocated with the view to generate 13179 man-days employment to the MNREGA Job card holders in the village panchayat Trilokpur of the Amethi Block.

7.28 Village Panchayats Ramdaipur

Water conservation, storage of water, construction of rural link road, land levelling and land development, minor irrigation work have been planned for which a sum of Rs. 31.85 lakh budget has been allocated with the view to generate 9757 man-days employment to the MNREGA Job card holders in the village panchayat Ramdaipur of Amethi.

7.29 Village Panchayat Gangauli

Construction of rural link road, land development, land levelling, flood control work have been planned for which a sum of Rs. 17.45 lakh budget has been allocated with the view to generate 7568 man days job for the MNREGA Job card holders in the village panchayat Gangauli of Amethi Block.

7.30 Village Panchayat Raidaipur

Construction of rural link road, land development, land levelling work have been planned for which a sum of Rs. 35.60 lakh budget has been allocated with the view to generate 22784 man-days employment to the MNREGA Job card holders in the village panchayat Raidaipur of Amethi.

7.31 Village Panchayat Kakawa

Water conservation, drought prone, afforestation, minor irrigation, construction of rural link road, land development, land levelling, flood control, horticulture plantation work have been planned for which a sum of Rs. 84.80 lakh budget has been allocated with the view to generate 42872 man-days employment to the MNREGA Job card holders in the village panchayat Kakawa of Amethi.

7.32 Village Panchayat Mahmadpur

Water conservation, construction of rural link road, minor irrigation, land levelling, land development, horticulture, plantation work have been planned for which a sum of Rs. 50.93 lakh budget has been allocated with the view to generate 32595 man-days employment to the MNREGA Job card holders in the village panchayat Mahmadpur of the Amethi Block.

7.33 Village Panchayat Agahar

Construction of rural link road, land development, land levelling, conservation of water, minor irrigation work have been planned for which a sum of Rs. 28.90 lakh budget has been allocated with the view to generate 14752 man-days employment to the MNREGA Job card holders in the village panchayat Agahar of Amethi Block.

7.34 Village Panchayat Saidpur

Water conservation, construction of rural link road, land development, land levelling, minor irrigation work have been planned for which a sum of Rs. 72.33 lakh budget has been allocated with the view to generate 34219 man-days employment for the MNREGA Job card holders in the village panchayat Saidpur of the Amethi Block.

7.35 Village Panchayat Bhusahari

Land development, land levelling, construction of rural link road, minor irrigation work have been planned for which a sum of Rs. 54.84 lakh budget has been allocated with the view to generate 34378 man-days job for the MNREGA Job card holders in the village panchayat Bhusahari of Amethi.

7.36 Village Panchayat Bhaganpur

Horticultural plantation, water conservation, minor irrigation, construction of rural link road, land development, land levelling, flood control, construction of *nali* work have been planned for which a sum of Rs. 100.95 lakh budget has been allocated with the view to generate 41399 man-days employment for the MNREGA Job card holders in the village panchayat Bhaganpur of the Amethi Block.

7.37 Village Panchayat Darakha

Construction of rural link road, land development, land levelling, construction of *nali* etc. work has been planned for and a sum of Rs. 26.29 lakh budget has been allocated with the view to generate 8282 man-days employment for the MNREGA Job card holders in the village panchayat Darakha of the Amethi Block.

7.38 Village Panchayat Loharata

Water conservation, water storage, construction of rural link road, minor irrigation, drought prone and afforestation, land levelling and land development work have been planned for which a sum of Rs. 70.25 lakh budget has been allocated with the view to generate 37760 man-days employment to the MNREGA Job card holders in the village panchayat Loharata of the Amethi Block.

7.39 Village Panchayat Mochawa

Construction of rural link road, land development, land levelling, minor irrigation, flood control work have been planned for which a sum of Rs. 69.44 lakh budget has been allocated with the view to generate 32194 man-days employment to the MNREGA Job card holders in the village panchayat Mochawa of the Amethi Block.

7.40 Village Panchayat Tala

Water conservation, water storage, construction of rural link road, flood control, minor irrigation, land development, land levelling work have been planned for which a sum of

Rs. 52.00 lakh budget has been allocated with the view to generate 29104 man-days employment to the MNREGA Job card holders in the village panchayat Tala of the Amethi Block.

7.41 Village Panchayat Saraiya Duban

Construction of rural link road, renovation of traditional water resources, land development, land levelling, minor irrigation work have been planned for which a sum of Rs. 33.65 lakh budget has been allocated with the view to generate 17048 man-days employment to the MNREGA Job card holders in the village panchayat Saraiya Duban of Amethi Block.

7.42 Village Panchayat Kushi Tali

Construction of rural link road, water conservation, water storage, drought prone and afforestation, land development, land levelling work have been planned for which a sum of Rs. 19.70 lakh budget has been allocated with the view to generate 10400 man-days job for the MNREGA Job card holders in the village panchayat Kushi Tali of Amethi.

7.43 Village Panchayat Kohara

Minor irrigation, construction of rural link road, land development, land levelling, drought prone work, water conservation and water storage work have been planned for which a sum of Rs. 63.03 lakh budget has been allocated with the view to generate 34560 man-days employment to the MNREGA Job card holders in the village panchayat Kohara of Amethi.

7.44 Village Panchayat Dhadhudhar

Water conservation, water storage, minor irrigation, construction of drainage, construction of rural link road, land development, land levelling work have been planned for which a sum of Rs. 82.29 lakh budget has been allocated with the view to generate 42898 man-days employment to the MNREGA Job card holders in the village panchayat Dhadhudhar of the Amethi Block.

It has been recorded that at village panchayat level in Amethi Block various activities planned under the Mahatma Gandhi National Rural Employment Guarantee Act (MNREGA) total estimated cost of the proposed work has been Rs. 2349.62 lakh for the Amethi Block of which Rs. 1576.27 lakh has been for the labour cost and sum of Rs. 733.34 lakh has been allocated for the material cost. Proposed works of 44 village panchayats of Amethi Block has proposed and allocated total budget of Rs. 234.62 lakh with the view to generate 1266645 man-days employment under the Mahatma Gandhi National Rural Employment Guarantee Act (MNREGA) job card holders belonging to different village panchayats of Amethi.

8. PEOPLE'S PARTICIPATORY NEED BASED VILLAGE DEVELOPMENT PLANNING

An effort has been made in this study to carry out door to door survey to obtain needs of the people, their willing consent and interest who have been deprived of the Welfare

Programme launched by the Government. The willing consent and interest of the village people has been incorporated for its inclusion in the work plan of the village panchayat-block panchayat-district panchayat.

It is known fact that three-fourth population of Amethi depends on agriculture in Amethi is agrarian economy, therefore, raising agricultural productivity is crucial for raising income and living standard of the rural people. An increase in the agricultural productivity and techno-scientific transformation in the agricultural activities may provide other benefits to an underdeveloped economy.

At the sustenance level, most of the output is for more consumption and a few stable foods and crops are the chief source of food intake. The agricultural productivity is low and only the simplest traditional methods and tools are used. The capital investment is minimal and the land labourers are principal factors of production. The law of diminishing returns is in operation as more labour is applied to shrinking parcels of land. With technological institutions, rigid social institutions, fragmented and non-availability of markets and infrastructure like warehousing, poor transportation net works between rural to urban markets of access to institutional credit facilities and irrigation tends to inhibit the process of transaction from traditional to commercial farming.

Despite the relative backwardness of agricultural production technologies, given the static nature of the present environment, the uncertainty that surround them, the farmers in subsistence sector do behave in a rational manner when confronted with stress alternative opportunities.

The retarded growth rate of agricultural productivity on the one hand and the increasing demand of food associated rapid population growth on the other and the growing need for additional income by the farmers in order to meet their other requirements have thus become a pressure on land.

The cropping pattern indicates, the production of different crops at a point of time, which undergoes changes with the change in the agricultural prices, technology, market demand, government policies and other related factors. It is also influenced by agro-climatic conditions. The changes in the cropping pattern may reflect the influence of changes in demand arising from an increase in income, population and also development of agro-industries. With the rising income the demand for non-food-crops, may increase relatively faster and among the crops, demand may shift towards relatively superior cereals. Thus, the changes in the cropping pattern may reveal the stage of agricultural development in the nature of the economy of Amehti.

In view of the above an effort has been made to analyse the need based people participatory village development planning for 44 village panchayats covering 82 revenue villages along with 377 purwas/tolas/hamlet villages of Amethi.

8.1 Required MNREGA Job Cards

During the door-to-door survey it has been observed that several Below Poverty Line poor people have not yet achieved the Mahatma Gandhi National Rural Employment Guarantee Act (MNREGA) Job Cards with the view to get benefit for 100 day guaranteed job under the MNREGA scheme. The deprived Below Poverty Line down trodden people surviving in the various village panchayats of Amethi are still awaiting to get MNREGA Job Card for sustained employment as per guidclines of Government. Interested Below Poverty Line persons interested to obtain MNREGA Job Card has been mentioned in Table 4.18. The proportionate distribution of needy MNREGA Job Card persons at village panchayat level in Amethi had been depicted in **Map 4.17.** It has been noticed

Table 4.18: Need Based Village Development Planning, Amethi

Sl. No.	Villages	MNREGA Job Cards	Schools	Tube-well Borings	Hand Pumps	Sports/Youth Programmes	Primary Health Centres	Women & Child Development Programe	Scheduled Caste Welfare Programmes
1	2	3	4	5	6	7	8	9	10
1.	Katra Maharani	60	1	25	15	1	2	1	1
2.	Sarai Khema	85	1	35	18	1	2	1	2
3.	Trilokpur	65	1	65	20	1	2	1	2
4.	Ramdaipur	80	2	50	25	1	2	1	2
5.	Jangal Ram Nagar	150	3	65	25	1	1	1	2
6.	Benipur	32	1	22	14	1	1	1	1
7.	Parsawan	50	1	25	15	1	1	1	1
8.	Mahmoodpur	50	1	35	15	1	2	1	1
9.	Raipur Fulwari	50	1	30	15	1	2	1	1
10.	Umapur Ganapatti	60	1	40	20	1	2	1	1
11.	Bhaganpur	80	2	15	30	1	1	1	1
12.	Tala	70	1	42	18	1	2	1	1
13.	Kushi Tali	60	2	40	20	1	2	1	1
14.	Loharta	40	1	10	15	1	1	1	1
15.	Darkha	75	1	28	25	1	1	1	1
16.	Mochwa	50	1	40	18	1	1	1	1
17.	Nuwawan	75	2	40	20	1	2	1	1
18.	Loniapur	42	1	22	18	1	2	1	1
19.	Kherauna	60	2	25	22	1	1	1	1
20.	Katra Phulkunwar	50	2	25	20	1	1	1	1
21.	Hathkila	50	1	20	32	1	1	1	1
22.	Rebha	60	1	30	18	1	2	1	1
23.	Raidaipur	45	1	25	10	1	2	1	1
24.	Korari Girdhar Shah	80	2	40	22	1	1	1	1
25.	Dedhpasar	60	1	25	30	1	2	1	1
26.	Mahaso	40	1	20	15	1	1	1	1
27.	Gangauli	75	1	35	40	1	2	1	1
28.	Dhadhudhar	60	1	30	15	1	1	1	1
29.	Gaderi	80	2	50	46	2	1	1	1
30.	Bhusahari	86	1	26	42	1	2	1	1
31.	Purabgaon	40	1	20	15	1	1	1	1
32.	Chaturbhujpur	85	2	25	45	2	1	1	1
33.	Mahrajpur	35	1	25	15	1	1	1	1
34.	Aghar	75	2	23	30	1	1	1	1
35.	Saidpur	45	1	32	48	1	1	1	1
36.	Kakwa	60	3	28	53	1	2	1	1
37.	Saraiya Duban	70	2	45	18	1	1	1	1
38.	Kohra	60	2	20	25	1	1	1	1
39.	Mahmadpur	50	1	25	15	1	1	1	1
40.	Naraini	75	2	40	20	1	1	1	1
41.	Nainaha	60	1	25	15	1	1	1	1
42.	Ramgarh	80	1	40	25	1	1	1	1
43.	Himmatgarh	45	2	35	18	1	1	1	1
44.	Dehara	75	1	40	35	1	1	1	1
	Amethi Block	**2775**	**62**	**1403**	**1035**	**46**	**61**	**44**	**48**

that the highest more than 100 number of needy MNREGA Job card holders has been found in the village panchayat Ram Nagar while medium between 70 to 100 number of needy MNREGA Job card persons has been found in Ramdaipur, Sarai Khema, Bhaganpur, Tala, Darakha, Nuwawan, Korari Girdhar Shah, Gangauli, Bhusahari, Ramgarh, Dehara, Gaderi, Chaturbhujpur, Naraini, Agahar and Saraiya Duban village panchayats. Low between 40 to 70 number of interested MNREGA Job card who have not been included in the MNREGA Job Card holders list has been found in Katra Maharani, Trilokpur, Parsawan, Raipur Phulwari, Kherauna, Katra Phulkunwar,

Hathkila, Dedhpasar, Rebha, Loniapur, Raidaipur, Mahaso, Umapur Ganapatti, Loharata, Purabgaon, Nainaha, Saidpur Kakawa, Kohara and Mahmadpur village panchayats while very low less than 40 number of need MNREGA Job card interested persons has been found in the Benipur and Mahrajpur village panchayats of the Amethi Block. It has been recorded that there are 2775 interested persons deprived of getting MNREGA Job Cards through village panchayats in the Amethi Block.

8.2 Required Number of Schools

In fact the Government has established schools at village level as per the population and other norms of the Government but the constantly and rapidly ever increasing population requires more number of schools at village level although some private schools have been opened but it could not fulfil the aspirations of the local people and the poor people cannot afford the hefty fees charged by these mushroomed schools at village level. Therefore, it is necessary to open and establish more number of schools at village level in Amethi. Required more number of schools at village panchayat level in Amethi has been mentioned in Table 4.18. It has been noticed that opening of 3 more schools are required in the village panchayats Kakawa, Jangal Ram Nagar and two number of more schools establishment are recorded in Himmatgarh, Naraini, Gaderi, Agahar, Chaturbhujpur, Korari Girdhar Shah, Katra Phulkunwar, Kherauna, Nuwawan, Kushi Tali, Bhaganpur, Ramdaipur village panchayats while establishment of one more new schools are required in the Katra Maharani, Sarai Khema, Trilokpur, Benipur, Parsawan, Mahmoodpur, Raipur Phulwari, Umapur Ganapatti, Tala, Loharata, Darakah, Mochawa, Loniapur, Hathkila, Rebha, Raidaipur, Dedhpasar, Mahaso, Gangauli, Dhandhudhar, Bhusahari, Purabgaon, Saidpur, Maharajpur, Nainaha, Ramgarh and Dehara Village panchayats of the Amehti Block. Thus there are 62 more new schools required to be established in the various village panchayats of the Amethi based on the ever increasing growing population at village panchayat level.

8.3 Required Tube-well Borings

Field to field level survey and individual interactions has been carried out for requirements of new Tube-well Borings because the minor irrigation department of Government of Uttar Pradesh has been engaged in the subsidized Tube-well Borings in the field of small and marginal farmers belonging to Below Poverty Line families. It has been desired by most of the farmers of village panchayats for getting support of Tube-well Borings as per the norms of the Government. The required number of Tube-well borings at village panchayat level in Amethi has been mentioned in Table 4.18. The proportionate distribution of required number of Tube-well borings at village panchayat level has been mentioned in **Map 4.18.** It has been recorded that more than 60 number of Tube-well borings are required in Trilokpur, Jangal Ram Nagar village panchayats while medium between 40 to 60 number of Tube-well borings are required in Ramdaipur, Kushi Tali, Tala, Umapur Ganapatti, Mochawa, Nuwawan, Korari Girdhar Shah, Gaderi, Ramgarh, Dehara, Naraini and Saraiya Duban village panchayats of Amethi. Low between 20 to 40 number of Tube-well borings are required in Katra Marahatni, Sarai Khema, Benipur, Mahmoodpur, Parsawan, Kherauna, Raipur Phulwari, Katra Phulkunwar, Dedhpasar, Rebha, Mahaso, Loniapur, Gangauli, Bhusahari, Himmatgarh, Dhandhudhar, Purabgaon, Nainaha, Mahrajpur, Chaturbhujpur, Agahar, Saidpur, Kakawa, Kohara and Mahmadpur village panchayats. Very low less than 20 number of Tube-well Borings has been required in the Bhaganpur and Loharata village panchayats of the Amethi Block.

8.4 Required Number of Hand Pumps

Government has installed India Mark-II Hand Pumps through its various schemes at village level in Amethi but the increasing demand of ever growing population in the newly developing settlements it has become an important task to install more number of Hand Pumps in the remote villages of Amethi. Required number of Hand Pumps at village panchayat level has been mentioned in Table 4.18. The distribution of required number of Hand Pumps at village panchayat level in Amethi has been depicted in the **Map 4.19**. It has been recorded that more than 45 required number of Hand Pumps installation has been recorded in Saidpur, Kakawa, Chaturbhujpur, Gaderi village panchayats while low between 30 to 45 number of required installation of Hand Pumps has been found in Bhaganpur, Agahar, Hathkila, Dedhpasar, Gangauli, Bhusahari, Dehara village panchayats of Amethi. Low between 15 to 30 number of required hand pumps has been recorded in Katra Maharani, Trilokpur, Sarai Khema, Ramdaipur, Jangal Ram Nagar, Mahmoodpur, Parsawan, Raipur Phulwari, Kherauna, Katra Phulkunwar, Rebha, Mahaso, Loniapur, Korari Girdhar Shah, Dhandhudhar, Mochawa, Nuwawan, Darakha, Loharata, Kushi Tali, Tala, Himmatgarh, Ramgarh, Purabgaon, Nainaha, Maharajpur, Naraini, Saraiya Duban, Kohara, Mahmadpur village panchayats of Amethi. It has been recorded that very low less than 15 number of new hand pumps installation has been found in Benipur and Raidaipur village panchayats of the Amethi Block. It has been observed that 1035 number of installation of more hand pumps are required at village panchayat level in Amethi to fulfil the ever increasing of the good quality drinking water of the growing population in Amethi.

8.5 Need of Sports and Youth Programmes

Prantiya Rakshak Dal (PRD), Prantiya Vikas Das (PVD) programmes are launched by the Government of Uttar Pradesh at village level with the view to form village level Khel Sangathan and Raksha Dal to promote sport's spirit among rural youth at grassroots level. It has been observed that on Khel Sangathan and village level Raksha Dal/Vikas Dal has been formed but the ever increasing population and unemployment has forced to develop such sports spirit and Prantiya Raksha/Vikas at village level in Amethi, so that the sports spirit at schools and village level can be promoted and rural youths are motivated to join the sports and Khel Sangathan at the grassroots level. It has been observed that 46 new sports centres or formation of Khel Sangathan is required at village panchayat level in Amethi. It has been noticed that two new Khel Sangathans or sports centres as per the support of Government are required to be opened in the Chaturbhujpur and Gaderi village panchayats while one new centres of sports and Khel Sangathan are required to be established in the rest of 42 village panchayats of Amethi.

8.6 Primary Health Centres

The ever growing population and constantly increasing number of patients and health problems due to health hazards contaminated water and water born diseases and other health problems are not properly cared by the existing health infrastructure at grassroots level. During the survey it has been noticed felt and desired/required by the common village people for new establishments of the Primary Health Centres in each village panchayats. In view of the population growth and increasing health problems establishment of two new Sub/Primary Health Centres are required in the Katra Maharani, Sarai Khema, Trilokpur, Ramdaipur, Mahmoodpur, Raipur Phulwari, Umapur Ganapatti, Tala, Kushi Tali, Nuwawan, Rebha, Ramdaipur, Dedhpasar, Gangauli, Bhusahari, Kakawa village panchayats of Amethi. The rest of the 27 village panchayats require at least establishment of new Sub or Primary Health Centres. Thus it has been observed that 61 establishment of 61 new Sub/Primary Health Centres are required at village panchayat level as per the demand and requirements of the down trodden, deprived, resourceless, rural poor multitudes facing acute health problems.

8.7 Women and Child Development Programmes

Anganbadi Kendra and rural health services have been made available at village level in Amethi, but it is insufficient according to the population growth. Thus the development of women and children at village level through Anganbadi Kendra, *Pushtahar* (Nutritious Food) etc. are required. It has been noticed that mostly all the village people desired and required for establishment of new women and child development centres including Anganbari Kendra and health centres and *Pushtahar* Kendra. Thus establishment of the women and child development programmes at village panchayat level in the Amethi Block has been required by the common village people at grassroots level.

8.8 Scheduled Caste Welfare Programmes

The Government of Uttar Pradesh has launched several programmes for the upliftment of down trodden scheduled caste persrons. It has been noticed that two scheduled caste welfare programmes especially education, health, vocational and income generating programmes are required in the Sarai Khema, Trilokpur, Ramdaipur, Jangal Ram Nagar village panchayat while one scheduled caste welfare programmes are required in the rest of the 40 village panchayats of the Amethi Block. Thus it has been recorded that 48 scheduled caste welfare programmes for their upliftment, betterment are required at village panchayat level in the Amethi Block.

8.9 Veterinary Centre

Animal health care system and establishment of new veterinary centres are required because the Animal Hospitals are very insufficient against the even increasing number of cattle at village level in Amethi. It has been desired by the animal husbandry workers at village panchayat level in Amethi for the establishment of new veterinary centres to control the diseases of the animals at the grassroots level in Amethi. The each village panchayat requires one veterinary centre. Thus 44 new veterinary centres are required as per the needs of the animal husbandry workers at village panchayat level in Amethi.

8.10 Food Supply Shops

It is known fact that Amethi is an agrarian area and the economy of the Amethi is agrarian economy which is dependent on agro-climatic conditions. Poor fertility status of soil, low agricultural productivity, usar/banjar land problem, water logging, poor irrigation system have caused low agricultural productivity and the increasing unemployment has caused hunger and difficult livelihood for the people of Amethi. Thus the establishment of Food Supply Shops and Public Distribution System at village panchayat level in Amethi has been required because the existing system of the Public Distribution System of Food Shops are insufficient against the extreme population growth at village level. Thus, it has been the need and demand of the local village people to establish at least one shop for food and ensure appropriate Public Distribution System to control the hunger problem. Therefore, at least one Food Shop/Public Distribution System must be established at village panchayat level in Amethi with the view to fulfil the vision and mission of the government to provide Food, Shelter, Cloth for everyone. Therefore, it is necessary to establish new more 44 shops under the Public Distribution System at village panchayat level in Amethi.

8.11 Needy Pension Beneficiaries

Government of Uttar Pradesh has been providing pensions to the old age persons, widows and handicapped persons but there are several old age persons, widows, handicapped persons who have not been included in the list of the pension facilities being distributed by the Government. It has been observed that 759 persons who require the pension benefits distribution by the Government. The needy pension beneficiaries at village panchayat level have been mentioned in Table 4.19. The proportionate distribution of needy pension beneficiaries have been depicted in **Map 4.20**. It has been recorded that more than 20 numbers of required pension beneficiaries are found in Sarai Khema, Jangal Ram Nagar, Korari Girdhar Shah, Chaturbhujpur and Saraiya Duban village panchayats. Medium between 15 to 20 number of required pension beneficiaries has been found in Katra Maharani, Trilokpur, Ramdaipur, Dedhpasar, Hathkila, Rebha, Raidaipur, Loniapur, Katra Phulkunwar, Kherauna, Raipur Phulwari, Parsawan, Benipur, Umapur Ganapatti, Tala, Kushi Tali, Loharata, Darakha, Mochawa, Nuwawan, Dhadhudhar, Dehara, Himmatgarh, Bhusahari, Ramgarh, Nainaha, Purabgaon, Naraini, Maharajpur, Saidpur, Kohara and Mahmadpur village panchayats of Amethi. Low between 10 to 15 number of needy pension beneficiaries has been found in the Bhaganpur, Mahaso, Gangauli, village panchayats, while very low less than 10 number of needy pension beneficiaries has been found in the Agahar and Kakawa village panchayats of the Amethi Block.

8.12 Required Number of Scholarships

It has been recorded that there are 4611 number of students who are deprived of scholarship support while these students belong to below poverty line and deprived section of the society. Required number of students eligible for scholarship has been mentioned in Table 4.19. The proportionate number of students who require scholarship at village panchayat level in Amethi has been depicted in **Map 4.21**. It has been recorded that more than 200 number of students needy for scholarship has been found in Trilokpur, Ramdaipur, Umapur Ganapatti, Ramgarh, Saidpur, Saraiya Duban village panchayats while medium between 130 to 200 number of students needy for scholarship has been observed in Sarai Khema, Jangal Ram Nagar, Kherauna, Raipur Phulwari, Rebha, Raidaipur, Korari Girdhar Shah, Tala and Naraini village panchayats of the Amethi Block. Low, between 60 to 130 number of students needy for the scholarship has been recorded in Katra Maharani, Mahmoodpur, Kherauna, Katra Phulkunwar, Loniapur,

Table 4.19: Need Based Village Development Planning, Amethi

Sl. No.	Villages	Veterinary Centre	Food Supply Shops	Pensions/ Beneficiaries	Scholar-ship	Construction of Road in km.	Small Scale Industries	Agro-Industries	Fish Ponds
1	2	3	4	5	6	7	8	9	10
1.	Katra Maharani	1	1	18	125	5	2	2	—
2.	Sarai Khema	1	1	25	130	5	3	5	—
3.	Trilokpur	1	1	20	215	5	2	5	—
4.	Ramdaipur	1	1	20	250	5	3	5	—
5.	Jangal Ram Nagar	1	1	25	138	5	4	7	1
6.	Benipur	1	1	20	31	2	2	3	—
7.	Parsawan	1	1	18	150	3	4	5	—
8.	Mahmoodpur	1	1	20	110	4	3	5	—
9.	Raipur Fulwari	1	1	20	200	4	4	6	—
10.	Umapur Ganapatti	1	1	20	225	5	2	5	—
11.	Bhaganpur	1	1	10	25	5	1	4	1
12.	Tala	1	1	20	186	5	3	6	—
13.	Kushi Tali	1	1	18	125	5	3	5	—
14.	Loharta	1	1	16	38	3	2	3	—
15.	Darkha	1	1	18	32	4	4	7	—
16.	Mochwa	1	1	15	103	3	2	4	—
17.	Nuwawan	1	1	20	105	5	4	6	—
18.	Loniapur	1	1	20	68	3	3	5	—
19.	Kherauna	1	1	16	78	4	2	3	—
20.	Katra Phulkunwar	1	1	18	65	10	1	3	—
21.	Hathkila	1	1	15	40	3	2	3	—
22.	Rebha	1	1	16	185	4	3	4	—
23.	Raidaipur	1	1	16	140	4	1	3	—
24.	Korari Girdhar Shah	1	2	22	150	7	8	10	1
25.	Dedhpasar	1	1	16	38	5	4	6	—
26.	Mahaso	1	1	10	60	5	2	3	—
27.	Gangauli	1	1	12	38	4	5	7	—
28.	Dhadhudhar	1	1	18	25	4	2	4	—
29.	Gaderi	1	1	18	45	5	3	5	—
30.	Bhusahari	1	1	18	25	7	3	6	1
31.	Purabgaon	1	1	15	85	5	1	3	—
32.	Chaturbhujpur	1	1	22	35	5	3	5	—
33.	Mahrajpur	1	1	20	65	5	2	3	—
34.	Aghar	1	1	5	50	10	1	3	1
35.	Saidpur	1	1	15	201	4	2	4	—
36.	Kakwa	1	2	4	86	15	2	3	1
37.	Saraiya Duban	1	1	25	225	4	3	5	—
38.	Kohra	1	1	18	78	5	2	4	—
39.	Mahmadpur	1	1	18	65	5	3	5	—
40.	Naraini	1	1	20	165	4	3	5	—
41.	Nainaha	1	1	15	115	3	3	5	—
42.	Ramgarh	1	1	15	201	5	2	4	—
43.	Himmatgarh	1	1	20	60	3	2	3	—
44.	Dehara	1	1	18	35	5	6	8	—
	Amethi Block	**44**	**46**	**759**	**4611**	**215**	**122**	**205**	**7**

Mahaso, Himmatgarh, Nainaha, Purabgaon, Maharajpur, Nuwawan, Mochawa, Kushi Tali, Kakawa, Kohara and Mahmadpur village panchayats. Very low less than 60 number of students needy for scholarship has been found in Benipur, Hathkila, Dedhpasar, Gangauli, Bhusahari, Dehara, Gaderi, Dhandhudhar, Chaturbhujpur, Agahar, Darakha, Loharata and Bhaganpur village panchayats of the Amethi Block.

8.13 Construction of Roads

No doubt rural road has been constructed under the schemes of the Government to connect the villages from one to another but the growing population and increasing pressure for transportation from rural to urban marketing centres has adversely affected the economy of the areas. It has been noted that rural/village connectivity plays an important role for the transportation of agricultural product to the urban marketing centres. It has been noted that 215 kilometres additional road construction is required in the Amethi Block. It has been recorded that the construction of 15 km. road in Kakawa, 10 km. rural road construction in Agahar and Katra Phulkunwar village panchayats has been required. It has been noticed that requirements of the additional construction between 5 to 10 kms. has been demanded in Katra Maharani, Sarai Khema, Trilokpur, Ramdaipur, Jangal Ram Nagar, Umapur Ganapatti, Bhaganpur, Tala, Kushi Tali, Dedhpasar, Mahaso, Gaderi, Purabgaon, Bhusahari, Chaturbhujpur, Maharajpur, Kohara, Mahmadpur Ramgarh and Dehara village panchayats while less than 5 km. construction of rural road has been required in Himmatgarh, Ramgarh, Naraini, Saraiya Duban, Saidpur, Dhandhudhar, Gangauli, Raidaipur, Hathkila, Rebh, Kherauna, Loniapur, Mochawa, Loharata, Darakha, Umapur Ganapatti, Mahmoodpur, Parasawan and Benipur village panchayats of the Amethi Block.

8.14 Small Scale Industries

It has been observed that 122 small scale industries are required to be established at village panchayat level in Amethi with the view to generate employment and increase the income of the people. It has been observed that 8 small scale industries are required in Korari Girdhar Shah, and 6 small scale industries are required to be established in Dehara and 5 small scale industries are required to be established in Gangauli and 4 small scale establishments are required in Jangal Ram Nagar, Parsawan, Raipur Phulwari, Darakha, Nuwawan, Dedhpasar village panchayats and 3 small scale industries are required in Ramgarh, Naraini, Mahmadpur, Saraiya Duban, Chaturbhujpur, Bhusahari, Gaderi, Rebha, Loniapur, Kushi Tali, Tala, Mahmoodpr, Ramdaipur and Sarai Khema village panchayats of Amethi. It has been observed that 2 small scale industries are required to established in Katra Maharani, Trilokpur, Benipur, Umapur Ganapatti, Loharata, Mochawa, Kherauna, Hathkila, Mahaso, Dhandhudhar, Maharajpur, Saidpur, Kakawa, Kohara, Ramgarh, Himmatgarh village panchayats while one small scale industry establishment has been needed in Agahar, Purabgaon, Raidaipur, Katra Phuklunwar and Bhaganpur village panchayats of the Amethi Block.

8.15 Agro-Industries

It has been observed that 205 agro-industries installations in different village panchayats have been required with the view to facilitate the agri-products processing for value addition, generating employment and increasing the income of the deprived rural poor people of Amethi village level. It has been noticed that 10 agro-industries are required in Korari Girdhar Shah, 8 agro-industries are required in Darakha, Gangauli and 6 agro-industries are required in Bhusahari, Dedhpasar, Nuwawan, Tala, Raipur Phulwari and 5 agro-industries are required for installation in Sarai Khema, Trilokpur, Ramdaipur, Parsawan, Mahmoodpur, Umapur Ganapatti, Kushi Tali, Loniapur, Gaderi, Chaturbhujpur, Saraiya Duban, Mahmadpur, Naraini, Nainaha, village panchayats while 4 agro-industries are required in Bhaganpur, Mochawa, Rebha, Dhandhudhar, Saidpur, Kohara, Ramgarh and 3 agro-industries are required to be established in Himmatarh, Kakawa, Agahar, Katra Phulkunwar, Loharata, Benipur, village panchayats and two agro-industries are needed for its establishment in Katra Maharani village panchayats and the installation of agro-industries are required to check the perish ability of agro-products and to provide its value addition, to generate employment and also increase the income of the people of Amethi.

8.16 Fish-Pond

It has been noticed that the construction of 7 fish pond has been required in the Amethi Block. It has been observed that construction of one fish pond has been required in the

Table 4.20: Need Based Village Development Planning, Amethi

Sl. No.	*Villages*	*Non-Conventional Sources of Energy*	*Electricity Connections*	*Low Cost Housing*	*Low Cost Sanitation*	*Dairy Centre*	*PMGSY Road in Km.*	*RGVY Households*	*Rural Health Programmes*
1	2	3	4	5	6	7	8	9	10
1.	Katra Maharani	10	80	4	2	1	4	—	2
2.	Sarai Khema	15	70	15	2	—	5	—	2
3.	Trilokpur	15	70	15	2	—	2	—	1
4.	Ramdaipur	15	80	15	2	—	4	—	1
5.	Jangal Ram Nagar	10	200	20	8	1	5	50	1
6.	Benipur	10	50	5	2	1	3	22	1
7.	Parsawan	15	25	15	2	—	3	30	2
8.	Mahmoodpur	10	48	11	2	—	4	50	1
9.	Raipur Fulwari	10	65	11	2	—	4	—	1
10.	Umapur Ganapatti	10	65	11	2	—	5	—	1
11.	Bhaganpur	10	30	5	3	1	4	25	1
12.	Tala	15	56	11	2	—	5	—	2
13.	Kushi Tali	10	60	11	2	—	5	40	1
14.	Loharta	6	25	15	1	—	2	—	1
15.	Darkha	25	52	15	9	1	5	30	1
16.	Mochwa	10	70	12	1	—	2	—	2
17.	Nuwawan	15	80	15	2	—	4	40	1
18.	Loniapur	10	40	12	2	—	3	—	2
19.	Kherauna	10	40	8	2	—	4	—	2
20.	Katra Phulkunwar	10	100	4	2	—	8	—	2
21.	Hathkila	12	30	6	2	1	2	30	2
22.	Rebha	10	60	12	2	—	3	—	1
23.	Raidaipur	10	70	6	2	—	2	4	2
24.	Korari Girdhar Shah	15	80	11	2	1	7	—	1
25.	Dedhpasar	20	43	11	3	1	4	35	1
26.	Mahaso	10	40	11	2	—	2	—	1
27.	Gangauli	25	53	5	2	1	3	40	2
28.	Dhadhudhar	10	20	12	3	—	2	52	1
29.	Gaderi	15	55	8	2	1	5	40	1
30.	Bhusahari	18	46	12	2	1	5	40	1
31.	Purabgaon	10	30	10	2	—	3	—	1
32.	Chaturbhujpur	20	42	10	2	1	4	40	2
33.	Mahrajpur	10	40	12	2	—	5	—	1
34.	Aghar	10	10	5	2	2	7	20	1
35.	Saidpur	15	45	11	2	—	4	—	1
36.	Kakwa	10	100	11	4	2	10	50	1
37.	Saraiya Duban	20	70	15	2	—	5	—	2
38.	Kohra	10	80	5	2	—	5	—	1
39.	Mahmadpur	10	80	20	2	—	5	—	1
40.	Naraini	10	75	20	2	—	4	40	1
41.	Nainaha	15	45	12	2	—	4	—	1
42.	Ramgarh	10	40	11	2	—	3	30	1
43.	Himmatgarh	12	45	8	2	—	3		1
44.	Dehara	18	38	11	2	1	4	40	1
	Amethi Block	**566**	**2543**	**735**	**104**	**18**	**182**	**784**	**57**

Jangal Ram Nagar, Korari Girdhar Shah, Bhusahari, Agahar, Kakawa and Bhaganpur village panchayats of the Amethi Block. The construction of ponds in the low-lying areas may be asset for appropriate conservation of land and water resources and conserving the environmental conditions and strengthening the infrastructural resources, generating employment and increasing the income of deprived resourceless Nishad Community in the different village panchayats of the Amethi Block.

8.17 Non-conventional Sources of Energy

The Non-conventional Sources of Energy plays an important role especially in the rural areas where electricity supply is very insignificant. The solar lights, solar water heater and solar water pump are an important assets to fulfil the day-to-day requirements of the village people. The requirements of the Non-conventional Sources of Energy of village panchayat level has been mentioned in Table 4.20. The proportionate requirements of the Non-conventional Sources of Energy at village panchayat level has been depicted in **Map 4.22**. It has been observed that more than 20 number of Non-conventional Sources of Energy has been required in Darakha and Gangauli while requirement of 15 to 20 number of Non-conventional sources of energy has been required in Trilokpur, Ramdaipur, Sarai Khema, Parsawan, Dedhpasar, Tala, Nuwawan, Korari Girdhar Shah, Gaderi, Chaturbhujpur, Bhusahari, Dehara, Himmatgarh, Nainaha, Saidpur and Saraiya Duban village panchayats. Low between 10 to 15 number of Non-conventional Sources of Energy has been needed in Katra Maharani, Benipur, Mahmoodpur, Bhaganpur, Kushi Tali, Raipur Phulwari, Kherauna, Katra Phulkunwar, Hathkila, Mahaso, Rebha, Raidaipur, Loniapur, Umapur Ganapatti, Loharata, Mochawa, Dhandhudhar, Purabgaon, Ramgarh, Naraini, Agahar, Kakawa, Kohara and Mahmadpur village panchayats. It has been noticed that less than 10 number of Non-conventional Sources of Energy has been required in Loharata village panchayat of Amethi. It has been recorded that 566 number of Non-conventional Sources of Energy are required for its installation in the different village panchayats of the Amethi Block.

8.18 Electricity

It has been recorded that 2543 number of additional electricity connection are require in the Amethi Block. Details of the required number of electricity connection at village panchayat level has been mentioned in Table 4.20. The proportionate number of required electricity connection at village panchayat level in Amethi has been depicted in **Map 4.23**. It has been recorded that more than 100 electricity connection are require in the Jangal Ram Nagar and new electricity connections between 75 to 100 connections are required in the Katra Phulkunwar, Ramdaipur, Korari Girdhar Shah, Nuwawan, Kakawa, Naraini, Kohara and Mahamadpur village panchayats, while 50 to 75 number electricity connections are required in the Sarai Khema, Trilokpur, Benipur, Raipur Phulwari, Rebha, Raidaipur, Gangauli, Gaderi, Mochawa, Darakha, Tala, Kushi Tali, Umapur Ganapatti, Gaderi and Saraiya Duban village panchayats of the Amethi Block. It has been noticed that less than 50 number of electricity connections are require in Bhaganpur, Loharata, Mahmoodpur, Parsawan, Kherauna, Lonaipur, Hathkila, Dedhpasar, Dhandhudhar, Mahaso, Bhusahari, Himmatgarh, Dehara, Ramgarh, Nainaha, Pubrabgaon, Chaturbhujpur, Mahrajpur, Agahar, and Saidpur village panchayats of the Amethi Block.

8.19 Low Cost Housing

Shelter is an important component of the survival of the man. Due to socio-economic backwardness of the Amethi most of the people are houseless and living hand to mouth. It has been observed that 735 number of low cost houses for the houseless persons are required in Amethi Block. The details of the required number of houses in Amethi has been mentioned in Table 4.20. The proportionate required number of low cost houses at village panchayat level has been depicted in **Map 4.24**. It has been noted more than 15 low cost houses are required in the Jangal Ram Nagar, Naraini and Mahmadpur village panchayats while 10 to 15 number of low cost houses for shelterless poor people are required in Trilokpur, Ramdaipur, Sarai Khema, Tala, Kushi Tali, Loharata, Darakha, Mochawa, Nuwawan, Umapur Ganapatti, Dhadhudhar, Korari Girdhar Shah, Loniapur, Raipur Phulwari, Mahmoodpur, Parsawan, Rebha, Dedhpasar Mahaso, Bhusahari, Dehara, Ramgarh, Nainaha, Purabgaon, Maharajpur, Chaturbhujpur, Kakawa, Saidpur and Saraiya Duban village panchayats of Amethi. It has been recorded that 5 to 10 number of low cost houses are required in Bhaganpur, Benipur, Kherauna, Hathkila, Raidaipur, Gangauli, Himmatgarh, Gaderi, Agahar and Kohara village panchayats while less than 5 number of low cost houses for houseless persons are required in Katra Maharani and Katra Phulkunwar village panchayats of the Amethi Block.

8.20 Dairy Centres

It has been observed very nominal households are engaged in the animal husbandry work but their milk produce has not been properly marketed due to which some of the milkman of the different village panchayats have desired dairy centres for the collection of milk to avoid the middlemen. It has been noticed that 18 number of dairy centres are required for the milk collection in the different village panchayats of the Amethi. It has been observed that the 2 dairy centres has been required in the Kakawa and Kohara village panchayats while one dairy centre for the milk collection has been required in the Korari Girdhar Shah, Dedhpasar, Gangauli, Gaderi, Bhusahari, Chaturbhujpur, Dehara, Hathkila, Darakha, Bhaganpur, Benipur, Jangal Ram Nagar and Katra Maharani village panchayats of the Amethi with the view to control the parish ability of milk products and to provide appropriate price for the milk of the animal husbandry workers and milkmen at the grassroots level.

8.21 Low Cost Sanitation

The construction of low cost sanitation has been an important programme of the Government to control the health hazards in the remote villages. It has been recorded that 104 number of low cost sanitation has been required in the different village panchayats of Amethi. Required number of low cost sanitation has been mentioned in Table 4.20. It has been observed that 9 low cost sanitation are required in Darakha and 8 low cost sanitation are required in Jangal Ram Nagar village panchayat and 4 number of low cost sanitation are required in Kakawa and 3 low cost sanitation are required in Bhaganpur, Dedhpasar and Dhandhudhar village panchayats of Amethi. It has been recorded that 2 low cost sanitation are required in Dehara, Himmatgarh, Ramgarh, Naraini, Mahmadpur, Saraiya Duban Saidpur, Agahar, Maharajpur, Chaturbhujpur, Purabgaon, Gaderi, Gangauli, Mahaso, Korari Girdhar Shah, Raidaipur, Rebha, Hathkila, Katra Phulkunwar, Kherauna, Loniapur, Nuwawan, Kushi Tali, Tala, Umapur

Ganapatti, Raipur Phulwari, Mahmoodput Parsawan, Benipur, Ramdaipur, Sarai Khema, Katra Maharani village panchayats of the Amethi Block. It has been observed that one low cost sanitation programme of the government has been required in Mochawa, Loharata village panchayats of the Amethi Block.

8.22 Pradhan Mantri Gram Sadak Yojana

The construction of rural road to connect the one village to another village through Pradhan Mantri Gram Sadak Yojana has been required in different village panchayats of the Amethi Block. The requirement of the rural road construction under Pradhan Mantri Gram Sadak Yojana has been mentioned in Table 4.20. The proportionate requirement of the construction of rural road under the Pradhan Mantri Gram Sadak Yojana at village panchayat level has been depicted in **Map 4.25**. It has been noticed that more than 9 km. rural road construction under Pradhan Mantri Gram Sadak Yojana has been required in the village panchayat Kakawa and 6 to 9 km. rural road construction under PMGSY has been required in Katra Phulkunwar, Korari Girdhar Shah and Agahar village panchayats while 3 to 6 km. rural road construction through Pradhan Mantri Gram Sadak Yojana has been required in Katra Maharani, Sarai Khema, Jangal Ram Nagar, Ramdaipur, Bhaganpur, Tala, Kushi Tali, Darakha, Nuwawan, Umapur Ganapatti, Benipur, Mahmoodpur, Parsawan, Raipur Phulwari, Kherauna, Rebha, Dedhpasar, Gangauli, Bhusahari, Himmatgarh, Dehara, Ramgarh, Nainaha, Purabgaon, Gaderi, Chaturbhujpur, Maharajpur, Naraini, Saidpur, Saraiya Duban, Kohara and Mahmadpur village panchayats. It has been noted that less than 3 km. rural road construction through Pradhan Mantri Gram Sadak Yojana has been required in the village panchayats Kakawa of the Amethi Block with the view to facilitate rural connectivity to the urban marketing centres for marketing of the agricultural product of the farmers of Amethi. It has been noted that 1182 km. rural road construction is required under Pradhan Mantri Gram Sadak Yojana in Amethi.

8.23 Rajiv Gandhi Vidyutikaran Yojana

The electricity connection through Rajiv Gandhi Vidyutikaran Yojana has been required by the villagers. It has been noted that 784 number of electricity connections has been required in Amethi, which has been mentioned in Table 4.20. It has been noted that 52 electricity connections in Dhadhudhar, 50 electricity connection in the Kakawa and Jangal Ram Nagar, and 40 electricity connections are required in Dehara, Naraini, Gaderi, Chaturbhujpur, Bhusahari, Gangauli, Nuwawan, Kushi Tali, village panchayats while 35 electricity connections in Dedhpasar and 30 electricity connections are required in Parsawan, Darakha, Hathkila, Ramgarh village panchayats of Amethi. It has been recorded that 25 electricity connections in the Bhaganpur, 22 electricity connections in Benipur and 20 electricity connections in Agahar and 4 electricity connection under the Rajiv Gandhi Vidyutikaran Yojana has been required in the Amethi Block.

8.24 Rural Health Programmes

Various rural health programmes have been launched by the Government including National Rural Health Mission Prgrammes. The rural health centres at village panchayat level are functional at village panchayat level, which is very insignificant and insufficient. it has been noticed that 57 new rural health programmes through National Rural Health

Mission (NRHM) programme has been required in Amethi. It has been recorded that two rural health programmes are required in Hathkila, Raidaipur, Gangauli, Chaturbhujpur, Saraiya Duban, Katra Maharani, Sarai Khema, Parsawan, Tala, Mochawa, Loniapur, Kherauna and Katra Phulkunwar village panchayats of the Amethi Block. It has been recorded that one National Rural Health Mission (NRHM) Programme has been required in Trilokpur, Ramdaipur, Jangal Ram Nagar, Benipur, Mahmoodpur, Raipur Phulwari, Umapur Ganapatti, Bhaganpur, Kushi Tali, Loharata, Darakha, Nuwawan, Rebha, Korari Girdhar Shah, Dedhpasar, Mahaso, Dhandhudhar, Gaderi, Bhusahari, Purabgaon, Maharajpur, Agahar, Saidpur, Kakawa, Kohara, Mahmadpur, Naraini, Nainaha, Ramgarh, Himmatgarh and Dehara village panchayats of Amethi with the view to provide better health services to the deprived resourcesless rural poor multitudes surviving in the remote villages of the Amethi Block.

In spite of the above, it has been recorded that there are several programmes launched by the Government of India and the State Government of Uttar Pradesh in co-ordination with the District Planning, District Panchayat → Block Panchayat → Village Panchayat could not reach appropriately as per the visions of the goals prioritized in the programmes. Therefore, it has become an important task to ensure the implementation of the planned programmes related to rural development, agricultures, employment generation, health, education, common basic amenities and various other day-to-day requirements of the common people for realizing the upgradation, better perception, actions and aspiration for good quality of life and also to fulfil the ever increasing demand of constant growth of the population for Food-Cloth-Shelter and Food grain, Fibre, Fruits, Fisheries, Fodder, Fuel Wood (F^6) and vegetables and also to improve the degraded land and environment and to improve to socio-economic-conditoins of the deprived resourceless rural poor multitudes of Amethi.

9. CONCLUSION

The planning is an organized process of the task of the people in which the planners can provide back up support to achieve their planning goals.

The development is basically a human enterprise and therefore, it requires, the combined efforts of all systems of knowledge to comprehend and articulate it. The fuel good perception of the development has to be not only from National-State level but also from District-Block-Village level perspective.

The priorities, visions, missions and goals of the Government for the formulation of the planning and the implementation of the planned programmes has been analysed.

It has been realized that there are is a quest for revolving a model for development planning and macro-level planning has been adopted in our country and it did not yield the requisite results due to in equities amongst people and disparities between one village to another village. During seventies integrated and sustainable planning at various levels has been ensured and conceptual changes in the planning process has been adopted at the grassroots level.

The development should be participatory tapping the local talent and resources in order to make the created assets self-sustained for optimum use of the village level beneficiaries. The village has been considered as the lowest unit of the plan formulation and the implementation of the peoples participatory and rural development activities.

The construction of infrastructural resources at the grassroots level has been launched through 'Bharat Nirman' by the Government of India. The computerization of the land records, watershed development, *Hariyali*, rural housing, National Social Assistance

Programme, Mahatma Gandhi National Rural Employment Guarantee Act (MNREGA) Mahila Kisan Sashaktikaran Pariyojana, Placement linked skill development, Swarnjayanti Gram Swarojgar Yojana, Pradhan Mantri Gram Sadak Yoana, National Bio-Gas, National Health Insurance Policy Scheme, Sampoorna Grameen Rojgar Yojana, Rajeev Gandhi Grameen Vidyutikaran Yojana, Rural Drinking Water Supply, Rural Sanitation, Pradhan Mantri Grameen Jal Samvardhan Yojana etc. has been launched by the Government of India with the view to facilitate fruits of the development programmes at the grassroots level.

The Government of Uttar Pradesh has also initiated various rural development programmes through 25 per cent state share and 75 per cent grants from the Government of India. The Government of Uttar Pradesh has also initiated various programmes, like Swarnjayanti Gram Swarojgar Yojana, Sampoorna Grameen Rojgar Yojana, Mahatma Gandhi National Rural Employment Guarantee Act, Pradhan Mantri Gram Sadak Yojana, Indira Awaas Yojana, Rural Drinking Water Supply, Community Development Programme, MLA & MLC-Local Area Development Fund, Ambedkar Vishesh Rojgar Yojana and National Bio-Gas Yojana, and some programmes have been re-nominated or changed but the target of the programme has been the same. The Department of Rural Development, Government of Uttar Pradesh and District Rural Development Agency play an important key role in the plan formulation and implementation of the various rural development programmes.

District development planning has been formulated, planned by the Zila Yojana Samiti. The agriculture, horticulture, assistance for small and marginal farmers, animal husbandry, fisheries, milk, forest, *sahkarita*, special programmes for village development, development of land and water resources, employment, Panchayati Raj, Community Development, Minor irrigation, Flood control, additional sources of energy, khadi and gramodyog hand loom, road and bridges, environment, science and technology, tourism, education, pradeshik Vikas Dal, Medical and Health, housing drinking water, sanitation and child development programmes, etc. has been planned and being implemented at grassroots level through various line departments.

Block Development planning has been done for the Mahatma Gandhi National Rural Employment Guarantee Act (MNREGA) construction of rural link road, digging of pond, *nali*, land development, land levelling, conservation of water, water storage, flood control, minor irrigation, renovation of traditional water resources, drought prone and afforestation, horticulture plantation, construction of kharanza, etc. work has been planned by the Village Panchayat and Block Panchayat Amethi with the view to generate employment and increase the income of the Below Poverty Line people living in the remote villages of the Amethi Block.

It has been noted that all 44 village panchayats of the Amethi Block has planned various activities under the Mahatma Gandhi National Rural Employment Guarantee Act the estimate budget of the proposed planned work has been Rs. 2349.62 lakh out of which Rs. 1576.27 lakh have been for the labour cost and a sum of Rs. 773.34 lakh has been allocated for the material cost and it has been planned create 1266645 man-days employment through Mahatma Gandhi National Rural Employment Guarantee Act (MNREGA) for the Below Poverty Line MNREGA Job card holders belonging to the 44 village panchayats and covering 82 revenue village along with 377 purwas/tolas/hamlet villages of the Amethi Block.

Peoples participatory need base planning survey has been carried out at grassroots level with the view to know and assess the interest and needs of the common village people who have been deprived of due to some reason or the other from the programmes launched by the Government. In view of the above, an attempt has been made to analyze the willing consent, interests, and need of the common people at village level in the Amethi Block.

It has been noted that there are 2775 needy interested Below Poverty Line persons looking forward to obtain Mahatma Gandhi National Rural Employment Guarantee Act (MNREGA) Job Card for getting 100 days ensured job for their livelihood and survival in the various village panchayats of the Amethi.

It has been noted that 62 more new schools are required to be established in different village panchayats of Amethi to fulfil the Sarva Shiksha Abhiyan (Campaign for Education for All) Mission of the Government.

It has been recorded that 1403 number of tube-well borings are required in different village panchayats of Amethi with the view to facilitate minor irrigation programmes launched by the Government.

To ensure appropriate rural drinking water supply programmes at village panchayat level 1035 number of hand pumps are required in the Amethi Block. Sports and Youth Welfare 46 programmes are needed to be established in Amethi.

In view of the growing population and increasing number patients and disease 61 sub/primary health centres are required to be established in Amethi and women and child development programmes are required one each in the very village panchayat of Amethi. Scheduled Caste Welfare Programmes has not been properly implemented and very insignificant people are benefited. Therefore, 48 number of scheduled caste programmes are required to established in the various village panchayats of Amethi.

At least each village panchayat of Amethi requires establishment of veterinary cenres for proper treatment of animals in Amethi. It has been noted that 46 supply shops are required to be opened under the Public Distribution System in Amethi. There are 579 old age, widow, handicapped pension beneficiaries who have not yet received pension facility of the Government and initiative must be taken to ensure to facilitate the pension benefits to the deprived resourcesless poor people surviving in the remote villages. It has been recorded that 4611 number of students deprived from scholarships and these students at school level belong to the Below Poverty Line family, effort must be ensured to provide scholarship to the needy interested school going students at village panchayat level in Amethi.

Construction of rural link road covering 215 km. distance linking one village to another and urban marketing centre are required in the different village panchayats of the Amethi Block.

It has been observed that 122 small scale industries and 205 agro-industries installation has been required in the different village panchayats of the Amethi Block with the view to process the agricultural products for the value addition and also to generate employment and increasing the income of the deprived rural poor people surviving in the remote villages of the Amethi Block. Construction of 7 fish the available water logged land and to generate employment for the interested Nishad and other communities of the Amethi Block.

The renewable sources of the Energy or the Non-conventional Sources of Energy including solar light, solar pump, solar water heater, solar lantern etc. total 566 number of solar items are required at village panchayat level in Amethi.

It has been recorded that 2543 number of electricity connections are required in different village panchayats of Amethi and 735 low cost houses under Indira Awaas Yojana are required for houseless Below Poverty Line people surviving the thatched roof, mud houses in different village panchayats of the Amethi Block. It has also been noted that 104 rural sanitation and low cost sanitation programmes are required at village panchayat level in Amethi. There is demand for the establishment of 18 dairy centre for the collection and marketing of milk at village panchayat level in the Amethi Block. It has been noted that 182 kilometre construction of rural road under the Pradhan Mantri Gram Sadak Yojana has been needed at village panchayat level in the Amethi. It has been noticed that 784 number of Below Poverty Line households required electricity connection under the Rajiv Gandhi Vidyutikaran Yojana in different village panchayats of Amethi. The National Rural Health Mission Programmes are not properly implemented and it has been desired by the common people of Amethi for initiation and establishment of 57 rural heath programmes at village panchayat level in Amethi wih the view to provide rural health services for needy, interested Below Poverty Line patient at the grassroots level.

In spite of the above, there are various programmes launched by Government of India and the State Government of Uttar Pradesh, it has been observed and realized that most of the rural development programme has not yet still reached upto the grassroots level, even, if same programmes are initiated but the implementation of such programmes could not yield the requisite results as per the visions targeted goals, aims, and objectives of the Government. Time bound peoples participatory need based formulation of the policy planning at the grassroots level, through tapping the available local talents and natural and human (Socio-Economic-Industrial) infrastructural resources and its optimum utilization, should be prioritised. The peoples participation in the implementation of the planned programmes must be ensured at the village level. Local village people must be trained, educated, motivated to know through awareness programmes being implemented for their betterment and upgradation of their socio-economic conditions of the deprived rural poor multitudes at village level in Amethi. The policy planning and formulation of the need based planning at the National Level-State Level-District Level has not been properly planned and implemented through ignoring the local people their needs, aspiration and actions for their better quality of life due to which it failed to yield the desired success of it completion at village level. In view of the above it is necessary to prioritize the needs and to innovate the available natural-human-infrastructural resources at the field level should be considered in the plan formulation and continued involvement of the local people should be given due importance in the implementation of the planning and various rural development programmes at the village level.

The people's participatory need base planning through optimum utilization of the available infrastructural resources may be an asset for the successful implementation of the planned programmes at the village level in Amethi with the view to increase the agricultural productivity through appropriate utilization and conservation of *Jal-Jangal-Zameen* (Land-Water-Forest) natural infrastructural resources to meet the ever increasing demand of the growing cattle and human population and conserve the available natural resources and improve the environmental conditions of the Amethi and to fulfil the growing demand of fuel wood, fodder, fibre, fruits, fisheries, food grains (F^6) and vegetables and also to improve the socio-economic conditions of the deprived resource-less poor multitudes surviving in the remote villages of Amethi through generating large scale employment among the unemployed rural youth and increasing their income and to realize their actions and aspirations for better quality of life with the view to move equally in the society along with the rich and elite class people because the implementation of the rural development programmes should reach to the rural poor *equally, effectively, efficiently* as per the constitutional rights and visions of the Father of the Nation.

5 Conclusions

Economics development has been realized at various levels and commendable advances have been made in the diversified of rural development. It has been noticed that several implemented rural development programmes failed to translate into better and dignified life for the majority of the people living in the remote rural areas.

It is known fact that more than three-forth population lives in the rural areas who are deprived of the basic common amenities and necessities required for the survival of the human being. It has been noticed that there is faster development of the rural areas followed by Rurban areas while rural areas are socially economically, educationally backward. The village people are isolated from the main streams and the villages are identified as an independent unit for implementation of rural development programmes.

In view of the above, an attempt has been made in this study to analyze the "Village Information System" — Development Planning at village panchayat level in Amethi, covering 377 Purwas/Tolas/Hamlet Villages and 82 Revenue Villages and 44 Village Panchayats of the Amethi Block.

The social structure of the village or gaon or gram is not just a physical space or settlement of a group of people. The social life in the village is organized through definite ritual and secular principals, such as those of castes, kinship, politics, economy and religion etc.

The physical characteristics of the village has a definite pattern of social relations based on traditional principles of kinship and marriage ceremony such as those of village exogamy. The social relations extend the interactive network and social space of a village well beyond it boundaries into surrounding village. The community institutions and organization are flexible and fail to adjust to the changing needs of villages. The communities traditional norms and conventions have been formed slowly over many many years.

It has been realized that the development should be participatory and it should be planned according to the local needs of the deprived rural resource less poor multitudes. The development should be planned through tapping the local level talent and available natural and human infrastructural resources. The planning process has been done from bottom to top. The real meaning of democracy is the importance of the people and village self-government is the main sould of the rural development. Governance-Management, Financial and Administrative Control of the Village panchayat, Continued participation, cooperation of the people to establish the village panchayat for the Self-Governance to ensure peoples participatory planning and the implementation integrated village development programmes are being ensured for the self-sustenance of the remote villages of Amethi Block.

The main objectives of this study is to analyse the policy, planning, programmes and to assess the implementation of rural development programmes and to explain the need based people's participatory development planning at village panchayat level in Amethi.

Effort has been made to explain the various policies, plannings initiated by the Government of India and State Government of Uttar Pradesh and the District Panchayat → Block Panchayat → Village Panchayat. Various indicators related to the rural development programmes and the need based village development planning of grassroots level has been selected and primary field survey at the field level has been carried out to collect the requisite data for an appropriate analysis and assessment of the implementation of various rural development programmes and also to explain the people's participatory need based village development planning at the village panchayat level in Amethi because the development is a multifaceted phenomenon. The development is basically a human enterprise and it requires the combined efforts of all the systems of knowledge, whether, by the physical, biological, social or human to comprehend and articulate it.

The development is one which is pursued with genuine concern for human values. The development means evolution of people in which the people acquires better perception and best control over its natural and human infrastructural resources.

The development has been fundamentally a process of change that involves the whole society its socio-economic, politico-cultural and physical structures as well as the value system and way of life of the people even living in the remote rural areas. The tools of measuring the levels of development ranges from assessing economic factors and other socio-cultural and political indicators realized against an accepted standard, norm and aspiration. The goals of development planning are to replicate the level of achievements of others which have been perceived as superior in the echelon of the development.

The development in the today's system is the modern advances in science, technology, democracy, values, ethics and social organization, fuse into the single humanitarian programme of producing a better quality of life for those people living in the remote villages.

The social scientists have attempted to seek to expand the understanding to seek to expand the understanding of the village level available social infrastructure and how it affects the welfare of the people and development of places. The scientists and research scholars have diverted their attention from conventional models of the village development to the alternative, community based models that put to the interest of works and the community sustainability over urban and rurban marketing centres. It has been realized that the clusters plays a significant role in the economic growth. It has also been advocated that in the peripheral development, the science and technology accompanied through the continuous changes in their social structure play a fundamental role for the integrated village development.

The human development has been a process of enlarging people's choices and need based preferences at the village level. The basic objectives of the human development has been to create an enabling environment in which the people can enjoy long life, healthy and creative livelihood at village level. The infrastructural indicators may together reflect the attainment of human development. In reality, there are various numbers of indicators for measuring human development which includes-Natural-Social-Economic-Institutions (Human) infrastructural resources available at the village level. The development is possible only when rural India or rural areas or remote rural villages are developed.

In spite of massive development efforts initiated, undertaken by the Government of

India, Government of Uttar Pradesh in different plan-periods, the problems of the malnutrition, mass poverty, malignment, growth of unemployed rural youth and large scale migration of people to the urban areas residing in the rural villages, unless we improve the rural economy, one cannot lessen the burden of poverty nor can we solve the problems of unemployment. It has been noticed that more than 40 per cent of our rural population still lives under the Below Poverty Line.

The problems of unemployment cannot be tackled by creating more jobs in the public sector and other government agencies and non-government organizations. The skill development, small scale entrepreneurship for self-employment, and expansion of the job-opportunities at the village level. The educated youths at the village level must be trained and involved in the entrepreneurship oriented vocations through different Entrepreneurship Development Programmes (EDP) and Skill Development Training Programme through Science and Technology at the village level with the view to generate employment and increase the income of the deprived rural poor multitudes for the overall economic growth and integrated village development.

It has been realized that there is a quest for evolving a model for planning at various levels. The Constitutional and Institutional changes has been brought to implement. The State Government has been empowered through the institutions of local self-governance, right from the Village Level → Block Level → District Level. The State Governments have accordingly constituted such local level bodies with definite mandates to collect revenues, to draw need based plan and to implement integrated rural development programmes through people's participation. It requires the capacity building at the institutions of local Self-Governance to prepare and implement the need based local area specific integrated village development programmes through assessing and utilizing the available Natural-Human (Social-Economic-Institutional) Infrastructural Resources available at the grassroots level.

The formulation of the policy, planning and implementation of the various integrated rural development programmes in the remote villages is an information oriented intensive tasks. The Government of India has initiated various programmes to develop the rural areas and also trying to ensure the faster development to bridge the gap between rural to urban. It has been realized that the development should be formulated according to the local needs of the villagers. The Government of India and State Government of Uttar Pradesh have launched various need based rural development programmes for upliftment and appropriate development of the deprived, downtrodden resourceless vulnerable sections of the society living in the remote villages.

The Panchayati Raj Institutions have been strengthened, financial and administrative powers has been allocated to the Village-Block-District Panchayat with the view to ensure people's participatory need based integrated village development. In view of the above an attempt has been made in the third volume of the Village Information System to analyse the various policy, planning and programmes initiated by the Government of India and State Government and District Level three-tier Panchayati Raj Institutions, i.e. District-Block-Village Panchayat and to assess the implementation of various rural development programmes at village panchayat level in the Amethi Block and to explain the peoples participatory need based village development planning at village panchayat level in Amethi Block, which will be a mile stone for the grassroots level policy planners, implementing agencies, research scholars and various government and non-government implementing institutions and local level villagers, Village Panchayat representative, Village Pradhan, Block Development Committee Members and Block Pramukh and District Panchayat Committee Members and Chairman and the District Rural

Development Agency, Amethi and others engaged in the implementation of various rural development programmes at grassroots level in Amethi.

Policy Planning

It has been realized that the commendable advances have been made in the diverse field of the development but it has been noticed that such development has been found incomplete in reality because the implemented programmes failed to translate into better and dignified meaning for the life of the majority of the people surviving in the remote villages.

The policy-makers and the planners must provide integrated development planning techno-scientific backup support to the grassroots level people's representatives. Thus the policy planning for the Integrated Development Programmes must be carried out as per the needs and requirements of local village people, with the involvement of the village people and with the sustained participation of the village people to achieve the formulated planned, integrated village developmental target.

It has been observed that there is a quest for evolving a model for the planning. The Macro-level resources management planning has been adopted in our country and it did not yield desired results due to inequities amongst the people and disparities between one area to another.

Initially the Government of India made policy for the poverty alleviation and "*Adhik Ann Upjao*" (Produce More Grain). Twenty-Points Programme, TRYSEM and Development of Women and Children in Rural Areas have been launched as per the policy of the Government of India.

The Eleventh and Twelfth Schedules of the Constitution while specifying the sectors for Panchayats and the local bodies.

It has been mentioned in the Constitution of India that, "The Government should evolve methods to unite the village panchayats and provide such powers and rights which can be helpful to work as a unit of self-governance."

In view of the above three-tier Panchayati Raj System has been established and administrative, financial powers have been allocated to the Panchayats. The village should be taken as lowest unit of planning and the implementation of the Development Programmes.

The planning is an organized process by which the people achieve their developmental goal. It has been noticed that the planning is formulated without the willing consent of the local people. The aspirations and the requirements of the people are not incorporated in the planning process. The planning is the task of the people by which the planners can provide techno-scientific back up support to achieve their planning goals.

The Government of India has initiated various Rural Development Programmes like Computerization of Land Records, Watershed Development, Hariyali Rural Housing, National Social Assistance Programmes, Mahatma Gandhi National Rural Employment Guarantee Act (MNREGA), Mahila Kishan Sashaktikaran Pariyojana, Placement linked Skill Development of Rural B.P.L. youth under Swarnjayanti Swarojgar Yojana, Pradhan Mantri Gram Sadak Yojana, Rajiv Gandhi Grameen Vidyutikaran Yojana, Rural Housing, Drinking Water Supply, Rural Sanitation and Pradhan Mantri Grameen Jal Samvardhan Yojana, Women Empowerment, and Rural Health Mission programmes at the grassroots level, i.e village panchayat level.

The Department of Rural Development of the Government of Uttar Pradesh has been engaged in the implementation of various Rural Development Programmes, like

Swarnjayanti Gram Swarojgar Yojana, Mahatma Gandhi National Rural Employment Guarantee Act, Pradhan Mantri Gram Sadak Yojana, Rural Drinking Water Supply and various other programmes have been launched for the deprived rural poor people.

It has been noticed that different rural Development Programmes are being implemented by the District Authorities through various line departments at various levels in Amethi.

The agriculture, horticulture, social-forestry, rural road, support to small and marginal farmers, animal husbandry, Mahatma Gandhi National Rural Employment Guarantee Act (MNREGA), Dairy Development, drinking water, irrigation support, rural sanitation, employment generation, pension, scholarships, social welfare, rural health, Indira Awaas Yojana and various other programmes are being implemented through concerned district level line departments.

Zila Panchayat Yojana, Block Panchayat Yojana and Village Panchayat Yojana have also been implemented through various implementing organizations. Zila Panchayat has been engaged in the implementation of the rural health, education, irrigation, women and child development, agriculture, horticulture, social forestry, drinking water, public works department and various other rural development programmes are also implemented through Zila Panchayat.

Block Panchayat has been engaged in the implementation of rural development, primary health centres, animal hospital, seeds and marketing centres, maintenance and management of the created assets.

Village Panchayat has also been engaged in the implementation of various rural Development Programmes including primary education, medical health, animal husbandry, agriculture, horticulture, social-forestry, rural development, panchayati raj system, all types of scholarships and pensions.

District Panchayat, Block Panchayat and Village Panchayat have been engaged in the implementation of various need based policy plans as per the decisions and willing consent of the grassroots level village people. The visions and mission of the Mahatma Gandhi has been ensured through implementing Panchayati Raj System and to strengthen the concept of local self-government. The Panchayati Raj System has been found successful on paper but at the field level, the concerned deprived rural poor village beneficiaries are still awaiting to achieve the people's participatory planning goals and to upgrade their living standards for the better quality of life through improving their socio-economic conditions of the resourceless deprived rural poor multitudes surviving in the remote villages of Amethi.

Rural Development

The development is a human enterprise and it requires combined efforts of the all systems of knowledge, be they physical, biological, social, economic, institutional with the view to comprehend and articulate it. The development is pursued with the genuine concern for human values, their actions and aspirations for the better quality of life. In the process of development the growth alone does not ensure the integrated development, because the development is after all a multifaceted phenomenon.

The existing process of development whether urban or rural development has neither been true nor good, nor beautify but it does not mean that everything is wrong. The progress of people and economic growth along with the socio-economic-institutional, infrastructural development, man has made and adopted destructive approach than constructive approach of development without incorporating the willing consent and interest of the deprived sections of the society and also ignoring the continued sustained participation of the grassroots level interested beneficiaries for its sustenance to fulfil the increasing demand of the growing cattle and human population at the grassroots level.

It has been realized that commendable advances have been made in the diverse fields of economic development. But there is a great question, whether, it would in reality be incomplete if such rural development programmes fail to translate into better and dignified life for the majority of the people living in the remote villages.

The implementation of the integrated rural development programmes can be made more effective through ensuring proper participation of the local village people. Need based people's participatory planning and the implementation of development programmes should be implemented at the grassroots level. The willingness, consent and needs of the local village people and their priorities should be given due consideration in the plan formulation at the grassroots level.

In view of the above an effort has been made in this study to analyse the progress of the implementation of various rural development programmes being implemented at Village-Block-District-Panchayat level.

The centrally sponsored programmes supported by the Government of India and the programmes supported by the State Government of Uttar Pradesh and the planned programmes supported by the District Planning Committee and Zila Panchayat - Block Panchayat - Village Panchayat and implemented by the various line departments and implementing institutions have been analysed at village panchayat level.

It has been noticed that the job card holders and the beneficiaries of the Mahatma Gandhi National Rural Employment Guarantee Act (MNREGA) have been recorded 15520 beneficiaries, belonging to the Below Poverty Line (BPL) category in Amethi. The landless agricultural labourers, skilled and non-skilled labourers and other labourers have been provided MNREGA Job card holders and they are provided 100 days guaranteed job employment to increase the income for their better livelihood.

It has been recorded that there are 10763 number of students studying in the Primary Junior School at village panchayat level in Amethi. The High School and Intrermediate school students have been found 1308 in the various villages of Amethi. It has been observed that 208 students are studying in the Higher Education including Graduate and Post Gradaute level education at village panchayat level in Amethi. The technical, engineering, management, medical and other vocational/professional education students are found very insignificant having only 41 students at village panchayat level in the Amethi Block.

It has been observed that the canal irrigated area has been found 418 hectares and the Private Tube-well irrigated area has been noticed 5109 hectares in the Amethi Block. The Government Tube-well irrigated area has been recorded 280 hectares while other sources of irrigation have been recorded 87 hectares in the Amethi Block.

The India Mark-II Hand Pumps have been an important source of drinking water for the village people. It has been noticed that 2380 India Mark-II Hand Pumps have been installed in Amehti. The rural drinking water supply and sanitation programmes have been implemented at village panchayat level in Amethi and *Swajaldhara* Drinking Water Yojana has been successfully implemented at village panchayat level in Amethi.

The Sports and Youth Welfare Programmes are implemented at village level. The Sports and Youth Welfare Centres and units at village panchayat level have been established at village panchayat level in Amethi.

The Community Health Care Centres, Primary Health Care Centres and Sub-Primary Health Centres have been established with the view to provide medical and health services to the needy and interested patients and villagers in the Amethi Block.

Various Women and Child Development Programmes have been launched in Amethi including Anganwadi Kendra and other women and child health care supporting programmes at village panchayat level in Amehti.

Animal Health Care Centres and Veterinary Hospitals have been established to facilitate and promote the animal husbandry programmes at village level in Amethi.

It has been noticed that there are 5914 Above Poverty Line Card holders and 3819 Below Poverty Line (BPL) Card holders at village panchayat level in the Amethi Block.

Various other rural development programmes have been launched which include cleaning and sanitation programmes supported by the Government of India. The individual Hand Pumps have been installed due to insufficient installation of the India Mark-II Hand Pumps in Amethi.

The rural housing programmes have been initiated with the view to provide shelters for the houseless downtrodden deprived rural poor multitudes in Amethi. It has been recorded that 422 rural houses have been constructed at village panchayat level in Amethi.

The old age pension, widow's pension, handicapped pension and the scholarship for the scheduled caste, backward caste and minorities students have been distributed at village panchayat level in Amethi. It has been observed that 643 old age pensions, 143 handicapped persons, 49 widows pensions and 6470 students scholarships have been distributed at village panchayat level in Amethi.

Various agro-afforestation programmes have been launched by the Agriculture-Horticulture-Social Forestry departments in Amethi. It has been noticed that 2453 people have been benefited under the Agro-afforestation programmes at village panchayat level in Amethi. It has been recorded that 11023 number of plants have been planted at village panchayat level to fulfill the increasing demand of the fuel wood, fodder and wood for the cattle and human population at village panchayat level in Amethi.

It has been noticed that 132 km. pucca road has been constructed in Amethi and 132 small scale industries have been installed at village panchayat level in Amethi. There are 225 agro-industries established in the Amethi Block.

The low cost latrines/low cost sanitation programmes have been launched at village panchayat level to facilitate clean environment and proper sanitation to control the health hazards at the grassroots level in Amethi.

It has been recorded that 6 dairy development programmes have been launched in Jangal Ram Nagar, Darakha, Korari Girdhar Shah, Gangauli, Himmatgarh and Dehara village panchayats of Amethi.

Various integrated rural development programmes including cleaning/sanitation, women and child development, rural health, Kishori Shakti Yojana, immunization and other welfare programmes have been launched in Amethi. There are 74 number of integrated rural development programmes which has been implemented at village panchayat level in Amethi.

Pradhan Mantri Gram Sadak Yojana has constructed at village panchayat level in Amethi to provide accessibility and movement from one village to another village including Block and District Headquarters of Amethi. It has been recorded that 1423 number of villagers has been facilitated under the Pradhan Mantri Gram Sadak Yojana at village panchayat level in Amethi.

National Rural Health Mission (NRHM) Programmes have been successfully launched and implemented at village panchayats in Amethi. Rajiv Gandhi Grameen

Vidyutikaran Yojana has been implemented and 847 households have been provided electricity connections in the various village panchayats of the Amethi Block.

Mahatma Gandhi National Rural Employment Guarantee Act (MNREGA) has been launched with Rs. 341.76 released amount for implementation of various programmes to generate guaranteed employment for the below poverty in MNREGA Job Card holders at village panchayat level in Amethi.

It has been recorded that a sum of Rs. 179.59 lakh has been incurred for non-skilled labour in Amethi while Rs. 5.79 lakh has been expended for the skilled labour work and a sum of Rs. 101.21 lakh has been spent on account of material cost for the various planned activities at village panchayat level in Amethi, and a sum of Rs. 5.80 lakh amount has been spent for the temporary administrative expenses for successful implementation of MNREGA programmes. It has been recorded that total amount of Rs. 292.36 lakh expenditure has been expended for the implementation of various planned programmees under Mahatma Gandhi National Rural Employment Guarantee Act (MNREGA) at village panchayat level in Amethi.

It has been noticed that the Self-Help Groups are fast emerging powerful tool of socio-economic empowerment of the rural people at village level. The Self-Help Groups are a small body formed by the people for meeting their specific, objectives particularly credit. There are 538 Self-Help Groups (SHGs) formed in Amethi out of which 393 SHGs are active Self-Help Groups in Amethi. There are 214 Self-Help Groups crossed Grade-II and financial files has been processed by the concerned service providing banks and financial assistance for 214 SHG has been sanctioned by the Banks. Out of which 203 Self-Help Groups financial assistance have been distributed by the respective Banks at village panchayat level in the Amethi and three Self-Help Groups financial assistance has been rejected by the concerned Bank.

It has been recorded that 26 Self-Help Groups (SHGs) covering 281 Members has been sanctioned Rs. 44.25 lakh loan and Rs. 28.70 lakh Grants Components sanctioned for the various projects implementation by the different service Banks in Amethi.

Swarn Jayanti Gram Swarojgar Yojana has been launched to generate employment and increase the income of the deprived weaker people. In this scheme 155 beneficiaries has been supported out of which 48 Buffaloes, 60 goats, 38 shops and 9 Dairy projects has been sanctioned to the selected Swarn Jayanti Gram Swarojgar Yojana in Amethi. There are 2 minority, 55 general category and 98 scheduled caste beneficiaries selected and financially supported under the Swarn Jayanti Gram Swarojgar Yojana in Amethi. It has been noticed that Baroda Purvi Uttar Pradesh Grameen Bank supported 98 beneficiaries, Oriental Bank of Commerce supported 17 beneficiaries, Central Bank supported 21 beneficiaries, and Bank of Baroda supported 13 beneficiaries under Swarn Jayanti Gram Swarojgar Yojana at village panchayat level in Amethi Block.

It has been recorded that 221 number of houses under Indira Awaas Yojana has been planned and financial assistance has been sanctioned as per the norms of the Government and such low cast houses has been constructed as per planned target in the selected villages of the Amethi Block.

It has been observed that 31 low cost houses under the Mahamaya Awaas Yojana of the State Government of Uttar Pradesh has been planned and sanctioned and the houses has been constructed as per guidelines and norms of the Government of Uttar Pradesh at village panchayat level in Amethi.

It has been noticed that 2352 Indira Mark-II Hand Pumps have been installed out of which 143 Indira Mark-II Hand Pumps are out of order and defective.

It has been recorded that 2 Bio-Gas has been installed out of sanctioned 3 Bio-Gas Plants in Amethi and 31 Government Tube-wells has been installed covering 26 village panchayats of the Amethi Block and 3 Government Tube-wells are out of order in the Amethi Block.

It has been recorded that 171 Kisan Credit Cards has been issued out of which 158 Kisan Credit Cards have been distributed at village panchayat level in Amethi.

It has been noticed that Rs. 90.10 lakh crop loans have been sanctioned out of which Rs. 75.50 lakh Crop loans have been distributed at village level in Amethi. It has been recorded that 151 free of cost Tube-well borings have been sanctioned out of which 126 Tube-well borings have been successfully at village level in Amethi and 25 Tube-well borings have been installed for the beneficiaries at village panchayat level in Amethi.

It has been observed that various rural development programmes have been launched at village panchayat level especially improvement, betterment and upgradation of the available infrastructure at village panchayat level in Amethi. Various employment generating and income increasing programmes have been launched without willing consent and needs of the deprived resourceless, weaker, poor section of the society because social infrastructure of Amethi is inter-woven with social fabric of the caste, religion etc. The caste system of Amethi has been based on their occupational structure, and the successful implementation of the employment generation must be based on the needs, willing consent and interest of their caste based occupation structure and agriculture development and its productivity should be ensured through application of better agricultural implements, appropriate irrigational system use of High Yielding Variety (HYV) Seeds, proper application of the organic and inorganic amendments and techno-scientific application of Post Harvest and Agro-processing technology for value addition of the Agricultural production and generating employment and increasing the income of the resourceless deprived downtrodden weaker section of the society. Appropriate quality education, including occupational/vocational/professional education must be ensured at grassroots level. Proper utilization of available infrastructural resources must be tapped and optimally utilized to meet the ever increasing demand of growing cattle and human population for the Food-Cloth-Shelter and Fuel Wood, Fodder, Fibre, Fruits, Food Grains, Fisheries (F^6) and vegetable at village panchayat level in Amethi.

Development Planning

The planning is an organized process of the task of the people in which the planners can provide back-up support to achieve their planning goals.

The development is basically a human enterprise and therefore, it requires, the combined efforts of all systems of knowledge to comprehend and articulate it. The fuel good perception of the development has not to be only from National-State level but also from District-Block-Village level perspective.

The priorities, visions, missions and goals of the Government for the formulation of the planning and the implementation of the planned programmes has been analysed.

It has been realized that there are a quest for revolving a model for development planning and macro-level planning has been adopted in our country and it did not yield the requisite results due to in equities amongst people and disparities between one village to another village. During seventies integrated and sustainable planning at various levels have been ensured and conceptual changes in the planning process has been adopted at the grassroots level.

The development should be participatory tapping the local talent and resources in order to make the created assets self-sustained for optimum use of the village level beneficiaries. The village has been considered as the lowest unit of the plan formulation and the implementation of the peoples participatory and rural development activities.

The construction of infrastructural resources at the grassroots level has been launched through 'Bharat Nirman' by the Government of India. The computerization of the land records, watershed development, Hariyali, rural housing, National Socila Assistance Programme, Mahatma Gandhi National Rural Employment Guarantee Act (MNREGA) Mahila Kisan Sashaktikaran Pariyojana, Placement linked skill development, Swarn Jayanti Gram Swarojgar Yojana, Pradhan Mantri Gram Sadak Yojana, National Bio-Gas, National Health Insurance Policy Scheme, Sampoorna Grameen Rojgar Yojana, Rajeev Gandhi Grameen Vidyutikaran Yojana, Rural Drinking Water Supply, Rural Sanitation, Pradhan Mantri Grameen Jal Samvardhan Yojana etc. have been launched by the Government of India with the view to facilitate fruits of the development programmes at the grassroots level.

The Government of Uttar Pradesh has also initiated various rural development programmes through 25 per cent state share and 75 per cent grants from the Government of India. The Government of Uttar Pradesh has also initiated various programmes, like Swarn Jayanti Gram Swarojgar Yojana, Sampoorna Grameen Rojgar Yojana, Mahatma Gandhi National Rural Employment Guarantee Act, Pradhan Mantri Gram Sadak Yojana, Indira Awaas Yojana, Rural Drinking Water Supply, Community development programme, MLA & MLC-Local Area Development Fund, Ambedkar Vishesh Rojgar Yojana and National Bio-Gas Yojana, and some programmes have been re-nominated or changed but the target of the programme has been the same. The Department of Rural Development, Government of Uttar Pradesh and District Rural Development Agency play an important key role in the plan formulation and implementation of the various rural development programmes.

District development planning has been formulated, planned by the Zila Yojana Samiti. The agriculture, horticulture, assistance for small and marginal farmers, animal husbandry, fisheries, milk, forest, *sahkarita*, special programmes for village development, development of land and water resources, employment, Panchayati Raj, Community Development, Minor irrigation, Flood control, additional sources of energy, khadi and gramodyog hand loom, road and bridges, environment, science and technology, tourism, education, Pradeshik Vikas Dal, Medical and Health, housing drinking water, sanitation, child development programmes etc. have been planned and being implemented at grassroots level through various line departments.

Block Development planning has been done for the Mahatma Gandhi National Rural Employment Guarantee Act (MNREGA), construction of rural link road, digging of pond, nali, land development, land levelling, conservation of water, water storage, flood control, minor irrigation, renovation of traditional water resources, drought prone and afforestation, horticulture plantation, construction of kharanza etc. work has been planned by the Village Panchayat and Block Panchayat Amethi with the view to generate employment and increase the income of the Below Poverty Line people living in the remote villages of the Amethi Block.

It has been noted that all 44 village panchayats of the Amethi Block has planned various activities under the Mahatma Gandhi National Rural Employment Guarantee Act the estimate budget of the proposed planned work has been 2349.62 lakh out of which Rs. 1576.27 lakh be for the labour cost and a sum of Rs. 773.34 lakh has been allocated for the material cost and it has been planned create 1266645 man-days employment through Mahatma Gandhi National Rural Employment Guarantee Act (MNREGA) for the Below Poverty Line MNREGA Job Card holders belonging to the

44 village panchayats and covering 82 revenue village along with 377 purwas/tolas/ hamlet villages of the Amethi Block.

People's participatory need based planning survey has been carried out at grassroots level with the view to know and assess the interest and needs of the common village people who have been deprived of due to some reason or the other from the programmes launched by the Government. In view of the above, an attempt has been made to analyse the willing consent, interests, and need of the common people at village level in the Amethi Block.

It has been noted that there are 2775 needy interested Below Poverty Line persons looking forward to obtain Mahatma Gandhi National Rural Employment Guarantee Act (MNREGA) Job Card for getting 100 days ensured job for their livelihood and survival in the various village panchayats of Amethi.

It has been noted that 62 more new schools are required to be established in the different village panchayats of Amethi to fulfil the Sarva Shiksha Abhiyan (Campaign for Education for All) Mission of the Government.

It has been recorded that 1403 number of tube-well borings are required in different village panchayats of the Amethi with the view to facilitate minor irrigation programmes launched by the Government.

To ensure appropriate rural drinking water supply programmes at village panchayat level 1035 number of hand pumps are required in the Amethi Block. Sports and Youth Welfare 46 programmes are needed to be established in Amethi.

In view of the growing population and increasing number patients and disease 61 sub/primary health centres are required to be established in Amehti and women and child development programmes are required one each in the very village panchayat of Amethi. Scheduled Caste Welfare Programmes has not been properly implemented and very insignificant people are benefited. Therefore, 48 number of scheduled caste programmes are required to established in the various village panchayats of Amethi.

At least each village panchayat of Amethi requires establishment of veterinary centres for proper treatment of animals in Amethi. It has been noted that 46 supply shops are required to be opened under the Public Distribution System in Amethi. There are 579 old age, widow, handicapped pension beneficiaries who have not yet received pension facility of the Government and initiative must be taken to ensure to facilitate the Pension benefits to the deprived resourcesless poor people surviving in the remote villages. It has been recorded that 4611 number of students deprived from scholarships and these students at school level belongs to the Below Poverty Line family, effort must be ensured to provide scholarship to the needy interested school going students at village panchayat level in Amethi.

Construction of rural link road covering 215 km. distance linking one village to another and urban marketing centre are required in the different village panchayats of the Amethi Block.

It has been observed that 122 small scale industries and 205 agro-industries installation has been required in the different village panchayats of the Amethi Block with the view to process the agricultural products for the value addition and also to generate employment and increasing the income of the deprived rural poor people surviving in the remote villages of the Amethi Block. Construction of 7 fish ponds are available in water logged land and to generate employment for the interested Nishad and other communities of the Amethi Block.

The renewable sources of the Energy or the Non-conventional sources of Energy including solar light, solar pump, solar water heater, solar lantern etc. total 566 number of solar items are required at village panchayat level in Amethi.

It has been recorded that 2543 number of electricity connections are required in the different village panchayats of the Amethi and 735 low cost houses under Indira Awaas Yojana are required for houseless Below Poverty Line people surviving the thatched roof, mud houses in different village panchayats of the Amethi Block. It has also been noted that 104 rural sanitation and low cost sanitation programmes are required at village panchayat level in Amethi. There is demand for the establishment of 18 dairy centres for the collection and marketing of milk at village panchayat level in the Amethi Block. It has been noted that 182 kilometre construction of rural road under the Pradhan Mantri Gram Sadak Yojana has been needed at village panchayat level in the Amethi. It has been noticed that 784 number of Below Poverty Line households required electricity connection under the Rajiv Gandhi Vidyutikaran Yojana in different village panchayats of Amethi. The National Rural Health Mission Programmes are not properly implemented and it has been desired by the common people of Amethi for initiation and establishment of 57 rural heath programmes at village panchayat level in Amethi with the view to provide rural health services for needy, interested Below Poverty Line patients at the grassroots level.

In spite of the above, there are various programmes launched by Government of India and the State Government of Uttar Pradesh, it has been observed and realized that most of the rural development programme has not yet still reached up to the grassroots level, even, if same programmes are initiated but the implementation of such programmes could not yield the requisite results as per the visions targeted goals, aims, and objectives of the Government. Time bound peoples participatory need based formulation of the policy planning at the grassroots level, through tapping the available local talents and natural and human (Socio-Economic-Industrial) infrastructural resources and its optimum utilization should be prioritised. The peoples participation in the implementation of the planned programmes must be ensured at the village level. Local village people must be trained, educated, motivated to know through awareness programmes being implemented for their betterment and upgradation of their socio-economic conditions of the deprived rural poor multitudes at village level in Amethi. The policy planning and formulation of the need based planning at the National Level-State Level-District Level has not been properly planned and implemented through ignoring the local people their needs, aspiration and actions for their better quality of life due to which it failed to yield the desired success of it completion at village level. In view of the above it is necessary to prioritize the needs and to innovate the available natural-human-infrastructural resources at the field level should be considered in the plan formulation and continued involvement of the local people should be given due importance in the implementation of the planning and various rural development programmes at the village level.

The people's participatory need base planning through optimum utilization of the available infrastructural resources may be an asset for the successful implementation of the planned programmes at the village level in Amethi with the view to increase the agricultural productivity through appropriate utilization and conservation of *Jal-Jangal-Zameen* (Land-Water-Forest) natural infrastructural resources to meet the ever increasing demand of the growing cattle and human population and conserve the available natural resources and improve the environmental conditions of the Amethi and to fulfil the growing demand of fuel wood, fodder, fibre, fruits, fisheries, food grains (F^6) and vegetables and also to improve the socio-economic conditions of the deprived resource-less poor multitudes surviving in the remote villages of Amethi through generating large scale employment among the unemployed rural youth and increasing their income and to realize their actions and aspirations for better quality of life with the view to move equally in the society along with the rich and elite class people because the implementation of the rural development programmes should reach to the rural poor *equally, effectively, efficiently* as per the constitutional rights and visions of the Father of the Nation.

6

References

I. BOOKS

Babarata, K.C., *Planning for Forest Resources and Bio-Diversity Management*, Concept Publishing Co. Pvt. Ltd., New Delhi.

Bhattacharya, J.P., *Study of Soil Conservation for Agricultural Land*, New Delhi, 1964.

Bland Fort, H.F., *The Climates and Weather of India, Cylon and Burma*, (London) 1889.

Browrigg, F.W., *Settlement Report, District Sultanpur*, 1898.

Chauhan, D.S., *Studies in Utilization of Agricultural Land*, Aggarwal Publication, Agara, 1966.

Ganguli, H.N., *Restoration of Soil Structures with Gypsum*, Bikaner Gypsum, Ltd., Bikaner, 1954.

Ginsbarg, M., *Sociology*, Better Birth, London, 1934, p. 50

Govinda Rajan, S.V. and Gopal Rao, H.G., *Studies on Soils of India*, New Dehli, 1978.

Iver, M.C. RMS. & Page, C.H., *Society*, Mac Millans & Company, New York, 1950, 348.

Krishnan, M.S., *Geology of India and Burman*, Madras, 1960

Kuldeep, K.P., *The Climates of Continents*, Oxford University Press, Oxford, 1927.

Leather, J.W., *Investigation of Usar Land in United Provinces,* Government Press, Allahabad, 1914.

Mishra, R.P., *Regional Planning*, Concept Publishing Co. Ltd., New Delhi, 1992.

Mishra, R.P. (Ed.), *Changing Deceptions of Development Problems*, Singapore, Maruze in Asia, 1983.

Mohammad, Ali, *Dynamics of Agricultural Development in India*, Concept Publishing Co. Pvt. Ltd., New Delhi, 1978.

Nevill, H.R., *District Gazetteer of the District Sultanpur*, Allahabad, 1903.

Rae Chaudhury, S.P., *Land and Soil*, National Book Trust, New Delhi, 1966.

Rao, K.L., *India's Water Wealth : Its Assessment, Uses and Projections*, Orient Longman, New Delhi, 1979.

Risley, H., *The People of India,* London, 1951, p. 1.

Shafi, M., *Land Utilization in Eastern Uttar Pradesh*, Aligarh Muslim University, Aligarh, 1960.

Shame, K.B. & Rae Chaudhary, S.P., *Rating of Soils of India*, IARI, New Delhi, 1960.

Singh, A.K. *et al.*, *Forest Resource Economy and Environment*, Concept Publishing Co., New Delhi, 1987.

Srivastava, K.G., *Agro Forestry*, Central Book House, Rajpur, M.P., 1995.

Tajwani, K.G., *Agro-Forestry in India*, Concept Publishing Co., New Delhi, 2001.
Wadia, D.N., *Geology of India*, London, 1960.
Yadav, H.R. *Village Information System*, Vol. II, (Innovation of Human Infrastructure), Concept Publishing Co. Ltd., New Delhi, 2012.
Yadav, H.R., *Agro-Afforestation Management on Wastelands*, Concept Publishing Co., New Delhi, 2011.
Yadav, H.R., *Dimension of Wastelands Development*, Concept Publishing Co., New Delhi, 1988.
Yadav, H.R., *Genesis and Utilization of Wastelands*, Concept Publishing Co., New Delhi, 1986.
Yadav, H.R., *Reclaiming Wastelands*, Concept Publishing Co., New Delhi, 1990.
Yadav, H.R., *Village Development Planning*, Concept Publishing Co., New Delhi, 2009.
Yadav, H.R., *Village Information System*, Vol. I, (Innovation of Natural Infrastructure), Concept Publishing Co. Ltd., New Delhi, 2012.
Yadav, H.R., *Wastelands Diagnosis and Treatment,* Concept Publishing Co., New Delhi, 1987.

II. ARTICLES

Abrol, I.P., "Reclamation of Wastelands and World Food Prospects", *Trans, Int. Cong. Soil Science*, New Delhi, 1982.
Aggarwal, L.I. & Mehrotra, C.L., "Soil Survey and Soil Work in U.P." Vol.I, Allahabad, 1952.
Aggarwal, R.R. & Mehrotra, C.L., "Quality of Water Irrigation Waters in U.P." *India J. Science*, 31, (1966).
Aggarwwal, L.I., "Soil Survey and Soil Work in U.P." Vol.II, Allahabad, 1952.
Aggarwwal, L.I., "Soil Survey and Soil Work in U.P." Vol.III, Allahabad, 1954.
Aggarwwal, L.I., "Soil Survey and Soil Work in U.P." Vol.IV, Allahabad, 1954.
Bland Food, H.F., "The Rainfall of India" *Mem.*, Indian Met. Deptt. Vol. 3, 1986-88.
Bland Ford, H.F., "Hotwinds of Northern India" *Mem.*, Indian Met, Deptt., Vol. 6, 1986.
Choudhary, Kamala, "Greening of India", *Indian Express*, 21 December, 1982.
Clark, K.G.T., "The Vicissitudes of Summer Rainfall of the Indo-Gangetic Plain and the Valley", *Geography*, 18 (Pt. IV) 1932.
Dhawan, C.L., "Land Reclamation", Central Board of Irrigation and Power, *Publication No. 43*, Vol. III, 1.
Eliot, J., "The Hot Winds of Northern India", Indian Met., *Mem.* 6 (Pt.) (III), 1980.
Hart, D.R.D. & Stands, M.W., "Sustainable Land Use System Research and Development" in *International Workshop on Sustainable Land Use System Research*, February, 12-16, p. 13.
Hill, S.P., "Variations of Rainfall in Northern India: Indian Met.", *Mem.* 1 (Pt. III) 1897.
Kanwar, J.S., "Reclaiming Retriorated Soils", *Fertilizer News*, 6 (21) 1961.
Leather, J.W., "Agriculture Soils" in *Agriculture Ledger* (3) 1898.
Mathur, R.K., "Economics of Agro-Forestry for wastelands Reclamation", *Agriculture Ledger*, 1983, (175-87).
Rae Chaudhary, S.P., "Extension of Cultivated Areas for Increased Agricultural Production" *Producing of Symposium of Science and India's Food Problem*, ICAR, New Delhi, 1971.
Rae Chaudhary, S.P., "Final Report of the All India Soil Survey Scheme", *Bulletina*, India Council of Agricultural Research, 1952, 13.

St. Duster, S.A., "Intervening Opportunities : A theory relating Mobilizing and Distance", *American Sociological Review*, Vol.-II, Dec. 840, pp. 845-67.

Stamp, L.D., "The Land Utilization Survey of Britain", *Geographic Journal*, London, and 78), 1931.

Taylor, C.C., "Weed Control", *Indian Farming*, 9 (4) 1948.

Tewari, D.N., "Technology for Sustainable Development" National Seminar on *Technology for Sustainable Development*, March 12-18, Guru Ghasi Das University, 1980, p. 17.

Wadia, D.N. & Auden, J.B., "Geology Structure of Northern India", *Mem.*, Geological Survey of India, 78 (1939).

III.

- Performance Budget-2011-12, Department of Rural Development, Govt. of Uttar Pradesh.
- Progress Report of the MNREGA - Amethi Block 2011-12.
- Progress Report of the MNREGA - Village Panchayat Level, 2011-12
- Work Plan of the District Amethi 2012-13.
- Work Plan 2012-13 Amethi Block.
- MNREGA Work Plan 2012-13, 44 Village Panchayats of Amethi Block.
- Programmes of the Ministry of Rural Development, Government of India.
- Agricultural Census of Uttar Pradesh, 1990-71, Agricultural Statistics of Uttar Pradesh, 1971.
- District Census Hand Book, Sultanpur District 2001.
- Economic Register, Block Development Office, Amethi.
- F.A.O. Framework for Land Evaluation Soil Bulletin No. 1, 1976.
- I.C.A.R., Final Report of All India Soil Survey Scheme, 1958.
- I.A.R.I., Resources Analysis of the District Sultanpur, 1989.
- I.A.R.I., Resources Analysis of the District Rae Bareli, 1989.
- I.C.A.R. Hand Book of Agriculture, 1969.
- National Thematic Maps Organisation (NATMO), Govt. of India.
- Land Revenue Records (Khasara Register and Khasara Maps) Amethi Tehsil, Distt. Amethi.
- State Soil Conservation Research, Annual Reprot, U.P. p. 61.
- Statistical Book, District Sultanpur, 2001.
- Statistical Book, District Rae Bareli, 2001.
- Survey of India, Topographical Sheets No. 63F/11, 63F/10, 63F/12, 63F/14, 63F/15, 63F/16, 63J/3, 63J/4, 63J/5, 63J/8, 63J/11, 63J/12, 63K/3, 63K/9.
- U.S.D.A., A Manual on Conservation of Soil and Water, Hand Book of Professional Agriculture Workers, Oxford Publishing Co., 1984.
- *The Imperial Gazetteer of India*, Vol. XXIII, Singhbhumi to Transhialchod-Zong, Reprint Edition, (Today and Tomorrow Printers and Publishers) New Delhi, 1974, 130-37.

Coloured Maps

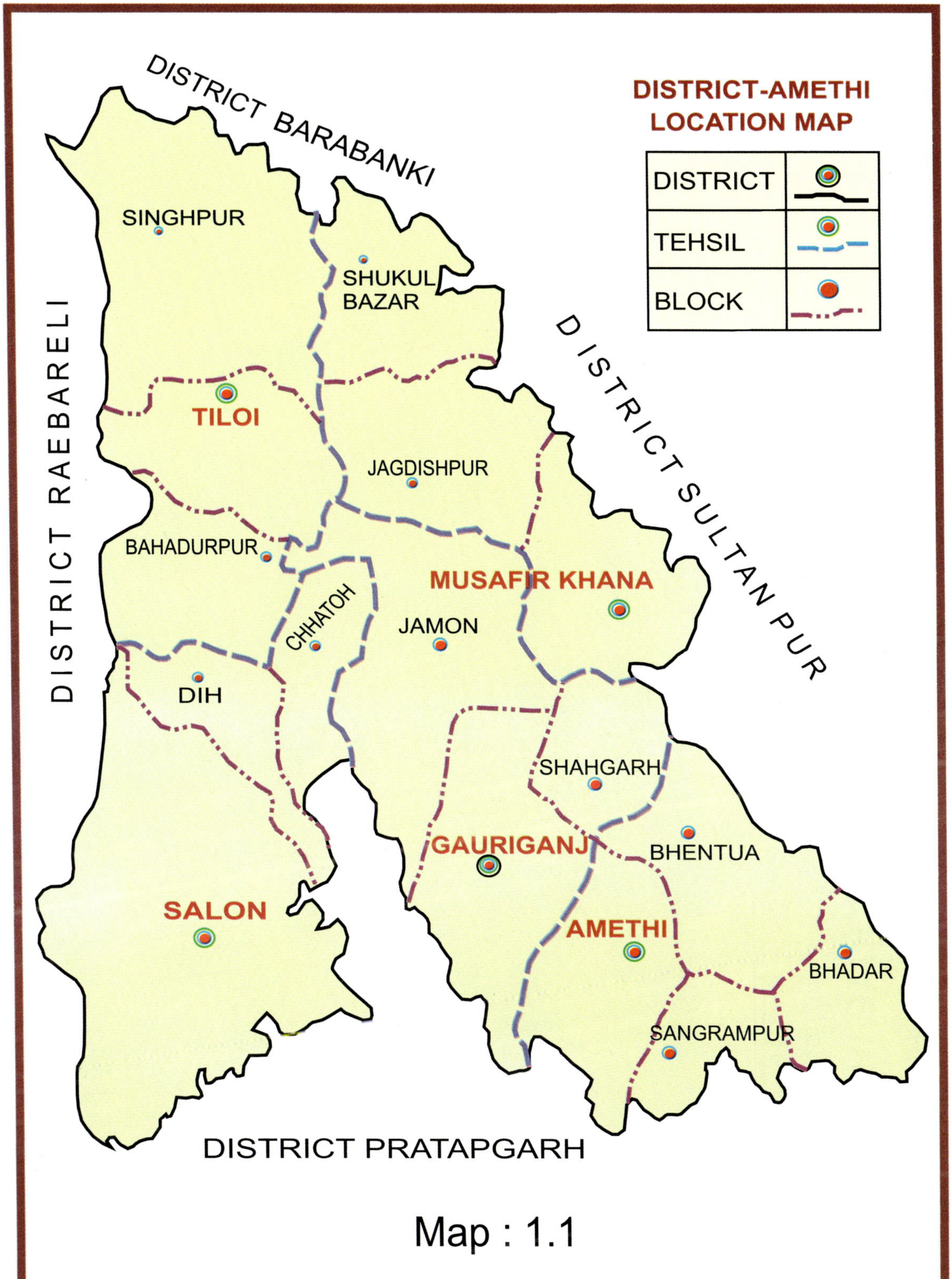

Map 1.1: Blocks and Tehsils, Amethi District

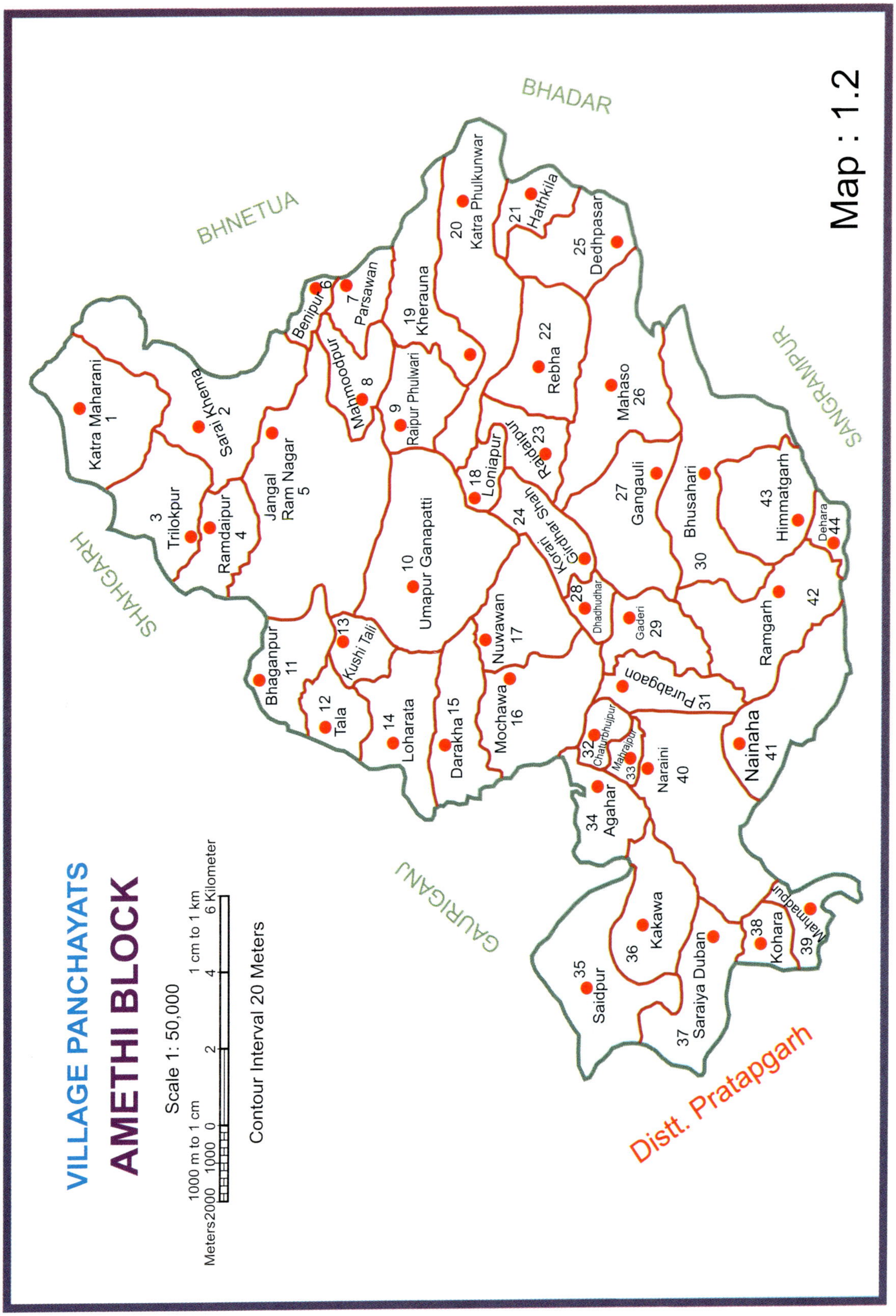

Map 1.2: Village Panchayats, Amethi Block

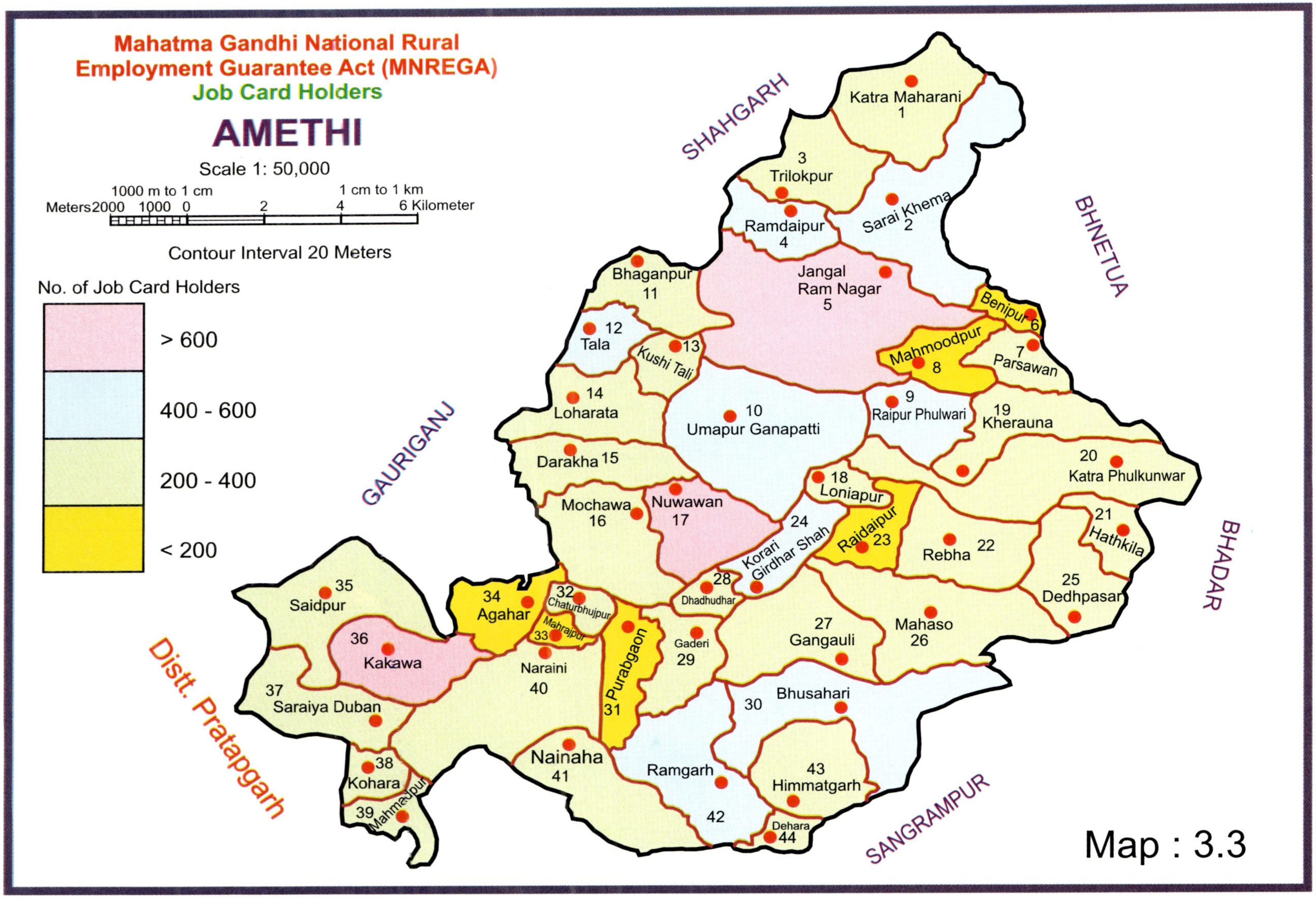

Map 3.3: Mahatma Gandhi National Rural Employment Guarantee Act (MNREGA) Job Card Holders, Amethi

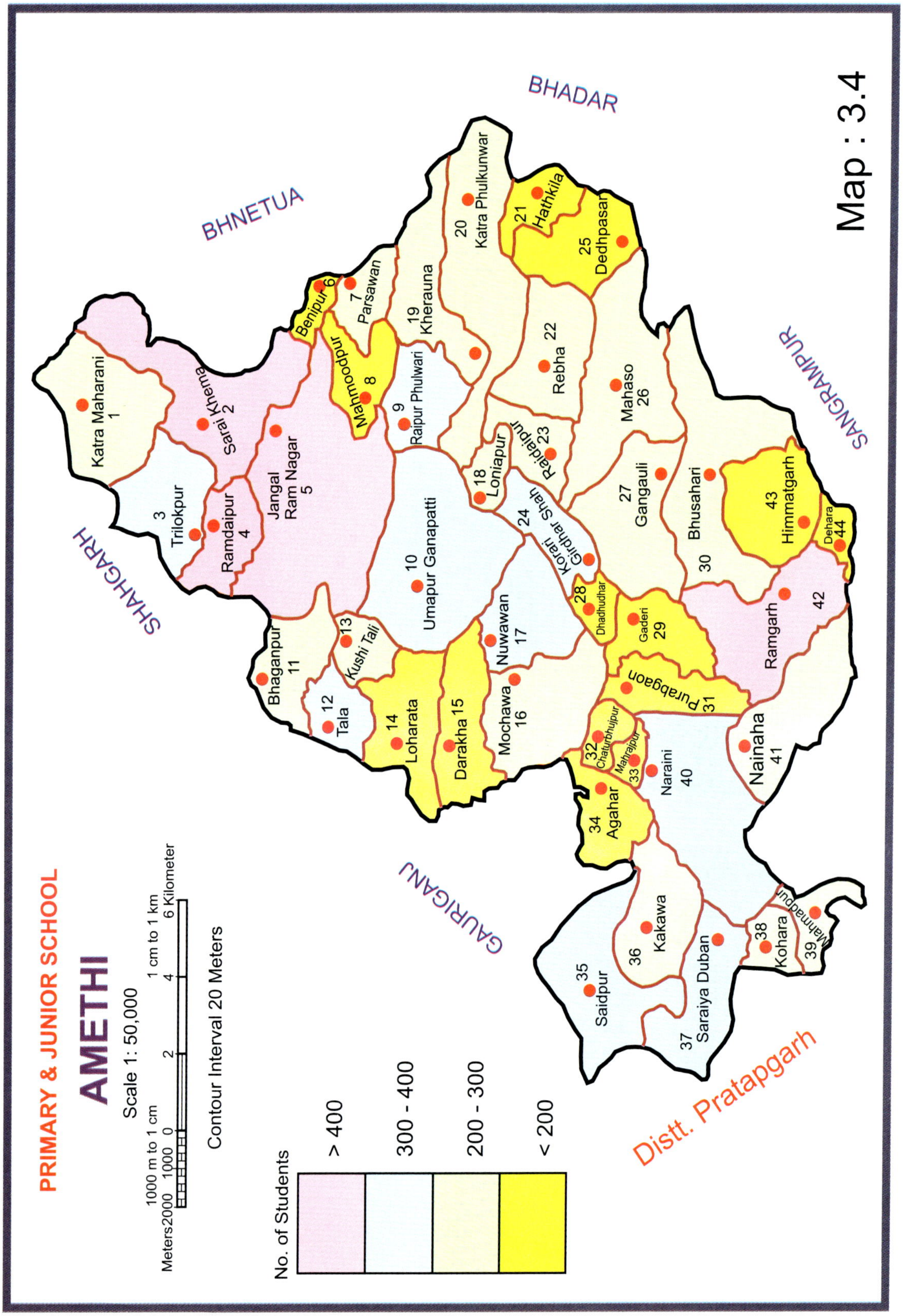

Map 3.4: Primary & Junior School, Amethi

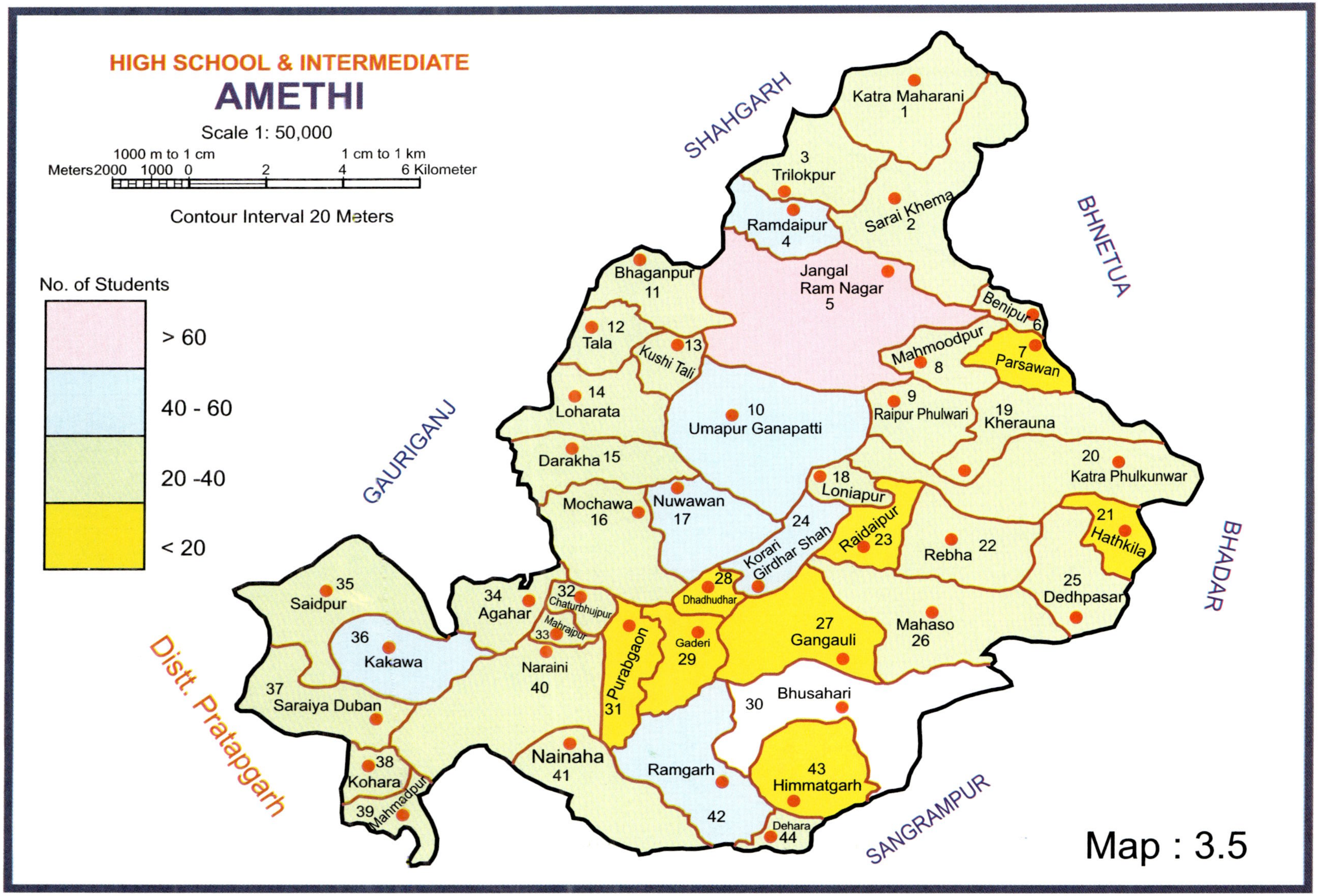

Map 3.5: High Schools & Intermediate Colleges, Amethi

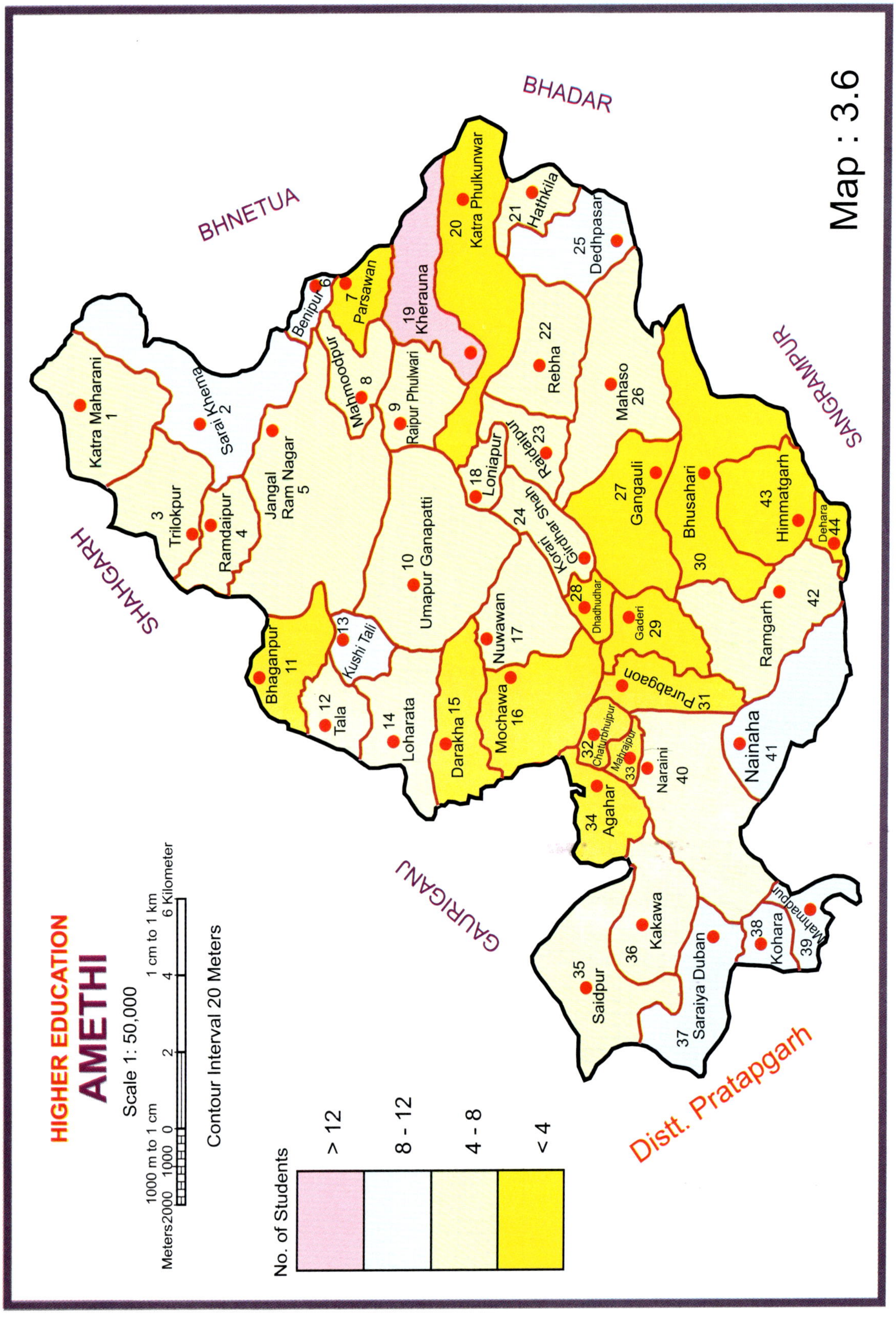

Map 3.6: Higher Education, Amethi

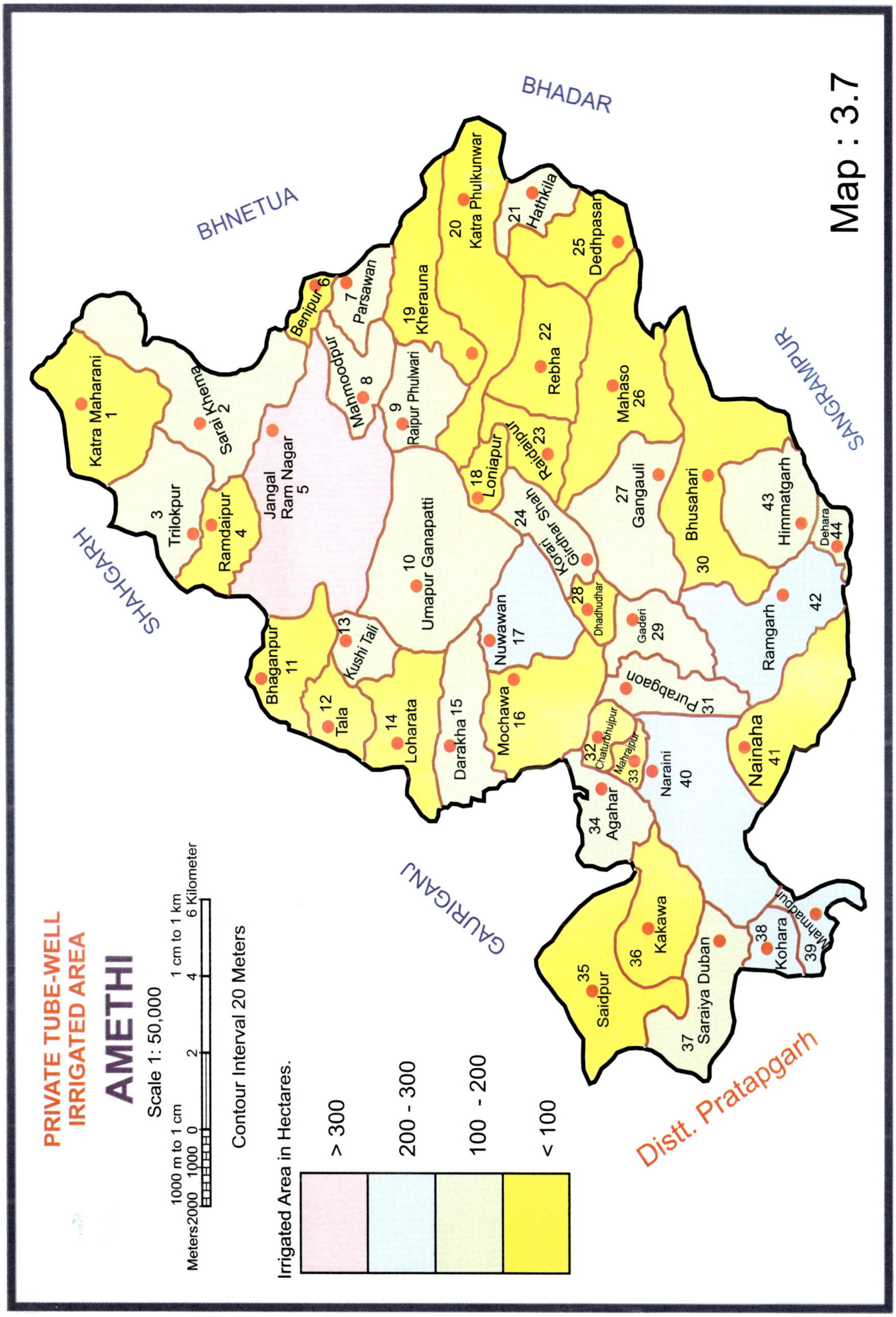

Map 3.7: Private Tube-well Irrigated Area, Amethi

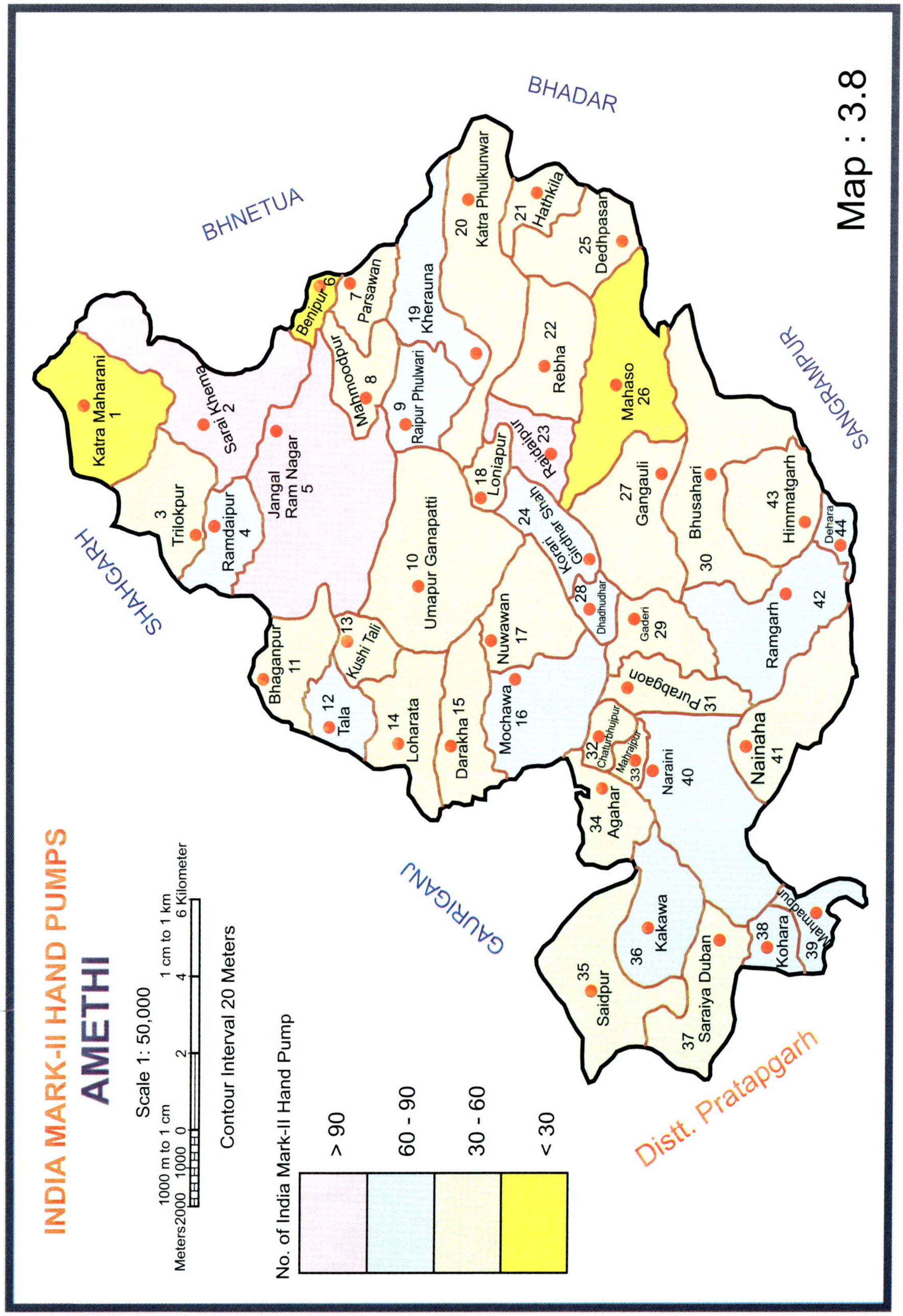

Map 3.8: India Mark-II Hand Pumps, Amethi

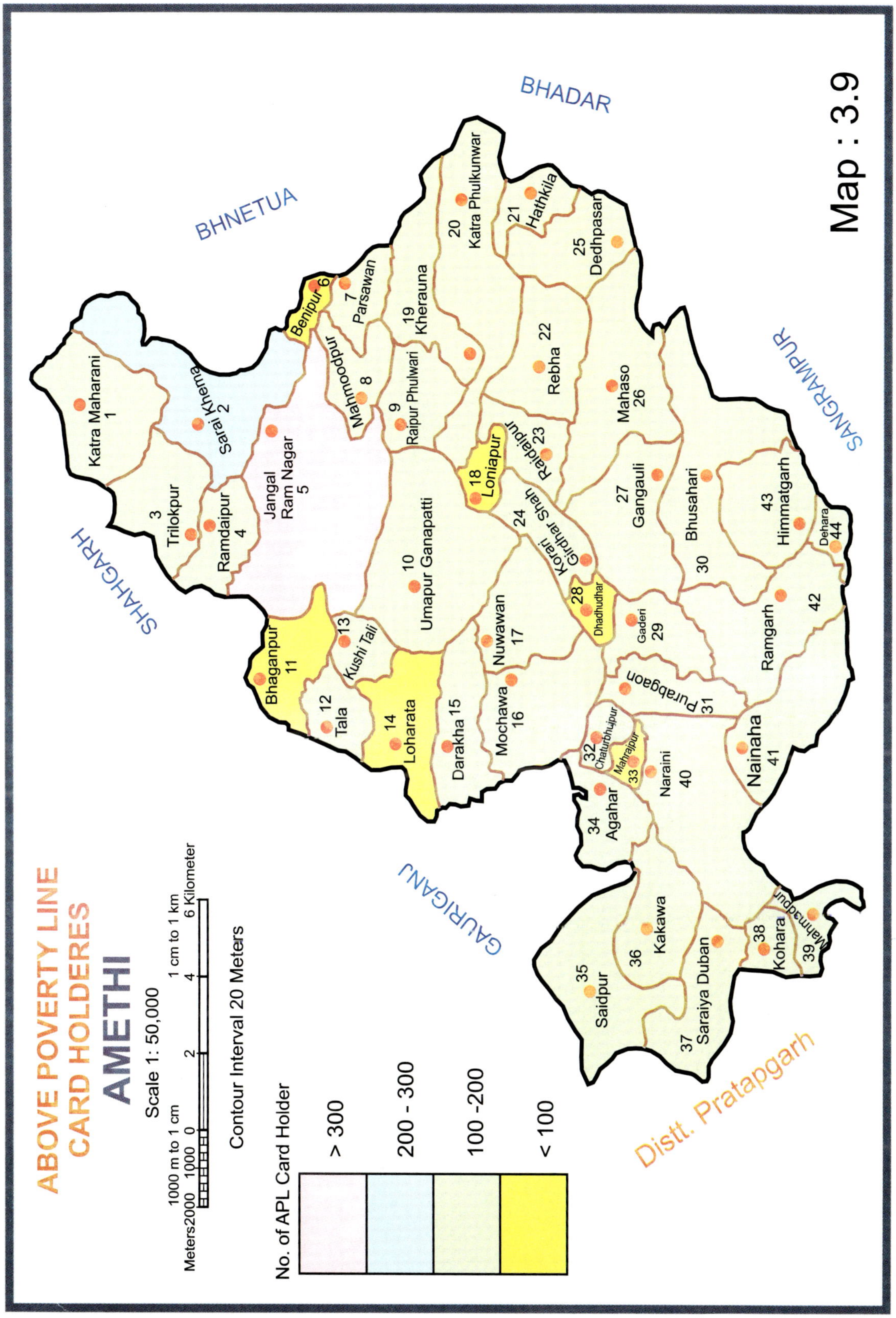

Map 3.9: Above Poverty Line Card Holders, Amethi

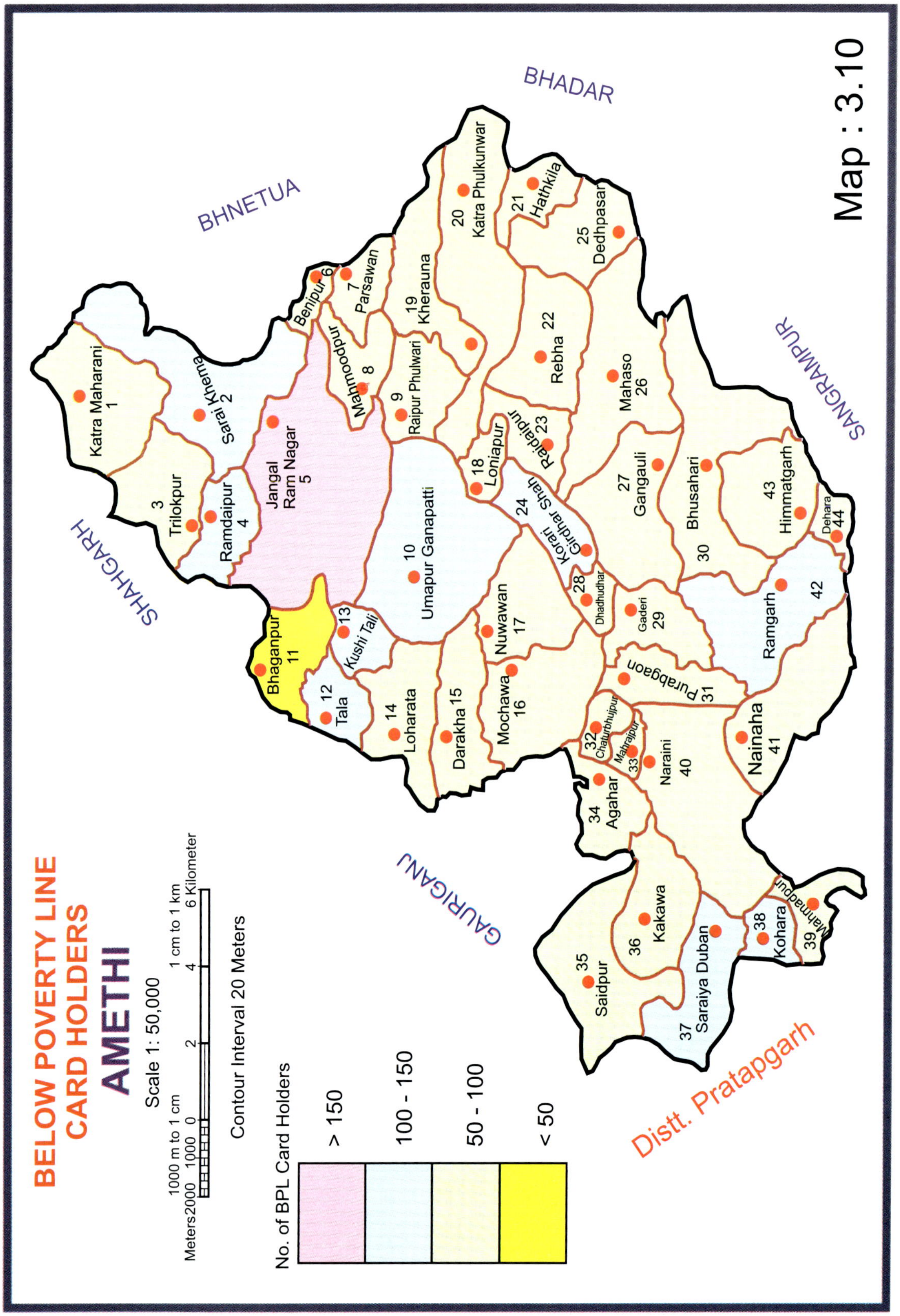

Map 3.10: Below Poverty Line Card Holders, Amethi

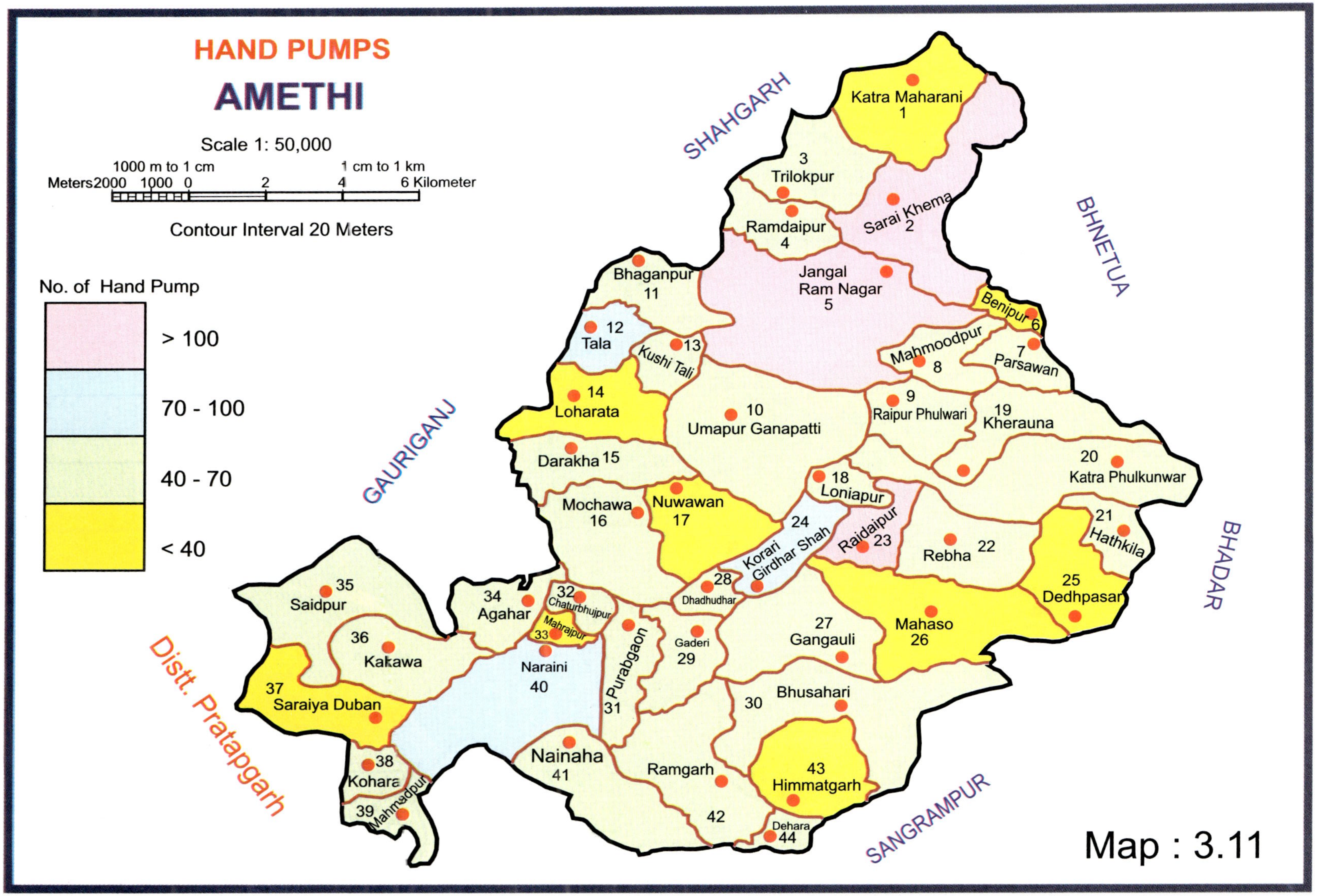

Map 3.11: Hand Pumps, Amethi

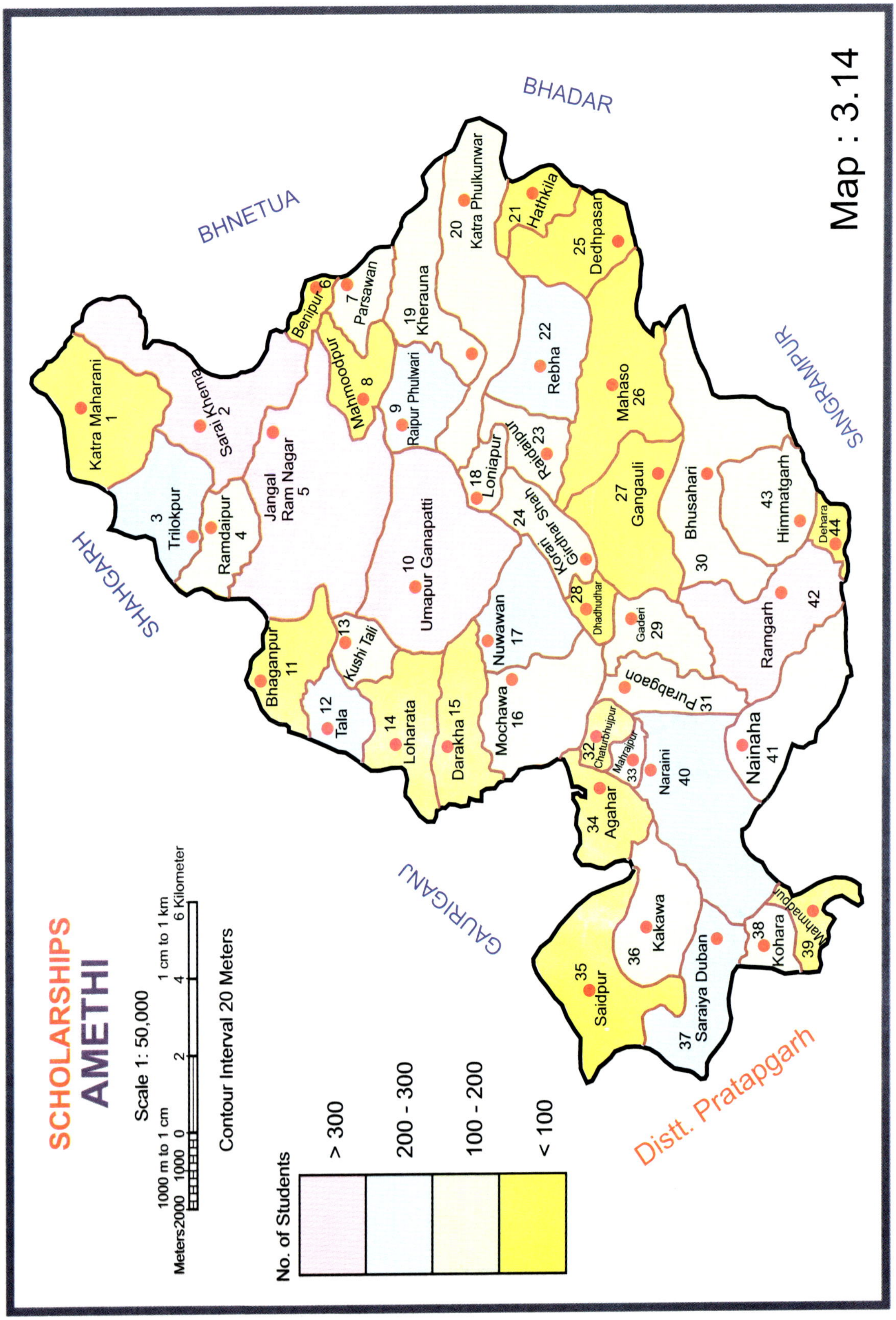

Map 3 .14: Scholarships, Amethi

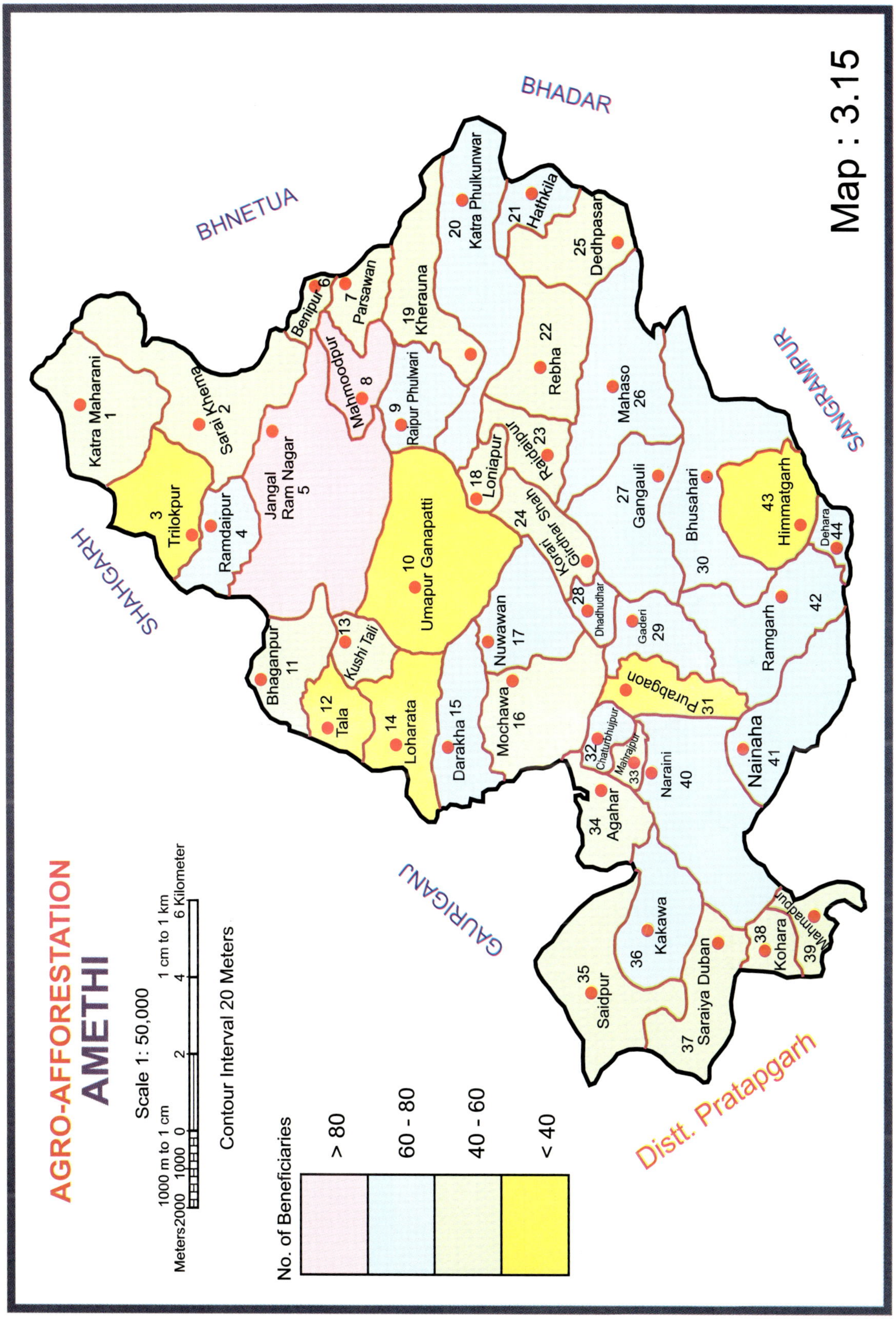

Map 3.15: Agro-Afforestation, Amethi

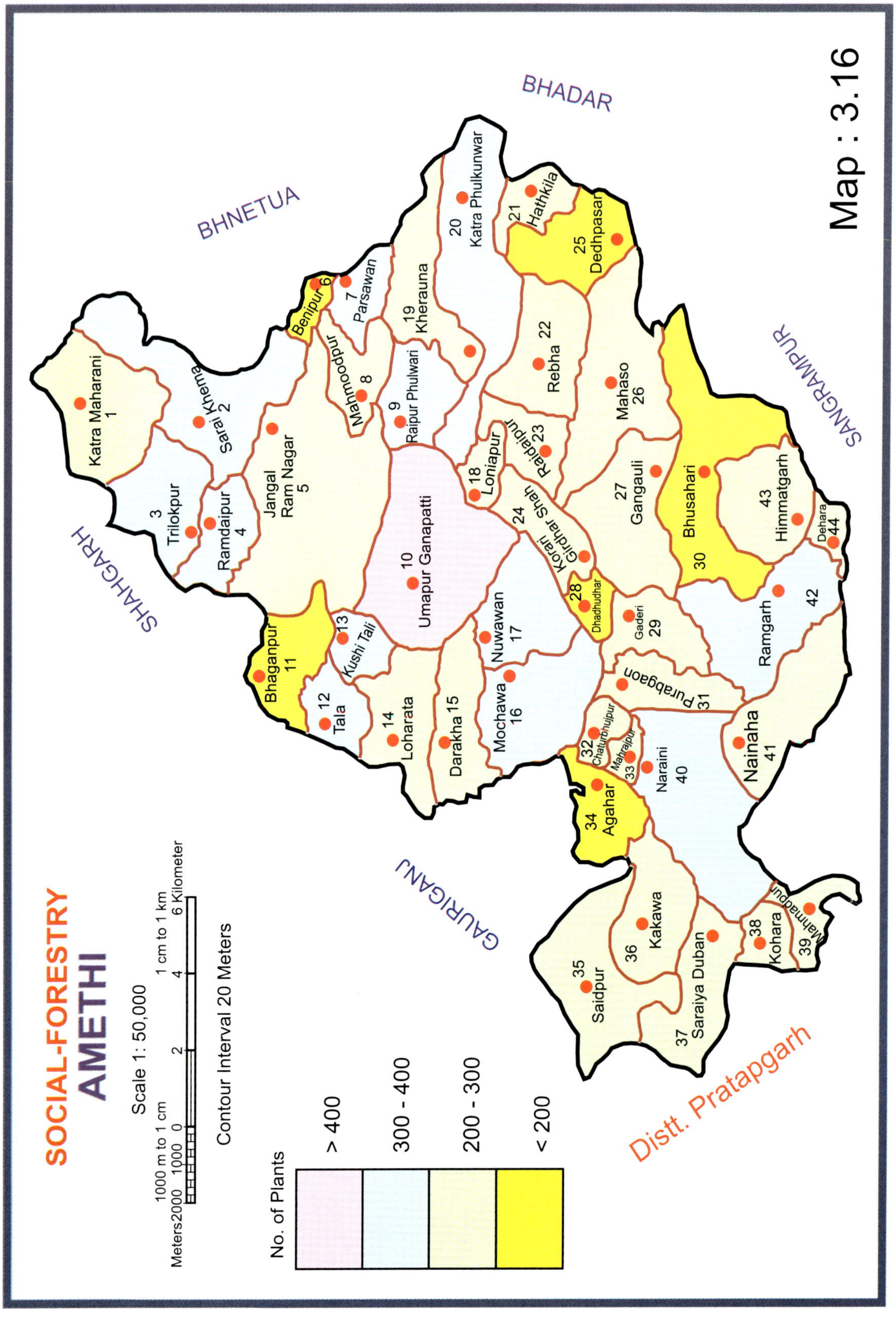

Map 3.16: Social-Forestry, Amethi

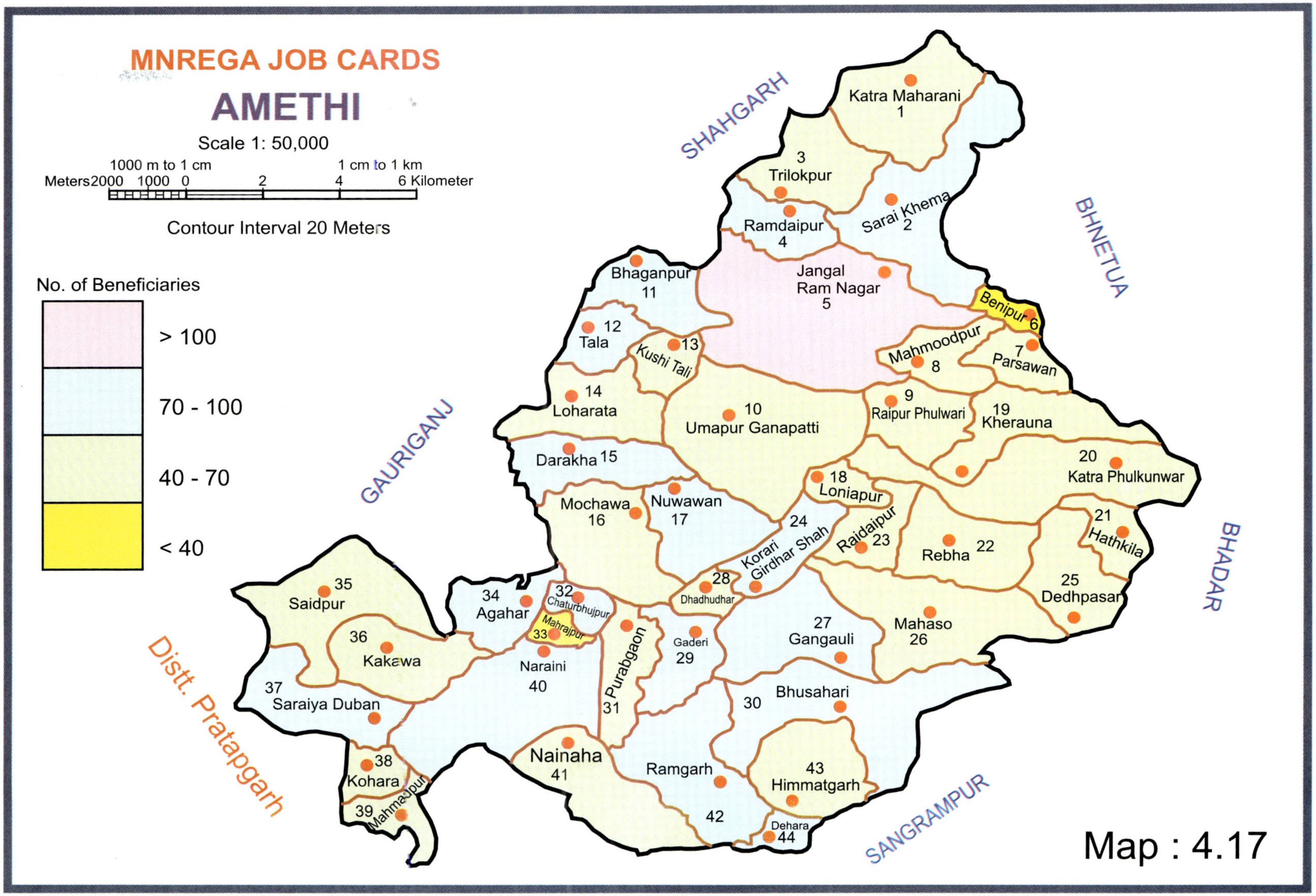

Map 4.17: MNREGA Job Cards, Amethi

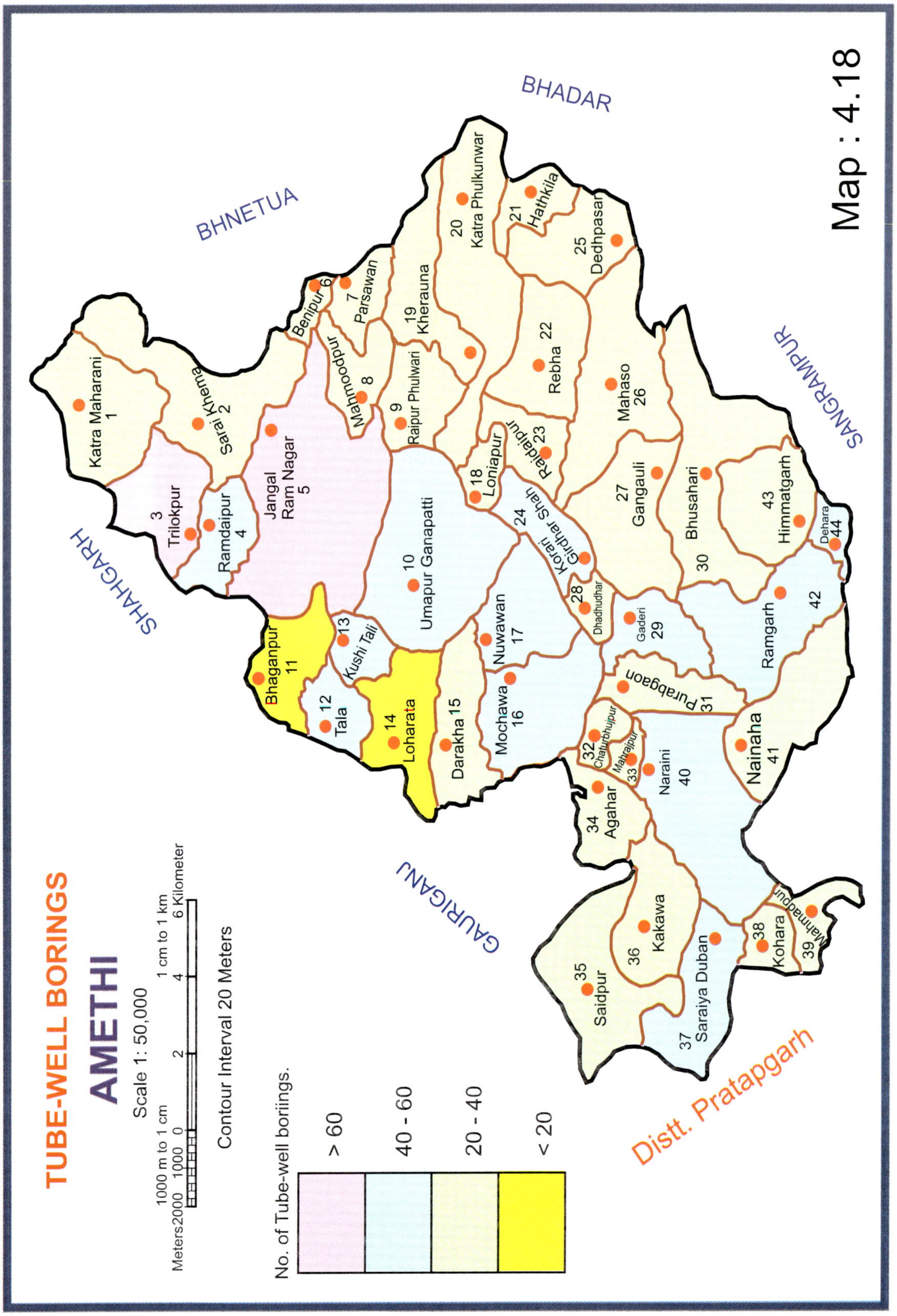

Map 4.18: Tube-well borings, Amethi

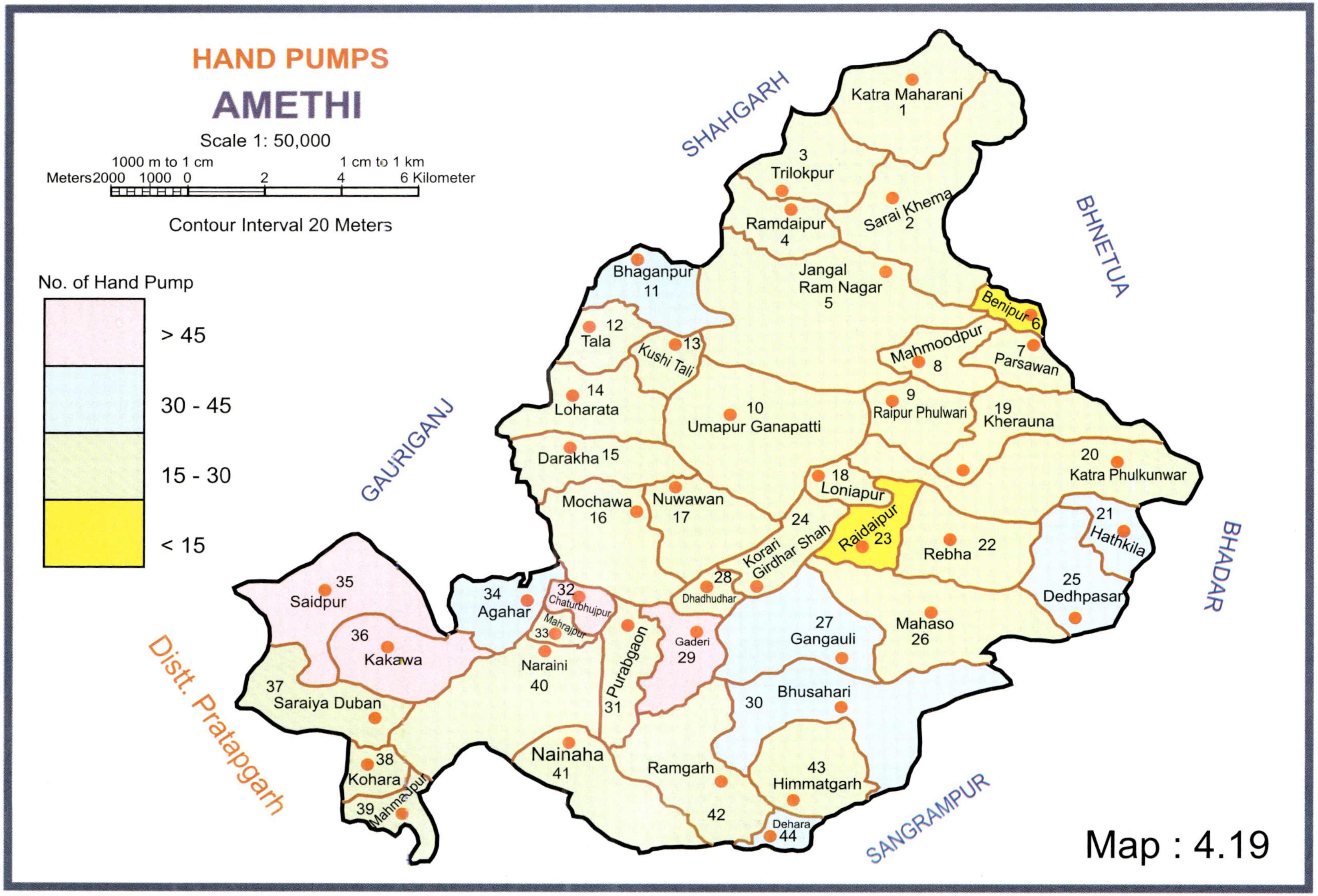

Map 4.19: Hand Pumps, Amethi

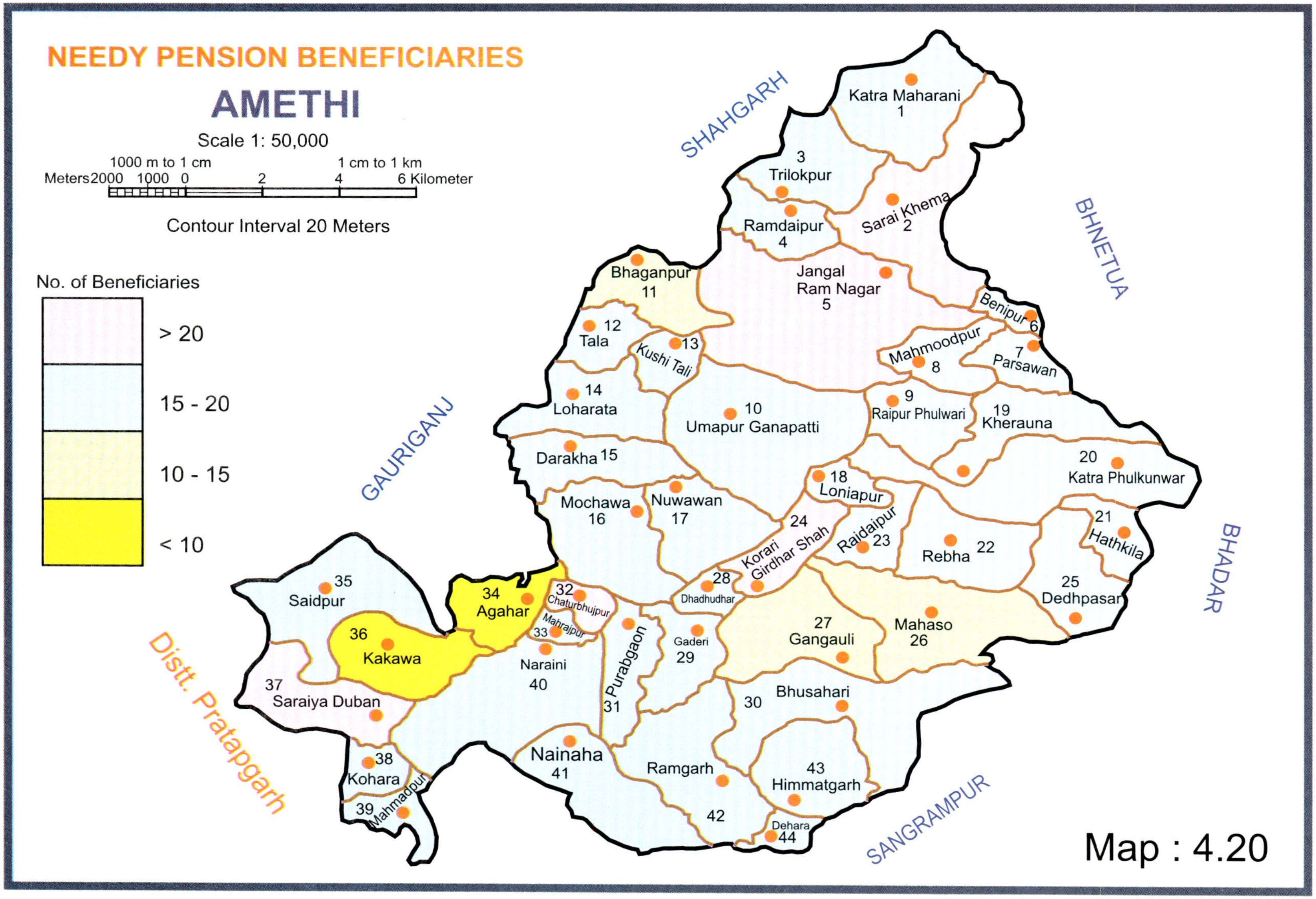

Map 4.20: Needy Pension Beneficiaries, Amethi

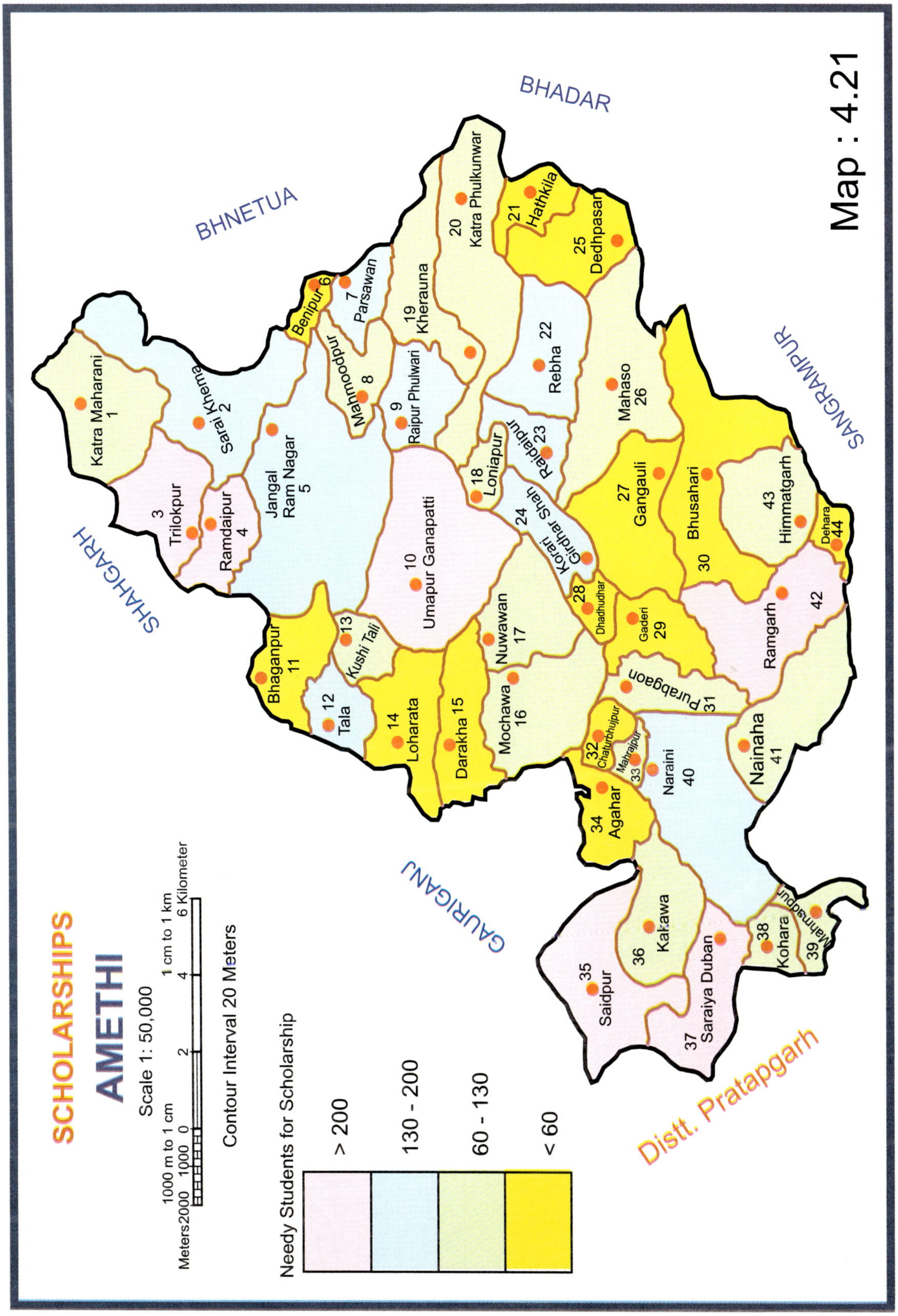

Map 4.21: Scholarships, Amethi

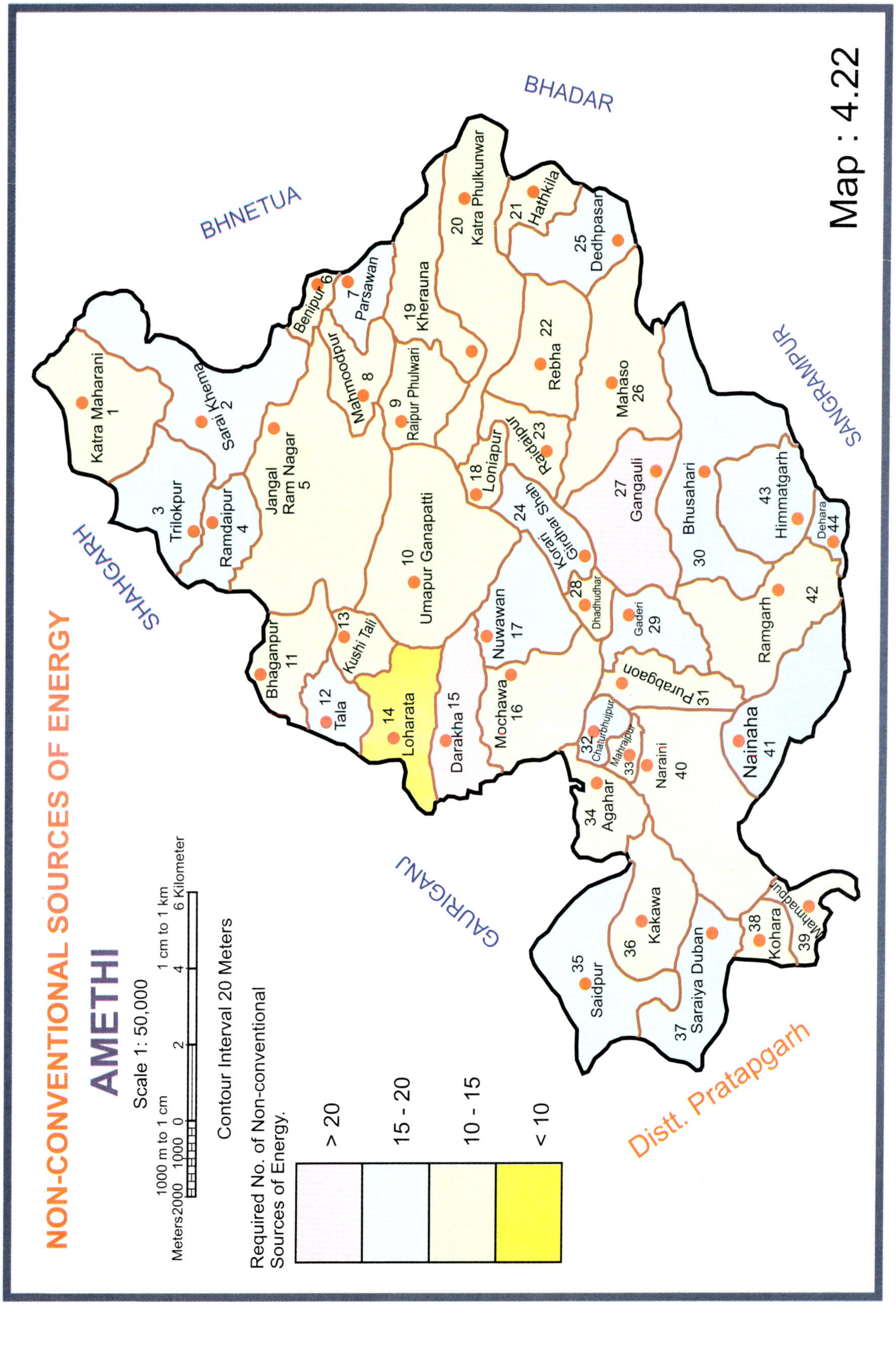

Map 4.22: Non-Conventional Sources of Energy, Amerhi

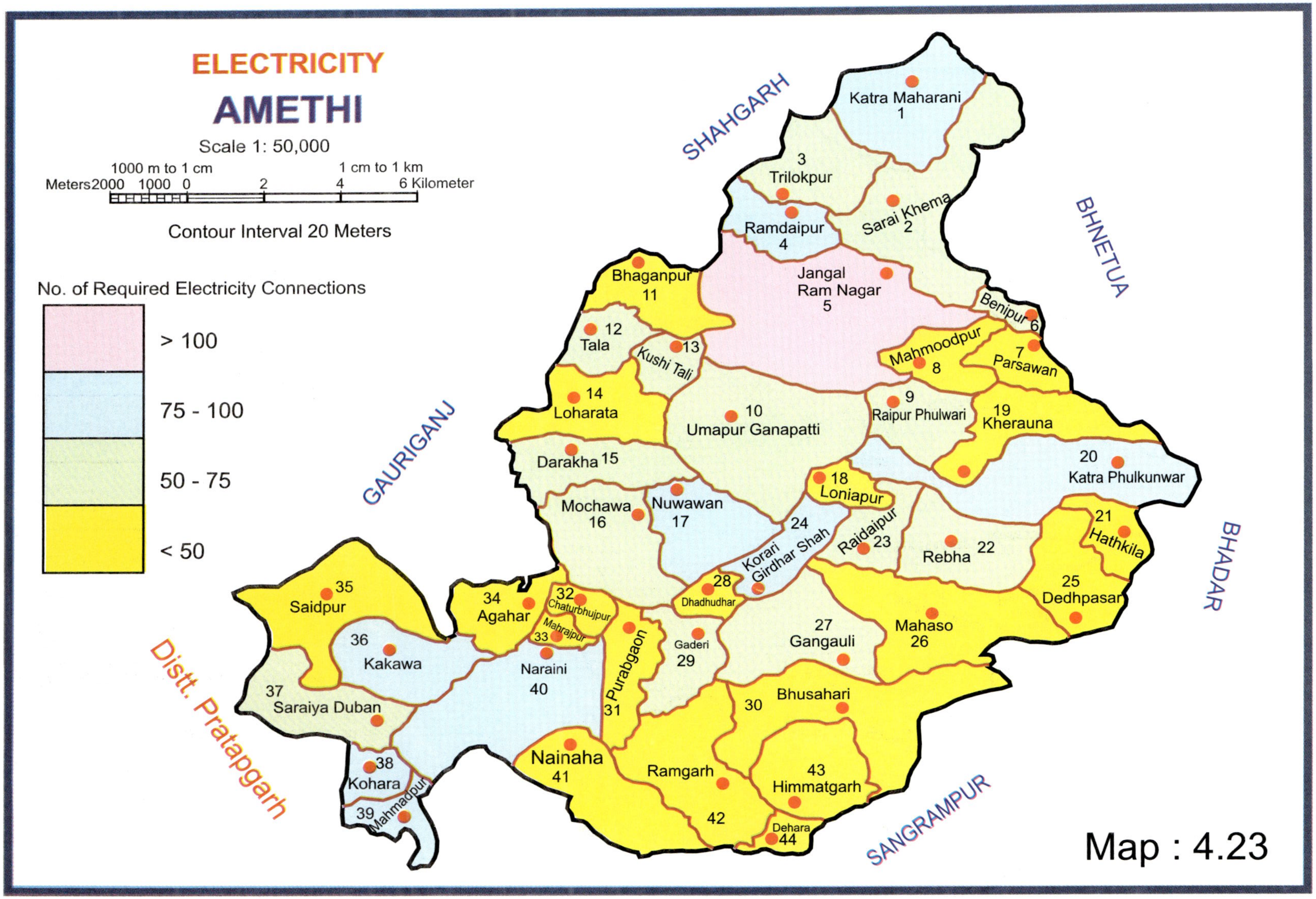

Map 4.23: Electricity, Amethi

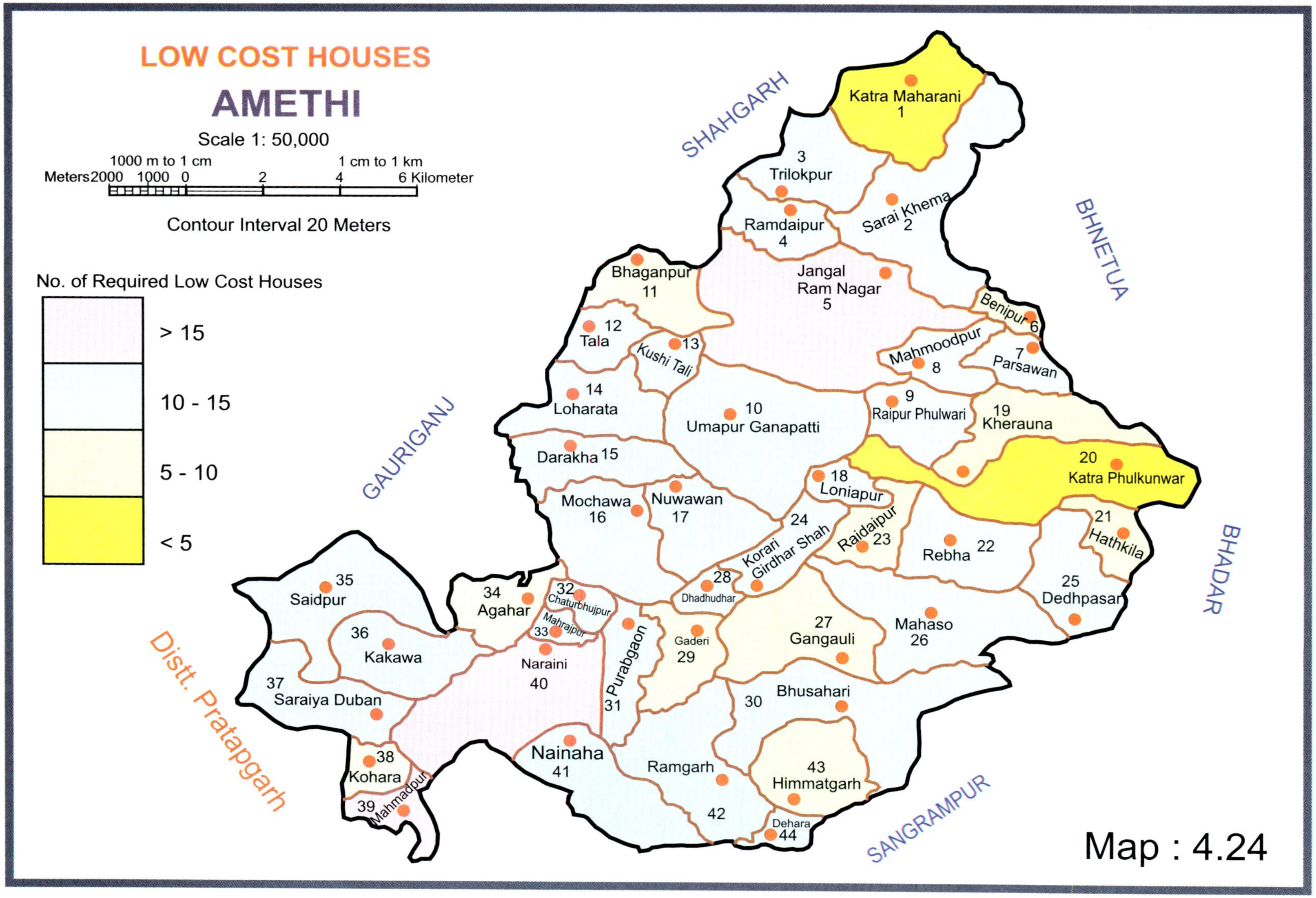

Map 4.24: Low Cost Houses, Amethi

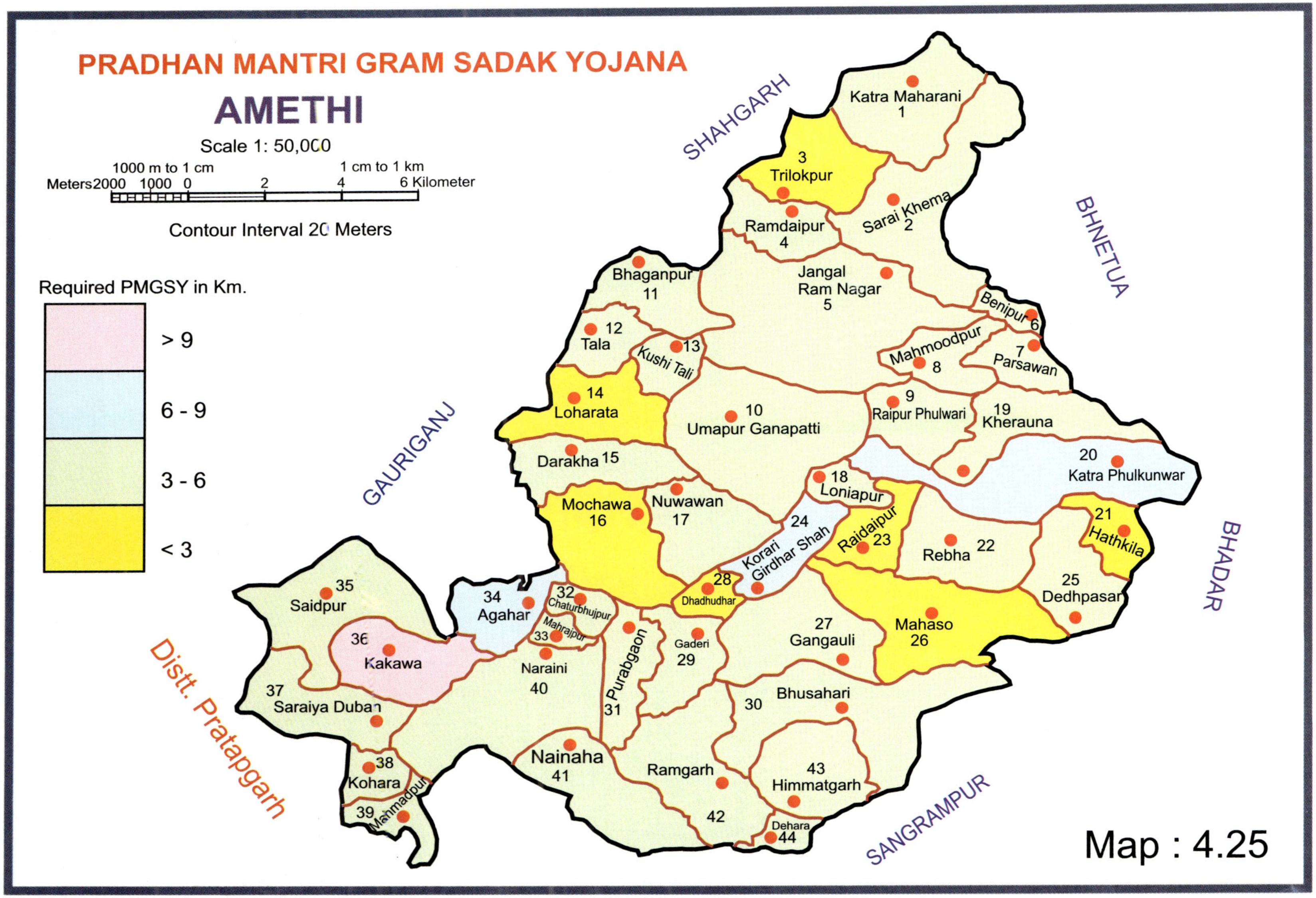

Map 4.25: Pradhan Mantri Gram Sadak Yojana, Amethi

Index